Britain TravelBook

Written by Christopher Somerville
Ninth edition verified by Jane Egginton
Project Editor: Sheila Hawkins Ltd

Published by AAA Publishing, 1000 AAA Drive, Heathrow, Florida 32746.
The *AAA Britain TravelBook* was created and produced for AAA Publishing by AA Media Limited, Fanum House, Basing View, Basingstoke, Hampshire, RG21 4EA, UK.

ISBN: 978-1-59508-518-4

Cover photos
Main cover photo and spine: Tower Bridge, London, England, Miles Ertman © 2012 Masterfile Corporation.
Back cover: Taxis and Union Jack Flags, Regent Street, London, England, Alan Copson © awl-images.

Cataloging-in-Publication Data is on file with the Library of Congress.

Color separations by Digital Department AA Publishing.
Printed in China by C & C Offset Printing Co. Ltd.

A04764

The Valley of Rocks seen from Hollerday Hill, Exmoor National Park, Devon

Foreword

Britain is steeped in history and dotted with castles and grand country houses. This book will help you discover its heart. Historic city centers, lush landscapes and smaller towns fill these pages, introducing you to this fascinating island's diverse regions. Visit world-class sights and museums, or follow one of the included driving or walking tours through the countryside.

Relish the cathedral cities of York and Canterbury and retrace the steps of the great playwright William Shakespeare in his hometown of Stratford-upon-Avon. You'll find plenty of reasons for the abundant national pride in Edinburgh, Scotland's premier city, and in Cardiff, the civic capital of Wales. Bath and the elegant towns of Cheltenham, Stamford and Harrogate are a pleasant contrast to big-city bustle. And London is renowned for its cultural legacy and sightseeing treasures. The capital of Britain also stepped onto the world stage in 2012 as the host of the Summer Olympic Games – officially, the Games of the XXX Olympiad – or more informally, London 2012.

Wherever you go – and you'll never have far to travel – you'll experience intriguing new aspects of the land and its people. Leave any preconceptions behind and let the AAA Britain TravelBook be your guide, whether along the well-trodden tourist trails or off the beaten track. There's plenty of practical information to smooth your path, such as tips on getting around and finding a place to stay. We've included maps, descriptions of the sights, and suggestions for eating, drinking and shopping. Our insider advice will help you get the most out of Britain, one of Europe's most charming countries.

Contents

Key to symbols

- map page number and coordinates
- address
- telephone number
- opening times
- nearest subway station
- nearest bus/trolley bus/tram/funicular route
- ferry
- restaurant
- admission charge
- information

For conversion charts, see the inside back cover

Warwick Castle, a medieval fortress, Warwickshire

Introduction to Britain

The image of Britain in the eyes of the world is a contradictory one. Here is a little ragged-edged cluster of islands, stuck out in the sea off the shoulder of Europe, which until recently wielded more power and influence than any other country on earth. These islands are some of the most densely populated in the world, yet they are famous for their tranquil green ruralism and the sense of space and leisure that they maintain. Their people are proverbially polite, yet notoriously pugnacious. The British are well known to be reserved and insular, yet they have spread their culture enthusiastically around the globe. They are said to be philistine to the core, yet have given rise to many artistic giants as diverse as Shakespeare, Wordsworth, the Beatles and the Brontës. And the British are famous for being tongue-tied in social situations, yet have had their language accepted as the lingua franca of the world.

Britain Explained

"Britain" refers to the countries of England, Scotland and Wales. "Great Britain" is Britain and its adjacent islands (except the Channel Islands and Isle of Man). To include Northern Ireland, the correct name is the "United Kingdom." The United Kingdom is the official unified entity, governed by the central parliament in London and (nominally) by Queen Elizabeth II. However, political boundaries are becoming increasingly blurred and Scotland and Wales – historically uneasy with what they saw as an English parliament (and Queen) in London – now have their own national assemblies and a degree of autonomy. The legacy of London remains, and when the British talk about "this country," they usually mean Britain.

A Historic Land

History has dealt a full deck to Britain, scattering aces across the land in the form of prehistoric stone monuments and Iron Age hill forts, historic castles and great country houses, medieval market towns and Georgian spa resorts. Here you can follow the stories of names as illustrious as Queen Elizabeth I, Sir Winston Churchill, Jane Austen and Charles Darwin, through the houses and landscapes where they were born and lived, worked and died. You may choose to plunge into London, one of the world's greatest cities, for a rich diet of pomp, pageantry, culture and fun. You can visit Windsor Castle to savor the heady scent of a thousand years of monarchy and gaze at the stunning stained-glass window of St. George's Chapel. You could photograph the scarlet-coated Beefeaters at the Tower of London, listen to a kilted bagpiper on the ramparts of Edinburgh Castle, muse among the dreaming spires of Oxford University or stroll through Stratford-upon-Avon, from the house where William Shakespeare was born to the church where he was buried.

An Explorable Country

Such potent symbols of Britain are unquestionably "must-see" attractions. The images of pageantry and history that they conjure up are what whets most people's appetite to visit Britain. And they are so seductive that it is easy to spend a couple of weeks here and never lift your nose from the well-worn tourist trail. But Britain is far more than a museum of ancient buildings and quaint costumes. Packed within its shores is an enormous variety of landscapes – a green and brown patchwork quilt, smooth and soft here, lumpy and rough there. In Britain, marshes blend with cornfields, chalk downs with mighty cliffs, and oak woods with mountains, all within a scrap of land that, at its most

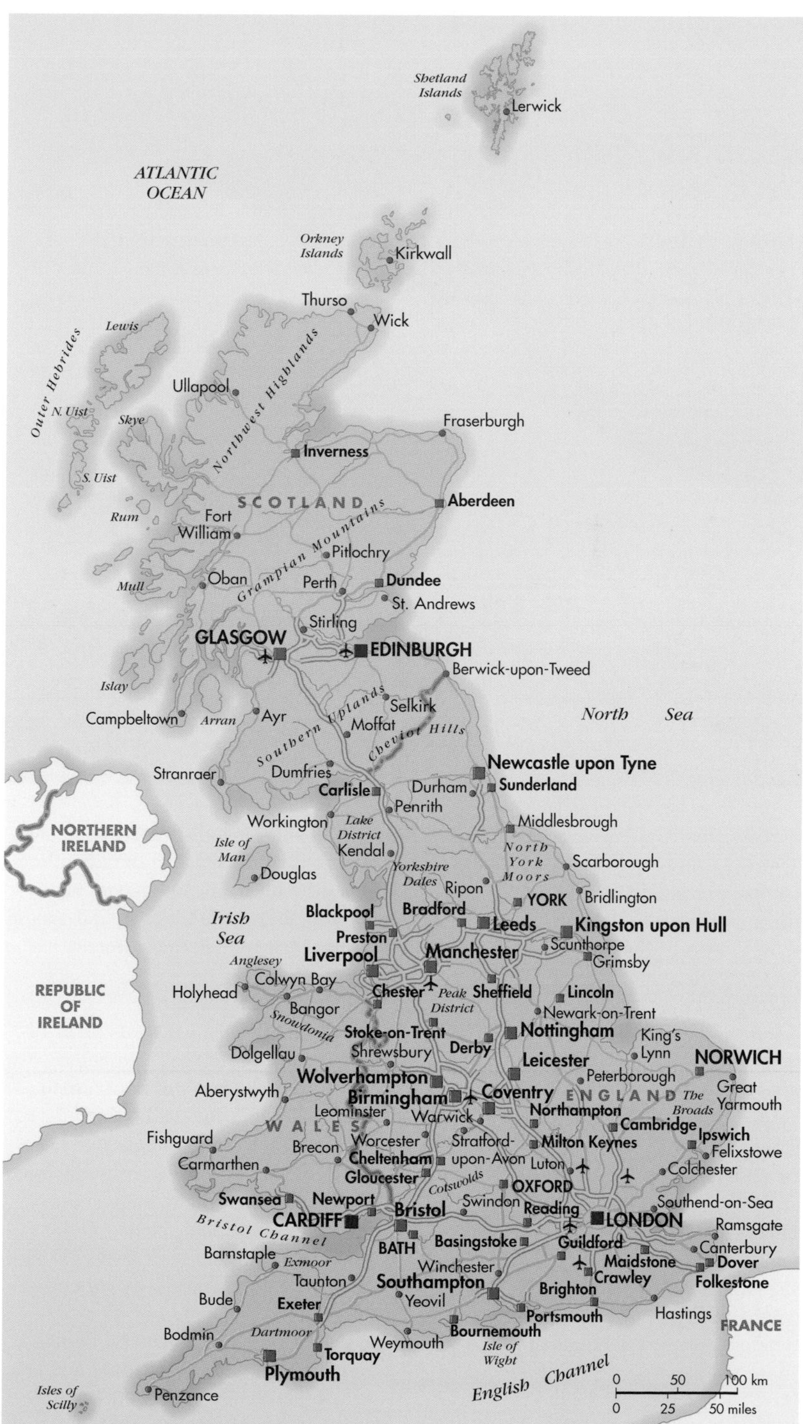
Shetland Islands
Lerwick
ATLANTIC OCEAN
Orkney Islands
Kirkwall
Thurso
Wick
Lewis
Outer Hebrides
N. Uist
Skye
S. Uist
Ullapool
Northwest Highlands
Fraserburgh
Inverness
SCOTLAND
Aberdeen
Rum
Fort William
Grampian Mountains
Pitlochry
Mull
Oban
Perth
Dundee
St. Andrews
Stirling
GLASGOW
EDINBURGH
Berwick-upon-Tweed
Islay
Southern Uplands
Selkirk
Campbeltown
Arran
Ayr
Moffat
Cheviot Hills
North Sea
Stranraer
Dumfries
Newcastle upon Tyne
Carlisle
Durham
Sunderland
Penrith
NORTHERN IRELAND
Workington
Lake District
Middlesbrough
Isle of Man
Kendal
North York Moors
Scarborough
Douglas
Yorkshire Dales
Ripon
YORK
Bridlington
Irish Sea
Blackpool
Bradford
Leeds
Kingston upon Hull
Preston
Manchester
Scunthorpe
Anglesey
Liverpool
Grimsby
REPUBLIC OF IRELAND
Holyhead
Colwyn Bay
Chester
Peak District
Sheffield
Lincoln
Bangor
Newark-on-Trent
Snowdonia
Stoke-on-Trent
Nottingham
King's Lynn
Dolgellau
Shrewsbury
Derby
Leicester
NORWICH
Wolverhampton
Peterborough
Aberystwyth
Birmingham
Coventry
ENGLAND
The Broads
Great Yarmouth
Leominster
Warwick
Northampton
WALES
Cambridge
Fishguard
Worcester
Stratford-upon-Avon
Milton Keynes
Ipswich
Brecon
Felixstowe
Carmarthen
Cheltenham
Luton
Colchester
Gloucester
Cotswolds
OXFORD
Swansea
Newport
Swindon
Southend-on-Sea
CARDIFF
Bristol
Reading
LONDON
Bristol Channel
Ramsgate
BATH
Basingstoke
Guildford
Canterbury
Barnstaple
Exmoor
Winchester
Maidstone
Dover
Taunton
Southampton
Crawley
Folkestone
Bude
Yeovil
Brighton
Exeter
Hastings
Portsmouth
Bodmin
Dartmoor
Weymouth
Bournemouth
FRANCE
Torquay
Isle of Wight
Plymouth
English Channel
Isles of Scilly
Penzance
0 50 100 km
0 25 50 miles

narrow, you could drive across in a day. There are more quiet villages, small woods, inviting footpaths and friendly pubs tucked away down country lanes than there are along the main roads and highways, and more memorable views hiding just over the horizon than you'll see from the window of a tour bus. Above all, Britain is an explorable country, a place where the traveling can be just as much fun as the arriving. So slow down, and give yourself the time to be taken by surprise.

Don't Rush the British

Don't rush Britain, and don't rush the British. A typical Brit (or "John Bull") might seem all buttoned-up and defensive on first acquaintance. But those who approach the British quietly have their reward as the reserve cracks away to reveal some of the oddest, warmest and most distinctive characters on earth. Bring a sense of the ridiculous and a taste for ironic understatement with you, and you'll like and understand Mr. and Mrs. Bull all the better.

The Bones of Britain

Britain lies off the northwest corner of Europe, with her ragged coat collar – the weatherbeaten islands of the Scottish coast – turned to the wild North Atlantic. The westerly winds, and the ocean waves they drive in from the open Atlantic, have cut the western coast of Scotland into dramatic clefts.

The underlying volcanic rocks of these most northerly and westerly regions – the Scottish Highlands and Islands, the Lake District in northwest England, Snowdonia in Wales, Dartmoor and the Cornish peninsula in the southwest – form the highest country in Britain.

The Seven Sisters chalk cliffs dip into the English Channel on the south coast in East Sussex

Light Limestone, Dark Gritstone

Other high country areas in both Scotland and Wales were formed by younger rocks, heaved several miles high during underground convulsions and then eroded into a muddle of fractured rocks with suitably slithery names: slates, shales, schists.

Moving south and eastward, you leave behind the great red sandstone cliffs of southwest Scotland and the Cumbrian coast to skim across the limestone of the Pennine hills and dales. To the south lie rolling moors bedded on gritstone, dark and dour when weathered and oxidized, clear and sparkly when newly cut or cleaned. These northern mountains, moors and dales – the wettest region of a country blessed with a generous amount of rain – make wonderful walking country, and so does the snaking band of speckly oolitic limestone that comes next in our southeasterly journey. The oolitic hill ranges are "wolds" – the Lincolnshire Wolds, the Cotswolds – and their towns, villages, farmsteads and field walls are constructed from stone that can vary from silver to a rich honey color. The city of Bath is the queen of the oolite, with gracious streets, avenues and crescents of houses and other buildings made of the golden stone.

Chalk Cliffs and Downs

The county of Dorset along England's southern coast is also the westernmost outpost of the great blanket of chalk that covers the southeastern corner of Britain. Up to 1,800 feet thick, this smooth white wedge of lime is entirely made up of the shells of microscopic sea creatures. Beech woods, herb-rich downlands (many now cultivated) and high white cliffs are the features of the chalk downs, rolling with a beautiful elasticity from the counties of Dorset through Wiltshire, Hampshire and East and West Sussex into Kent.

A Bleak Beauty

Easternmost of all – and driest, being sheltered from Britain's prevailing westerly winds – are the flat lands of gravel and silt washed down by melting Ice Age glaciers into what is now the Thames Estuary and the bulging rump of East Anglia. This level countryside, so rich in churches built from flint, produces wonderful wheat and vegetables. The salt marshes and pebbly shores where southeast England meets the North Sea have a bleak beauty all of their own. Wildfowl congregate in huge numbers here, along the best birding coast in Britain.

Ordnance Survey Maps

The Ordnance Survey (OS), based in the south coast city of Southampton, is a national institution of which the British are rightly proud.

Drivers, cyclists, hikers and lovers of landscape and the open air acknowledge the superior quality of the maps produced by the OS.

The most useful for finding your way around small sections of Britain, and appreciating what you see while you do so, are the crimson-covered, 1:50,000-scale Landrangers. They cover the entire country in a series of over 200 maps.

For countryside rambling, more serious hiking and off-road cycling, it's advisable to use the orange-covered 1:25,000-scale Explorers, which cover the entire country in a series of more than 400 maps.

All footpaths and other public off-road rights of way are marked on both series of maps. You can buy laminated waterproof versions of most maps, as well as digital versions to load onto PCs and GPS units.

OS maps are for sale at tourist offices, bookstores and on the internet. They are also kept for reference at most town libraries.

Pioneers

Ten thousand years ago, as the great ice sheets of the last Ice Age steadily retreated northward, the hunter-gatherer pioneers of the current phase of British civilization arrived across land bridges from the Continent. Acres of great forests fell to stone tools as the newcomers began to clear the land. More foreign immigrants arrived as the

Hadrian's Wall runs across the country just to the south of the Scottish border

millennia went by – late Stone Age farmers from the Mediterranean, bronze workers from Spain and the Low Countries (present-day Belgium, Luxembourg and The Netherlands), along with iron-smelting Celts from France. Each contributed new skills to the community, and fresh genes to the human pool. They raised stone monuments and tombs, worked gold, worshiped the sun and the trees, and sowed and reaped the land. This was the state of things when the Romans invaded in AD 43.

Roman Efficiency

For nearly 400 years Britain was the northernmost outpost of the Roman Empire. The impact of the Romans on the country was profound. These practical-minded overlords began to put into place a serviceable legal system. They organized agriculture, built sumptuous country houses and public buildings, and laid down a network of roads that were the envy of the empire. They mined, smelted, crafted, ditched and drained. This was the beginning of an efficiently governed Britain.

Bath's Circus is an elegant Georgian sweep of town houses built between 1754 and 1768

However, the Roman Empire rotted from within and crumbled in the face of barbarian attacks. By AD 420 the last of the Romans were gone, their influence dwindled, and the Dark Ages rolled in to cover their traces.

Saxons and Danes

Fair-haired Saxons arrived around AD 450 from the Low Countries of continental Europe, bringing with them hugely improved farming techniques. They plowed the land with ox teams and settled the river valleys with villages, managing their affairs through decision making by discussion in council rather than by decree.

Saxon civilization was rocked when Danish raiding parties began to arrive on the east coast around the end of the eighth century. But King Alfred rallied the Saxons and defeated the Danes at Edington in AD 878. Uneasy compromise and adjustment followed, although stability and unification of the country would not really be established until long after the Norman invasion of 1066.

The Norman Conquerors

The energetic and self-confident Normans snuffed out resistance in northern and eastern England. In 1086 King William I ordered the compilation of the definitive Domesday Book to record exactly what his new possession was worth. The Normans made sure they maximized their investment (and stayed on top of it) by means of the feudal system, which guaranteed the Norman nobleman a place at the top of the pile and peasants a subsistence-level existence in his shadow.

The feudal system eventually softened and then faded out after the disastrous depopulation caused by the Black Death plague of 1348–49. Prosperity in the later Middle Ages of the 15th century came through wool exporting, but the medieval era also saw Britain lose all its land held in France.

In 1455 the aristocratic warlords of the houses of Lancaster and York led their peasant followers into the bloody civil strife of the Wars of the Roses.

Golden Age, Civil War

The Tudors formed a short dynasty from 1485 to 1603. The five rulers – in particular Henry VII, Henry VIII and Elizabeth I – presided over a golden age for Britain, an exciting century of exploration and discovery, national confidence and pride, embodied in such figures as Sir Francis Drake and Sir Walter Raleigh. A remarkable artistic flowering culminated in the genius of William Shakespeare.

But the country suffered during the 17th century when religious and political tensions, set simmering by the rejection of Roman Catholicism during the Reformation, boiled over in the bitter Civil War of 1642–46. The Stuart king Charles I was executed in 1649, and 11 years of quasi-republican "Commonwealth" followed – mostly under the stern eye of the Puritan leader Oliver Cromwell – until Charles II returned from exile in 1660 to restore the monarchy.

Georgian Flowering, Victorian Pomp

There was another cultural flowering during the 18th and early 19th centuries under four successive King Georges – particularly in philosophical thought and in the wonderful uncluttered squares and crescents, town houses and grand Palladian country houses of Georgian architecture. The Industrial Revolution got under way, and Britain went to the top of the world tree of enterprise and innovation. Waterpower was harnessed, then steam. The French-Corsican dictator Napoleon Bonaparte, conqueror of most of Europe, was defeated by the British in 1815, which pushed national confidence to an all time high.

During the reign of Queen Victoria (1837–1901) Britain went from strength to strength, dominating world manufacturing and ruling a vast overseas empire. Yet there were cracks in the edifice. Britain had lost its biggest colony in North America in the 1775–83 War of Independence. At home, rich landowners dispossessed the rural population. The manufacturing towns became a byword for hellish conditions, crowded, unhealthy and ugly. Mineral extraction scarred the landscape. Poverty and inequality underpinned the pomp of late Victorian Britain.

Loss and Gain

The two cataclysmic World Wars of the 20th century cost Britain dearly, both in loss of life (2 million dead) and in global influence. By the turn of the third millennium, one of the greatest empires the world had ever seen had been dismantled, and Britain seemed like a diffident shadow of its former proud self. Yet a largely harmonious multiethnic society has been forged; the fragile countryside and wildlife are both vigilantly protected; and a reputation for tolerance and fairness remains intact – not inconsiderable achievements to celebrate as the country faces the new age.

The Pilgrim Fathers

The first of Britain's shaky attempts to settle North America was Sir Walter Raleigh's foundation of a colony in 1584 in Virginia. It heralded a trickle of migration through the 17th century, mostly by religious dissenters in flight from Catholic or Protestant intolerance. The first and best known of these pioneers were the Pilgrim Fathers. Led by William Brewster and William Bradford, they had first tried to emigrate from the Lincolnshire river port of Boston in 1607, but were captured and jailed for their pains. The following year, however, they did get away. In 1620 the little group of dissenting families sailed from Holland to Britain, intending to use the old country as a stepping-stone to the new. In two tiny ships, the *Mayflower* and the *Speedwell*, they departed from the south coast port of Southampton on August 15, 1620. A storm in the English Channel forced them into Dartmouth for emergency patching up. The leaky little *Speedwell* proved beyond repair, so the Pilgrim Fathers crammed into the *Mayflower,* finally setting out from Plymouth on September 6, 1620. Just over 100 passengers and crew, under the command of Captain Christopher Jones of Harwich, sailed across the Atlantic and found a new world in New England.

Britain today is a multicultural society – one of the most profound and conspicuous changes in these islands since World War II. Alongside the influence of the modern media and the internet, in broadening perspectives and opening eyes, this ethnic diversity has made the British a far less insular and narrow-minded people. The old sense of superiority, of being a cut above "Johnny Foreigner," is gone. This liberating effect can be seen in a range of international influences on British cuisine, on the pop music that dominates the charts, on people's dress, speech and manners, on the way they react to strangers and to each other, and on the schooling and leisure pursuits of their children.

Class Caricature

The British are no longer (if they ever were) the condescending, tight-lipped puritans of familiar stereotype. They are black, white, straight, gay, conventional, off-the-wall: a thoroughly mixed bunch with – on the whole – a relaxed and easygoing attitude toward each other. The class system is still alive inside most British heads, but more in caricature than actuality nowadays. It surfaces from time to time – when there is a proposal to abolish the House of Lords, for example, or when one of the tabloid newspapers sends a

London is a multicultural city

The Changing the Guard ceremony takes place at Buckingham Palace in London

photographer to mock the moneyed spectators parading in their finery at Henley Regatta or Royal Ascot. But the British themselves treat class more as a joke these days.

Party Place

Where a social divide does show is in the increasingly divergent lifestyles of the old and young. For young people, especially those in the cities, Britain has become a 24-hour party place over the last couple of decades. Its clubbing scene is famous throughout Europe. The centers of big provincial cities such as Bristol, Manchester, Leeds and Newcastle, which would have been deserted after midnight only a few years ago, now come to life in the wee hours, with revelers dancing into the night – and the street – for hours.

Young Brits drink cappuccino at sidewalk tables or stroll, beer bottle to lips, through lively enclaves. They are far less concerned than their parents were about settling down early to a regular job and a sensible family life – partly because, in common with most of the developed world these days, the steady job-for-life is becoming increasingly rare.

North and South

Many parts of Britain are facing a new start in the 21st century, forced on them by the collapse of industries – coal mining, steelmaking, shipbuilding, textile manufacturing, heavy engineering – on which their prosperity and daily ways of life were founded at the beginning of the 20th century. Most heavily industrialized regions are in the northern part of the country, and the industrial decline and high unemployment that plagued them in the 1970s and late in the 20th century have helped to reinforce the idea of a "north–south divide."

There certainly are strong regional differences, very noticeable as you travel through Britain. Accent and dialect tend to be more marked the farther away from London you go, speech becomes plainer and more direct, and each region is more proudly championed by its natives.

The debating chamber at the Scottish Parliament building in Edinburgh was first used in 2004

Softer Left, Harder Right?

British politics used to be polarized. Rural areas and the southeast of England could be characterized as conservative, and their political party was the Conservative Party. It was the party of Benjamin Disraeli, Winston Churchill (for most, but not all of his career) and Margaret Thatcher. Scotland, Wales, the northern cities of England and the poorer areas of London leaned to the political left – characterized by Labour politicians such as Ramsay MacDonald, Clement Atlee and Harold Wilson.

At the end of the 1990s, the distinctions softened. Labour leader Tony Blair swept to power with a program that combined elements of both traditions. He was succeeded after 10 years by his former lieutenant and finance minister Gordon Brown. The 2010 election resulted in a coalition of Conservatives and Liberal Democrats, who appeared in many respects to be the heirs to the Blair era. While it appears that a political middle ground has been reached, the British still have not fully embraced the European Union, and cling doggedly to beloved national institutions – the pint of beer, the mile, the pound sterling and driving on the left.

Breakup of Britain

However, these national institutions may soon lack a nation to symbolize. The political union between Scotland, England and Wales has slackened after several centuries of tight bonding. Scotland now has its own parliament, with considerable power, and Wales has a national assembly with somewhat less power.

The mood of independence in both countries is stronger than at any time in the 300-year history of the union. Northern Ireland, too, has its own assembly. Whether this fragmenting of the national conglomeration that was once proud to call itself Great Britain will be a strengthening or enfeebling

development remains to be seen. So, too, does the future of the monarchy under which these islands have lived more or less willingly for a thousand years. The Royal Family, an unassailable icon since Victorian times, has come under sharp criticism in more recent years – partly through a series of self-inflicted indignities, partly due to obsessive interest on the part of a salacious media, and partly a reflection of the changing identity and allegiances of Britons themselves.

Britain has always considered itself a land of tradition and stability. Now it stands on the threshold of great changes. All in all, there has never been a more interesting time to pay a visit to this grand old dame who is discovering a new spring in her step.

Music, Mystery and the Muse

Writing for the printed page and for the theater is far and away Britain's most significant contribution to the world of the arts, and here the past casts a long shadow. William Shakespeare still bestrides the theater like a god, selling out performances not only at the Royal Shakespeare Theatre in Stratford-upon-Avon and the brilliant replica of his Globe Theatre on London's South Bank, but at provincial theaters across the country. He is still the man to catch when you visit Britain.

Poetry has been similarly dominated by William Wordsworth, although both the late poet laureate Ted Hughes and the brilliant Irish Nobel Prize winner Seamus Heaney have succeeded in turning the contemporary spotlight on this neglected art form.

As for novelists, who would not pale in the mighty 19th-century shadows of Jane Austen, the Brontë sisters, Charles Dickens and Thomas Hardy?

Modern writers keeping the flag flying include the dark and subtle Ian McEwan, the lighter but quintessentially English Joanna Trollope, and the hugely successful J. K. Rowling – all well worth seeking out.

No one seems quite sure what art is anymore. Is it the readily appreciated

The Café Royal bar in Edinburgh dates from the 1860s and has a number of original Victorian features

paintings of David Hockney or the bulgy, enigmatic sculptures of Henry Moore? The crumpled and soiled unmade bed displayed by Tracey Emin or the body fluids of Gilbert and George? Or Damien Hirst's sliced cow in formaldehyde? If the function of modern art is to get people talking and keep them at it, then contemporary British artists are doing their job brilliantly. London's Tate Modern is one of the world's leading museums of modern art.

You are on less contentious ground with the musical arts. The sumptuous renovation of the Royal Opera House in Covent Garden has given London an opera and ballet venue to rival any in the world. The Beatles are still the yardstick by which rock bands are judged, and the club scene has its own dividing and specialized groupings and sub-groupings.

Eating and Drinking

The now multicultural society has revolutionized British cuisine, and in the big cities you can sample the very best of literally hundreds of different national favorites, from Afghan to Zambian. Country pubs with any pretensions offer blackboard menus of up to 50 dishes. The best of British fare – fresh fish, game and beef, together with their traditional trimmings – is hard to beat, as long as it's top quality.

Wines and spirits from every corner of the world can be sampled. And the famous British pint of beer – pulled from

a hand-pump or straight out of a barrel, and drunk slowly – has subtleties of flavor that can spoil you for all those chilled, pasteurized, fizzy concoctions passing for beer elsewhere.

Quintessentially British

To see the English at their most characteristic, drop in on a church fête in summer or attend one of the eccentric village festivals, such as the Hare Pie Scramble and Bottle Kicking at Hallaton, Leicestershire on Easter Monday. Catch the Scots at their nationalistic and cheery best on Hogmanay (New Year's Eve – but not New Year's Day, a national day of mourning in Scotland!), or on Burns Night, January 25, when they celebrate their national poet, Robert Burns. For the Welsh, it should be St. David's Day, March 1, in a small country church or village school, or the Royal National Eisteddfod, the Welsh language pride and musical joy, during the first week of August.

As for the *English* – try the Notting Hill Carnival in London during the last weekend (Saturday–Monday) in August, a crowded and noisy celebration with fantastic costumes and ear-splitting music, based on Caribbean tradition but now infused with Asian and Latin American strands. Or you could join the thousands of boating enthusiasts who crowd along the shores of tiny Isle of Wight to enjoy the annual Cowes regatta week, also in August.

For English land lovers, there are no greater spectacles than the big race meetings that bring all members of society together in the common thrill of the racetrack. All of these events throughout the year attract the great and the good, the rich and the poor in an extraordinary array of color and glamor, passion and enthusiasm.

Wherever you go in Britain, whatever time of the year, there will be a local or national festival taking place, usually complete with costumes, singing and dancing, but always with enjoyment.

Heritage Pass

The English Heritage Overseas Pass (not available to UK residents) offers unlimited free entry to more than 400 historic houses, castles and gardens, including almost all the major sites listed in this book. A map and guidebook to the properties is included in the price. The pass is valid for seven (£20.40) or 14 (£25) consecutive days for one adult. Family tickets are available. Tickets must be purchased online at: www.britishheritagepassbritain.com. An E-ticket will be issued, which should be printed and taken to the redemption point at any English Heritage Property where it will be exchanged for a pass. Vouchers are valid for one year from the date of issue.

Timeline

AD 43	Romans invade and conquer Britain.
AD 407	Roman legions withdraw from Britain.
AD 450	Saxons and others begin waves of invasion and settlement from the Low Countries.
AD 563	St. Columba begins spreading Christianity in Britain.
AD 878	King Alfred of Wessex defeats invading Danes at Battle of Edington.
1066	Normans invade and conquer England.
1215	Barons force King John to sign Magna Carta, Britain's first bill of civil liberties and political rights.
1348–49	Black Death plague wipes out a third of Britain's population.
1381	Peasant's Revolt is put down with savagery; feudal system crumbles.
1485	Tudor dynasty (1485–1603) begins, a Golden Age for Britain.

Parts of Arundel Castle were built at the end of the 11th century

1534–40	Henry VIII breaks with Rome and founds the Church of England.
1642–46	Civil War is fought between King Charles I and Parliament.
1649	King Charles I is executed; Commonwealth (Republic) of England initiated; Oliver Cromwell governs from 1653.
1660	Charles II is restored to the throne.
1707	Act of Union between England and Scotland.
1746	Scot rebels under Bonnie Prince Charlie defeated at Battle of Culloden; collapse of the clan system and way of life follows.
1769	James Watt patents the first efficient steam engine, heralding the Industrial Revolution.
1783	American independence is achieved.
1815	Twenty-five years of war with France ends with Napoleon Bonaparte's defeat at the Battle of Waterloo.
1837	Queen Victoria ascends the throne for her 64-year reign.
1851	The Great Exhibition reflects Imperial Britain's 19th-century pride and prosperity.
1914–18	A million British die during World War I.
1939–45	World War II (see below).
1947	India achieves independence, beginning the dissolution of the British Empire.
1952	Elizabeth II becomes queen at the age of 25 on the death of her father, George VI.
1969	Start of "The Troubles" in Northern Ireland, which continue for 30 years.
1973	Britain joins the European Community (now the European Union).
2002	The Queen Mother dies at age 101; celebrations for Queen Elizabeth's Golden Jubilee.
2010	The general election in Britain results in a coalition government for the first time in 30 years.
2011	Prince William marries Catherine Middleton.
2012	The nation celebrates the Queen's Diamond Jubilee and London hosts the summer Olympic Games.

Effects of World War II

The British have only recently begun to put World War II and its long-term effects on their society into perspective. This war saw many of Britain's cities badly damaged and 58,000 civilians killed by bombs. The devastation of important industrial cities and ports is graphically recorded in their museums.

Five million volunteers from the British Empire joined 6 million Britons in the Allied services; the experiences of these "colonials" provided a great impetus toward postwar independence movements that saw the empire disappear. Weakness, introspection and exhaustion after the war, not to mention the financial drain, caused Britain to lose its place among the most prosperous and influential of the world's nations.

With 275,000 British servicemen and women dead, the war also had a profound effect at the personal level.

Survival Guide

- Don't forget to pack your raingear, an umbrella and some sensible walking shoes – it rains quite a lot in Britain.
- If you enter central London by car Monday through Friday (except public holidays and Christmas through New Year) 7 a.m.–6 p.m. you will incur a daily Congestion Charge of £10, which must be paid in advance or on the day of travel, or £12 if you pay by midnight of the following day. For additional information phone 0845 222 1234; www.tfl.gov.uk. For most other big cities in the U.K. use the anti-congestion "park and ride" plans; you leave your car in a parking lot on the outskirts, and frequent buses (every 10 to 15 minutes) take you into the center.
- Many of the famous scarlet telephone boxes were replaced during the 1990s by smaller booths – cheaper to maintain and functional but much harder to spot. A few can still be found in London and in some town and village centers.
- The British police are still among the world's friendliest and most helpful.
- Baked potatoes and other take-away (to go) foods have become immensely popular, but probably the best fast-food bet is still good old fish and chips – cheap and delicious.
- How to buy a drink in a pub: Walk to the bar, order your drink and pay for it when you receive it. No one tips the bar staff, but if you are feeling particularly friendly the offer of a drink is often welcome.
- Famous tourist attractions such as Shakespeare's birthplace at Stratford-upon-Avon, the Crown Jewels in the Tower of London or the ancient monument of Stonehenge on Salisbury Plain become very crowded on summer weekends – particularly on public holidays. Try to visit early in the day, before the crowds gather.
- For London's most popular attractions, it is a good idea to pre-book admission tickets through the attraction's website, usually at least 24 hours in advance.

Shakespeare's Birthplace in Stratford-upon-Avon has been attracting visitors since the 18th century

- The British are generally relaxed about dress codes when eating out, but in high-end restaurants and hotels you may feel more comfortable in a suit and tie or a dress and high heels. Also, many clubs outside of London operate a "no jeans and sneakers" policy.
- For both women and men, it has become acceptable to greet female acquaintances with a kiss on one cheek, or both, provided that you know them well enough. However, between men a handshake is the usual greeting.
- Don't stick to the main roads and highways. Buy a book of road maps (available at all big service stations) or better still, an Ordnance Survey Landranger map for your area (see page 10), and take time traveling the side roads and country lanes. Don't worry about becoming lost: Britain is a small country full of people to ask.
- Consider taking a boat trip to one of the islands just off the coast of Scotland (page 248) or Northumberland (page 206). You'll see more seabirds and wildflowers than you could dream of and have the pleasure of being entirely out of the everyday world for a few hours.
- Beggars – many damaged by drugs or drink – have become a feature of most British cities and large towns. They rarely make a nuisance of themselves, but sooner or later you will have to decide on your policy. To give or not to give? That's up to you, but it is worth remembering that many of these unfortunates are very young and vulnerable, and many are homeless.
- Walking in the country: Britain boasts the world's most extensive and well-maintained network of legal rights-of-way for walkers. Don't be afraid to try out the footpaths. You can go it independently with the right map, or take one of the thousands of short circular hikes for which there are easy-to-follow leaflet guides – just ask at the nearest tourist office.

A network of footpaths cross Britain's countryside

- Be aware that Scottish and Welsh people do not like to be referred to as "English."
- Some of the more famous cathedrals now ask for standard donations from visitors – generally £3 to £5. A determined visitor can get in without paying, but without such donations no diocese can maintain these wonderful buildings in the condition in which everyone likes to see them.

Southeast England

Opposite: Beachy Head in East Sussex, the highest cliff along the south coast

Southeast England

Southeastern England is the country's most populous region and the richest in per capita income. Its beautiful landscapes, founded on chalk and greensand, are the most threatened by building development, and the most jealously championed by well-heeled local residents. In London it boasts one of the best-known, liveliest and most historic national capitals in the world. The main roads and railroad lines are notoriously congested, thanks to a very high proportion of London commuters. More horses are ridden in this countryside than anywhere else, more gin-and-tonics drunk, more personal bodyguards employed. It is the driest and sunniest region in Britain. Southerners seem, to those from less well-favored regions, to have things soft and easy.

Billowing Chalk

It is the chalk and greensand that give the southeast its gentle elasticity of shape. Gilbert White, the great 18th-century English naturalist, wondered whether the chalk downs might not in ancient times have been quickened by some singular moisture, as bread dough is quickened by yeast, and thus bulged skyward like fungi out of the level plains. It's an attractive idea; the chalk downs do have a dip and roll to them, as they undulate from Kent through Surrey and Sussex into Hampshire, which makes them look as if they are in just-suspended motion. Beech woods known as hangers grow well on the chalky ridges of the North Downs below London, and farther west are wide tracts of heathland, sandy wildernesses dark with heather and pine trees, exuding an atmosphere of lonely mystery. Farther west again, the greensand and gravel flatten into the classic shallow valleys of southern Hampshire, where trout-filled rivers hurry over gravel and flint beds, teeming with healthy green waterweed.

Southeastern Landscapes

The coastline of the southeast starts in industrial confusion and muddle along the flat south shore of the Thames Estuary as it straggles seaward out of London. At the easternmost tip of Kent it rises to form the bulbous nose of the North Foreland. Here, fine chalk cliffs run south and west into the narrows around Dover and Folkestone, where the English Channel meets the North Sea. Then come the strange, and sometimes eerie, flat grazing lands of Romney Marsh, reclaimed centuries ago from the sea, and the even stranger landscape of pebbly Dungeness, the arrowhead-shaped spit of land that forms the largest shingle beach in the world.

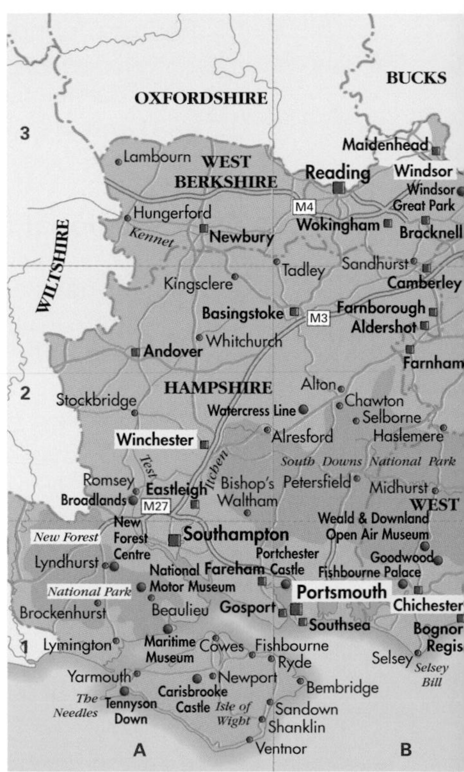

Farther west along the Channel coast the chalk reappears, rising to Beachy Head and the magnificent Seven Sisters cliffs, before declining again into the built-up holiday coast of Sussex, with its beautiful sand and shingle beaches and the wide inlet of Chichester harbor. Still farther west, a charmless mess of docks and development has a little jewel in its center: Portsmouth Historic Dockyard, where Admiral Nelson's famous flagship H.M.S. *Victory* is superbly maintained.

Historic Region

Historic sites lie thick in this corner of Britain, so close to London and to the Continental seaports. Kent, with its Channel ferries and sub-Channel rail tunnel, is the gateway into Britain from Europe for non-air travelers. The county is full of the castles and fine houses of noble and influential figures of the past. It also boasts the lovely medieval city and cathedral of Canterbury, whose archbishop is the Church of England's supreme clergyman. The Chatham Historic Dockyard and the harbors at Dover and Folkestone have sustained Britain's seafarers through the centuries.

Tame and Wild

The counties of Surrey and Berkshire have a rich, opulent feel to them, with some of England's prettiest villages tucked away in the well-wooded folds of the North Downs. This is commuter country, which accounts for the carefully manicured and slightly unreal atmosphere of some of these gorgeous places. It also is the site of the monarch's out-of-town residence – mighty Windsor Castle, near the River Thames west of London. The river scenery here is glorious, celebrated in Kenneth Grahame's *The Wind in the Willows* and

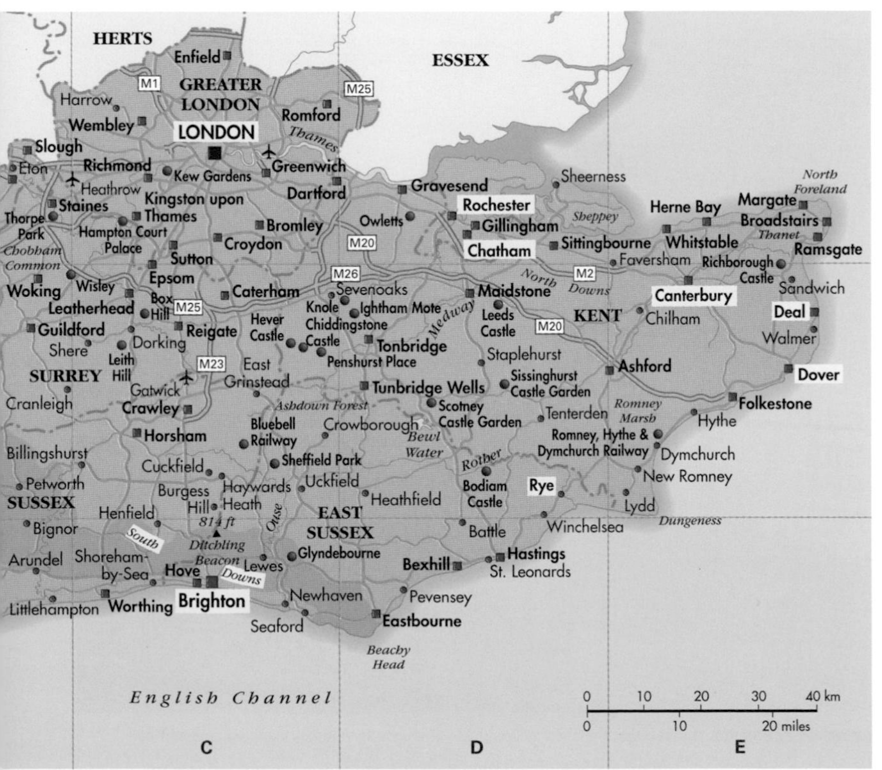

Jerome K. Jerome's *Three Men in a Boat*.

If you want a taste of something lonely and wild, however, head for the dark heathery wastes of Chobham Common, on the Surrey-Berkshire border. "A vast tract of land given up to barrenness," wrote Daniel Defoe in the 1720s. Today it is a nature reserve and a favorite with Sunday strollers.

In July 2012, the quiet streets of Surrey came to life as thousands of spectators lined the roads to cheer on the competitors of the Olympic cycling road races. The courses included a punishing ride many times up and down steep Box Hill in the beautiful Surrey Hills.

Resorts and Romans

Sussex has the beautiful South Downs, now a national park, villages of flint and brick, and a coast dedicated to seaside pleasures, where the queen of the resorts is undoubtedly the now chic and trendy, "old Ocean's Bauble, glittering Brighton." Chichester is a small cathedral town at the feet of the downs. Superb mosaic floors have been unearthed in the ruins of Roman buildings at Fishbourne, on Chichester harbor, and at Bignor, up in the downs northeast of the city.

Walk, Fish, Read

You can stride the South Downs Way along the crest of the downs for over 100 miles, from Eastbourne in East Sussex west to Winchester in Hampshire. Don't forget to pack your fly-fishing rod, for Hampshire's clear, gravel-bedded rivers of Meon and Test are among the best in the world for trout fishing. Pack your Jane Austen, too, so that after you have visited her house in Chawton and her memorial in Winchester Cathedral, you can walk the beech woods and downland paths in the company of Mr. Darcy and the rest of the Austen gang.

Above: Away from towns and cities, thatched buildings are still seen in villages, like here in East Meon
Opposite: The rolling South Downs were declared a national park in 2010

London

London, the capital of Britain, is one of the great cities of the world. The Tower of London, Westminster Abbey, Big Ben, Buckingham Palace and the Mall, Horse Guards Parade and St. Paul's Cathedral: The city boasts dozens of famous architectural showpieces. Today, added to these, is the excellent Olympic Park at Stratford, east London, the major venue for the 2012 Summer Olympic Games, along with other Olympic sporting venues at Wimbledon and on the River Thames at Eton Dorney (see page 64).

But London is far more than a collection of historic buildings, essential viewing though these are. Taking in a show in the West End, shopping in the grand stores of Knightsbridge, dining

out in a range of restaurants that span the culinary globe, strolling in attractive Kensington Gardens or on the walkways along the Thames – it's no wonder so many visitors who come to explore Britain never get any farther than London. Tourist information, tickets for transportation and for city attractions are available from 21 tourist information offices in the city (see page 34).

A Sharp Bunch

Londoners are a mixed lot, becoming more culturally and racially mixed with every passing decade. You'll find Londoners themselves a witty and eclectic bunch of people and the city a safe and pleasant place to explore, provided that you follow the common sense rules that apply when visiting any major city.

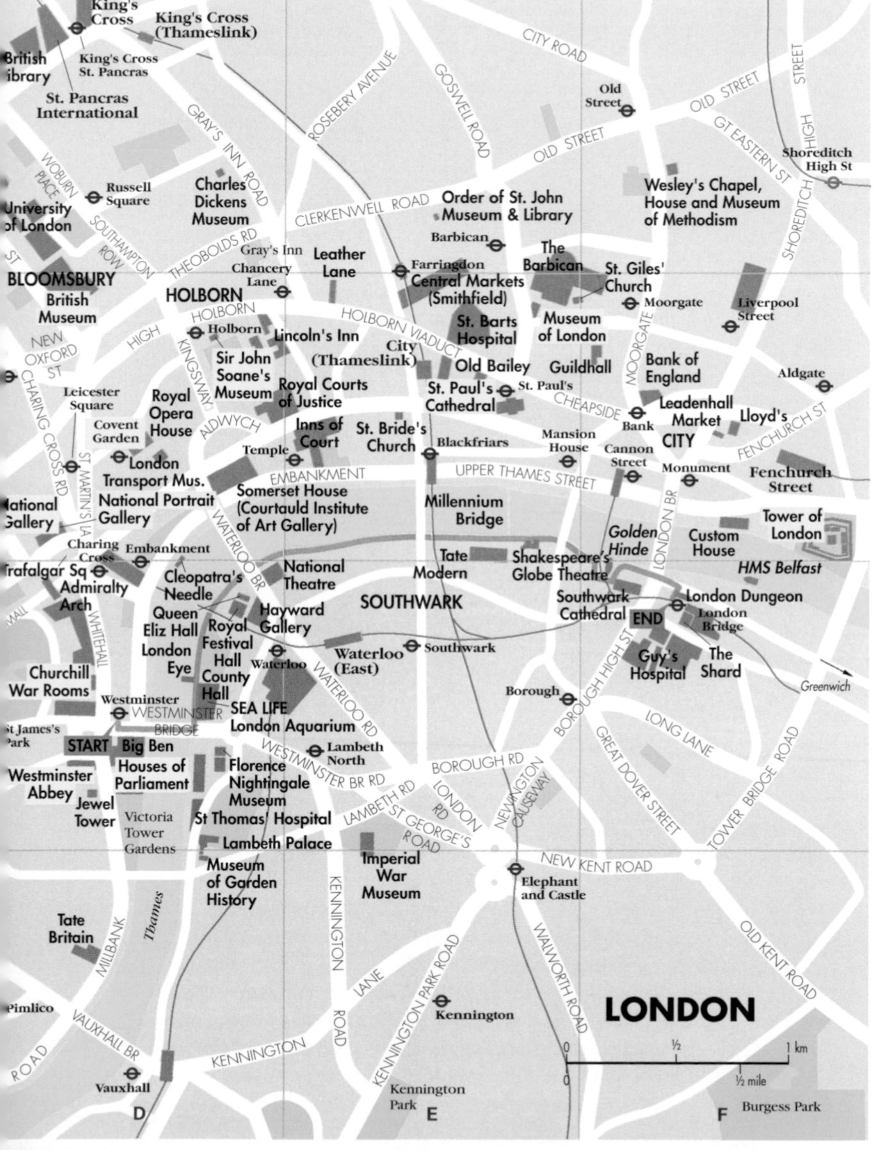

The London "Clock"

Orienting yourself in the city is not too difficult and fixing your bearings in your mind's eye is well worth it. Begin by imagining a clockface with Trafalgar Square at the clockface center. Trafalgar Square itself contains the National Gallery, the National Portrait Gallery, Nelson's Column and wild pigeons in their thousands.

At 12 o'clock north from Trafalgar Square is the West End and its theaters and Leicester Square and its movie theaters; elegant Bloomsbury and the British Museum lie beyond. At 1 o'clock you will find Covent Garden and the Royal Opera House. At 2 o'clock are the city's financial quarter and St. Paul's Cathedral, with the Barbican Centre and the Museum of London a little to the

Essential Information

Tourist Information

■ Visit London

Some 21 tourist information centers in London offer information, tickets for transportation and popular London attractions and sightseeing tours. The most central office is: Piccadilly Circus Underground Station, London W1D 7DH.

Urban Transportation

London Underground or "Tube" (subway) trains operate Mon.–Sat. 4:30 a.m.–12:40 a.m., Sun. 7 a.m.–1 a.m. and serve central stations every 5–10 minutes. Lines are color coded and maps are displayed in stations. Tickets can be bought at ticket booths or machines in station entrance halls. The subway symbol is a red circle crossed by a blue horizontal line and is marked on the London city map. London's distinctive red buses serve the city and suburbs from 5 a.m.–12:30 a.m., but with a 24-hour service on most major routes. The most economical and convenient way to travel by bus and tube is to purchase a pay-as-you-go Oyster card. Alternatively, tickets can be bought at bus and Tube stations: ☎ 0843 222 1234 (24hrs); www.tfl.gov.uk. London's cabs are metered and are ready for passengers when the yellow light is on. They can be flagged down on the street or found at taxi stands.

Airport Information

London is served by two main airports: Heathrow, 20 miles west of the city (☎ 0844 892 0322; www.heathrowairport.com), and Gatwick, 30 miles south (☎ 0844 335 1802; www.gatwickairport.com). Services below operate daily from around 5 a.m.–midnight (less frequently outside these times). The Heathrow Express train goes to London's Paddington Station every 15 minutes (travel time 15–20 minutes). The subway's Piccadilly line departs to central London every 4–5 minutes (travel time 1 hour). Buses to London's Victoria Coach Station depart every 30 minutes (travel time 35–60 minutes). The Gatwick Express train goes to Victoria Station every 15 minutes (travel time 30–40 minutes). Southern trains also travel to Victoria Station every 15 minutes (travel time 40 minutes). There are First Capital Connect trains to London Bridge and St. Pancras International stations every 15 minutes (travel time 30 minutes). There are also buses to Victoria Coach Station, departing hourly (travel time from 130 minutes).

Climate – average highs and lows for the month

Jan.	Feb.	Mar.	Apr.	May	Jun.	Jul.	Aug.	Sep.	Oct.	Nov.	Dec.
6°C	6°C	10°C	13°C	16°C	20°C	21°C	21°C	18°C	14°C	10°C	7°C
43°F	43°F	50°F	55°F	61°F	68°F	70°F	70°F	64°F	57°F	50°F	45°F
2°C	2°C	3°C	5°C	8°C	11°C	13°C	13°C	11°C	7°C	5°C	3°C
36°F	36°F	37°F	41°F	46°F	52°F	55°F	55°F	52°F	45°F	41°F	37°F

Detail of the exterior of London's Albert Hall

north. From 3 o'clock to 5 o'clock is the River Thames. The north Embankment runs east toward the Tower of London, while the South Bank is lined with attractions that include the London Eye (a giant Ferris-wheel with glass-enclosed observation capsules), Royal Festival Hall, the Tate Modern art gallery and the replica Shakespeare's Globe Theatre.

At 6 o'clock are Westminster Abbey, Big Ben and the Houses of Parliament. At 7 o'clock, it's the Churchill War Rooms on the edge of St. James's Park. At 8 o'clock comes Buckingham Palace, with the upper-crust districts of Knightsbridge and Kensington a little farther out. Here you will find Harrods department store and three splendid museums: Victoria & Albert, Science, and Natural History. At 9 o'clock lie the parks – Green Park, Hyde Park and then Kensington Gardens. Also here is the exclusive Mayfair district. Finally, Oxford Street brings you from 10 o'clock back to 12, with Madame Tussauds and Regent's Park beyond.

Getting around in London is simple, provided you don't try to drive. Public transportation consists of the underground subway system, known as the "Tube." London's red buses offer frequent service, and the famed black taxicabs are everywhere, though not all are black now. Note that you are expected to tip the cab driver.

From Breakfast to Dinner

The cuisines of the world meet and mingle in London, and some of the most exciting cooking stems from this creative infusion of different cultures. You could start the day at your hotel with a full English breakfast (bacon, eggs and all the trimmings), have lunch at one of London's burgeoning food markets, take afternoon tea at The Savoy, and dine at any one of the hundreds of brasseries.

Of course, you would need to work up an appropriate appetite – and what better way than shopping? Harrods is a realm unto itself. Fortnum & Mason has all you need in the food and drink line. Harvey Nichols and the boutiques of Knightsbridge keep ladies in classic fashion style; gentlemen should seek out Gieves & Hawkes on Savile Row and Bates Gentlemen's Hatter on Jermyn Street for their apparel requirements. Cheaper and maybe more cheerful shopping flourishes in the ragbag atmosphere of the street markets in Camden (daily, with the main market on Sunday) and Petticoat Lane (daily except Saturday; with the main market on Sunday), while Charing Cross Road is lined with bookstores of every size and description.

Plays and Pubs

What to do in the evening? Those organized enough to reserve seats well in advance can enjoy world-class opera and ballet at the Royal Opera House in Covent Garden. Shakespeare fans will revel in the open-air Shakespeare's Globe Theatre on the South Bank. There are also dozens of plays and shows in the West End around Shaftesbury Avenue. Concerts at the Royal Festival Hall and the Royal Albert Hall are worth checking out. Or you could just walk into one of the thousands of London pubs and sit chatting over a pint of beer.

London Sights

Key to symbols

map coordinates refer to the London map on pages 32–33 admission charge: $$$ more than £6, $$ £2–£6, $ less than £2

See page 5 for complete key to symbols

British Museum

The British Museum, founded around the private collection of royal physician Sir Hans Sloane (1660–1753), has grown over 250 years to become one of the world's premier museums, with a collection of more than 8 million items. The British Library has now moved to St. Pancras, but the famous cylindrical Reading Room (where Karl Marx, Mahatma Gandhi and George Bernard Shaw all studied) remains.

There are more than 2 miles of galleries. The best approach is to select a few must-see items from the museum plan at the information desk, and then to enjoy whatever crosses your path as you seek them out. Among the treasures are the controversial Elgin Marbles, a group of 5th-century BC sculptures brought from the Parthenon in Athens to London in 1801 (the Greek government is still trying to have them returned); the famous Rosetta Stone, carved with hieroglyphic, demotic and Greek script that proved the key to understanding Eygptian hieroglyphics; the Sutton Hoo Treasure, a hoard of gold and bronze items from Saxon times; and the fine Portland Vase, a masterpiece of Roman glassware. On the ground floor, The Great Court is spanned by a vast glass roof making it the largest covered square in Europe. A World Conservation and Exhibition Centre with state of the art laboratories is planned for 2014.

D3 Great Russell Street, WC1 020 7323 8299; www.britishmuseum.org Daily 10–5:30 (also Fri. 5:30–8:30 p.m.). Great Court: Sat.–Thu. 9–6,

The Great Court of the British Museum was designed by Foster and Partners

Fri. 9–8:30 Restaurant and cafés Tottenham Court Road, Holborn, Russell Square, Goodge Street Free (charge for special exhibitions)

Churchill War Rooms

The Churchill War Rooms were built as a subterranean command center in 1939 in the expectation that London would be badly bombed. Visiting with an audio guide, you peer into the bleak rooms from which Winston Churchill and Britain's other notable wartime leaders conducted the war. The fascinating memorabilia here includes maps, communication devices and scramblers, huge radio sets, and Churchill's personal bedroom, complete with ashtray for the famous cigar. A series of rooms contains the Churchill Museum, charting the life of the great man.

D2 Clive Steps, King Charles Street, SW1 020 7930 6961; http://cwr.iwm.org.uk Daily 9:30–6. Last admission at 5 Café Westminster, St. James's Park $$$

Covent Garden

The centerpiece of Covent Garden is the old Market Hall, a working vegetable market until 1973 and now a vibrant mall and open-air plaza, with shops, cafés and bars. You can stroll around the hall by day, taking in the atmosphere and enjoying the wealth of creative talent displayed by the street performers. Across the traffic-free plaza, the Floral Hall, a sunny cast-iron-and-glass shed where flowers were sold during the area's heyday is now part of the Royal Opera House complex – Britain's finest venue for opera and ballet. There are exhibitions and back-stage tours to give you the full story. Look, too, for the lunchtime recitals.

Royal Opera House D3 Bow Street, Covent Garden, WC2 020 7304 4000; www.roh.org.uk Tours: Mon.–Fri. at 10:30, 12:30 and 2:30, Sat. at 10:30, 11:30, 12:30 and 1:30; check website to confirm times Restaurants and bars Covent Garden Free; tours $$$

Today, arts and crafts can be found on sale in Covent Garden's Apple Market

Houses of Parliament

The finest view of the Houses of Parliament, and the clock tower that houses the great bell known as Big Ben, is from across the Thames on the South Bank; best of all, from the London Eye (see page 40). Close up, from Parliament Square, you see the work of architects Augustus Pugin and Sir Charles Barry, replacing the original building, which survived Guy Fawkes' Gunpowder Plot of November 5, 1605 but burned down in 1834.

Inside, the Houses of Parliament are a labyrinthine maze. Business takes place in two Houses, the House of Commons (elected by the public) and the House of Lords (theoretically appointed by the Queen). In the scarlet and gold somnolence of the House of Lords, manners are better and the tone quieter. When the Houses are in session, you can ascend to the public galleries and view the proceedings below. Entrance is on a first-come, first-served basis; line up outside the Cromwell Green Entrance. Tours of Parliament are available during the summer recess (when Parliament does not sit). Another must is a look into 1,000-year old Westminster Hall, with its wonderful, detailed medieval timber roof.

D2 St. Margaret's Street, Westminster, SW1 020 7219 4272; 0844 847 1672 (tours); www.parliament.uk Mon.–Thu. and some Fri. when Parliament is sitting (times vary; phone for details). Tours: Sat. 9:15–4:40, Jul.; Mon.–Tue., Fri.–Sat. 9:15–4:30, Wed.–Thu. 1:15–4:30, Aug.; Mon., Fri., Sat. 9:15–4:30, Tue.–Thu. 1:15–4:30, Sep.–Oct. Café in Westminster Hall Westminster Westminster Millennium Pier Free; tours $$$

Kensington Palace

These days Kensington Palace is inextricably associated with Diana, Princess of Wales, who lived here until her death in 1997.

Kensington Palace, built in 1605, was the principal royal London residence from 1689 until King George III's move to Buckingham Palace in the 1760s. Parts of the building are still maintained as royal apartments; the remainder, open to the public, contains 18th-century

Westminster Abbey and the Houses of Parliament are silhouetted against the night sky

state rooms with notable murals and painted ceilings, and an exhibition of court dress since 1760 that includes some Diana-related exhibits. Outside is a charming sunken garden, and nearby an 18th-century orangery with decorations by master carver Grinling Gibbons.

A £12 million improvement project completed in 2012 saw the opening of several new permanent exhibitions including Victoria Revealed and a display of Diana's dresses.

A2 Kensington Gardens, W8 0844 482 7777; www.hrp.org.uk Daily 10–6, Mar.–Oct.; 10–5, rest of year. Last admission 1 hour before closing Restaurant High Street Kensington, Notting Hill Gate, Queensway $$$; free under 16 years

Madame Tussauds

This is one of London's top tourist attractions – beware long lines! Madame Tussauds offers a bizarre collection of waxwork dummies of the rich, the famous and the infamous, ranging from brilliant likenesses to inexplicable aberrations. The business was started in 1835 by Madame Tussaud herself, an emigrée Frenchwoman who had arrived in London 30 years before with a case full of wax death masks she had molded from the faces of executed victims of the French Revolution.

Some of the originals are on display, along with thousands more recently made. It's fun to visit "Blush" and have your picture taken hobnobbing with the stars. In "World Stage" come face to face with world leaders including Barack Obama, or join Queen Elizabeth II for a private audience.

Visitors need a morbid curiosity to enjoy the horribly gory "Chamber of Horrors," where effigies of serial killers and their victims are confronted. They can experience a live re-enactment at "SCREAM," where actors play the part of mass murderers. Far more sedate, and offering a chance to sit down for a short while, is "The Spirit of London," a time-travel ride in a London "taxi" through the sights, sounds and smells of 400 years of London history.

B4 Marylebone Road, NW1 0871 894 3000; www.madametussauds.com Mon.–Fri. 9:30–5:30 (9–6 during school holidays), Sat.–Sun. 9–6 Café (Café Nero at exit) Baker Street $$$

Museum of London

This is one of London's most enjoyable museums, taking you on a chronological stroll through the history of the city, enlightening you on events from earliest prehistory to the present day. It could be a dry-as-dust history lesson, but it isn't.

Highlights include Roman marbles and wall paintings salvaged nearby, jewelry and leatherwear from Shakespeare's London, a grim mock-up of a cell in the notorious Newgate prison, and Victorian shops. You can hear Samuel Pepys' account of the Great Fire of 1666 while watching the city burn (in miniature), relive the miseries of the Blitz bombings of 1940–41, and groove through swinging London of the 1960s.

E3 150 London Wall, EC2 020 7001 9844; www.museumoflondon.org.uk Daily 10–6. Last admission at 5:40 Restaurant and café St. Paul's, Barbican, Moorgate Free (charge for special exhibitions)

Walk:
The South Bank of the Thames

Refer to route marked on city map on page 33

This short walk along the South Bank of the River Thames, designated the Millennium Mile (it's actually closer to 2 miles), offers a variety of attractions, and stunning vistas to the skyline of central London. A brisk walk takes half an hour, but you could easily devote at least half a day. The paving throughout is suitable for all types of footwear.

Start from Westminster tube station. Coming out of the station, you are confronted by the full majestic height of Big Ben's clock tower, with the Houses of Parliament beyond.

Turn left and cross Westminster Bridge. Pause on the bridge to have a good look at the parliamentary buildings. Britain's most illustrious poet stopped here, too, to admire the view on a still morning in 1802. "Earth hath not anything to show more fair," wrote William Wordsworth, recalling the "ships, towers, domes, theatres and temples" he saw that day, "all bright and glittering in the smokeless air."

Turn left along the south bank of the river. You will pass below the giant 433-foot London Eye. A ride in one of its glass pods will give you a unique view of London's famous landmarks and the surrounding countryside. Dwarfed in its shadow is County Hall, housing all manner of marine creatures of the SEA LIFE London Aquarium.

The London Eye on the South Bank is beautifully lit at night

The Turbine Hall of Tate Modern

Follow the river wall path past strings of rusty barges, modern cruise boats and the stocky little launches of the river police. Pass under Waterloo Bridge, where there are secondhand book stands, then under Blackfriars Bridge. Note the gaudy cast-iron company badge of the London, Chatham and Dover Railway, known to Victorian travelers as the "Smash 'em and Turnover" because of its frequent accidents (Charles Dickens was almost killed in one of them).

Next on your right is the huge, dark bulk of Bankside Power Station. It opened in 1963 but supplied power to the capital for fewer than 30 years. Now it has taken a glorious new lease on life as the Tate Modern, featuring 20th-century works by Andy Warhol, Henry Moore, Pablo Picasso and others of the older guard, as well as those by up-to-the-minute artists. The original Tate Gallery, west of here at Millbank, has been reinvented as Tate Britain, exhibiting the world's greatest collection of British art.

Stretching across the Thames outside Tate Modern is the Millennium Bridge, opened in 2000, the first pedestrian crossing to be built over the Thames in more than a century.

In the shadow of Tate Modern, on the east side, stands a dignified little pair of 17th-century houses, Cardinal's Wharf. Here, architect Sir Christopher Wren lived while he was supervising the building of St. Paul's Cathedral after the disastrous Great Fire of London in 1666. Here also stood the Globe Theatre, partly owned and made famous by William Shakespeare – and it stands once more, beautifully reconstructed and putting on plays in Elizabethan open-air style.

Beyond the Globe, duck into the Anchor Bankside pub for a pint of beer and a bite to eat; then continue along narrow, dark Clink Street past the Clink Prison Museum, once the grimmest of jails. Farther along lie the *Golden Hinde*, a replica of Sir Francis Drake's famed vessel, and lovely Southwark Cathedral, both worth a visit before you return to London Bridge Tube station.

London Eye ✚ D2 ✉ Jubilee Gardens, South Bank ☎ 0871 781 3000; www.londoneye.com 🕑 Daily 10–9:30, Jul.–Aug.; 10–9, Apr.–Jun.; 10–8:30, rest of year. Last admission 1 hour before closing; closed 10 days mid-Jan. 🍴 Café 🚇 Waterloo 💲 $$$

SEA LIFE London Aquarium ✚ D2 ✉ County Hall, Westminster Bridge Road ☎ 0871 663 1678; www.sealife.co.uk 🕑 Mon.–Thu. 10–6, Fri.–Sun. 10–7 🍴 Restaurants and cafés 🚇 Waterloo, Westminster 💲 $$$

Tate Modern ✚ E2 ✉ Bankside ☎ 020 7887 8888; www.tate.org.uk 🕑 Sun.–Thu. 10–6, Fri.– Sat. 10–10. Last admission 45 minutes before closing 🍴 Restaurant and cafés 🚇 Blackfriars, Southwark ⛴ Bankside Pier 💲 Free (charge for special exhibitions) ℹ Guided tours daily at 11, 12, 2 and 3 (free); audio tours ($$)

Shakespeare's Globe ✚ E3 ✉ 21 New Globe Walk, Bankside ☎ 020 7902 1400; www.shakespearesglobe.com 🕑 Performances: late Apr.–early Oct. Exhibition and theater tour: daily 9–5, mid-Oct. to late Apr.; Mon.–Sat. 9–12:30 and 1–5, Sun. 9–11:30 and noon–5, late Apr. to mid-Oct. 🍴 Restaurant and café 🚇 London Bridge, Mansion House, Blackfriars ⛴ Bankside Pier 💲 $$$ ℹ Audio tours (free)

Southwark Cathedral ✚ F2 ✉ London Bridge ☎ 020 7367 6700; http://cathedral.southwark.anglican.org 🕑 Mon.–Fri. 8–6, Sat.–Sun. 8:30–6 🍴 Café 🚇 London Bridge 💲 Free (suggested donation $$)

National Gallery

Britain's premier art gallery faces the lions, fountains and Nelson's Column in Trafalgar Square. It tells the story of painting in western Europe from 1250 to 1900. There is an embarrassment of riches here (around 2,300 works), so take a while to familiarize yourself with the layout and to pick a few special treats from the catalogue.

Particular treasures include Leonardo da Vinci's drawing of *The Virgin and Child with St. Anne and St. John the Baptist*, Botticelli's *Venus and Mars*, and a beautiful unfinished *The Nativity* by Piero della Francesca. The gallery contains several Titians, a moody *The Agony in the Garden of Gethsemane* by El Greco, and Michelangelo's *The Entombment*. In the North Wing (1600–1700), you will find glorious fleshy Rembrandts and a sexy post-coital *Samson and Delilah* by Rubens. In Room 34 you will find the flower of England's Golden Age of landscape painting – including John Constable's great East Anglian scenes filled with water, trees and light, and J.M.W. Turner's increasingly wild and impressionistic seascapes. The gallery also has a superb collection of French Impressionists, from Degas (*Ballet Dancers*) to Monet (*Bathers at La Grenouillère*), Renoir (*The Umbrellas*), Gauguin (*Faa Iheihe*) and Van Gogh (*A Wheatfield, with Cypresses and Sunflowers*).

D3 Trafalgar Square, WC2 020 7747 2885; www.nationalgallery.org.uk Daily 10–6 (also Fri. 6–9 p.m.) Restaurant and café Charing Cross, Leicester Square Free (charge for special exhibitions) Guided tours (free) daily at 11:30 and 2:30; audio guides (free; suggested donation)

National Portrait Gallery

The best-known British men and women from the Middle Ages onward are depicted here: ascetic (composer Frederick Delius), powerful (Margaret Thatcher, Queen Elizabeth I), soulful (poets William Cowper and William Wordsworth), suffering (AIDS-reduced film director Derek Jarman) and confident (Victorian engineer Isambard Kingdom Brunel), among others.

The imposing National Gallery sits majestically overlooking Trafalgar Square

The whole family will enjoy the excellent selection of dinosaur exhibits at the Natural History Museum

D3 St. Martin's Place, WC2 020 7306 0055 or 020 7312 2463 (recorded information); www.npg.org.uk Daily 10–6 (also Thu.–Fri. 6–9 p.m.). Last admission 45 minutes before closing Restaurant and café Charing Cross, Leicester Square Free (charge for special exhibitions) Audio guide $$

Natural History Museum

The Natural History Museum is one of the world's leading museums of natural history. Housed in a fine 19th-century Victorian building (the modern walkways inside allow you to appreciate all the hitherto obscured architectural and decorative details), the museum is divided into four zones: Red, Blue, Green and Orange.

The high-tech Red Zone explores the natural forces that shape the planet and features an escalator ride through the center of the earth. The Blue and Green Zones are a fine blend of traditional but fascinating glass-cases and interactive exhibitions based on a variety of themes inspired by nature. Pride of place here goes to those perennial favorites with all visitors – the magnificent dinosaurs, viewed from every possible angle from the walkway layout. Don't miss the roaring *T. rex*.

The Orange Zone is home to a wildlife garden (Apr.–Oct.) and the Darwin Centre, a state-of-the-art research center.
A1 Cromwell Road, SW7 020 7942 5000; www.nhm.ac.uk Daily 10–5:50. Last admission is at 5:30 Restaurant and cafés South Kensington Free (charge for special exhibitions)

Science Museum

The Science Museum adjoins the Natural History Museum and was opened, like its sister museum, to satisfy the public thirst for knowledge created by London's Great Exhibition of 1851. This it still achieves through exhibitions covering a wide variety of topics. They range from space exploration to the earliest attempts at flight, from steam engines to microchips, from advanced nuclear physics to children's puzzles. Don't miss the excellent Wellcome Wing with its IMAX 3D movie theater or the display of bygone surgical and dental equipment that makes you glad that medical science has moved on.
A2 Exhibition Road, SW7 0870 870 4868; www.sciencemuseum.org.uk Daily 10–6. Last admission 45 minutes before closing Restaurant and café South Kensington Free (charge for special exhibitions). IMAX 3D Cinema $$$; simulator rides $$$

London's Parks

London is proud of its parks, a wide network of open green spaces with plenty of trees and water features. Here locals and visitors can escape traffic noise and crowded sidewalks to stroll, laze, flirt, run, go boating or fly a kite.

Nearest to Trafalgar Square is St. James's Park (Tube: St. James's Park), London's oldest park. These green wooded acres were used as a royal deer-hunting forest in the time of King Henry VIII. Across the park on a January day in 1649 walked King Charles I, on his way to execution in Whitehall. The land was opened to the public by Charles II and it quickly became a favorite resort of Londoners. Architect John Nash landscaped it, complete with lake, around 1828, when he was redesigning Buckingham Palace for King George IV. Look west from the elegant bridge across the waist of the lake for a fine view of the palace.

Just north of Buckingham Palace, and separated from St. James's Park by The Mall, a broad, straight avenue, is Green Park (Tube: Green Park), rich in beautiful trees and a more informal open space than its manicured neighbor. The gallant and hot-tempered young bloods of 18th-century London fought their duels here. During World War II the park was plowed up and turned over to vegetable production, but all traces of such rough treatment have long since vanished.

Walking west from Green Park, you come to the vast open space of Hyde Park (Tube: Hyde Park Corner) and its twin sister Kensington Gardens (Tube: Lancaster Gate). Together they preserve 600 acres of quiet green ground on the flank of London's most exclusive districts: Mayfair, Kensington and Knightsbridge. Hyde Park formed a part of the lands belonging to Westminster Abbey, which were confiscated by King Henry VIII in the 1530s at the time of the Reformation. It was King James I who opened the land to the public. The bridle path along the south side, known as Rotten Row, quickly became a hangout for duelists, highwaymen and prostitutes. Around the turn of the 18th century lamps

London parks burst into color in spring providing a relaxing escape from the metropolitan bustle

were installed to deter the worst criminals; the prostitutes retaliated by taking to the saddle and displaying their charms for hire on horseback during the day. There's no such excitement these days, but plenty of enjoyment is still available at Speakers' Corner in Hyde Park's northeast corner, where anyone with a cause can climb on a soapbox and state their case at length – often to wisecracking crowds. It's fun, too, to boat on the curved lake called The Serpentine, created in Georgian times by damming the Westbourne River.

Kensington Gardens, the more westerly of these twin parks, once formed the grounds of Kensington Palace (see page 38). Queen Victoria gifted the land to the nation in 1841. Nowadays, model boats set sail on Round Pond; there is a beautiful Flower Walk and acres of open grassland for kite-flying and ball games. Also in Kensington Gardens is George Frampton's celebrated 1912 statue of Peter Pan, an object of pilgrimage for children of all ages.

Holland Park, a 10-minute walk west of Kensington Gardens (Tube: Holland Park), is small and well-wooded. Holland House was destroyed by bombs during World War II; this pleasant little park with its small café and open-air theater was opened in 1952 on what remained of the grounds.

A 15-minute walk north of Hyde Park is central London's other great green space, Regent's Park (Tube: Regent's Park or Baker Street). This elegant park was laid out in the early 19th century by John Nash, landscaper of St. James's Park, at the behest of George, Prince of Wales. At that time the self-indulgent "Prinny" – later to become King George IV – was acting as a proxy monarch, owing to his father's mental incapacity. He wanted something nice to look at when he drove out from his house in St. James's: hence the superb Nash-designed terraces that flank the park. ZSL London Zoo is in the park's northern corner and has some interesting architectural features. There is also a boating lake and an open-air theater where you can enjoy alfresco performances in summer.

The dome of St. Paul's Cathedral viewed from the pedestrian Millennium Bridge

St. Paul's Cathedral

Sir Christopher Wren's great baroque church (built 1675–1710) rose like a phoenix from the ashes of the 1666 Great Fire of London to become the symbol of the city, an image reinforced when it miraculously survived ferocious bombing during the 1940–41 Blitz.

The central dome is 364 feet high and 157 feet across; the summit lantern alone weighs 850 tons. Heavy statistics, and the whole church has a bulky, solid atmosphere. In the crypt, some of Britain's national heroes are buried: Admiral Horatio Nelson (1805), the Duke of Wellington (1852) and Florence Nightingale (1910).

Climb to the Whispering Gallery inside the dome – sounds carry around the curve of the wall to someone listening on the opposite side. It was from here in 1981 that TV cameras filmed the wedding of Prince Charles and Lady Diana Spencer. Climb to the Stone Gallery and ascend the iron staircase for a grand view of London.

E3 St. Paul's Churchyard C4 020 7236 4128; www.stpauls.co.uk Mon.–Sat. 8:30–4.

Galleries: Mon.–Sat. 9:30–4:15 Restaurant and café St. Paul's $$$ Guided tours at 10:45, 11:15, 1:30 and 2 ($$); audio tours ($$)

Sir John Soane's Museum

Three modest-looking, though elegant, row houses on the north edge of Lincoln's Inn Fields contain London's oddest museum, unknown to most visitors but a genuine delight. One of the world's great private collections, it was put together by Sir John Soane (1753–1837), architect of the Bank of England. Exhibits range from the impressive sarcophagus of an Egyptian pharaoh to fine Roman marbles and urns, Italian busts, and paintings by such artists as Canaletto, J.M.W. Turner and Joshua Reynolds, along with William Hogarth's complete sequences of *An Election* and *A Rake's Progress.*

D3 13 Lincoln's Inn Fields, WC2 020 7405 2107; www.soane.org Tue.–Sat. 10–5 (also 6–9 p.m. first Tue. of every month. Last entry at 4:30 Holborn Free (donations recommended) Guided tours ($$) on Sat. – tickets available from 10:30 a.m. for tour at 11

Tower of London

The Tower of London is one of London's premier attractions, drawing millions of visitors a year. They come to see the Yeoman Warders – better known as Beefeaters – in their red dress uniforms and white Elizabethan neck ruffs, to admire the resident ravens (mythology has it that if the birds ever leave, the Tower will fall), and to thrill to tales of torture, murder and beheadings.

On Tower Hill hundreds found guilty of treason died in public under the axe; a privileged handful (including King Henry VIII's second and fifth wives, Anne Boleyn and Catherine Howard) were beheaded in private on Tower Green. You will see the spot on a guided tour, as well as the Bloody Tower, where in 1483 the young heir to the throne, Prince Edward, and his younger brother, Prince Richard, were killed. The boys were probably smothered with pillows on the orders of their uncle Richard, Duke of Gloucester, crowned King Richard III shortly afterward.

Overlooking the Thames is St. Thomas' Tower; those accused of treachery were brought here through its arched and barred gateway, known as Traitors' Gate, to be incarcerated. At the Jewel House you can line up to see the Crown Jewels – a fabulous monarchical treasure of gold, crowns, orbs and scepters.

F3 Tower Hill, EC3 0844 482 7777; www.hrp.org.uk Tue.–Sat. 9–4:30, Sun.–Mon. 10–4:30. Last admission 30 minutes before closing Restaurants and cafés Tower Hill; DLR Tower Gateway Tower Millennium Pier $$$ Tours (free)

The White Tower, built by William the Conqueror, is the central building of the Tower of London

The view along the choir stalls toward the ornate gilt altar of Westminster Abbey

V&A Museum

The V&A Museum was founded after the 1851 Great Exhibition to inspire the British with examples of artistic achievement, and extends through some 7 miles of galleries on six floors.

You will find life-size plaster casts of famous sculpture, from Michelangelo's *David* to the door of Santiago de Compostela's cathedral; impressive Raphael drawings for his Sistine Chapel paintings; Islamic and Japanese treasures; and some English painting, silverware and 18th-century furniture. After visiting the Frank Lloyd Wright Gallery you can relax in a Victorian Arts and Crafts tearoom.

B1 Cromwell Road, SW7 020 7942 2000; www.vam.ac.uk Daily 10–5:45 (also Fri. 5:45–10 p.m.). Last admission 10 minutes before closing Cafés South Kensington Free (charge for special exhibitions) Guided tours at 10:30, 11:30, 12:30, 1:30, 2:30 and 3:30 (free)

Westminster Abbey

Westminster Abbey is the meeting place of the nation's religious, political and monarchical life. It has seen every coronation but two of the 38 since William the Conqueror's on December 25, 1066. Here you will find the tombs and memorials of monarchs, poets such as Alfred, Lord Tennyson, writers like Charles Dickens and politicians such as Sir Winston Churchill.

D2 Broad Sanctuary, SW1 020 7222 5152; www.westminster-abbey.org Mon.–Fri. 9:30–4:30 (also Wed. 4:30–7 p.m.), Sat. 9:30–2:30 (last admission 1 hour before closing). Cloisters: daily 8–6; Museum: Mon.–Sat. 10:30–4. Pyx Chamber: Mon.–Sat. 10:30–4. Chapter House: daily 10:30–4. College Garden: Tue.–Thu. 10–6, Apr.–Sep.; Tue.–Thu. 10–4, rest of year. St. Margaret's Church: Mon.–Fri. 9:30–3:30, Sat. 9:30–1:30 and Sun. 2–5 Westminster, St. James's Park Westminster Millennium Pier Abbey $$$; Other parts free Guided tours ($$); audio tours (free)

Thames Cruises: Greenwich, Kew and Hampton Court

River cruises make a great day out, and London has a couple of classics along the Thames in each direction.

Downriver, a boat ride of less than an hour from Westminster Millennium Pier will take you to Greenwich, with one of London's finest waterfront vistas. Get your camera out on the boat – the best views are from the river. The Old Royal Naval College flanks the National Maritime Museum (begun by Inigo Jones as a house for King James I's wife, Anne of Denmark). Alongside this museum is Queen's House, England's first classical Palladian building and the architectural ancestor of Washington D.C.'s White House. Nearby are the masts and rigging of the famous Victorian tea clipper *Cutty Sark* (badly damaged by fire in 2007, but restored and reopened in 2012), dwarfing the tiny yacht *Gipsy Moth IV*, in which Sir Francis Chichester made the first solo circumnavigation of the world in 1966–67. Inland rises the hill of Greenwich Park, where, in the yard of the Royal Observatory, you can straddle the famed Meridian Line.

Upriver from Westminster Millennium Pier, it is a seven- to eight-hour round-trip along the Thames to some of London's loveliest riverside scenery to the west of the city. At Kew you'll find the Royal Botanic Gardens, with two giant Victorian conservatories. Farther upriver sprawls the mighty Hampton Court Palace, the grandest Tudor building in Britain. King Henry VIII embellished it for his beloved (but soon executed) second wife, Anne Boleyn.

To Greenwich F2 (off map) Thames River Services Westminster Millennium Pier, Victoria Embankment 020 7930 4097; www.thamesriverservices.co.uk Sailings daily 10–6 (every 30 minutes), Apr.–Oct.; 10:20–4 (hourly), rest of year $$$

To Kew, Richmond and Hampton Court A1 (off map) Westminster Passenger Services Association (Upriver) Westminster Millennium Pier, Victoria Embankment 020 7930 2062 or 020 7930 4721 (recorded information); www.wpsa.co.uk Sailings daily at 10:30, 11, noon and 2, mid-Mar. to Sep. (timings are tidal dependent, may vary); by appointment in Oct. $$$

The formal gardens of Hampton Court Palace enhance the Tudor palace of King Henry VIII

The murder of Archbishop Thomas Becket in 1170 turned Canterbury into the country's foremost pilgrimage site. Much remains of the medieval city that grew up catering to the millions of penitents who came each year to pray at the saint's shrine.

The centerpiece of Canterbury is the great cathedral. Some of the Norman church in which Becket was killed still stands, incorporated into the cathedral that developed over the centuries. Stimulated by Canterbury's success as a pilgrimage destination, the impressive cathedral was remodeled and expanded several times.

Most visitors make for The Martyrdom, a commemorative slab in the northwest transept marking the spot where four knights cut Becket down on what they thought were the orders of King Henry II. The question of whether Church or Crown should wield ultimate authority had caused an angry division between Henry and his erstwhile friend, but the king probably did not expect to be taken

Canterbury Cathedral evolved over the centuries to become the city's imposing centerpiece

Fan vaulting inside the cathedral's nave

literally when he gave vent to the notorious outburst: "Of all the cowards who eat my bread, are there none to rid me of this turbulent priest?" Henry came to Canterbury to be scourged in expiation of the murder; within three years Becket had been canonized as a saint, and the pilgrimages began.

Becket's spirit pervades this great church, mother cathedral of the Church of England. The martyr's golden shrine in Trinity Chapel at the east end, an object of wonder to pilgrims all through the Middle Ages, was destroyed during the Reformation in 1538. The knees of penitents during the four centuries of medieval pilgrimage wore hollows in the stone steps; their shadows flicker in the light of candles still kept burning in the chapel. Among the scenes depicted in Canterbury Cathedral's renowned display of stained glass are images of pilgrimages and portrayals of miraculous healing performed by the saint. Don't miss the beautiful fan vaulting, and be sure to descend into the Norman-era crypt to see the 12th-century wall paintings and carved columns.

You can stroll around the medieval center of Canterbury city in an hour. Parts of the old city walls still stand, along with one of the 14th-century gates. Streets like Mercery Lane are lined with attractive houses, some half-timbered, with glimpses over their red-tiled roofs of the four rocket pinnacles on the cathedral's central tower. Worth visiting are the excellent Canterbury Heritage Museum, housed in the 900-year-old Poor Priests' Hospital on Stour Street, and the smell-and-sound-enhanced tableaux recounting five of Chaucer's tales at The Canterbury Tales, in former St. Margaret's Church.

E2

Tourist information 12–13 Sun Street, The Buttermarket 01227 378100; www.canterbury.co.uk

Cathedral The Precincts 01227 762862; www.canterbury-cathedral.org Mon.–Sat. 9–5:30, Sun.12:30–2:30, Apr.–Oct.; Mon.–Sat. 9–5, Sun.12:30–2:30, rest of year $$$ Audio tours ($$)

Canterbury Heritage Museum Stour Street 01227 475202 Daily 10–5 Apr.–Dec.; Mon.–Sat. 11–5, rest of year. Last entry 1 hour before closing $$

The Canterbury Tales St. Margaret's Church, St. Margaret's Street 01227 479227; www.canterburytales.org.uk Daily 9:30–5, Jul.–Aug.; 10–5, Mar.–Jun. and Sep.–Oct.; 10–4:30, rest of year Restaurant (adjacent) $$$ Audio tours

The South Downs

This billowing ridge of chalk downland forms the spine of Sussex and extends west into Hampshire. It became a national park in 2010. "On the Downs the mind becomes more aerial," wrote naturalist W.H. Hudson in 1900. "Standing on one great green hill and looking across vast intervening hollows to other round heights and hills beyond and far away, I can almost realise the sensation of being other than I am – that in a little while I shall lift great heron-like wings and fly..."

You can enjoy such aerial sensations by tramping the South Downs Way, a National Trail that runs 106 miles west from Eastbourne to Winchester.

Henry VIII built Deal Castle and instaled a powerful cannon as a deterent to French invaders

Chatham, The Historic Dockyard

The naval base at Chatham, on the River Medway in north Kent, was founded by King Henry VIII. With its sheltered dockyard and easy access to the Thames Estuary and the open sea, it became a mainstay of Britain's naval strength. The dockyards closed in 1984 and then took a new lease on life as The Historic Dockyard Chatham.

Here are historic shipbuilding sheds, warships, a ropery, sawmills that produced sailing ship timbers, a museum of shipbuilding, displays of knotting and nautical crafts, and one of the world's most comprehensive collections of old ships' figureheads. No. 1 Smithery showcases maritime artifacts and also interactive and educational areas.

During the Napoleonic Wars of the early 19th century, French prisoners of war were forced to carry out extensions to Fort Amherst from Chatham upriver. You can take a guided tour through its fascinating labyrinth of tunnels.

D3

Historic Dockyard Dock Road, Chatham 01634 823800 or 01634 823807 (recorded information); www.thedockyard.co.uk Daily 10–6 (or dusk if earlier), late Mar.–early Dec.; 10–4 mid-Feb. to late Mar. $$$ (valid 12 months) Restaurant and café

Fort Amherst Dock Road, Chatham 01634 847747 Visitor Center 10–4 or consult www.fortamherst.co.uk Café $$$ Tours at 11 a.m. and 2 p.m.

Chichester

Brighton (see page 51) may be the flashiest town in Sussex, but Chichester, 30 miles west, is the county's true heart, an elegant small Georgian city at the foot of the South Downs. The slim spire of Chichester Cathedral, 277 feet tall, is a landmark for many miles around. The nave is tall, too, giving the whole building an uplifting atmosphere. The furnishings range from medieval (12th-century stone sculpture in the choir, including Lazarus being raised from the dead) to modern (a John Piper tapestry, large paintings by Graham Sutherland, beautiful Marc Chagall stained glass); all seem to meld in harmony.

If you want to see how a well-to-do Sussex wine merchant lived in the Georgian era, take a look at Pallant House Gallery on North Pallant Street, just off East Street, though the gallery has now spilled into an ultra-modern

Chichester Cathedral's spire can be seen from villages many miles around

space next door. To get a glimpse of how similarly affluent people lived 1,500 years ago, Fishbourne Roman Palace, just 2 miles west of Chichester, will get your imagination going. Here are superb mosaic floors, bathrooms and an original heating system excavated in the 1960s. B1

Tourist information 29A South Street 01243 775888; www.visitchichester.org

Chichester Cathedral West Street 01243 782595; www.chichestercathedral.org.uk Daily 7:15–7, Apr.–Oct.; 7:15–6, rest of year Café Donation ($$) suggested Free guided tours Mon.–Sat. at 11:15 a.m. and 2:30 p.m.

Pallant House Gallery 9 North Pallant 01243 774557; www.pallant.org.uk Tue.–Sat. 10–5 (also Thu. 5–8 p.m.), Sun. 11–5 Restaurant $$$

Fishbourne Roman Palace B1 Fishbourne 01243 789829; www.whitecliffscountry.org.uk Daily 10–5, Mar.–Oct.; daily 10–4, in Feb. and Nov. 1 to mid-Dec.; Sat.–Sun. 10–4, rest of year Café $$$ Guided tours ($)

Deal

With the French coast only 30 miles away, the little town of Deal became prosperous during the 18th century as much through smuggling as fishing. These days Deal makes a charming place to stroll through or along its pebbly beach. On the seafront stands Deal Castle, built by King Henry VIII against the threat of French invasion, and designed in the shape of a Tudor rose.

Deal's sister town of Sandwich was medieval England's foremost port before the harbor silted up. With its ancient town walls and merchants' houses, Sandwich is a delightful town to explore. E2

Tourist information Landmark Centre, High Street 01304 369576; www.whitecliffscountry.org.uk

Sandwich E2

Tourist information Guildhall, Cattle Market 01304 613565; www.whitecliffscountry.org.uk Open Apr.–Oct. only

Blodwit and Fledwit

Medieval Sandwich was one of the Cinque Ports; the others were Hastings, Dover, Romney and Hythe. In return for defending the coast, the five towns were granted exemption from certain taxes and rights over fishing and wrecks. These privileges had resonant titles such as blodwit and fledwit, sac and sol, infangentheof and outfangentheof, pillory, mundbryce and tumbril.

Natural erosion at Dover's white chalk cliffs keep them looking pristine

Dover

Dover is the chief cross-Channel ferry port on this stretch of the south coast, but its real claim to fame and interest for the visitor resides in its Norman castle, which stands high on cliffs honeycombed and burrowed into tunnels by French prisoners during the Napoleonic Wars. Dover Castle – known in medieval times as the "Key to England," because whoever held it controlled entry to the country – is one of the most interesting in England to explore, with its still-standing Roman lighthouse, restored Saxon Church of St. Mary-in-Castro, and keep with walls 20 feet thick.

The castle saw dramatic action in both world wars. During World War I it was the base from which anti-submarine strategies were carried out, and in World War II it was the headquarters from where the evacuation of the retreating British army from Dunkirk was co-ordinated. This was an extraordinary venture during which 338,226 men were brought home in a ramshackle flotilla consisting of every conceivable kind of vessel.

Hellfire Corner, so named because it endured intense wartime bombardment, is a section of cliff tunnels refurbished to give a vivid idea of conditions in an emergency hospital and in the co-ordinating nerve center. The cliffs themselves, ramparts of solid chalk hundreds of feet high, are famous as the White Cliffs of Dover.

The Dover Museum and Bronze Age Boat Gallery traces the development of the town and port and has a Bronze Age-era boat, said to be the world's oldest seagoing vessel. A footpath runs west for some 7 miles along the edge of the cliffs, a breezy walk that brings you to the Channel Tunnel rail entrance near the old Victorian resort and port town of Folkestone.

E2

Tourist information Old Town Gaol, Biggin Street 01304 205108; www.whitecliffscountry.org.uk

Dover Castle Castle Hill 01304 211067; www.english-heritage.org.uk Daily 9:30–6 in Aug.; daily 10–6, Apr.–Jul. and Sep.; daily 10–5 in Oct.; daily 10–4, Feb.–Mar.; Thu.–Mon. 10–4, rest of year. Last admission 1 hour before closing Restaurant and café $$$

Dover Museum and Bronze Age Boat Gallery Market Square 01304 201066 Mon.–Sat. 10–5, Sun. 10–3 Apr.–Sep.; Mon.–Sat. 10–5, rest of year $$

Folkestone E2

Tourist information 01303 258594; www.discoverfolkestone.co.uk

The New Forest

The 150 square miles of the New Forest, on the Hampshire/Dorset border, form the oldest royal hunting forest in the country. Poachers of the king's deer in olden days could expect no mercy; even to disturb the animals carried a penalty of blinding, while to kill one meant death. Not only poachers died in the New Forest: King William Rufus, son of William the Conqueror, had his reign cut short by an arrow while hunting here in August 1100.

This ancient patchwork of woodland, farms, wetlands and heaths looks, and works, as the countryside used to before the mechanization of farming. Everyone loves the free-roaming New Forest ponies, and there are fallow deer, butterflies, foxes, birds and wildflowers to delight any amateur naturalist.

At Beaulieu (pronounced "Bew-ly"), in the southeast corner of the forest, is the splendid car collection at the National Motor Museum. Here you can see around 250 vintage vehicles, from gleaming Rolls-Royces to monsters that have broken the world land-speed record. Farther down at the mouth of the Beaulieu River is the charming small village of Buckler's Hard, which has a remarkably wide main street. Oak timber from the New Forest was stacked high in the street to season, in the days of the Napoleonic Wars 200 years ago, when Buckler's Hard was an important shipbuilding center. The village's excellent Maritime Museum tells the tale.

A1

Tourist Information New Street, Lymington, Hampshire 01590 689000; www.thenewforest.co.uk

Lyndhurst Centre Main Car Park, High Street, Lyndhurst, Hampshire 023 8028 2269 Daily 10–5 $$

National Motor Museum A1 Beaulieu, Brockenhurst, Hampshire 01590 612345; www.beaulieu.co.uk Daily 10–6, late May–Sep. 30; 10–5, rest of year Restaurant and café $$$

Maritime Museum A1 Buckler's Hard, Hampshire 01590 616203; www.bucklershard.co.uk Daily 10–5:30, Jul.–Aug.; 10–5, Mar.–Jun. and Sep.–Oct.; 10–4:30, rest of year $$

Two fallow deer graze near Stoney Cross in the New Forest National Park

Drive
Great Houses and Castles of Kent

Distance: 90 miles

This drive through Kent from Tunbridge Wells passes eight fine castles and houses.

From Tunbridge Wells proceed north on A26; at B2176 turn left, passing through Bidborough to the medieval and picturesque village of Penshurst.
Here is one of Britain's oldest country houses, Penshurst Place, built in 1341 for merchant Sir John de Pulteney. The vast Baron's Hall under its splendid wooden roof still exists. Constructed at a time when architecture was based on religious buildings, the original window frames and doorways seem more ecclesiastical than secular. Sir Philip Sidney, ideal of all that was manly and courtly in Elizabethan England, was born here in 1554.

Continue north on B2176. Turn left onto B2027 past the Penshurst railroad station, then left again after 1 mile.
Chiddingstone Castle is a 17th-century country house retaining many original fixtures, with others added in 1805 when the house was turned into a mock-Gothic castle.

Continue for 3 miles to Hever Castle.
Moated Hever Castle is set in wide grounds. King Henry VIII dallied with the young Anne Boleyn here, and later gave Hever Castle to his fourth wife, Anne of Cleves. Essentially a Tudor house, it was refurbished early in the 20th century when American newspaper magnate William Waldorf Astor bought it.

Continue 2 miles eastward, pass through the village of Leigh and go under A21. Immediately turn left, proceed 1 mile, turn left again on B245 (which becomes A225) to the outskirts of Sevenoaks.
Turn right onto the extensive grounds of Knole, one of Britain's finest country houses. Begun in 1456 by Archbishop Thomas Bourchier, it was altered by King Henry VIII and remodeled in 1603 in the Jacobean style it exhibits today.

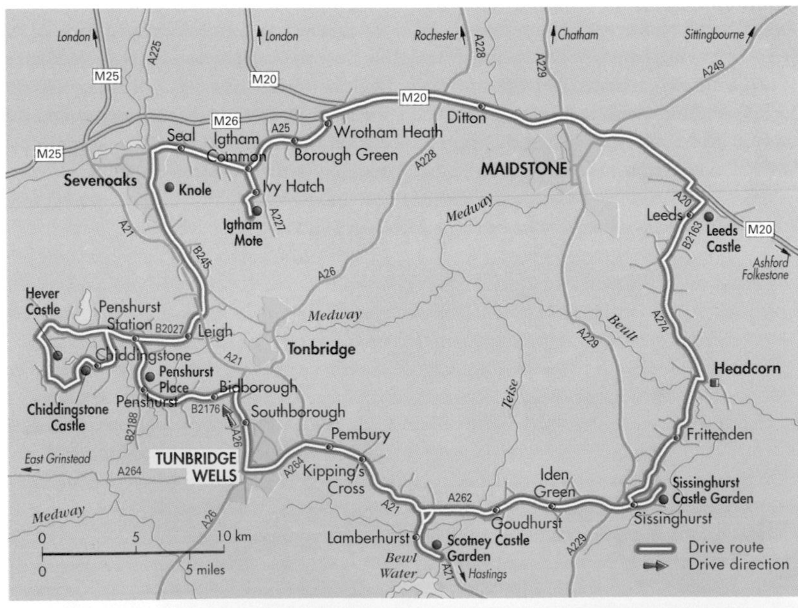

One of the most beautiful castles in England, Leeds Castle sits serenely above its extensive moat

The Sackville family has owned Knole since Tudor times; the horticulturalist and poet, Vita Sackville-West (see Sissinghurst below) was born here.

From Sevenoaks proceed east on A25, then south at Ightham Common through Ivy Hatch to Ightham Mote.

The moated medieval manor house of Ightham Mote is a picturesque half-timbered building dating from the 14th century.

Backtrack to A25 and join M26/M20 at Wrotham Heath. Proceed east 10 miles to A20 beyond Maidstone.

Leeds Castle lies just off the road and is described by some as the most beautiful castle in England. The 500-acre, equally lovely, grounds were landscaped by Lancelot "Capability" Brown.

B2163 and A274 take you south to Headcorn. Turn right and proceed on local roads through Frittenden to Sissinghurst.

At Sissinghurst in the 1930s, Vita Sackville-West and her husband created a garden around the ruin of a Tudor castle. The printing press off which Virginia Woolf ran the first copies of T.S. Eliot's *The Waste Land* in 1922 is in the gatetower.

A262 leads west to Goudhurst. Southwest near Lamberhurst is Scotney Castle.

Scotney Castle is a 14th-century island fortress in picturesque ruin amid grounds that were landscaped in the 19th century.

A21 and then A264 return you to Tunbridge Wells.

Penshurst Place ✉ Penshurst, near Tonbridge ☎ 01892 870307; www.penshurstplace.com 🕔 House: daily noon–4, late Mar.–Oct.; Sat.–Sun. noon–4, early Mar.–late Mar. Gardens: daily 10:30–6, late Mar.–Oct.; Sat.–Sun. 10:30–6, early Mar.–late Mar. Last admission 1 hour before closing 🍴 Café ✋ $$$ (gardens only $$) ℹ Guided tours $$$

Chiddingstone Castle ✉ Hill Hoath Road, Chiddingstone ☎ 01892 870347; www.chiddingstonecastle.org.uk 🕔 Sun.–Wed. 11–5; last admission 4:15 🍴 Café ✋ $$$; Grounds free

Hever Castle ✉ Hever, near Edenbridge ☎ 01732 865224; www.hevercastle.co.uk 🕔 Gardens: daily 10:30–5, Apr.–Oct.; Wed.–Sun. 10:30–4, Mar. House: daily noon–5, Apr.–Oct.; Wed.–Sun. noon–4, Mar., Nov.–Dec. 24 🍴 Restaurants ✋ $$$ (gardens only $$) ℹ Audio tour $$

Knole ✉ Sevenoaks ☎ 01732 462100; www.nationaltrust.org.uk/knole 🕔 House: Wed.–Sun. noon–4, mid-Mar. to Oct. Garden: Tue. 11–4, Apr.–Sep. 🍴 Café ✋ House $$$; Garden $$

Ightham Mote ✉ Ivy Hatch, Sevenoaks ☎ 01732 810 378; www.nationaltrust.org 🕔 Wed.–Mon. 11–5, Jun.–Aug.; Thu.–Mon. 11–5, mid-Mar. to May, Sep.–Oct.; Thu.–Mon. 11–3, Nov. to mid-Dec. Estate: daily dawn–dusk 🍴 Restaurant ✋ $$$

Leeds Castle ✉ Near Maidstone ☎ 01622 765400; www.leeds-castle.com 🕔 Daily 10–5:30 🍴 Restaurant and café ✋ $$$

Sissinghurst Castle Garden ✉ Near Cranbrook ☎ 01580 710700; www.nationaltrust.org 🕔 Fri.–Tue. 10:30–5, mid-Mar. to Oct. 🍴 Restaurant ✋ $$$

Scotney Castle ✉ Lamberhurst ☎ 01892 893820; www.nationaltrust.org 🕔 House: Wed.–Sun. 11–5, Mar.–Oct. Garden: Wed.–Sun. 11–5:30, mid-Feb. to Oct. Estate: daily dawn–dusk ✋ $$$ (gardens only $$); Estate free

Portsmouth

"Pompey," as generations of naval men have nicknamed Portsmouth, has been the home port of the British Royal Navy for hundreds of years. Because of this, much of the city was bombed flat during World War II. However, its naval spirit is fittingly preserved around the waterfront and its historic atmosphere at Portsmouth Historic Dockyard.

The docks themselves are of the size and complexity of a small town. There you will find miles of impressive Victorian and fine Georgian naval architecture – storehouses, offices, barracks, chapels, houses – a Royal Naval Museum, and some classic veteran ships. Queen of the docks is HMS *Victory*, the battleship in which Lord Nelson flew his flag and in whose cockpit he died of wounds at the moment of victory during the Battle of Trafalgar on October 21, 1805. Nearby is the Tudor battleship *Mary Rose*, sunk on her maiden voyage in 1545 and raised from Portsmouth Harbour with dazzling technical skill in 1982. Housed in a boat-shaped museum since 2012, the displays include many of the military and everyday objects that sank with the ship, which were well-preserved in the harbor mud. The world's first iron-hulled armored battleship, HMS *Warrior* (1860), is also docked here.

In the D-Day Museum at Southsea, a few minutes' drive away, you can admire the amazing Overlord Embroidery, a tapestry 272 feet long, which depicts the epic events of the Allied landings in Normandy in June 1944.

B1

Tourist information The Hard, Portsmouth, also Clarence Esplanade, Southsea 023 9282 6722; www.visitportsmouth.co.uk

Portsmouth Historic Dockyard Entry through Victory Gate (corner of Queen Street and The Hard) 023 9272 8060; www.historicdockyard.co.uk Daily 10–6, Apr.–Oct.; 10–5:30, rest of year Several Site ticket (valid for one year) $$$

D-Day Museum B1 Clarence Esplanade, Southsea 023 9282 7261; www.ddaymuseum.co.uk Daily 10–5:30, Apr.–Oct.; 10–5, rest of year Café (mid-Mar. to early Nov. only) $$$ (children under 17 free with an adult)

Rochester and Charles Dickens

Rochester stands on the River Medway at the heart of the countryside immortalized in the novels of Charles Dickens – most notably in *Great Expectations*. The city's Norman cathedral has a beautiful west doorway;

Elevators whisk you to the top of Portsmouth's Spinnaker Tower for fine views of the harbor

in the choir are stalls and a wall painting 800 years old. Rochester Castle also is Norman, and has a giant keep.

Dickens knew Rochester well as a boy, and settled at nearby Gads Hill from 1856 until his death in 1870. *Great Expectations* sites around town include the timber-framed building on High Street, which Dickens used as the shop of self-important Uncle Pumblechook, and Restoration House on Crow Lane, which became the cobwebbed Satis House, Miss Havisham's abode. Close to High Street, this is a fine example of a city mansion and is beautifully furnished and decorated.

Northwest of Rochester, St. Mary's Church at Higham is the marsh church where Pip first met the convict Magwitch. In the village of Chalk, a pretty white wood-slatted cottage on the A225 road is Joe Gargery's forge, where Pip lived as a boy. At Cobham, the Dickens connections are Pickwickian. At the Leather Bottle Inn Mr. Pickwick dissuaded Mr. Tupman from suicide.

D3

Tourist information 95 High Street 01634 338141; www.visitmedway.org

Rochester Castle The Esplanade 01634 335882; www.english-heritage.org.uk Daily 10–6, Apr.–Sep.; 10–4, rest of year $$

Rye

The charming town of Rye huddles on a hilltop on the East Sussex/Kent border. Streets are crooked, cobbled and steep; houses are whitewashed, red-tiled and hung with flower baskets. Fine views over ancient Rye can be enjoyed from St. Mary's Church tower, the Ypres tower, the town wall or the Landgate. Crisscross the town to visit many of its welcoming old inns, where you can still sample some locally brewed real ales.

American novelist Henry James settled at Lamb House on West Street in 1898; he lived here until his death in 1916.

D2

Tourist information 4/5 Lion Street 01797 229049; www.visitrye.co.uk

Lamb House West Street 01580 762334; www.nationaltrust.org.uk Thu. and Sat. 2–6, late Mar.–late Oct. $$

St. Mary's Church Church Square 01797 224935 Daily 9:15–5:15, Apr.–Sep.; 9:15–4:15, rest of year. Tower closes 30 minutes before rest of church (or dusk if earlier) Free (tower $$)

The exterior of Restoration House in Rochester was Dickens' inspiration for Miss Havisham's home

Winchester

Winchester, the capital of the Saxon kingdom of Wessex before the Norman Conquest, is a delightful and historic cathedral city set among meadows along the River Itchen in central Hampshire.

Winchester Cathedral, the highlight of the city, has the longest medieval nave in Europe (556 feet), and one of the most impressive. Memorials include those to Jane Austen; to King Alfred's old teacher, St. Swithun; and to King William Rufus, son of William the Conqueror. Rufus was shot dead by his companion's arrow while out hunting – the arrowhead itself was found within Rufus' remains inside his tomb in Victorian times. There are some early 14th-century misericords (wood carvings on the underside of seats) in the choir, fine stained-glass windows and a library of medieval books.

In the Great Hall on Castle Avenue, the only surviving part of Winchester Castle, hangs the famous 13th-century Round Table. Romantics insist this is the one magically created by the wizard Merlin for King Arthur, in order to avoid squabbles over seating precedence among the knights at Camelot.

Walk through the meadows along the riverbank to the 12th-century Hospital of St. Cross. Visitors who knock at the Porter's Lodge will receive the traditional "wayfarer's dole" of ale and bread.

Leafy streets and parks surround Winchester Cathedral, which stands at the heart of the historic city

Eighteen miles northeast of Winchester, just off the A31, lies the little village of Chawton, where Jane Austen lived during her most prolific years from 1809 until her death in 1817. You can visit her plain, square redbrick house, now a museum, and see the rooms where she wrote some of her best-loved books, including *Mansfield Park*, *Emma* and *Persuasion*, and revised some of her other books.

A2

Tourist information Winchester Guildhall, High Street 01962 840500; www.visitwinchester.co.uk

Cathedral The Close 01962 857200; www.winchester-cathedral.org.uk Mon.–Sat. 9:30–5, Sun. 12:30–3. Restaurant $$$ Guided tours Mon.–Sat. 10–3 (free)

Dedicated Diver

Built on water meadows, the mighty cathedral in Winchester has an uneasy relationship with the water table. Between 1906 and 1911, diver William Walker worked beneath the cathedral in darkness and cold water in order to prevent the rotting Norman timber foundations from sinking into the mud, inserting around 1 million bricks and sacks of concrete under the collapsing east end of the church.

A statue of Walker stands in the company of St. Swithun and William of Wykeham.

Great Hall Castle Avenue 01962 846476 Daily 10–5 Free ($ donation suggested)

Hospital of St. Cross St. Cross Road 01962 851375; www.stcrosshospital.co.uk Mon.–Sat. 9:30–5, Sun. 1–5, Apr.–Oct.; Mon.–Sat. 10:30–3:30, rest of year Café (Apr.–Sep. only) $$

Jane Austen's House Chawton, near Alton 01420 83262; www.jane-austens-house-museum.org.uk Daily 10–5, Jun.–Aug.; daily 10:30–4:30, Mar.–May and Sep.–Dec.; Sat.–Sun. 10:30–4:30, rest of year Café opposite $$$

The Round Table in Winchester's Great Hall

The approach through Windsor Great Park to Windsor Castle, one of the British monarch's official residences

Windsor

This town beside the Thames west of London and its castle have been the monarch's out-of-town residence for almost a thousand years. If the Royal Standard (flag) is flying from the flagpole, the ruling monarch is in residence. The town itself is an attractive place for a stroll, but it is the castle that draws visitors. Its distinctive Round Tower, originally of wood, was rebuilt in stone along with the rest of the castle in the mid-12th century and forms the eye-catching focus of an ensemble laid out in two wards, or great walled enclosures. Many rooms have been meticulously restored after a disastrous fire in 1992.

The Upper Ward contains the State Apartments, full of opulent furnishings and art treasures. Here you can see Queen Mary's Dolls' House, designed at a scale of 1:12 by architect Sir Edwin Lutyens in 1923. The water runs, the electric lights work, even the books and pictures are genuine miniatures. In the Lower Ward is the Tudor masterpiece of St. George's Chapel, where 10 monarchs lie buried – among them King Henry VIII.

South of the castle stretches Windsor Great Park, 5,000 acres of beautifully tended and thickly wooded parkland crisscrossed with footpaths open to the public. Walking here among ancient trees and across wide grassland spaces is a pleasure. North of Windsor, across the Thames, is the village of Eton, home of Britain's most exclusive and prestigious private school, Eton College. The school was founded in 1440, and has since accrued a roll call of distinguished former pupils, including 19 prime ministers. Its pupils wear a distinctive uniform of top hat and tails on public occasions. There is a museum dedicated to the school, and a Gothic chapel.

Nearby, the village of Eton Dorney, on the River Thames, became famous in 2012 when the rowing competitions of the Summer Olympics took place here.

B3

Tourist information Old Booking Hall, Windsor Royal Station, Thames Street 01753 743900 (24 hours); www.windsor.gov.uk

Windsor Castle Castle Hill 020 7766 7304; www.royalcollection.org.uk Daily 9:45–5:15, Mar.–Oct.; 9:45–4:15, rest of year. Last admission 1 hour, 15 minutes before closing; opening times subject to change at short notice $$$ (includes audio tour) Changing of the Guard takes place Mon.–Sat. 11 a.m., Apr.–Jul.

Eton College Eton High Street 01753 671177; www.etoncollege.com Daily 10:30–4:30, mid-Feb., Apr., Jul. to mid-Sep.; Wed., Fri.–Sun. 1:30–4:30, early Feb., Jun., mid-Sep. to early Oct. $$ Guided tours ($$) daily at 2 and 3:15 during school holidays (Wed. Fri., Sat., Sun. at other times)

Along the Pilgrim's Way

The Pilgrim's Way along the heights of the North Downs was followed by millions of penitent (and not so penitent) travelers riding or tramping to the tomb of St. Thomas Becket at Canterbury (see page 52).

The pilgrims – Geoffrey Chaucer's *Canterbury Tales* yarn-spinners among them – traveled this way for the best part of four centuries, coming northeast from Winchester to bypass London along the high chalk downs of Surrey before sloping off into Kent toward Canterbury. The route they followed was far older than the cult of the martyred saint, however. For thousands of years this old road was used as a thoroughfare connecting the great Stone Age and Bronze Age centers on Salisbury Plain to the Kentish coast and its short sea connections to the Continent.

Today the 153-mile North Downs Way National Trail from Farnham to Dover keeps company with the Pilgrim's Way for much of its length along the downs south of London. The modern trail runs through beautiful woodland, pastoral hillsides and fields, generally keeping to the crest of the ridge and offering spectacular views. The original route tends to be lower: Ancient travelers preferred to journey above the dangers of the valley floor but below the skyline, where their silhouettes would give them away.

Some of the small villages around the Pilgrim's Way in Surrey are particularly attractive. Shere, 6 miles east of Guildford along the A25 Dorking Road, has charming 16th- and 17th-century village houses overhanging the streets, a Tudor pub and the really exceptional Norman parish church of St. James. The central tower is early Norman, as is the south doorway, and the oaken door it holds is 800 years old. Some of the stained glass dates back to the 14th century and features symbols of the Four Evangelists. Also on display is a beautiful little bronze statuette of the Virgin and Baby Jesus, only the height of a thumb – probably an icon mislaid by some Canterbury-bound penitent on the Pilgrim's Way, which runs along the downs above the village.

From here it is a very fine 7-mile walk eastward to Box Hill, an escarpment with a wonderful view to the south. Footpaths and bridleways are clearly marked on Ordnance Survey maps that cover this region (see page 10), and by using these you can devise your own trips.

North Downs Way, a free leaflet giving introductory information about the trail, is available from all local tourist information centers; call 01622 221525 or go online at www.nationaltrail.co.uk/northdowns.

The ancient North Downs Way footpath leads through East Warren Woods, near Compton

The West Country

Opposite: Ruins of Wheal Coates Tin Mine sit above the cliffs near St. Agnes in Cornwall

The West Country

For the British, images of the West Country always include dairy cattle grazing in sloping green fields, a glass of strong cider on a hot day, thatched cottages clustered around churches of golden stone, seaside vacations on a coast of rocky coves and sandy beaches.

The southwestern corner of Britain forms a long peninsula like an outstretched leg, its toe tip dipping into the Atlantic at Land's End in westernmost Cornwall. Plentiful rainfall gives the countryside of the interior a lush appearance, smooth and green. The coast, on the other hand, is famous for its ruggedness and for the wild danger of the seas that have carved it.

It is a superb vacation coast, with a handful of big resorts and hundreds of smaller villages and hamlets. Visitors come in their millions during the summer months. But in the less crowded spring and fall you can see the small coast villages at their best, while lovers of furious seas and storms can get all the thrills they want on the cliffs and headlands of the West Country in winter.

Farmers and Fishermen

Fishing and farming are this intensely rural region's mainstays, together with tourism. West Country people have a well-earned reputation for being easy-going and mild-mannered, with little use for bureaucracy and a lot of time for conversation and bucolic leg-pulling. They are not always in good humor when their village centers and local services are overrun with busloads of tourists – "grockles" or "emmets," as they call them – on holiday weekends. Since any visitor to the West Country is bound to spend a lot of time exploring, strolling or driving around the glorious countryside, the observance of such common courtesies as shutting field gates behind you when out walking, or negotiating the narrow, high-banked lanes at appropriate speeds, is always appreciated.

County of Antiquities

Five counties make up the West Country – Wiltshire, Somerset, Dorset, Devon and Cornwall. Wiltshire, in the northeastern part of the region, is founded on chalk. At the heart of this county lies the great grassland of Salisbury Plain, much of it untouched by modern intensive farming methods

and thus providing a haven for wildlife. In southern Wiltshire is the handsome small city of Salisbury; its famous 404-foot cathedral spire is the tallest in Britain.

Prehistoric antiquities are scattered thickly around and across Salisbury Plain; most celebrated among them are the double stone circle enclosing Avebury village, the man-made hill of Silbury, and Britain's best-known stone monument, the enigmatic structure of Stonehenge.

From Mendip to the Moors

Of the West Country's five counties, Somerset has the greatest variety of landscape. The soft golden limestone of the Cotswolds rolls south to meet the harder gray limestone of the Mendip Hills. Here lies the beautiful and popular World Heritage city of Bath, rightly admired for its matchless Georgian architecture and Roman sites. Much of central Somerset is low-lying flat country known as the Levels, with the legend-encrusted knoll of Glastonbury Tor rising from the surrounding fields. The muddy tidal waters of the wide Severn Estuary wash its western flank.

Farther west, Somerset rises into the moorland hills of Quantock and Exmoor, while to the south it rolls into Dorset on a tide of deep gold stone, known as "hamstone" after Ham Hill, where it is quarried.

Thomas Hardy's Wessex

The chalk landscape ends with a flourish in the southern half of Dorset, with fine billowing downs. The limestone here is a hard but easily worked white rock called "freestone," or Portland stone, and it can be seen in some spectacular cliffs. It provided stone for the rebuilding of London through the centuries, resulting in some harshly scarred land.

The Dorset beaches and coves west of Bournemouth are beautiful, and there are some stunning fishing villages to explore and pause in for refreshment, including East and West Lulworth, which lead to Lulworth Cove. This area of coast is thick with fossils, and known by many as the Jurassic Coast, but visitors are discouraged from removing them as souvenirs. The chalk pokes through the green fields here and there – most notably on the hillside above Cerne Abbas, where a rampantly phallic giant is as clearly outlined as when he was cut out of the turf 2,000 or more years ago (see page 86).

Coastal erosion at West Bay, Dorset

Dorset's literary hero is Thomas Hardy; you can visit the cottage where he was born, at Higher Brockhampton near Dorchester; the house in which he lived the last 43 years of his life; the churchyard where his heart is buried; and scenes from all his great Wessex novels – from *Under The Greenwood Tree* to *Jude the Obscure*.

Easygoing Devon

Dorset's westerly neighbor is Devon, often thought of as the "softest" of the five West Country counties. It is true that these rolling fields of red earth are clothed in rich grassland, and produce champion thick cream, beef and milk. It's also true that the "combes," or valleys, of mid-Devon, west Exmoor and the South Hams are wonderful places for easy, sheltered idling.

But Devon has a wild enough coastline, and plenty of harsh drama in the dark granite moorland of Dartmoor, with its mists and moody weather. This is a historic seafaring county, with the famous ports of Dartmouth and Plymouth, and charming fishing towns such as Brixham and Appledore. Sailing in small boats is extremely popular. Picturesque coast settlements like Combe Martin and Clovelly in the north and Sidmouth and Salcombe in the

The granite cliffs of Land's End in Cornwall, mainland England's most westerly point

south have become vacation havens, but there also are plenty of out-of-the-way places where tourists don't throng.

Cornwall – A Land Apart

Granite-boned Cornwall, Britain's southwesternmost county, really is a land apart, a harsh place to make a living on a small farm or in small-scale fishing. Yet it possesses much weatherbeaten beauty and a sandy, cliff-walled coast. The Southwest Coast Path runs along the coast's perimeter, offering unforgettable views and steep up-and-down hiking. Swimming is superb, from beaches as expansive as the 3-mile Penhale Sands to diminutive coves. Inland there are more delights: prehistoric standing stones and tombs, hidden villages and sheltered valleys where subtropical gardens flourish.

But it is that tremendous, storm-carved coast, narrowing to the final full stop of Land's End, that really holds the ancient spirit of this dramatic outpost of the West Country.

West Country Flavors

The West Country boasts some culinary delights, too. This is the home of the traditional cream tea: scones served with strawberry preserves and piled high with "clotted" cream (thick Devonshire or Cornish cream), accompanied by a pot of tea. Fudge also is excellent here, and don't miss the local pies known as Cornish pasties. Of course, seafood abounds in every town and village along the coast, from traditional fish and chip shops to top-quality, elegant fish restaurants. Try the local cheeses, such as cheddar and Somerset brie.

The county of Somerset is also famed for its cider, an alcoholic drink made from apples, in particular, scrumpy. Stop at a village pub for a "ploughman's lunch" consisting of cheese, pickles and fresh bread, and taste a glass of the locally brewed ale.

Artists and Craftsmen

If you're looking for local crafts, St. Ives in south Cornwall is a magnet for artists and craftspeople. Don't miss Dartington Hall estate, located just outside the Devon town of Totnes. A wonderful collection of glass, pottery and wood-carvings made by local craftspeople is sold here. The hall itself is home to an arts and education center, set up by American millionaire Dorothy Elmhirst in 1925. There is a program of movies, concerts, plays and talks here during the summer months.

Bath

Bath is Britain's best-known small city, famous for its Georgian architecture. Its beauty is framed to perfection in its setting among seven hills where the Cotswold and Mendip ranges converge. It is the underlying oolitic limestone, with its lovely gold finish, that lends Bath its unique good looks. The city was fortunate to experience its 18th-century apex of prosperity as a spa resort at a time when British architecture also had reached a high point in the clean lines and symmetry of the Palladian style. In Bath it attained its peak, transforming a quiet and unremarkable market town into the supreme example of classic Georgian elegance.

From Leper King to Social Dictator

Bath's hot springs have had a long history of healing. Back in the mists of mythology it was the leper Bladud, a king turned swineherd, who discovered their powers in about 850 BC, when he noticed his pigs wallowing in the mud to ease their itchy skins. Following their example, Bladud found himself cured. When the Romans arrived in about AD 44 they built magnificent baths here. Their spa city of Aquae Sulis flourished, and parts still remain.

It was the 18th-century preoccupation with "taking the waters" that really launched Bath as Britain's premier spa town. The social side of this activity, far more important to most spa-goers than anything medical, had its origin here under the benign dictatorship of Beau Nash (see page 77). Soon the rich, famous and marriageable all came flocking, and the city prospered.

Delectable Small City

With its graceful crescents, squares and terraces rising and falling across the hillsides, Bath is an absolute must for

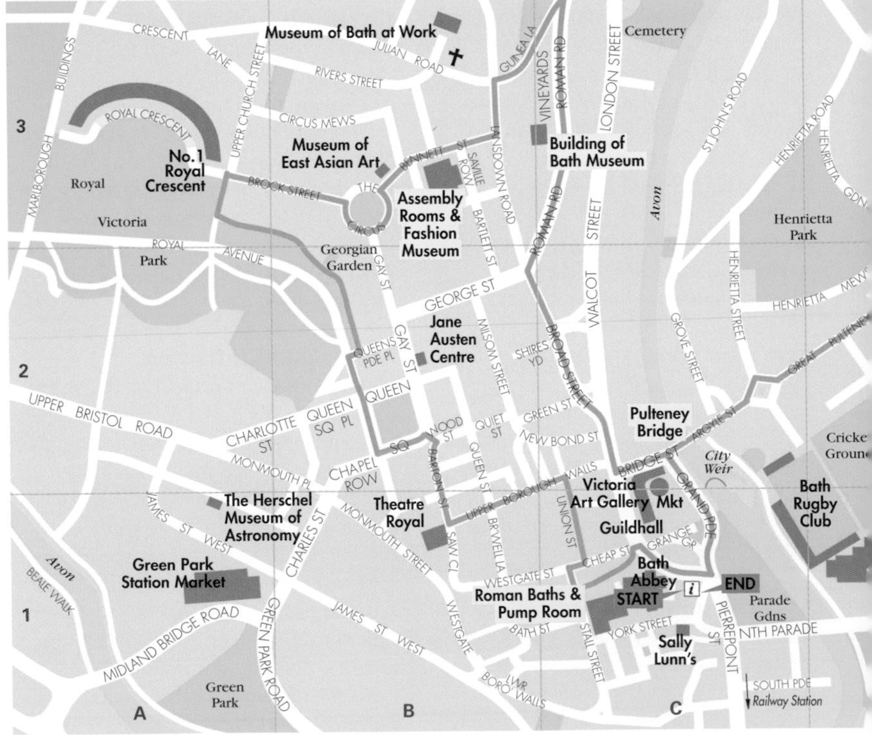

any visitor to Britain. The city has controlled modern development effectively and retains a low-rise, human scale. As one of the country's most delectable small cities, it has attracted well-heeled and sophisticated inhabitants. Bath is an ideal size city for strolling around, although it can become horribly crowded on some holidays and sunny weekends.

Lay of the Land

Orienting yourself in the city is not difficult. Bath Abbey, the Pump Room and the Roman Baths all flank Abbey Churchyard, the lively focus of the city. East of here, the River Avon flows south under Pulteney Bridge, then curves west by the railroad station to mark the southern boundary of the city center. North of Abbey Churchyard a warren of little streets gives way to Milsom Street, where you'll find Bath's most exclusive shops. North of Milsom Street are the Assembly Rooms and Fashion Museum; farther to the west lies the elegant Circus, and then the stunning sweep of the Royal Crescent at the crown of Royal Victoria Park.

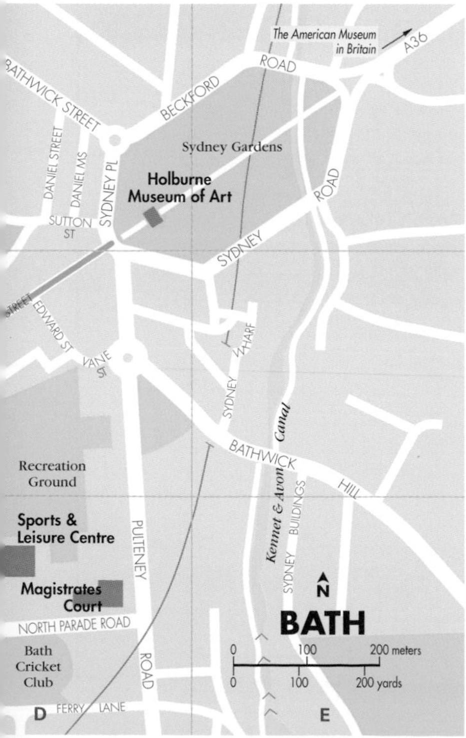

Park and Ride

If you bring a car into the city center, park in the big Charlotte Street parking lot. Some on-street "Pay-and-display" parking is also available. You'll need to buy a ticket from a machine and display it in your vehicle. Another option is to leave your car at one of the big "park and ride" lots on the city's outskirts and make your way to and from the center aboard one of the frequent special buses.

The historic sections of Bath can be seen comfortably in approximately two hours. The train station at the south end of Manvers Street is a 10-minute walk from Abbey Churchyard.

Try a Bath Bun

Bath has plenty of elegant restaurants, as you'd imagine, and many intimate bistros that come and go in the wink of an eye. Lunch at Demuths vegetarian restaurant, tucked away down North Parade Passage, or satisfy your hunger with a giant Sally Lunn Bun, baked according to a secret recipe, at Sally Lunn's, a couple of doors down the same street. Take tea in the Pump Room to

Festival!

The Bath International Music Festival brings the cream of the musical world to Bath for just over 12 days in late May and early June. Classical, traditional, jazz, ethnic and blues music mix with art shows and theater, either formally staged or erupting spontaneously in the street. This is Bath at its liveliest, and also at its most crowded.

Reserving accommodations and tickets well in advance is essential.

For information and tickets contact the Bath Festivals Box Office (☎ 01225 463362) or consult www.bathfestivals.org.uk.

the tinklings of a piano trio; it will wash away the bad-egg flavor of the healing hot-spring mineral waters. There is a plethora of coffee shops as well as wine bars and atmospheric places to take a load off after a hard day's sightseeing, many at reasonable prices.

Shopping and Street Entertainment

Upscale establishments – antiques, jewelry, clothes – can be found on and around Milsom Street, and cheaper and more cheerful shops in the warren of streets around Abbey Churchyard.

For entertainment, the 18th-century Theatre Royal Bath on Sawclose has been superbly restored and offers plays, concerts and tours of the interior. There are lunchtime recitals in the abbey.

The *Venue* website (www.venue.co.uk) gives reviews and details of what's on in Bath and Bristol. Entertainment, often baffling, hilarious or just plain weird, is provided by street performers around Abbey Churchyard. The amusement comes free, but a coin in the hat is always appreciated.

Cycling the Railroad

If the crowds of sightseers are getting you down, why not try a bicycle ride along the Bristol and Bath Railway Path (for information, ☎ 0117 922 4325; www.bristolbathrailwaypath.org.uk)?

The long-abandoned railroad track between Bath and Bristol has been turned into a 13-mile bicycle and walking path, which runs through attractive countryside and is perfect for a bike ride or hike.

Bicycles can be rented from the Bath and Dundas Canal Company, Brass Knocker Basin, Monkton Combe, Bath (☎ 01225 722292; www.bathcanal.com).

Essential Information

Tourist Information

✉ Abbey Chambers, Abbey Churchyard
☎ 0906 711 2000 (costs 50p per minute for this call); 0844 847 5257; www.visitbath.co.uk

Urban Transportation

Bath Spa railroad station is on Dorchester Street, a short walk from the city center. There are regular train services to London's Paddington station and other destinations in Britain. For information and reservations ☎ 08457 484950; www.nationalrail.co.uk. National Express operates regular long-distance buses from London Victoria station to Bath (some services stop at Heathrow airport). For information ☎ 08717 818178; www.nationalexpress.com. Buses in and around Bath start from the bus station on Dorchester Street (☎ 0845 6064446).

Airport Information

Bristol International Airport (☎ 0871 334 4444; www.bristolairport.co.uk) is 7 miles southwest of the city center and 15 miles from Bath. A regular express bus service, the Bristol Airport Flyer, travels from the airport to Bristol train station (Temple Meads) and Bristol bus station (every 10 minutes peak times; daily 2:30 a.m.–12 a.m.; travel time 40 minutes), from which trains and buses operate to Bath.

Climate – average highs and lows for the month

Jan.	Feb.	Mar.	Apr.	May	Jun.	Jul.	Aug.	Sep.	Oct.	Nov.	Dec.
8°C	7°C	10°C	12°C	17°C	19°C	22°C	21°C	18°C	14°C	11°C	8°C
46°F	45°F	50°F	54°F	63°F	66°F	72°F	70°F	64°F	57°F	52°F	46°F
3°C	3°C	5°C	6°C	9°C	12°C	14°C	14°C	12°C	9°C	6°C	4°C
37°F	37°F	41°F	43°F	48°F	54°F	57°F	57°F	54°F	48°F	43°F	39°F

Bath Sights

Key to symbols
map coordinates refer to the Bath map on pages 72–73 admission charge: $$$ more than £6, $$ £2–£6, $ less than £2
See page 5 for complete key to symbols

The American Museum in Britain

At 19th-century Claverton Manor is The American Museum in Britain, not a trivial Disneyfication but a well thought-out series of reconstructed interiors. They show the development of American home life from early pioneer rooms, with their plain furnishings, through elegant 18th-century woodwork that compares favorably with some of the best that Bath itself offers, to overblown 19th-century grandeur. There are displays of venerable quilts, needlework samplers, elegant Shaker furniture, indigenous American art, and cookies baked on the premises according to original pioneer recipes.

The grounds of Claverton Manor, which include an arboretum, are beautiful; don't miss the painstaking reconstruction of the garden George Washington tended at Mount Vernon.

E3 (off map) Claverton Manor, Claverton Down 01225 460503; www.americanmuseum.org Tue.–Sun. noon–5, mid-Mar. to Oct. (also Mon., in Aug. and public holidays); Tue.–Sun. noon–4:30, late Nov. to mid-Dec. Café $$$ (grounds and exhibition gallery only $$)

Assembly Rooms

The Assembly Rooms were built in 1769–71 by John Wood the Younger at the height of his fame. His father, John Wood the Elder, died in 1754. The Woods were the most illustrious architects of their day, and between them they shaped the face and character of Georgian Bath.

The Assembly Rooms consist of three harmonious rooms – a lofty, chandelier-lit ballroom, a tearoom and a galleried, octagonal card room. Here, all of fashionable Bath would gather in the evenings to play cards, dance and size up potential lovers.

The Fashion Museum is a display of dress that spans 400 years from Elizabethan hand embroidery to modern synthetics. Some of the 18th- and

The Tearoom is one of the three Assembly Rooms that were the focus of Georgian Bath's social scene

The Italianate-style Pulteney Bridge, designed by Robert Adam, is set above a terraced weir

19th-century gowns are beautiful examples of master craftsmanship.

Assembly Rooms and Fashion Museum

B3 Bennett Street Assembly Rooms: 01225 477789; www.nationaltrust.org.uk. Fashion Museum: 01225 477173; www.museumofcostume.co.uk Daily 10:30–6, Mar.–Oct.; 10:30–5, rest of year. Last admission 1 hour before closing Café Assembly Rooms $; museum $$$ (with audio guide) Assembly Rooms may close for private functions

Building of Bath Museum

If you want to appreciate what you see as you stroll around the city, then you can't do better than to start with a visit to the Building of Bath Museum, housed in an old chapel behind the beautiful curved terrace of the Paragon. It relates the story of how the medieval wool-trading town of Bath was changed into the most chic and elegant resort in Britain, brilliantly transformed chiefly at the hands of the talented father and son team of John Wood the Elder and John Wood the Younger.

Fascinating details include the nitty-gritty of plumbing, heating and lighting in the Georgian era, and how the Woods designed and built the most harmonious and carefully balanced facades for their terraces and crescents while leaving the body of each house to the design whim of individual builders. Disciplined order without, multiple eccentricities within: The architecture of Bath stands as a metaphor of sorts for the British personality.

C3 The Countess of Huntingdon's Chapel, The Vineyards 01225 333895; www.bath-preservation-trust.org.uk Sat.–Mon. 10:30–5, Feb.–Nov. $$

Pulteney Bridge

This is one of the finest town bridges in Britain, built across the River Avon to link the city with the east bank of the river, which Sir William Pulteney intended to develop into a residential area in the 1770s. He called in the eminent architect Robert Adam, who finished the bridge in 1774 in splendid Italianate style with two rows of flanking shops and dwellings supported above a terraced weir on three great round arches. Pulteney's funds would not stretch to accomplishing his ambitious plans, however. Today he is remembered through Great Pulteney Street, the fine, wide thoroughfare on the east bank, and by the bridge that carries his name.

C2

Life in Georgian Bath

Picture this – a morning stroll along Milsom Street, with one eye on the shop windows and the other on one's fellow strollers, followed by a glass or two of warm mineral water fresh from the hot springs in the Pump Room to the genteel sound of a string ensemble. In the afternoon, a saunter along the gravel walks of the park to display one's new walking gown, before tea and civilized conversation in the drawing room of one of Mr. Wood's elegant new houses. And at night, perhaps a game of cards and a few dances in the Assembly Rooms, with the chance to indulge in a little flirtation while – of course – observing the strict rules of etiquette laid down by that arbiter of good taste, Beau Nash...

When Richard "Beau" Nash became Bath's Master of Ceremonies in 1704, he wisely saw that when strangers gathered together for pleasure in one small town – lords and ladies, prosperous farmers, London swells, local traders all cheek by jowl – they needed some agreed-on rules to abide by if they were to get along amicably. Most of Beau Nash's rules were commonsense recommendations: no swearing or smoking in public places, no wearing of swords, and entertainments such as balls to end by 11 o'clock at night.

There was plenty of gossip in Georgian Bath, and plenty of ritual. This was Britain's premier spa, unsurpassed for elegance and gentility. Good manners and an obligation to conform were imposed on all who stayed at Bath. Visitors came under the civilizing influence of superb architecture, plenty of green spaces and a social life with unwritten but very definite rules.

The daily round of family walks, taking the waters in the Pump Room, courting in the public gardens, tea drinking, visiting, and card parties and dances in the Assembly Rooms suited almost everyone. It was easy and pleasant to follow the set course, which gave maximum opportunity to flirt, make and break alliances, secure one's next step up the social ladder – and, of course, exchange endless gossip.

Visitors can still take the waters at the Pump Room in Stall Street

The base of the pillars of the Great Bath date from Roman times, but the upper structure is more recent

Pump Room

The cornerstone of the Georgian social scene in Bath faces the south side of Abbey Churchyard and was built in the 1790s in Classical style. Around five glasses of mineral water a day was the recommended dose for liverish Georgians, although once you have choked down a single glass of the warm spring water (which tastes awful) you may wonder how anyone completed the course. The water wells up from the King's Spring and jets down through spouts from a handsome stone samovar.

A statue of Beau Nash, Bath Master of Ceremonies in the early 18th century and ultimate arbiter on all matters of taste and behavior, keeps a stern eye on water drinkers, cream tea guzzlers and lunchers as they browse and quaff to the tinkling of the Pump Room's music ensemble. Through a side window you can look down to view the sacred spring of the Romano-Celtic goddess Sulis-Minerva, steaming and bubbling in the King's Bath.

C1 Stall Street 01225 477785; www.romanbaths.co.uk Daily 9 a.m.–10 p.m., Jul.–Aug.; 9–6, Mar.–Jun. and Sep.–Oct.; 9:30–5:30, rest of year. Last admission 1 hour before closing Restaurant Free

Roman Baths

This is one of Britain's prime Roman relics, and a very popular tourist attraction. If crowds in narrow spaces bother you, don't visit on summer holiday weekends.

These splendid baths were built around AD 65–75, shortly after the Romans came to Britain. With their departure in the early fifth century the baths fell into disrepair and lay all but forgotten 20 feet under the ground until excavations in 1878 revealed them.

The elevated terrace with statues of Roman heroes that overlooks the Great Bath is a Victorian addition, but the baths themselves are much as the Romans would have known them. The lead-lined Great Bath itself, measuring 39 feet by 78 feet, is fed with steamy green water at a constant 115 degrees Fahrenheit from the largest of the three hot springs, welling from 10,000 feet deep in the earth. The stumps of masonry that surround it would have supported columns holding up a great barrel roof, but nowadays the bath lies open to the sky.

In chambers off the Great Bath are other baths and rooms – a little circular bath for medicinal bathing, a sauna whose heat came from a well-stocked furnace blowing hot air beneath the floor, and the handsome structure known as the King's Bath, which was built above a Roman reservoir and dates from 1100.

In locating their baths at the hot springs, the Romans made the wise diplomatic decision to incorporate the locally worshiped water goddess Sulis in their dedication of the spring, as well as to their own Minerva. The Baths Museum holds fascinating relics from the temple to Sulis-Minerva that the Romans built here, chief among them a beautiful gilt bronze head of the goddess and a giant stone sculpture of the head of a Gorgon-like god, wildly bearded and fiercely staring, that once adorned the pediment of the temple.

C1 · Stall Street · 01225 477785; www.romanbaths.co.uk · Daily 9 a.m.–10 p.m., Jul.–Aug.; 9–6, Mar.–Jun. and Sep.–Oct.; 9:30–5:30, rest of year. Last admission 1 hour before closing · Restaurant in Pump Room · $$$ (includes audio guide) · Guided tours on the hour (free)

Royal Crescent

This wonderful sweep of 30 houses bends in a graceful golden bow of stone, at the upper end of Royal Victoria Park. John Wood the Younger, its architect, was not quite 40 when building started in 1767. The crescent, completed in 1774, is the finest in Britain and the jewel in the crown of Wood's achievements. It was a hollow triumph, literally, since Wood followed his usual practice of constructing only the facade: Other builders completed the dwellings as they saw fit.

Number One and its elegant reception rooms and cheerful basement kitchen give a good idea of the lifestyle of visitors to Bath, who would rent houses like this for the season.

No. 1 · A3 · 1 Royal Crescent · 01225 428126; www.bath-preservation-trust.org.uk · Tue.–Sun. 10:30–5, mid-Feb. to Oct.; Tue.–Sun. 10:30–4, Nov. to mid-Dec. Last admission 30 minutes before closing · $$

Some houses along the Royal Crescent are still privately owned, although there is a hotel and a museum

Walk:
Around Bath

Refer to route marked on city map on pages 72–73

Bath is the right size for a stroll, and this walk passes a number of interesting places – if you want to visit some of these the excursion could easily last all day.

Start at the Tourist Information Centre on Abbey Churchyard.

Stop to explore the adjacent Bath Abbey, a beautiful Tudor church, completed in 1499 by Bishop Oliver King after a dream about angels. The abbey is fan-vaulted inside, with a wonderful collection of memorials and inscriptions from Bath's Georgian heyday.

Walk across Abbey Churchyard past the Pump Room, turn right onto Union Street, then left along Upper Borough Walls to Barton Street.

To your left is the Theatre Royal Bath, a Georgian building dating from 1805, plush and well gilded within. Plays are performed here, and it is the city's cultural hub.

Turn right to reach elegant Queen Square.

This beautiful square was built in 1728–34 by John Wood the Elder.

Walk up the left-hand side of the square,

Bath Abbey, completed in 1611, replaced earlier religious buildings that had been on the site since AD 757

cross to the steps and continue ahead beside fine stone gateposts to the Gravel Walk, which curves to the left through Royal Victoria Park.

Veer to the right to reach Royal Crescent. Leave the east end of the crescent along Brock Street to get to The Circus. There are 30 houses, as in the Royal Crescent, but these form a stylish circle with a carved frieze of magical symbols, instruments and animals.

Continue along Bennett Street (the Assembly Rooms and Fashion Museum are to your right), turn left onto Lansdown Road (enjoy the views behind you), and right down Guinea Lane, before turning right onto The Paragon.

Jane Austen lived at No. 1 in 1801; the Building of Bath Museum (see page 76) is in the Old Chapel halfway along the curve.

Continue past the traffic lights and then down Broad Street.

Have a pint at the Saracen's Head pub on the left, the oldest pub in Bath.

Bear right at the bottom of Broad Street, then left over graceful Pulteney Bridge and along Argyle Street, and then the grand avenue of Great Pulteney Street to the Holburne Museum of Art in Sydney Gardens, at the end of the street.

The museum contains fine furniture, silver and paintings.

Return over Pulteney Bridge, turning left along the river. Grand Parade and Grange Grove return you to the tourist office.

Try a bun at Sally Lunn's (Bath's oldest house), to your left in North Parade Passage.

Jane Austen's City

Jane Austen enjoyed several family vacations in Bath before coming to live at No. 1, The Paragon, in 1801. The Austens moved around the city during the next five years, and Jane could observe the rituals and pretensions of Bath society. She wrote about them in the novels *Northanger Abbey* and *Persuasion*. In *Persuasion*, for example, Anne Elliot meets Captain Wentworth in the octagonal room of the Assembly Rooms.

Austen enthusiasts can imagine themselves present at Miss Elliot's side as they explore these same rooms today, and guided walking tours (Sat.–Sun. and public holidays at 11 a.m.; also Fri.–Sat. at 4 p.m., Jul.–Aug.; $$), which begin at the KC Change Visitor Information Centre in Abbey Churchyard, follow in Jane's footsteps around Bath (tours last 90 minutes).

Sally Lunn's is the home of the Bath bun

Bath Abbey C1 Abbey Churchyard 01225 422462; www.bathabbey.org Mon.–Sat. 9–6, Sun. 1–2:30 and 4:30–5:30, Apr.–Oct.; Mon.–Sat. 9–4:30, Sun. 1–2:30 and 4:30–5:30, rest of year Free (suggested donation $$); Tower $$

Holburne Museum of Art D3 Great Pulteney Street 01225 388588; www.holburne.org Mon.–Sat. 10–5, Sun. 11–5 Café $$$

Jane Austen Centre B2 40 Gay Street 01225 443000; www.janeausten.co.uk Daily 9:45–5:30 (also Thu.–Sat. 5:30 p.m.–7 p.m.), Apr.–Oct.; Sun.–Fri. 11–4:30, Sat. 9:45–5:30, Nov.–Mar. Café $$$

Regional Sights

Key to symbols
map coordinates refer to the West Country map on pages 68–69 admission charge: $$$ more than £6, $$ £2–£6, $ less than £2
See page 5 for complete key to symbols

Bradford-on-Avon

Set beside the River Avon in northwest Wiltshire, Bradford-on-Avon is a charming stone-built town whose name derives from "broad ford." Its crooked streets, lined with old wool merchants' houses, rise to fine hillside churches, and down along the river are handsome water mills. West of town on the south bank of the Avon is a splendid 14th-century tithe barn at Barton Farm, built to store the tenth of the tenants' produce that was due to the local abbey. Afternoon tea is served here.

Toward the town center north of the river is a complete Saxon church, a great rarity. It functioned as a school and then a cottage, until recognized for what it was in the 1850s by the Vicar of Bradford.

E3
Tourist information 50 St. Margaret's Street
01225 865797; www.bradfordonavon.co.uk

Bristol

Bristol is the West Country's liveliest city. Its hilly streets slope down past Georgian sea captains' houses to the harbors and docks, where you will find two good art centers.

Attractions include the 14th-century church of St. Mary Redcliffe, which has an imposing spire. The elegant Regency district of Clifton perches on the lip of the Avon Gorge beside engineer Isambard Kingdom Brunel's handsome Clifton Suspension Bridge, finished in 1864. In the dock area sits Brunel's restored, great pioneering steamship, the SS *Great Britain*. Also on the waterfront is At-Bristol, an interactive science center with a planetarium.

D3
Tourist information E Shed, 1 Canons Road
0906 711 2191; www.visitbristol.co.uk
Brunel's SS *Great Britain* Great Western Dockyard, Gas Ferry Road 0117 926 0680
Daily 10–5:30, Apr.–Oct.; 10–4:30, Nov.–Mar. Last ticket sales 1 hour before closing Café
$$$ Audio guides (free)
At-Bristol Anchor Road 0845 345 1235; www.at-bristol.org Mon.–Fri. 10–5 (5–6 during school holidays), Sat.–Sun. 10–6 Café $$$

Devonshire Moors

The county of Devon possesses two national parks, Exmoor and Dartmoor. The two moors are twins, but are entirely dissimilar. Exmoor is the more northerly, with the Devon/Somerset border dividing it into an eastern and a western half (two-thirds of the park lies within Somerset). The moor is founded on red sandstone from which it takes a light and open character, with rounded hills blanketed with grass or heather. Outside the park, wooded valleys known as "combes" lead to a varied coast – sandy surfing beaches

Opposite: Dartmoor's granite outcrops are known as tors
Right: The Clifton Suspension Bridge spans the Avon

The view of the Valley of Rocks from Hollerday Hill within Devon's Exmoor National Park

and dunes along the Atlantic-facing west, pebbly shores under high cliffs on the north coast that looks at Wales across the Bristol Channel.

Just outside the national park to the west, between the towns of Barnstaple and Lynton, Arlington Court is a fine house worth visiting for its objets d'art, woodland walks and its horse-drawn carriage collection.

Dartmoor, in southern Devon, is associated with the classic Sherlock Holmes tale *The Hound of the Baskervilles* (1902). In this exciting fable, Sir Arthur Conan Doyle caught the grim atmosphere of Dartmoor and its gray, misty granite moorland. The standing stones and beehive huts of primitive pre-Roman moor dwellers highlight the lonely aspect of the landscape in these parts.

Southeast of Dartmoor is historic Dartmouth, tucked away up the Dart Estuary. This is a good base for exploring the area; it's packed with restaurants and inns, and pretty shops in which to browse.

Beyond Plymouth is Morwellham Quay (tel 01822 832766; www.morwellam-quay.co.uk), a former copper-mining village on the River Tamar. You can explore a reconstructed mine, a Victorian schoolroom, draft horse stables as well as an Edwardian farm project, all accompanied by informed and period-costumed guides.

Exmoor National Park Authority C2–C3 Exmoor House, Dulverton, Somerset 01398 323665; www.exmoor-nationalpark.gov.uk

Dartmoor National Park Authority C1–C2 Parke, Haytor Road, Bovey Tracey, Newton Abbot, Devon 01626 832093; www.dartmoor-npa.gov.uk

Arlington Court C3 Arlington, near Barnstaple, Devon 01271 850296; www.nationaltrust.org House: daily 11–3, mid-Feb., mid-Mar. to Oct. Garden: 11–3, mid-Feb.; 10:30–5, mid-Mar. to Oct. Other times vary, see the website Café $$$ Horse-drawn carriage rides

The End of England

At the southwest tip of the West Country peninsula lies Cornwall, a county famous for its superb seaside – sandy beaches, granite cliffs and coves, and fishing villages piled into clefts in the cliffs. The south coast is rich in fishing villages such as Polperro, Mevagissey, Portloe, Portscatho and Mousehole, and in pretty, old-fashioned gray stone towns – Fowey, St. Mawes, Falmouth – sheltered in deep-cut estuaries.

In the north the settlements tend to be less cozy. Here you will find windswept villages such as Zennor, which has a fascinating church. The biggest and cheeriest resort is Newquay, set behind fine beaches. The atmospheric little town of Padstow has an internationally renowned waterside fish restaurant and hosts a ceremonial "Mayday" of madness on May 1, when thousands pack the narrow streets to cheer a comical prancing horse ("Obby Oss") through town in a festive parade.

The mild Cornish climate encourages the growth of beautiful gardens. Many feature exotic species, such as the gardens in Trelissick and Trewithen, both near Truro, and farther west at Glendurgan and Trengwainton. Other delights include the causeway island of St. Michael's Mount, near Penzance, crowned with a magnificent house and church; and beautiful St. Ives, on the north coast. An artists' haunt, St. Ives contains the Barbara Hepworth Museum and Sculpture Garden, with works by this celebrated sculptor. There are historic sites inland, such as tiny Iron Age houses and gardens at Chysauster, near St. Ives.

Trelissick Garden A1 Feock, near Truro 01872 862090; www.nationaltrust.org.uk Daily 10:30–5:30, mid-Feb. to early Nov.; 11–4, rest of year. Closes dusk if earlier Restaurant $$$

St. Michael's Mount A1 Marazion, near Penzance 01736 710507 Sun.–Fri. 10:30–5, Apr.–Oct. Last admission 45 minutes before closing Restaurant and café $$$

Barbara Hepworth Museum and Sculpture Garden A1 Barnoon Hill, St. Ives 01736 796226; www.tate/org.uk/stives/hepworth Daily 10–5:20, Mar.–Oct.; Tue.–Sun. 10–4:20, rest of year. Garden closes at 4:20 (or dusk if earlier). Last admission 30 minutes before closing $$

Chysauster Ancient Village A1 Off B3311, Newmill, Penzance 07831 757934; www.english-heritage.org.uk Daily 10–6, Jul.–Aug.; 10–5, Apr.–Jun. and in Sep.; 10–4, in Oct. Last admission 30 minutes before closing $$

The picturesque village of Mousehole lies only a few miles from Penzance

Drive:
Thomas Hardy's Dorset

Distance: 80 miles

This 80-mile drive around Hardy-related sites takes in many of the most interesting and beautiful parts of Dorset. The names that Hardy gave to various locations in his famous "Wessex novels" appear in parentheses after their real names.

A thatched cottage at Milton Abbas

Start in Dorchester ("Casterbridge").
Dorchester is the county capital, and the Dorset County Museum preserves the manuscript of *The Mayor of Casterbridge* and a mock-up of Hardy's study. Visit Max Gate on Alington Avenue; Hardy designed it and lived here from 1885 until his death in 1928.

Proceed east along A35 to Stinsford.
Hardy's heart lies buried in the churchyard in the grave of his first wife, Emma. The National Trust maintains Hardy's Cottage, the author's birthplace, at nearby Higher Bockhampton. Bockhampton and Stinsford together form "Mellstock" in *Under the Greenwood Tree*.

Continue east along A35.
Puddletown ("Weatherbury" in *Far From The Madding Crowd*) is where Hardy's grandfather played bass viol in the local church. A little farther on is Tolpuddle, from where the six iconic "Tolpuddle Martyrs" were transported to Australia in 1834 for membership of a "secret society." They were, in fact, poor farm laborers trying to form a union.

Continue along A35.
The village of Bere Regis ("Kingsbere-sub-Greenhill" in *Tess of the D'Urbervilles*) has a Saxon church with tombs and a stained-glass lion crest of the Turbervilles, the name that inspired Hardy.

Go north on minor roads via Milborne St. Andrew to Milton Abbas.
This charming thatched estate village used to be next to the Gothic mansion and 14th-century abbey church of Milton Abbey a mile away, but in 1780 the house's owner, the Earl of Dorchester, had the village removed and rebuilt so that it did not intrude on his view.

From Milton Abbas proceed west to Hilton, then north to Bulbarrow Hill.
Standing on top of the hill are the ramparts of the Iron Age hill fort of Rawlsbury Camp; to the northwest is Blackmoor Vale.

From Bulbarrow Hill, work your way southwest on minor roads past Melcombe Bingham, Cheselbourne and Piddletrenthide to Cerne Abbas.
A 2,000-year-old chalk outline on the hillside depicts a priapic giant wielding his club.

Continue southwest via Sydling St. Nicholas to Maiden Newton, then turn northwest along the ridgeback A356. After 6 miles, bear left to Beaminster.
Look for the beautiful medieval church.

A3066 brings you south to the town of Bridport; from here, B3157 ambles southeast near the coast of Lyme Bay.
Here stretches pebbly Chesil Beach, which shelters brackish Fleet lagoon. Abbotsbury is a golden stone village; its

Chesil Beach is an 18-mile stretch of pebbles that links Portland to Abbotsbury

attractions include the longest tithe barn in Britain, a subtropical garden and a long-established Swannery.

From Abbotsbury minor roads bring you back to Dorchester by way of the enormous and spectacular Iron Age ramparted hill-fort of Maiden Castle.

Dorchester D2

Tourist information 11 Antelope Walk 01305 267992; www.westdorset.com

Dorset County Museum

High West Street, Dorchester 01305 262735; www.dorsetcountymuseum.org Mon.–Sat. 10–5, Apr.–Oct.; Tue.–Sat. 10–4, rest of year $$$

Max Gate Alington Avenue, Dorchester 01305 262538 Wed.–Sun. 11–5, Apr.–Oct. $$

Hardy's Cottage E2

Higher Bockhampton, near Dorchester 01297 489481 Call for opening times $$

Abbotsbury Swannery New Barn Road, Abbotsbury 01305 871858 Daily 10–6 (5 at start and end of season), mid-Mar. to Oct. Last admission 1 hour before closing Café $$$

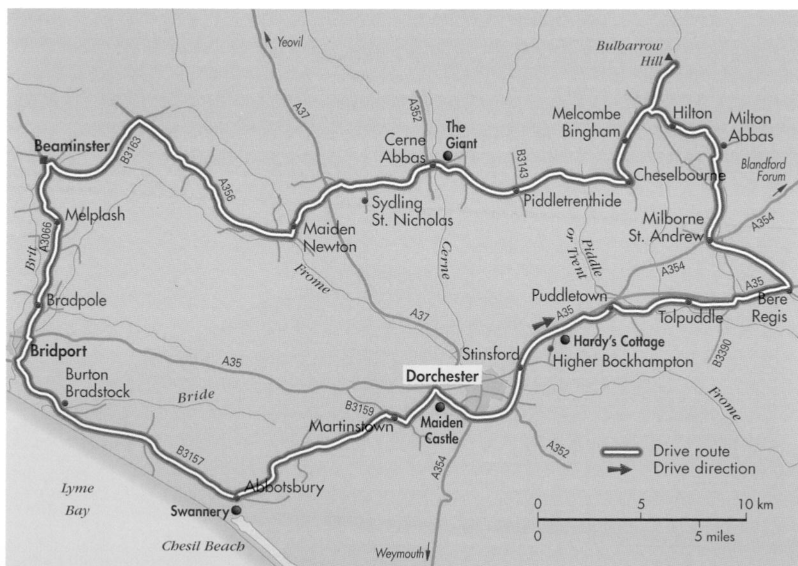

Glastonbury

Few places in the British Isles have attracted so many legends as Glastonbury. This unremarkable town sits amid the flat peat moors of the Somerset Levels, which some say is the location of the Vale of Avalon, legendary valley of healing and rebirth.

Above the town rises Glastonbury Tor, a dragon-shaped mass of rock crowned with a landmark church tower. Legend recalls how King Arthur, mortally wounded after his final battle, was rowed to Glastonbury in a barge to be healed. The king is said to lie with his knights under the Tor in an enchanted sleep, from which all will be roused to save England from some calamity yet to come.

The last abbot in England, Richard Whytyng, was hanged on the Tor in 1539; his abbey and monastery buildings lie in scenic ruin in the center of Glastonbury. The 14th-century, octagonal-roofed Abbot's Kitchen still stands, and the former monastic tithe barn now houses the excellent Somerset Rural Life Museum. Here, displays illustrate traditional rural ways of life such as cider- and cheese-making, thatching and farming.

Another legend tells how Joseph of Arimathea brought Jesus Christ to Glastonbury as a boy. In about AD 60, as a very old man, Joseph allegedly returned to Avalon with either the chalice used at the Last Supper, or the holy cup that caught the blood from Christ's side at the Crucifixion. On Wearyall Hill just outside town you can see the Holy Thorn Tree, said to bloom only at Easter and Christmas. Legends say that the tree is a cutting from a tree that took root from the spot where Joseph of Arimathea stuck his staff – made of a piece of Christ's cross – into the ground. Below the Tor lies the Chalice Well, an ancient well from which healing water springs; some say the holy cup lies buried in the surrounding gardens.

D3

Tourist information The Tribunal, 9 High Street 01458 832954; www.glastonburytic.co.uk

Glastonbury Abbey Magdalene Street 01458 832267 Daily 9–9, Jun.–Aug.; 9–6, Mar.–May; 9–5, Sep.–Nov.; 9–4, rest of year Café (outdoor) early May through Sep. $$

Somerset Rural Life Museum Abbey Farm, Chilkwell Street 01458 831197 Tue.–Sat. and public holidays, except Good Fri., 10–5 Café (Apr.–Sep.) Free

The distinctive silhouette of Glastonbury Tor can be seen from miles around

Lacock

Lacock is an 18th-century gray stone village that has been preserved by the National Trust, the country's conservation organization.

Among the Elizabethan, Jacobean and Georgian houses stands the 15th-century Church of St. Cyriac, with the vast, elaborate tomb of Sir William Sharington, who bought up the estate in 1539. As old as the church is the village pub, The Sign of the Angel.

Lacock's chief attraction, however, is the lovely abbey complex, which has many medieval features. Here you can see reproductions of a smeary photograph of the oriel window in the abbey's south gallery, snapped in 1835 by William Henry Fox Talbot and claimed to be the first photographic negative ever taken. The Fox Talbot Museum, located in the barn near the entrance, tells the story.

E3

Lacock Abbey and Fox Talbot Museum High Street
01249 730459; www.nationaltrust.org.uk
Abbey: Wed.–Mon. 11–5, mid-Feb. to Oct.; Sat.–Sun. noon–4, rest of year. Museum: daily 10:30–5:30, mid-Feb. to Oct.; 11–4, rest of year. Last admission 45 minutes before closing Restaurants and cafés in the village $$$ ($$ museum only early Nov.–Jan.)

Longleat

Sir John Thynne bought an Augustinian priory, Abbey Farm and more than 900 acres of land in 1541 on which he then built the grand Elizabethan mansion of Longleat.

Today you can visit the great hall, with its hammerbeam roof, seven libraries containing more than 40,000 books, and an art collection that includes Titian's *Rest on the Flight into Egypt*. There are also murals painted by the present owner, the 7th Marquess of Bath.

The 6th Marquess was the first homeowner in Britain to open his house to the public on a fully commercial basis, and the first to establish a drive-through wildlife safari park, on the "Capability" Brown-landscaped grounds. At the Journey into Jungle Kingdom exhibition you can see meerkats, monkeys and rainbow lorikeets. Amusement park rides and attractions now dominate the scene.

E3

Longleat Longleat, Warminster, Wiltshire
01985 844400; www.longleat.co.uk Safari Park: Mon.–Fri. 10–5, Sat.–Sun. 10–6 (to 7:30 p.m. public holidays and mid-Jul. to Aug). Last admission 1 hour before closing. House: check website for details
Restaurants $$$

Longleat House stands on extensive grounds designed by "Capability" Brown

The immense 13th-century Salisbury Cathedral is an architectural marvel

Salisbury

The symbol, pride and glory of Salisbury is its wonderful cathedral, set among the meadows of the River Avon in a hollow of the Wiltshire downs. The most famous part of this building is its immense spire, a graceful slim javelin of stone rising 404 feet into the sky. Salisbury Cathedral was completed in less than 40 years (1220–58), a tight time-frame that lent a unity of design and purpose so often lacking in medieval cathedrals that evolved through several centuries.

Any visit should start there, at the heart of Salisbury. Stand outside the cathedral, looking up at the tip of the spire with clouds scudding above, and you may feel the whole structure leaning over you. That seeming illusion is actually real: The foundations of the church go down no more than 6 feet into the soft alluvial soil of the river valley, and the top of the spire leans forward 2 feet.

Statues of saints and kings adorn the ornate west front. Inside, the church seems austere, its clustered marble pillars framing the tall emptiness of the nave. A glance upward reveals pillars bowed under the 6,000-ton weight of tower, spire and roofs, all built of solid stone. The late 13th-century cloisters, the most spacious in Britain in their day, are handsomely vaulted. In the late 13th-century Chapter House are biblical sculptures and one of only four surviving copies of England's Bill of Rights, the 1215 Magna Carta. There is a glorious 13th-century Tree of Jesse in stained glass in the south aisle (installed as the cathedral was built), and a delicate little fan-vaulted Tudor chantry (chapel) in which Masses were sung for the soul of Bishop Edmund Audley.

The cathedral stands at the center of the Close, a tranquil green space of trees and grass surrounded by fine buildings. The Bishop's Palace, the Deanery and the crooked old Wardrobe are all more than 700 years old. The Wardrobe, dating from 1254 and with many period features, now houses military artifacts from four local regiments. Mompesson House, dating from 1701, displays a collection of late 18th-century furniture and furnishings.

Salisbury itself was laid out in a grid pattern in early medieval times. A walk around town will show you the Poultry Cross, where laying birds were sold, and the strange display of a gambler's severed hand in a wall niche at the Haunch of Venison pub. In the Church of St. Thomas carved angels hold up the 15th-century roof, and demons drag down sinners in a vividly painted Day of Judgment mural from Tudor times. There are bookstores and craft shops to explore, and every Tuesday (except the third Tuesday in October) and Saturday a market is held on Market Square. The city is also a lively cultural center for theater and concerts, crowned by the annual Salisbury International Arts Festival for two weeks from late May to mid-June.

On the western outskirts of town stands the splendid baroque Wilton House, re-created by celebrated architect Inigo Jones for the Earl of Pembroke out of the ashes of a previous house, which burned in a fire in 1647. The art treasures inside are impressive (Rembrandt, Breughel, Van Dyck, Reynolds, Rubens), and on the grounds is a stylish Palladian bridge. There is also an excellent display about Tudor kitchens and Victorian laundry, neatly bringing the history of ordinary people to life.

Wilton gained world fame for its Wilton carpets, which can be seen in the Wilton Carpet Factory Shop at the Wilton Shopping Village, set in old factory buildings.

North of Salisbury you can climb the ramparts of the ancient hillfort of Old Sarum, the original city. The Normans built a cathedral here in 1092; a century later, lack of water and space drove the inhabitants to the river meadows.

E2

Tourist information Fish Row 01722 334956; www.visitwiltshire.co.uk

Cathedral The Close 01722 555120; www.salisburycathedral.org.uk Mon.–Sat. 9–5, Sun. noon–4 Restaurant Free ($$ donation suggested); tower tour $$$; guided tours (except tower) free Access may be restricted during services

The Wardrobe: The Rifles (Berkshire and Wiltshire) Museum 58 The Close 01722 419419; www.thewardrobe.org.uk Daily 10–5, Apr.–Sep.; Tue.–Sat. 10–5, Feb., Nov.; Mon.–Sat. 10–5, Mar. and Oct. Restaurant $$; garden only $

Mompesson House The Close 01722 420980 Sat.–Wed. 11–5, mid-Mar. to Oct. Café $$; garden only $

Wilton House Wilton 01722 746700; www.wiltonhouse.com Grounds: daily 11–5, early May to early Sep. House: Sun.–Thu. and Sat. before public holidays in May 11:30–4:30, mid-Apr. to Aug. Restaurant $$$ (grounds and exhibition only $$)

Wilton Shopping Village King Street, Wilton 01722 741211; www.wiltonshoppingvillage.co.uk Mon.–Sat. 9:30–5:30, Sun. 10:30–4:30 Restaurant and café Free

Old Sarum Castle Road 01722 335398; www.english-heritage.org.uk See website for details and events $$ Guided tours (Jun.–Aug.)

The grounds at Wilton House include formal gardens and architectural features

Some of Stonehenge's stones were brought more than 240 miles from Wales

Stonehenge and Prehistoric Wiltshire

The chalk downs of Wiltshire teem with prehistoric monuments, the richest collection in Britain. Best known of all is Stonehenge, 10 miles north of Salisbury, a remarkable 5,000-year-old double ring of stones that attracts the fanatical devotion of hippies, druids, New Age dreamers, archeologists and historians.

The earliest stones in the structure came from Wales, 200 miles away. The great trilithons, or "doorways," which still stand on the site, are built of stones brought here from Marlborough Downs to the north. A great effort of organization, labor and willpower, sporadically rekindled over the centuries, must have been required to transport and erect such enormous slabs of stone. The frequently asked question here is, "what was the structure actually for?" The answer to that question has eluded the investigations of curious minds for many centuries. Some say that Stonehenge is akin to a vast computer, built to calculate the cycle of the seasons: This is perhaps the most likely theory.

A few miles west of Marlborough is Avebury, a village literally surrounded by prehistory. A giant circle 1,400 feet in diameter encloses the settlement with great stones, around which dark legends have gathered. One of the stones is said to spit smoke if sat on; others to roll off for a drink at times. Under one was found the skeleton of a medieval surgeon-barber, complete with scissors and leather purse, who may have been caught unaware when the stone was toppled by superstitious locals.

The story of the stones is told in Avebury's excellent Alexander Keiller Museum, maintained by the National Trust. Also here are displays relating to other nearby monuments, including a ceremonial avenue of standing stones; the notable chambered tomb of West Kennet Long Barrow, dating from around 3250 BC; and the enigmatic, flat-topped Silbury Hill, built 130 feet high from chalk blocks that conceal a remarkable interior shaped like a spoked wheel.

Stonehenge E3

Off A303, near Amesbury, Wiltshire 01722 343834; www.english-heritage.org.uk Daily 9–7, Jun.–Aug.; 9:30–6, mid-Mar. to May and Sep. to mid-Oct.; 9:30–4, rest of year Café $$$ (includes audio tour)

Avebury E3

Avebury, near Marlborough 01672 539250; www.nationaltrust.org.uk Stone circle: daily dawn to dusk. Alexander Keiller Museum: daily 10–6, Apr.–Oct.; 10–4 (closes at dusk if earlier), rest of year Restaurant Stone circle free; Museum $$

The cloisters at Wells Cathedral

Stourhead

Banker Henry Hoare built the splendid Palladian mansion of Stourhead, in western Wiltshire, between 1721 and 1725. Wings were added later, and in 1840 a grand portico completed the house. The fine Chippendale furniture was made specifically for the house. Landscape paintings by Nicolas Poussin and Claude Lorrain influenced Hoare's son, Henry Hoare "the Magnificent," when he was laying out gardens, lakes and temples on the grounds. Strolling among the rhododendrons, tulip trees and beeches, venturing into a cave to pay your respects to the sculpture of the Spirit of the River Stour, or visiting the Pantheon or the Temple of the Sun, you'll get an idea of the high style in which the rich and powerful lived in 18th-century England.

E2

Stourton, near Warminster 01747 841152; www.nationaltrust.org.uk Garden: daily 9–6. House and Tower: Fri.–Tue. 11–5, mid-Mar. to early Nov Restaurant House $$$; garden $$$ (combined ticket available); Tower $$ Audio tours for garden

Wells

The pride of Wells is its magnificent Gothic cathedral, begun in 1180. The twin-towered west facade, with its 300 statues of saints, priests and kings, is considered the finest in Europe. Inside, the scissor arch under the central tower strikes many visitors as modern, although it was installed nearly seven centuries ago. There is a fine astronomical clock dating from 1392 and featuring knights on horseback who joust as each hour strikes, and a beautiful 14th-century Chapter House.

Also worth seeing in Wells are the moated Bishop's Palace; the 14th-century Vicar's Close, opposite the cathedral (the oldest intact medieval street in Europe); and the Wells Museum alongside it.

The limestone Mendip Hills north of the city are riddled with caves; some of the most impressive can be seen on a guided underground walk at Wookey Hole, a couple of miles west of Wells.

D3

Tourist Information Wells Museum, 8 Cathedral Green 01749 671770

Cathedral Cathedral Green 01749 674483; www.wellscathedral.org.uk Daily 7–7, Apr.–Sep.; 7–6, rest of year Restaurant Free ($$ donation suggested) Guided tours Mon.–Sat. (free)

Bishop's Palace Off Market Place 01749 988111; www.bishopspalacewells.co.uk Daily 10–6, Apr.–Oct.; 10–4, early Feb.–Mar. and Nov.–Dec. Restaurant $$

Wookey Hole D3 Wookey Hole 01749 672243; www.wookey.co.uk Daily 10–5, Apr.–Oct.; 10–4, rest of year Restaurant and café $$$

Albert
VICTORIA
SHELLEY

Eastern England

Opposite: Colorful beach huts at Southwold, Suffolk

Eastern England

England's eastern side is a vast area of country extending from the fringes of London as far north as Yorkshire, defined by a coast as rounded as a rump that stretches south into tatters of creeks and north to a line of crumbling low cliffs and marshes. The country's major highways all lie west of this region, as do the big manufacturing cities. In many ways it is England's least "touristy" rural area, a region of small towns and villages rooted in agriculture. The landscape is undramatic, flat in the western part of the district, gently rolling as you travel farther east. It takes time and tuning to appreciate the east of England for what it is: a subtle, slow-paced place where villages, pubs, paths, woods and beaches lie tucked away for the traveler to discover a little off the beaten track.

Undiscovered Delights

The Chiltern Hills, that rampart of beechwood downs that guard London to the northwest, offer a taste of the east in the chalk and flint that underlie them, and in the vast flat claylands of Bedfordshire over which they look. Essex is generally considered as too flat and too built-up to be of interest, but that is only really true of the towns that sprawl out eastward along the main roads from London. Away from this urbanized area you come upon a coast of quiet, muddy creeks and bird-haunted marshes, dotted with flat islands that are the cruising ground of boaters, bird-watchers and painters. Inland, too, there are delights such as the charming medieval buildings in Thaxted, Coggeshall and Saffron Walden; the great Jacobean mansion of Audley End; and footpaths through ancient, carefully tended woodlands.

Cleethorpes
0 10 20 30 40 km
0 10 20 miles
Ludborough
Louth
Mablethorpe
Sutton on Sea
North Sea
Alford
Ulceby
Ingoldmells
Lymm
Skegness
Mareham le Fen
Sibsey
Old Leake
North Norfolk Coast
Scolt Head Island
Wells-next-the-sea
Cley next the Sea
Sheringham
Boston
The Wash
Hunstanton
Burnham Market
Holkham Hall
Blakeney
Cromer
Sutterton
Heacham
Holt
Felbrigg Hall
Mundesley
Welland
Gedney Drove End
Dersingham
Fakenham
Bure
North Walsham
Sandringham House
Houghton Hall
Blickling Hall
Aylsham
Stalham
Sea Palling
Holbeach
Castle Rising
Salle
Hickling Broad
Horsey
Walpole St. Peter
King's Lynn
NORFOLK
Bawdeswell
Hoveton
Wroxham
Potter Heigham
Hemsby
The Fens
Great Ouse
Castle Acre
Taverham
Ranworth
Nar
Dereham
Broadland Conservation Centre
Caister-on-Sea
Wisbech
NORWICH
Norfolk Broads
Great Yarmouth
Thorney
Downham Market
Swaffham
Yare
Reedham
Nene
Guyhirn
Oxburgh Hall
Watton
Wymondham
Belton
March
Wissey
Loddon
Mundford
Attleborough
Lowestoft
Ouse
Grime's Graves
Long Stratton
Beccles
Chatteris
Brandon
Bungay
Kessingland
Ramsey
Ely
Lakenheath
Thetford
Little Ouse
Diss
Waveney
Wenhaston
Southwold
CAMBRIDGESHIRE
Mildenhall
Blythburgh
Walberswick
Great Ouse
Cam
Wicken Fen
Ixworth
SUFFOLK
Dunwich
Minsmere Reserve
Girton
Anglesey Abbey
Ickworth
Framlingham
Saxmundham
Cambridge
Newmarket
Bury St. Edmunds
Stowmarket
Snape
Thorpeness
Wimpole Hall
Great Shelford
Needham Market
Deben
Snape Maltings
Aldeburgh
Kentwell Hall
Lavenham
Gipping
Orford Castle
Orford
Sawston
Cavendish
Long Melford
Woodbridge
Orford Ness
Duxford Air Museum
Melford Hall
Kersey
Ipswich
Royston
Gainsborough's House
Sudbury
Hadleigh
Audley End House
Saffron Walden
Orwell
M11
Nayland
Stour
Dedham
Felixstowe
Thaxted
Halstead
Wissington
Brain
Buntingford
Flatford Mill
Harwich
Great Dunmow
Braintree
Copford
The Naze
HERTFORDSHIRE
Colchester
Stansted
Coggeshall
Walton on the Naze
Bishop's Stortford
Witham
Tiptree
West Mersea
Hertford
ESSEX
Clacton-on-Sea
Harlow
Hoddesdon
Chelmsford
Maldon
Hatfield House
Bradwell-on-Sea
Danbury
Epping
Greensted
Dengie
Burnham-on-Crouch
Crouch
Brentwood
Southend-on-Sea
Foulness
GREATER LONDON
Basildon
M25
Canvey Island
Stanford le Hope
C
D
E

Draining the Fens

Until the Middle Ages, the counties of Cambridgeshire and Lincolnshire were one vast fen, or reed-filled swamp, flooded regularly by rivers and by inward surges from the sea over an unprotected coast. Monasteries were established on the silty low islands that rose above the swamp, and it was their inhabitants who organized the area's first big drainage efforts.

Dutch engineers completed the job in the 17th century, bringing into being a huge, flat region of fertile farmland that still produces plentiful, excellent crops today.

Riches from Wool

North of Essex lie the twin counties of Suffolk and Norfolk, the heart of East Anglia. These were the most populous and prosperous counties in medieval England, thanks to the excellence of their wool and the talent of the weavers who brought their skills from continental Europe when they arrived as refugees from religious persecution.

The splendor and magnificence of the lifestyle of East Anglian wool merchants and landowners in the Middle Ages is reflected in the sumptuous architecture of the parish churches they paid for (see page 116). It also is seen in the rich beauty of the timber-framed houses they built and the even grander redbrick halls their heirs so proudly constructed in the 16th, 17th and 18th centuries. The attractive churches at Long Melford and Blythburgh (Suffolk) and Salle and Cley (Norfolk) are good examples, as are the great houses of Kentwell Hall (Suffolk), and Blickling Hall and Holkham Hall (Norfolk).

Lonely Coasts

The Suffolk coastline is windblown, lonely and beautiful, with an outstanding bird reserve at Minsmere, and the quaint little coastal towns of Aldeburgh and Southwold. The composer Benjamin Britten founded the Aldeburgh Festival in 1948, and now the Maltings concert hall (in the village of Snape) is the focus for a series of

The windmill at Wicken Fen lies within the 1,500-acre nature reserve

East Anglian musical events held in churches throughout the region.

The clay cliffs of Norfolk's coast curve as northwest to charming Cromer, an easy-paced resort with a pier and good beaches, then along a strange shore with little villages stranded inland by the growth of the marshes. The area offers superb bird-watching and boating; it is also renowned for amber, which is still collected on the beaches.

Local crafts are available all over the region – "Made in Cley" is worth a stop (in Cley-next-the-Sea, a beautiful village on the North Norfolk coast). A craft co-operative produces beautiful handmade pottery, jewelry, prints and sculpture; the gallery and workshops on High Street are open Mon.–Sat. 10–5, Sun. 11–4.

King's College Chapel, Cambridge

Fenland Heritage

The broad, horizon-filling acreage of grain crops in northern Cambridgeshire and southern Lincolnshire is not the only feature of fenland. The silhouettes of towering windmills are regularly visible on the horizon, and great cathedrals, churches and monastic ruins still straddle their islets of silt, dominating the level landscape – among them Ely, Ramsey, Thorney, Crowland and Boston.

Churches in the fens are the setting for some wonderful musical events, crowned by the Festival of Nine Lessons and Carols, held on Christmas Eve in King's College Chapel, Cambridge.

The world-famous and architecturally stunning university town of Cambridge has a wonderful cluster of medieval colleges, chapels and grounds. It's a great place to walk around, and small enough to explore on foot. Just north of the city, in the nature reserve at Wicken Fen, you can enjoy an unspoiled green corner of genuine old Fenland as the whole region would have looked before the drainers got to work. This little haven for wildlife is of ever-increasing value considering the implacable march of mechanized and intensive agriculture across eastern England since World War II.

Little-known Lincolnshire

Farther north lies Lincolnshire, its southern fens rising into the gently rolling chalk uplands of the Lincolnshire Wolds. This is one of Britain's most overlooked counties – all the better for discerning travelers who seek out the delightful Georgian town of Stamford, with its winding streets of golden houses; the unfrequented coast; the town of Boston, with its immense tower of St. Botolph's Church, known as the "Boston Stump"; and the city of Lincoln itself, where there is a magnificent Norman cathedral, one of the finest examples of Gothic architecture in the world.

Norwich

Norwich, the capital of Norfolk and of East Anglia, is one of the most agreeable cities in Britain. Yet surprisingly few visitors explore the city's delights, perhaps because it is located beyond the reach of the country's major highway systems. Like East Anglia itself, Norwich has remained a little behind the times, and is all the better for that. But the city is a long way from being run-down or boring. On the contrary, it has a well-looked-after medieval center, more fascinating medieval churches than any other British city of comparable size, and a thriving arts scene thanks to the lively, and popular, University of East Anglia.

The medieval center of Norwich

Past Riches

There was a market at Norwich in Saxon times, more than 1,000 years ago. The Normans thought it an important enough place to build a castle here; the great keep still looms on its mound.

In the Middle Ages an influx of emigrants from the Low Countries just across the North Sea helped Norwich become the most prosperous town in England, as local wool was woven and decorated with the skills passed on by these Flemish and Dutch settlers. The city's rich monastic communities and merchants built dozens of fine churches, scores of handsome flint and timber-framed houses, and a truly magnificent cathedral with an ornate, 315-foot spire. Norwich's location gave it a trading advantage with the rest of Europe, and the town scarcely needed to glance back over its shoulder at London and the rest of the country.

Marooned in Time

But for exactly these geographic and economic reasons, Norwich languished when the Industrial Revolution got underway early in the 18th century. Suddenly the well-to-do city – still confined within medieval walls – was isolated and out on a limb when the woolen and textile trades moved north to the new factories. Norwich had no mineral resources to exploit, and a big decline set in as it sank into a geographical and cultural backwater.

One happy effect of this was that the city was too poor to replace its old churches and townscape with modern architecture. It has therefore retained a great deal of its medieval character, in spite of a recent return to prosperity thanks to the establishment of high-tech industry and the university.

Getting your Bearings

Finding your way around Norwich can be a bit of a puzzle, since the city still retains a haphazard jumble of streets. But you soon get used to the shape of the center, defined by the great Norman keep and the open space of the market square, the latter indicated by the clock tower that is part of City Hall. From here the medieval streets run north to meet the River Wensum as it curls around the north and east flanks of the old city. Norwich Cathedral is northeast of the city center, but well inside the loop of the river. The bus station is a five-minute walk south of the market, while the railroad station lies just across the river to the east.

Dining and Shopping

Eating in Norwich can be as cosmopolitan as you like, with a choice of French, Italian, Chinese, Thai, Mexican, Indian and more. You can dine in a floating restaurant housed in a barge on the River Wensum, or lunch in the Refectory of Norwich Cathedral. There is also a great choice of cafés and many independent stores. Be sure to try the pungent Colman's mustard, made in town. Use it sparingly to start with; it is fierce enough to sting your tongue unless approached with caution. At The Mustard Shop and Museum in the Royal Arcade you can buy tiny yellow square cans of the stuff and learn all about this 180-year-old local tradition.

Another characteristic purchase in Norwich is an antique or piece of bric-a-brac from one of the many antiques shops on medieval Elm Hill. And don't forget to browse under the "tilts" of Norwich market (see pages 103–104) while enjoying the ambience and gossip. As for entertainment, the

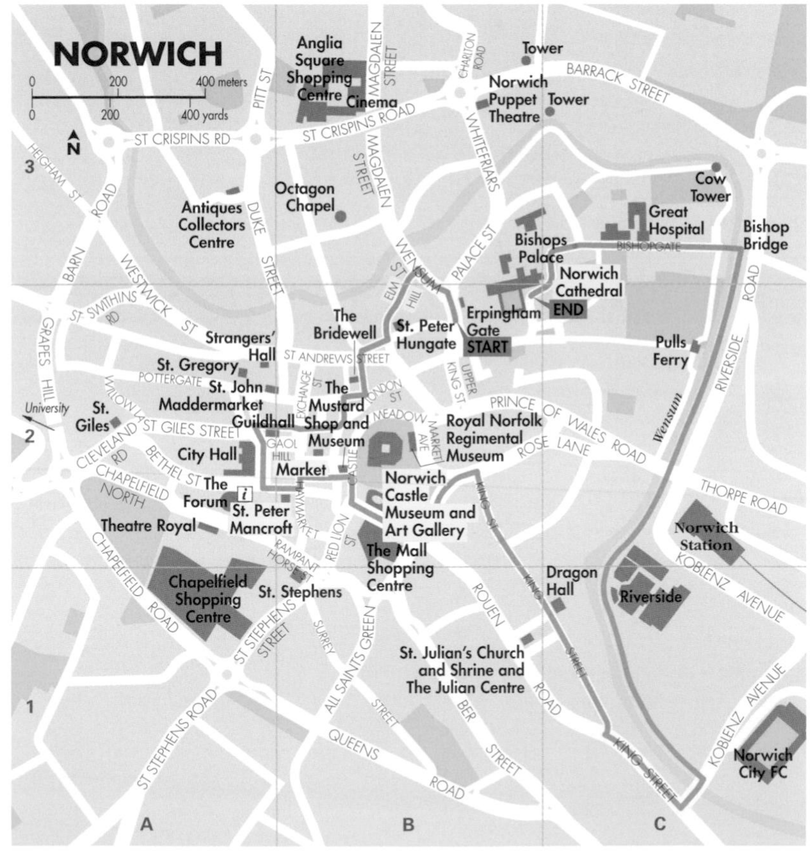

presence of the university guarantees a lively atmosphere. For theater, try the Norwich Theatre Royal on Theatre Street, or the Norwich Puppet Theatre in the converted St. James' Church in Whitefriars, just across the river to the north, with performances for children and adults. There is live music at the Norwich Arts Centre in Reeves Yard, off St. Benedict's Street. The Norfolk and Norwich Festival is held during May and features performances in a wide range of arts, from classical music to comedy; events are staged all over the city.

Colman's famous Mustard Shop and Museum in Norwich is a great place to buy an unusual souvenir

Essential Information

Tourist Information

✉ The Forum, Millennium Plain
☎ 01603 213999; www.visitnorwich.co.uk

Urban Transportation

Norwich's railroad station is on Thorpe Road. For information and reservations ☎ 0845 600 7245 or 0870 333 4876. The bus station is on Surrey Street. For information ☎ 0871 200 2233. Take taxis from the bus and railroad stations and in front of the Guildhall.

Airport Information

Norwich International Airport (☎ 01603 411923; www.norwichairport.co.uk) is 4 miles north of the city. Bus No. 27 runs to the city center and there is also a park and ride facility available Mon.–Sat.

Climate – average highs and lows for the month

Jan.	Feb.	Mar.	Apr.	May	Jun.	Jul.	Aug.	Sep.	Oct.	Nov.	Dec.
7°C	7°C	10°C	12°C	16°C	19°C	22°C	22°C	19°C	14°C	10°C	8°C
45°F	45°F	50°F	54°F	61°F	66°F	72°F	72°F	66°F	57°F	50°F	46°F
2°C	2°C	3°C	4°C	7°C	10°C	13°C	12°C	10°C	7°C	4°C	3°C
36°F	36°F	37°F	39°F	45°F	50°F	55°F	54°F	50°F	45°F	39°F	37°F

Norwich Sights

Key to symbols
map coordinates refer to the Norwich map on page 101 admission charge: $$$ more than £6, $$ £2–£6, $ less than £2
See page 5 for complete key to symbols

Elm Hill and Medieval Norwich

West of Norwich Cathedral the picturesque cobbled thoroughfare of Elm Hill rises as it runs south from Wensum Street. This is the best preserved of Norwich's many medieval streets, its crooked buildings overhanging the sidewalks.

Fragments of medieval Norwich are thickly scattered. Dragon Hall on King Street (southeast of the market) and Strangers' Hall on Charing Cross both retain handsome 15th-century halls. In Bridewell Alley is the Bridewell, once a prison; its crypt, with massive vaulting, dates back to 1325 and is now a fascinating museum of local trades and industries.

The cathedral close (grounds) exhibits some fine medieval architecture; the most striking is the entryway, Erpingham Gate. In a niche above the archway kneels Sir Thomas Erpingham in full armor. He directed the fire of the English archers as they crushed their French foes at the 1415 Battle of Agincourt, Erpingham built the gateway in 1420 as a thanksgiving – and to laud his own achievements, too.

Elm Hill B2
Dragon Hall C1 115–123 King Street 01603 663922; www.dragonhall.org Tue.–Thu. 10–4, Sun. noon–4 $$
Strangers' Hall A2 Charing Cross 01603 667229; www.museums.norfolk.gov.uk Wed.–Sat. 10:30–4, mid-Feb. to late Dec. $$
The Bridewell B2 Bridewell Alley 01603 629127; www.museums.norfolk.gov.uk Tue.–Sat.10–4:30 $$

Market and St. Peter Mancroft Church

Norwich Market has been a fixture in the big, sloping Market Place west of the castle for 900 years, having been moved there from its Saxon site in Tombland, near the cathedral. Here is another place where you will quickly reach for your camera, for the market stands are covered with dozens of awnings known as "tilts," each tilt striped in bright colors contrasting with its neighbors. Under the tilts you will

More than 200 stalls trade Monday to Saturday at Norwich's covered market

Cherry blossom complements impressive Norwich Castle, which stands tall over the city

find a bustling collection of stands selling everything from dried fruit to underwear and tools to animal feed. The narrow lanes are as crowded as a bazaar and the atmosphere buzzes with jokes and gossip.

Market Place is surrounded on all sides with notable buildings. On the west side is the plain-faced, 20th-century City Hall, with its 200-foot clock tower; on the north side is the fine 15th-century Guildhall, patterned in black knapped (cut) flint and white freestone to form a striking checkerboard pattern (access only to Caley's Cocoa Café within). East across Gentlemen's Walk is the art nouveau elaboration of the Royal Arcade, connecting market and castle.

It is the medieval Church of St. Peter Mancroft, dominating the south side of the square, that takes the breath away. Inside, carved angels hold up the hammerbeam roof. In the lovely east window, beautiful pre-Reformation stained glass depicts the Nativity, Crucifixion and Resurrection scenes, with many of the characters resplendent in 15th-century costume.

Church of St. Peter Mancroft B2 Market Place 01603 610443; www.stpetermancroft.org.uk Mon.–Sat. 10–3:30 Free (donation suggested)
Guildhall A2 Gaol Hill Café: 01603 629364 Café: Mon.–Sat. 9–4:30 Guildhall free

Norwich Market B2 Market Place 01603 213537; www.norwich-market.co.uk Mon.–Sat. 8–5

Norwich Castle Museum and Art Gallery

Norwich's Norman castle keep was built around 1100. The smooth facade seen today is the result of an 1834 facelift. Guided tours show you around the massive walls, battlement walkways and chambers. It was the county jail for nearly 700 years, and the dungeons and cells are grim. The Prison Stories exhibit recounts the realities of the time.

Now Norfolk's principal museum, the castle contains archeological treasures unearthed all over the county, plus what is said to be the world's largest collection of ceramic teapots.

Also on display is a fine collection of paintings – mostly of 19th-century East Anglian landscapes by open-air painters of the Norwich School.

The Royal Norfolk Regimental Museum, which narrates the story of the battles fought by the regiment since 1685, moved into the castle in 2011.

The Norwich School art galleries were extensively refurbished in 2012.

Castle B2 Castle Meadow 01603 493625 or 493648 (24-hour recorded information); www.museums.norfolk. gov.uk Mon.–Sat. 10–5, Sun. 1–5, Jul.–Oct.; Mon.–Sat. 10–4:30, Sun. 1–4:30, rest of year Café $$ Guided tours

Churches of Norwich

Like any self-respecting bunch of successful medieval men, the wool and trade merchants of Norwich expressed their gratitude to God and proclaimed their self-satisfaction through the building of fine churches. Norwich is well endowed with medieval churches: More than 30 survive inside the old city, most in decent states of repair. In these more secular days, more than half are now out of commission as religious buildings; some are now used as arts venues, museums, shops or community centers. Together they make a fascinating display of the art of medieval church architecture in East Anglia, particularly in their use of the local flint, either in cobble form or cut smooth and black to lie level with the surrounding stonework in a style known as flushwork.

St. Peter Mancroft, in the market (see pages 103–104), is the finest of them all, but there are others worth visiting. West of the market, on the corner of St. Giles Street and Upper St. Giles Street, stands St. Giles under its great tower, with an impressive angel roof. North of the market are St. Gregory's (just off St. Benedict Street), which has pre-Reformation frescoes, and St. John Maddermarket (built beside the market square, where madder, a Eurasian herb, was sold for the dyeing of cloth), boasting a beautiful tower and some fine monuments.

To the northeast, near the top of Elm Hill, is St. Peter Hungate. South of the market, off the intriguingly named Rampant Horse Street, the tower of St. Stephen's displays good flushwork, and there is brilliantly colored 16th-century glass from Germany in the east window.

A poignant oddity is St. Julian's Church, in St. Julian's Alley, a small lane between King Street and Rouen Road, where St. Julian of Norwich had her reclusive cell (see page 107). Next door, The Julian Centre is a study center dedicated to St. Julian.

St. Julian's Church and Shrine B1 St. Julian's Alley, Rouen Road 01603 622509; www.julianofnorwich.org Mon.–Sat. 8:30–5 (closes at 4 in winter months) Free Check opening hours with the tourist information center before visiting any of Norwich's churches

The Julian Centre B1 St. Julian's Alley, Rouen Road 01603 767380 Mon.–Fri. 10:30–3:30 Free

St. Peter Mancroft, the finest of Norwich's churches, was rebuilt in the 15th century

Norwich Cathedral

Norwich Cathedral was built of beautiful silvery-white French stone in Norman times. The blunt east end is supported by graceful flying buttresses. The spire, soaring 315 feet, is the second tallest in Britain after Salisbury (see pages 90–91).

Inside, delicate columns rise to the nave roof to burst out in fan vaulting that resembles stone-carved treetops. This is a place to bring your binoculars, to admire the beautiful ornamental carvings in the roof. They unroll the entire biblical story, from the Garden of Eden through the Flood (Mr. and Mrs. Noah and family, peeping out of the Ark in company with a smiling unicorn), the infant Moses in a golden basket, the terrified Pharaoh's army drowning in the Red Sea, and on to scenes from the New Testament.

There are more richly carved roof bosses (ornamental projections) in the cloisters, too, closer above your head for ease of inspection; they incorporate several faun-like Green Men (see page 120) peering out of leaves. There is also 20th-century artistry to admire in the Stations of the Cross, inlaid in wood.

The most remarkable artwork in the cathedral, however, is the haunting Despenser Reredos in St. Luke's Chapel at the east end, a 14th-century depiction of Christ's Passion and Resurrection. We see Christ being scourged by brutish guards, hanging helpless but with dignity on the cross while his mother swoons into the arms of St. John, and stepping purposefully out of his tomb over the heads of cringing soldiers. During the 17th century this rare treasure was used as a table, its painted face downward, to hide it from the Puritan zealots who would have destroyed it.

Outside, nestling closely against the cloisters of the cathedral, is the grave of Edith Cavell, a Norfolk-born nurse who tended both friend and foe alike while working in Belgium during World War I. Cavell was eventually executed by the Germans in 1915 for helping many Allied prisoners to escape from the German-occupied country.

B2–B3 · The Close · 01603 218300; www.cathedral.org.uk · Daily 7:30–6:30 · Restaurant · Free ($$ donation suggested) · Guided tours depart from the nave: Mon.–Sat. at 11, 12, 1, 2 and 3 (free; donation suggested)

Norwich Cathedral and its soaring spire

Pulls Ferry is a 15th-century watergate and is one of Norwich's best-loved buildings

Walk:
Central Norwich

Refer to route marked on city map on page 101

This stroll around the best parts of Norwich could be done in a couple of hours, but half a day is better if you want to visit the cathedral and stop en route.

Starting at Erpingham Gate west of the cathedral, turn down Wensum Street and left up medieval Elm Hill (see page 103). Browse among the enticing shops here. **Turn right onto Princes Street at the top of the hill, and cross St. Andrew Plain to turn left up narrow Bridewell Alley.** An interesting museum, The Bridewell (see page 103), is located here. **Continue across Bedford Street and up Swan Lane, then go right down London Street to the market, Guildhall and St. Peter Mancroft. Bear left through Royal Arcade, past the The Mustard Shop, to Norwich Castle. Bear right out of the arcade to curve left around the castle by Farmer's Avenue and Cattle Market Street. Turn right onto King Street; on your left you pass Dragon Hall (see page 103). Opposite the hall is St. Julian's Alley, leading to St. Julian's Church (see page 105).** This plain and over-restored flint building houses a shrine to a remarkable woman, Mother Julian of Norwich, who spent 43 years voluntarily confined to a tiny cell here after receiving heavenly visions. Her writings about them, published later as *The Revelations of Divine Love*, mark the first book written in English by a woman. She sees Christ crucified, a pure white baby rising to heaven out of a dead body, and a demon with "a young man's face, long and lean, the colour of a tilestone newly fired, and a foul and nauseating stench." Mother Julian is unsure about their meanings, but asserts:

"All I know is that the joy I saw surpasses all the heart could wish for, or the soul desire."

Continue along King Street, then bear left over Carrow Bridge to cross the River Wensum. Turn left up the riverside path and pass the medieval watergate of Pulls Ferry. Bear left across Bishop Bridge. Go up Bishopgate back to the cathedral.

Regional Sights

Key to symbols
map coordinates refer to the Eastern England map on pages 96–97 admission charge: $$$ more than £6, $$ £2–£6, $ less than £2
See page 5 for complete key to symbols

Aldeburgh and the Suffolk Coast

Aldeburgh is a delightful small resort-cum-fishing town, where local fishermen still launch their boats off the shingle beach and sell their catch fresh from the sea. The Tudor church contains a fine stained-glass window honoring Benjamin Britten, one of England's most celebrated 20th-century composers, who lived in the town for many years and lies buried in the churchyard. His house on the beach is marked by a commemorative plaque.

On the street a block off the beach, you'll find cafés, restaurants and shops. There are also art galleries featuring watercolor paintings of the regional landscape. Music lovers can attend concerts inland at Snape Maltings, converted by Britten into a splendid concert hall in the 1960s and now including the Hoffman Building and Britten-Pears building, rehearsal and performance space. It plays host to the annual Aldeburgh Festival in June and Snape Proms in August and the Aldeburgh Poetry Festival in November.

South of town stands Orford Castle, with a polygonal 12th-century keep overlooking Aldeburgh; it is now separated from the sea by a 10-mile-long shingle spit. Take a ferry over to the "elbow" of the spit, Orford Ness, for a wonderful nature walk among seabirds and old military buildings.

North of Aldeburgh you will find the Royal Society for the Protection of Birds' superb nature reserve at Minsmere (don't forget your binoculars), as well as remnants of magnificent monastic buildings on the cliffs at Dunwich, once the finest town in Suffolk but long since eaten by the sea. A good local museum tells the story.

A shingle beach leads farther north to the village of Walberswick, beloved by landscape painters, and to the small upscale resort of Southwold, with its lovely color-washed houses and picturesque bay. There are plenty of pubs to choose from in Southwold and, for real ale fans, Adnams Bitter (an uncarbonated, dark beer) is brewed in the town. Some say it's the tastiest in the country; try not to leave without sampling it.

Aldeburgh E2
Tourist information 48 High Street 01728 453637; www.thesuffolkcoast.co.uk
Snape Maltings Concert Hall Snape 01728 687110 Restaurant
Orford Castle Orford 01394 450472; www.english-heritage.org.uk Daily 10–6, Jul.–Aug.; daily 10–5, Apr.–Jun. and Sep.; Thu.–Mon. 10–4, rest of year $$ Audio tours (free)
Orford Ness E2
Orford Ness National Nature Reserve Orford Quay, Orford 01394 450900; www.nationaltrust.gov.org.uk Tue.–Sat., Jul.–Sep.; Sat., mid-Apr. to Jun. and Oct. Access by ferry, regular departures 10–2; return latest 5 p.m. $$$ (including crossing)
Southwold E3
Tourist information 69 High Street 01502 724729; www.visitsunrisecoast.co.uk

Opposite: The windmill at Wicken Fen stands in an artificial landscape, developed over centuries
Right: The beach at Aldeburgh

Dutch gables, corner turrets and a dominant clock tower mark Blickling Hall

Blickling Hall and Estate

This is one of north Norfolk's finest country houses, a redbrick Elizabethan mansion altered and extended in Jacobean times with curly-edged gables and tall chimneys, its wings flanked by square-built towers. The long approach drive offers a superb view.

The ceiling of the long gallery is a triumph of plasterwork, set with allegorical figures. If there is a ghost around, it is probably Anne Boleyn, ill-fated second wife of King Henry VIII, who spent part of her childhood here.

D4

Blickling, Norfolk 01263 738030; www.nationaltrust.org.uk House: Wed.–Mon. 11–5, mid-Jul. to early Sep.; Wed.–Sun. 11–5, late Feb. to mid-Jul. and early Sep.–Oct. Garden: daily 10:–5:30, Mar.–Oct.; Thu.–Sun. 11–4, rest of year. Park: daily dawn–dusk Restaurant and café $$$ (garden only $$)

Burghley House

A mile southeast of Stamford (see page 121) stands Burghley House, in a vast deer park centered on a lake and laid out by the 18th-century landscape architect, "Capability" Brown. A five-story gatehouse is enhanced by domes, cupolas, pediments and towers that bristle from the heights of Burghley.

The house – much altered in later centuries – was built in 1555–87 in grand style for William Cecil, 1st Lord Burghley, who was a confidant and favored counselor to Queen Elizabeth I. The 240-room house contains much fine artwork, notably the fresco paintings by 17th-century artist Antonio Verrio. His Hell staircase depicts the fate of sinners, while his Heaven Room shows gods and nymphs from classical mythology.

B3

Stamford, Lincolnshire 01780 752451; www.burghley.co.uk Sat.–Thu. 11–4:30, late Mar.–late Oct. Restaurant and café $$$ (gardens only $$) Audio guides $

Bury St. Edmunds

Bury St. Edmunds is a charming market town with fine ecclesiastical buildings. The abbey (now ruined) was built to house the shrine of the martyred St. Edmund, the last Saxon king of East Anglia, slain in AD 870. The abbey gardens run down to the River Lark. In town, the Angel Hotel (see page 263) was featured in Charles Dickens' *Pickwick Papers*, while The Nutshell is said to be the world's tiniest pub.

C2

Tourist information 6 Angel Hill 01284 764667; www.visit-burystedmundsbury.co.uk Audio guides $

Norfolk Broads

Long thought to be natural, these interconnected lakes in the flat country east of Norwich are in fact flooded medieval peat diggings. When locals connected them with a network of water channels, a unique way of life came into being. The marshmen made a subsistence living out of fishing, shooting wildfowl and cutting reed and sedge for thatching. It was a lonely, idiosyncratic lifestyle that persisted until Victorian pleasure boaters "discovered" the Broads. Soon the area turned into a playground for yachtsmen and riverboat parties – not so bad during the days of sail, but once diesel engines came on the scene the Broads quickly became grossly polluted.

Over the last two decades the Broads have been restored to their former glory with extensive maintenance and dredging work ongoing, and the area is now one of the most popular inland waterways in Europe, offering around 125 miles of boating, both sail and motor.

The Broads are Britain's only national park wetlands, famous for the rich variety of plants, animals and birds that can be found there. At nature reserves such as Ranworth Broad, Hickling Broad and Horsey Mere you can see rare water spiders, swallowtail butterflies, marsh harriers and hen harriers, reed buntings and other thriving wildlife. The Broads have a unique ecosystem, which is explained as you wander the boardwalk trails at the Broads Wildlife Centre in Ranworth.

The main boating centers include Wroxham and Potter Heigham, where you can rent a boat or take a boat tour. The Museum of the Broads in Stalham has displays on the history of the area and the local crafts.

There are plenty of churches and pubs to divert you on your voyages around the area. Visit the Broads to enjoy huge skies spread over a flat horizon, pierced by windmills, willows and the sails of boats.

Broads Information Centre D4
Station Road, Hoveton 01603 756097; www.broads-authority.gov.uk Daily 9–1 and 1:30–5, Apr.–Oct.

Broads Wildlife Centre D3 Ranworth 01603 270479; www.norfolkwildlifetrust.org.uk Daily 10–5, Apr.–Oct.; nature trails open all year Café Free (donations welcome) Boat trips on Ranworth Broad ($$$); ferry from Ranworth Staithe

Broads Tours D3 The Bridge, Wroxham 01603 782207; www.broads.co.uk Boat tours

Museum of the Broads E4 The Staithe, Stalham 01692 581681; www.broads-authority.gov.uk Daily 10:30–5, Apr.–Oct. Last admission 30 minutes before closing $$

A sailing boat picks up a slight breeze on Hickling Broad in the Norfolk Broads National Park

Punting along the River Cam toward the Bridge of Sighs, built in 1831

Cambridge

Probably the best way to see the city of Cambridge is by renting the most sedate mode of transportation known to man – a slow and creaky wooden punt. A soporific June afternoon spent poling one of these flat-bottomed boats gently along the River Cam – with university undergraduates basking on the green lawns on one hand and the stately towers and pinnacles of mellow chapels and colleges on the other – will soon convince you that Cambridge is a form of heaven. It is a conclusion reached by many through the centuries.

This almost perfect medieval university town originated when disgruntled scholars and teachers from Oxford University established a settlement by the river in the early 13th century. A whole range of splendid and beautiful colleges came into being over the ensuing centuries, endowed by the pious or seriously rich. Most are laid out along traditional monastic lines: a quadrangle (known here as a "court") surrounded by chapel, cloisters, dining and sleeping quarters.

Radical politics and cutting-edge research have always been the hallmarks of Cambridge University. Here Protestant bishop-martyrs Thomas Cranmer, Hugh Latimer and Nicholas Ridley were educated; here Isaac Newton calculated the speed of sound; and here in the 20th century the atom was split by Ernest Rutherford and the DNA double helix structure was identified by James Watson (an American geneticist) and Francis Crick (an English biophysicist).

Cambridge contains more than 30 colleges spread out over a large area. The finest and oldest are concentrated along the east bank of the River Cam (except Magdalene, pronounced "Maudlin," which is on the west bank). Their elegant gardens are connected to the meadows and lawns (known as The Backs) on the other side of the river by an assortment of bridges. Phone ahead to check opening times if you plan to visit any of the colleges, since schedules vary during the academic year.

Walking south from Magdalene Bridge, the first college you'll come to is St. John's, founded in 1511 by the mother of King Henry VII, Lady Margaret Beaufort, with a turreted and tabernacled gateway leading to beautiful courts. The Bridge of Sighs, a covered bridge of pale stone, was built in 1831 to connect St. John's with its new extension across the river. The bridge was named after the original in Venice (although it's not a faithful copy). The Church of the Holy Sepulchre, just across Sydney Street from St. John's, was built with a round nave in imitation of the original, which had been most admired in Jerusalem by Crusaders.

Trinity College boasts Great Court, the scene of a traditional undergraduate race against the clock (famously re-enacted in the film *Chariots of Fire*), and Nevile's Court, where Isaac Newton stamped his foot and timed the echo to calculate the speed of sound. Clare College, whose lovely Jacobean buildings and courts stand in beautifully tended grounds, has one of the oldest and most graceful of the city's bridges – Clare Bridge, which is a perfect place to stand and survey the surrounding glories.

King's College has a widely renowned chapel, built 1446–1515, with glorious fan-vaulting and Tudor stained glass. It is the site of an internationally broadcast Christmas Eve service.

Queens' College is one of Cambridge's most memorably beautiful, with its Tudor courts and gatehouse, and the charming, half-timbered President's Lodge. The Mathematical Bridge, built in 1749, connects Queens' College with The Backs.

If you tire of the colleges, Fitzwilliam Museum on Trumpington Street is one of the world's great small museums. Its granite and marble halls contain paintings by Old Masters (Titian, Hals), English landscape artists (Gainsborough, Constable, Wilson), Impressionists (Renoir, Monet, Cézanne, Gauguin) and modernists (Modigliani, Picasso, Spencer, Hockney). Here, you will also find superb collections of antiquities, illuminated manuscripts, folios, detailed ceramics and armor.

And, as if all this intellectual stimulation weren't enough, Cambridge also boasts an impressive range of cafés, pubs and nightlife.

C2

Tourist information Peas Hill
0871 226 8006; www.visitcambridge.org

St. John's College St. John's Street
01223 338600

Trinity College Trinity Street 01223 338400

Clare College Trinity Lane 01223 333200

King's College King's Parade 01223 331100

Queens' College Silver Street 01223 335511

Fitzwilliam Museum Trumpington Street
01223 332900; www.fitzmuseum.cam.ac.uk
Tue.–Sat. 10–5, Sun. noon–5 Café Free

Chiltern Hills

The Chiltern Hills arch around the northwestern outskirts of London, a great wall of high downland with a fine escarpment sloping down and out into the lower lands of Oxfordshire, Bedfordshire and Hertfordshire. They grow superb stands of beech and oak, and nourish many kinds of wildflowers.

Chiltern villages are kept neat by their proud residents. Among the most charming are Hambleden, West Wycombe (cared for by the conservation organization, the National Trust) and Chalfont St. Giles, with its beautiful church and the cottage where John Milton finished writing *Paradise Lost*. All are located in Buckinghamshire.

In Hertfordshire are the fine villages of Aldbury and Much Hadham, and tiny Ayot St. Lawrence, where George Bernard Shaw lived at Shaw's Corner; now kept as a shrine to the playwright.

Tourist information A1
Library, 5 Eden Place, High Wycombe 01494 421892; www.visitbuckinghamshire.org

Milton's Cottage B1
Deanway, Chalfont St. Giles 01494 872313
Tue.–Sun. 10–1 and 2–6, Mar.–Oct. Last admission 1 hour before closing $$

Shaw's Corner B1
Ayot St. Lawrence, near Welwyn, Hertfordshire
01438 820307; www.nationaltrust.org.uk
Wed.–Sun. noon–5:30 (house: 1–5), mid-Mar. to Oct. $$ (cyclists and taxibus users $)

Colchester

"The oldest recorded town in Britain" is Colchester's proud boast and, below the Norman castle, you can see the foundations of the temple established here by the Romans in AD 44 and burned by Queen Boudicca in AD 61. The castle is now an excellent museum that tells the story of the town. Evidence of the centuries lies all around: sections of

Paradise found: John Milton's cottage is in the Chiltern village of Chalfont St. Giles

2,000-year-old city wall; the Saxon tower of Holy Trinity Church; ruins of the Norman Priory of St. Botolph; the medieval Dutch Quarter, where refugee weavers started up the cloth trade that would enrich the town; and dozens of handsome Georgian and Victorian buildings. The Town Hall is a decent specimen of the latter. On the culinary front, Colchester's oysters are famed. Also of note, the Colchester Arts Centre hosts a program of music and dance.

D2

Tourist information 1 Queen Street 01206 282920; www.visitcolchester.com

Colchester Castle Museum Castle Park, High Street 01206 282939 Mon.–Sat. 10–5, Sun. 11–5. Last admission 30 minutes before closing $$$

Ely

Ely is a beautiful small town in the middle of the black Cambridgeshire peat fenlands, its crooked medieval streets running off the summit of a low "island" and down into the surrounding flat corn-growing country. From 1636 to 1646 – through the years of the English Civil War – Oliver Cromwell's family, and occasionally the man himself, were based in a black-and-white 14th-century house in the town. Part of Oliver Cromwell's House is now in use as Ely's Tourist Information Centre. The rest is given over to an exhibition about the domestic life of this serious-minded but far from curmudgeonly parliamentary leader who became Lord Protector of England – king in all but name – after ordering the execution of King Charles I in 1649.

Ely Cathedral is a mighty Norman edifice that literally overshadows and dominates the town. From whichever direction you approach Ely, the cathedral looms on the skyline like an enormous ship. It is a glorious building from the outside, sporting a 217-foot tower at the west end and an enormous central wooden octagon with a 62-foot lantern on top, which was hoisted to its crowning position in 1348. Inside, solid rounded Norman arches contrast with a couple of delicately ornate Tudor chantry chapels. There is beautiful Victorian painting on the nave roof, and a Stained Glass Museum with examples of the craft from the early Middle Ages onward. As a testimony to the subversive wit of the medieval woodcarvers, there are dozens of "Green Men" (see page 120) to spot: strange, often savage faces sprouting from or consumed by foliage, peeping out from roof trusses. The cathedral gardens make a pleasant place to stroll, and the market square is usually bustling with stands.

C3

Tourist information 29 St. Mary's Street 01353 662062; www.visitely.org.uk

Oliver Cromwell's House 29 St. Mary's Street 01353 662062 Daily 10–5, Apr.–Oct.; Sun.–Fri. 11–4, Sat. 10–5, rest of year $$

Ely Cathedral The College 01353 667735; www.elycathedral.org Daily 7:30–6:30, Easter–late Oct.; Mon.–Sat. 7–6:30, Sun. 7–5:30, rest of year Restaurant and café $$$ Guided tours (included in admission)

Stained Glass Museum South Treforium, Ely Cathedral 01353 660347; www.stainedglassmuseum.com Mon.–Fri. 10:30–5, Sat. 10:30–5:30, Sun. noon–6, Easter–late Oct.; Mon.–Sat. 10:30–5, Sun. noon–4:30, rest of year Restaurant and café $$

Looking down the aisle of Ely Cathedral

The "Wool Churches" of East Anglia

The remarkable parish churches of East Anglia, more than 2,000 of them, came into being because of the successful wool trade.

It was the enormous wealth generated by the woolen cloth trade during the Middle Ages that allowed merchants, abbots and wealthy Londoners to build these sumptuous "wool churches." Some used imported limestone, but most were built of the local flint and chalky rubble, ragstone, brick or abandoned Roman tiles. Embellishment was the key to a successful trumpeting to God and (perhaps more importantly at the time) your peers of just how well you had done in business.

The darkness of beautifully knapped (cut) flint contrasted with the whiteness of limestone, pinnacles were raised from the corners of towers, and one's initials were set into the fabric of tower or porch. Statues, frescoes, painted screens and clerestory windows would flood the church with clear East Anglian light. Stained-glass windows were set in flowing stone frames; wonderfully balanced hammerbeam roofs were seemingly upheld by sublime wooden angels; and pulpits were carved in slender-stemmed "wineglass" style. Eternity would be spent in an elaborate tomb of marble, surmounted by one's effigy lying or in kneeling pose with hands piously folded and every intricate crinkle of lace or link of chain mail faithfully and perfectly depicted.

The first-time visitor to East Anglia marvels at the sheer number, size and quality of parish churches, and the fact that so many of them grace tiny villages that can hardly muster enough worshipers these days to fill the front row of pews, let alone to raise the mighty shout of praise to God for which these splendid buildings were so obviously intended. The dedication of the small bands of volunteer parishioners who clean, maintain and raise funds for them is a remarkable thing in its own right.

Wandering from village to village through Essex, Suffolk and Norfolk you will discover your own particular favorite among the parish churches of East Anglia. Following are some suggestions; each has special features over and above its general beauty.

Essex

St. Michael's, Copford (southwest of Colchester): fine early medieval wall and roof paintings.

St. Peter-on-the-Wall, Bradwell (3 miles east of Bradwell Waterside): a seventh-century Saxon church in a beautiful, bleak coastal location.

St. Andrew's, Greensted (off A414 east of Harlow): log-built 11th-century nave, reputedly the oldest in the world.

St. John's, Thaxted: a mighty spire and a riot of medieval stone carvings.

Suffolk

Holy Trinity, Blythburgh (on A12 near Southwold): called "The Cathedral of the Marshes," is filled with light, has a wooden angel roof and Seven Deadly Sins bench-ends offering humorous warning.

St. Michael's, Framlingham: a striking collection of elaborate Tudor tombs, chiefly of the Howard family.

St. Peter and St. Paul, Lavenham: Tudor church with memorable carved screens, crowning Suffolk's purest medieval town.

Holy Trinity, Long Melford: probably the county's finest church. How did such wonderful stained glass survive the Reformation and Puritan vandalism?

St. Mary and St. Andrew, Mildenhall: astonishing carved roof with angels, saints, beasts and foliage.

St. Edmund's, Southwold: ship-like church with impressive flushwork.

St. Peter's, Wenhaston (just west of Blythburgh): a dramatic medieval painting of the Last Judgment.

St. Mary's, Wissington (pronounced "Wiston"; off A134 near Nayland): Norman arches, very early medieval wall paintings.

Norfolk

St. Nicholas', Blakeney (on A149 north Norfolk coast road): a really welcoming church; the light in its extra tower guided sailors and travelers at night.

St. Margaret's, King's Lynn: full of character, this church's architecture is spread over eight centuries; medieval stone carvings, elaborate wooden screens.

St. Helen's, Ranworth (off B1140 northeast of Norwich): superb medieval painted screen; great view across the Broads from the tower.

St. Peter and St. Paul, Salle (off B1145 near Reepham): finest of all the Norfolk churches – flooded with light and beautified with stone carvings and glorious wood-carving in the roof.

St. Peter's, Walpole St. Peter (off A47 between Wisbech and King's Lynn): the "Queen of the Marshlands," with many treasures; ancient screens and pews.

Above left to right: The seventh-century chapel of St. Peter-on-the-Wall, near Bradwell Waterside; 15th-century church of St. Peter and St. Paul, Salle

Hatfield House

William Cecil, 1st Lord Burghley, close confidant and adviser to Queen Elizabeth I, built Burghley House in Lincolnshire (see page 110); it was his son Robert, 1st Earl of Salisbury, who built the splendid Jacobean mansion Hatfield House in Hertfordshire from 1607–11. Robert had become Elizabeth's adviser after his father's death in 1598 and went on to be secretary of state to the new king, James I. All the power and prestige of the man are reflected in the giant C-shaped house with its domes and enormous cupola-crowned entrance. The gardens have been restored to reflect their Jacobean origins. Nearby stands the mellow redbrick remnant of Hatfield Palace, where Queen Elizabeth I spent much of her childhood. Inside are portraits of her in later life.

B1

Hatfield, Hertfordshire 01707 287010; www.hatfield-house.co.uk Wed.–Sun. and public holidays 11–5:30 (house noon–5), Easter–Sep. Last admission 1 hour before closing Restaurant $$$; park and west garden only $$$; east garden only $$; park only $$ Audio tours; pre-arranged guided tours can be booked online

Lavenham

Lavenham was one of Suffolk's most prosperous wool towns until Tudor times, but slumped into a depression when the trade moved north. Lavenham's loss is the visitor's gain, however, for there was never enough money in the town to replace the crooked old timber-framed houses with anything more convenient or up-to-date. Thus Lavenham survives as the finest collection of medieval vernacular buildings in Britain, a feast of crooked doorframes and overhanging upper stories.

Particularly notable are the half-timbered The Swan pub, the handsome church (see page 117), 14th-century Little Hall, the Priory on Water Street and the elaborately carved Guildhall,

The Jacobean East Gardens at Hatfield House have been restored to their former glory

dating from 1529, in the marketplace, which houses exhibitions on the wool industry and local railways.

D2

Tourist information Lady Street 01787 248207; www.visitsuffolk.com

Guildhall Market Place 01787 247646; www.nationaltrust.org.uk

Daily 11–5, Apr.–Oct.; Wed.–Sun. 11–4 Mar.; Sat.–Sun. 11–4, Nov. Café $$

Lincoln

Lincoln Cathedral stands on a 200-foot rocky eminence dominating the town, a position it shares with Lincoln Castle. The cathedral dates mostly from the 13th century, with two great towers flanking the broad west front and a third soaring behind. Don't miss the 13th-century rose windows, the slim arcades and the graceful Chapter House. Up at the top of a column squats the cheeky Lincoln Imp, supposedly turned to stone for flirting with the 30 angels that support the wonderful 1280 choir roof.

The Norman castle encircled by the city walls, offers a rather chilling, but interesting, time-trip. In the prison chapel the pews are so tall that felons could not see or hear each other.

Halfway up cobbled Steep Hill a second-hand bookshop – The Reader's Rest – gives visitors an excuse to catch their breath before continuing uphill to the cathedral, past some arts, craft and jewelry shops. For a taste of local cuisine, stop for a game pie at the Wig and Mitre (see page 263).

B5

Tourist information 9 Castle Hill 01522 545458; www.visitlincolnshire.com

Lincoln Cathedral Minster Yard 01522 561600; www.lincolncathedral.com Mon.–Fri. 7:15 a.m.–8 p.m., Sat.–Sun. 7:15–6, late Jun.–late Aug.; Mon.–Sat. 7:15–6, Sun. 7:15–5, rest of year Restaurant $$ Guided tours (Mon.–Sat.) free

Lincoln Castle Castle Hill 01522 511068 Daily 10–6, May–Aug.; 10–5, Apr. and Sep.; 10–4, rest of year. Last admission 45 minutes before closing Café $$ Guided tours (free)

A statue of Alfred, Lord Tennyson lies within the grounds of Lincoln Cathedral

Eroded cliffs are reflected in the Tidepool near Hunstanton

North Norfolk Coast

A strange thing has happened to many of the seaside settlements along the coast of north Norfolk. They have been left high, dry and up to two miles from the sea by the growth of marshes on the rich silt brought down by rivers. At the same time, the phenomenon known as longshore drift has dragged silt and pebbles westward to form 3-mile spits at Blakeney Point and Scolt Head Island. Wildfowl flock here to spend the winter, and pass through in their millions while migrating – hence the area's reputation for bird-watching.

Gems along this lonely coast include the seaside resorts of Cromer, Sheringham and Hunstanton. There are notable churches at Salthouse, Cley-next-the-Sea, Blakeney and Snettisham. Burnham Thorpe is the birthplace of Admiral Lord Nelson, the hero of the 1805 Battle of Trafalgar – enjoy mementos of this great sailor in the church, and a glass of "Nelson's Blood" (rum) in the local pub. South of Snettisham is the Royal Family's country residence of Sandringham. There's an exhibition of royal memorabilia in the house, and there are attractive grounds.

Cromer ✚ D4

Tourist information ✉ Louden Road ☎ 0871 200 3071; www.visitnorthnorfolk.com

Sheringham ✚ D4

Tourist information ✉ Station Approach ☎ 0871 200 3071; www.visitnorthnorfolk.com 🕑 Daily

Sandringham House ✚ C4

✉ Sandringham, Norfolk ☎ 01485 545408; www.sandringhamestate.co.uk 🕑 Daily 10:30–5 (house and museum open at 11), Easter–late Jul. and

Green Men

As you're exploring Norfolk, look for the "Green Man." He can be found vomiting tendrils of leaves or wreathed in foliage, staring out with a troubled frown or a salacious leer from church roofs and pillars, or from pew ends and screens. But he is not confined exclusively to churches. You can spot him painted on pub signs and carved into old inn paneling. He is thousands of years old. Who is he? A representation of man's untamed inner nature? A wild god from the woods? Christ giving the Word of God? No one knows.

early Aug.–early Nov.; visitor center only 9:30–4:30, rest of year. Park: daily dawn to dusk Restaurant and café $$$ (museum and gardens only $$); visitor center and park free

Saffron Walden

Saffron Walden is certainly the best-looking small town in Essex. An excellent Town Trail booklet is available from the tourist office in the Market Place. For sale each August from the tourist office and the museum on Museum Street are the saffron crocus bulbs that made the town's fame and fortune in the Middle Ages – they produced yellow dye for the woolen cloth spun all over East Anglia then.

You'll also find the saffron crocus flower honored in carved stone in the Church of St. Mary. From Gold Street there is a memorable exterior view of the church with its 193-foot spire. Take a look inside to admire the angel roof. Other sights include the medieval houses along Bridge Street and in Myddylton Place; the peaceful haven of Bridge End Gardens, with lawns, rose pergolas and trees; and the rich plasterwork molding (known as pargeting) that adorns the Old Sun Inn. There are a number of book and antiques shops on Church Street, and a network of alleyways and shops around the Market Place. Don't leave without trying to figure your way out of the brick-paved maze on the town common; it has baffled people for 800 years!

C2

Tourist information 1 Market Place, Market Square 01799 524002; www.visitsaffronwalden.gov.uk

A classic example of pargeting on the Old Sun Inn in Saffron Walden

Stamford

Stamford, down in the southwest corner of Lincolnshire, is a beautifully preserved town of 17th- and 18th-century buildings constructed from attractive cream-colored limestone. Filmmakers love to set period costume dramas here, and no wonder. There are many cobbled lanes, and on Barn Hill and Broad Street are rows of houses with dignified stone door and window frames, porches and chimneys. Several church spires rise from the roofscape.

Stamford Arts Centre, built in 1776, is one of the oldest provincial theaters in the country and puts on a lively program of arts and cultural events throughout the year.

Daniel Lambert (1770–1809), who rejoiced in the title of "Britain's Fattest Man" is buried in the graveyard of the Church of St. Martin's. Inside the church is an alabaster effigy of William Cecil, adviser to Queen Elizabeth I and builder of Burghley House (see page 110), just southeast of town.

B3

Tourist information Stamford Arts Centre, 27 St. Mary's Street 01780 755611; www.southwestlincs.com

Drive:
Constable Country

Distance: 85 miles

If you're a fan of British painter John Constable, this drive through the low-lying countryside of the Stour Valley, on the borders of Suffolk and Essex, may give an odd sense of déja vu. If several of the artist's landscapes seem surprisingly similar to the real thing, it was because Constable celebrated so effectively the richness and subtle beauty of his native East Anglian countryside.

Just east of the sprawling town of Haverhill you join A1092, a lazy road with plenty of bends that winds eastward along the north bank of the Stour.

The River Stour rises across the county border in Cambridgeshire, and winds down into Suffolk as a stream almost small enough to step over, then wends its way through a string of lovely villages enriched and beautified by medieval wool wealth. First comes Stoke by Clare. Then you pass through Clare, with its castle mound, little Nethergate Brewery, priory remains and the richly pargeted (plasterworked) 15th-century former priest's house on the churchyard corner. Cavendish is next, its thatched houses exuding pink-faced charm. Then comes Long Melford and its great church (see page 117).

At Long Melford turn right on B1064, passing the broad village green to navigate a straggling main street lined with handsome old houses.

Set back from the road are two fine Tudor houses, Kentwell Hall and Melford Hall.

Continue south on A131 to Sudbury.

The 18th-century portrait and landscape painter Thomas Gainsborough was born here; his house is now a museum.

From Sudbury, B1508 wanders south along

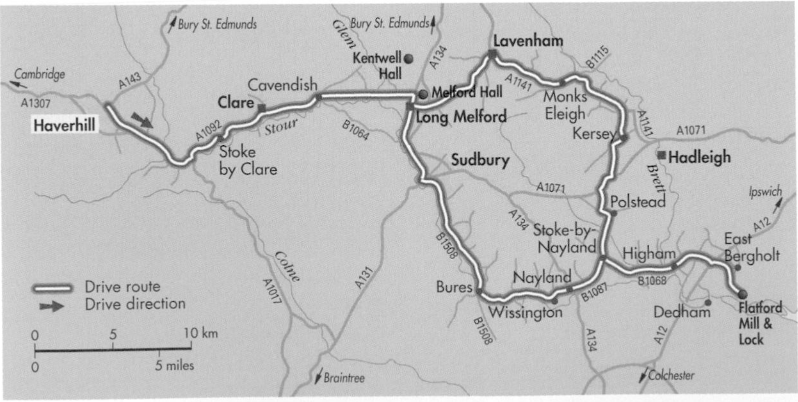

The familiar outline of Flatford Mill, made famous by John Constable's paintings

the east bank of the Stour (or you can take an even prettier and narrower road along the west bank) for 5 miles to Bures, one of the smallest and sleepiest of the Stour Valley towns. From Bures, you remain just within the southernmost border of Suffolk as you take the 5-mile local road east along the north bank of the river.

This is a really beautiful stretch in a shallow, rolling valley. Don't forget to look into the Norman church at Wissington (pronounced "Wiston"), with its ancient wall paintings.

Cross A134 to reach Nayland.

There are picturesque old houses, and an altarpiece by John Constable in the village church.

Continue on B1087 to Stoke-by-Nayland.

This village has a commanding church tower on the ridge. The Angel Inn (see page 265), at the crossroads here serves superb pub food.

From Stoke-by-Nayland, bear right on B1068 toward the A12 highway. Turn left onto A12, then immediately take B1070 to East Bergholt, John Constable's birthplace. Turn right in the village (watch for the sign) to reach a parking lot and walk down to Flatford Mill.

Scenes from Constable paintings surround you here: *Flatford Mill* (1817), *Boat-building near Flatford Mill* (1815), and at the end of the lane, the whitewashed gables of Willy Lott's Cottage and the tree-hung pool by the mill as shown in *The Hay Wain* (1821).

From the Flatford parking lot return to Stoke-by-Nayland. From here, a local road leads north past Polstead and its pond. Turn right along A1071 (in the direction of Hadleigh), leaving it after a short distance to take a local road on the left that dips through Kersey, an unspoiled and enchanting medieval village. Just north of here, turn left on A1141 to much-visited Lavenham (see page 118). Leave the village along B1071, Great Waldingfield/Sudbury road; in a mile a local road on the right returns you to Long Melford, and then A1092 back to Haverhill.

Kentwell Hall C2 Long Melford, near Sudbury 01787 310207 Daily 11–5 (phone or consult www.kentwell.co.uk for details); House noon–4 Restaurants $$$

Melford Hall C2 Long Melford, near Sudbury 01787 376395; www.nationaltrust.org.uk Wed.–Sun. 1:30–5, May–Sep.; Sat.–Sun. 1:30–5, Apr. and Oct.; Wed.–Mon. 1:30–5, at Easter Café $$$

Gainsborough's House C2 46 Gainsborough Street, Sudbury 01787 372958; www.gainsborough.org Mon.–Sat. 10–5 $$ (free Tue. 1–5)

Heart of England

"Heart of England" is essentially a tourist board label, intended to soften the unflattering image of grimy manufacturing cities associated with the traditional reference to England's central area: the Midlands. It is certainly true that this region was the birthplace of Britain's Industrial Revolution. And the growth of huge manufacturing cities such as Birmingham and Leicester and their various accompanying roads, railroads and canals have detracted from the rural idyll in some places. But the Heart of England covers a lot of ground. Here, too, are the beautiful Cotswold Hills with their perfect little limestone villages; the lift and sweep of the Herefordshire and Shropshire hills along the Welsh Border; and the green lowlands of woods and fields in Warwickshire, where William Shakespeare spent his formative years.

Rivers and Hills

Toward the western part of the region you will find the most dramatic landscapes, the red stone that underpins the Welsh Border hills and the red earth that covers them. The sister rivers of Severn and Wye wind a lazy course through much of this countryside.

The River Severn flows from Wales through Shropshire and on through Worcestershire, widening toward the start of its mighty estuary that splits the edges of southern Gloucestershire. The River Wye snakes to meet the Severn through the lush cattle-grazing country of Herefordshire.

Shropshire has the fine whaleback uplift of the Long Mynd, and to the east a succession of narrow gorges along the River Severn. Here, in 1709, an iron-master named Abraham Darby discovered how to smelt iron cheaply with coke, and this set in motion the monstrous juggernaut of the country's Industrial Revolution.

Worcestershire looks to its mini-mountain chain of the Malvern Hills, aptly nicknamed the "English Alps." Gloucestershire and neighboring

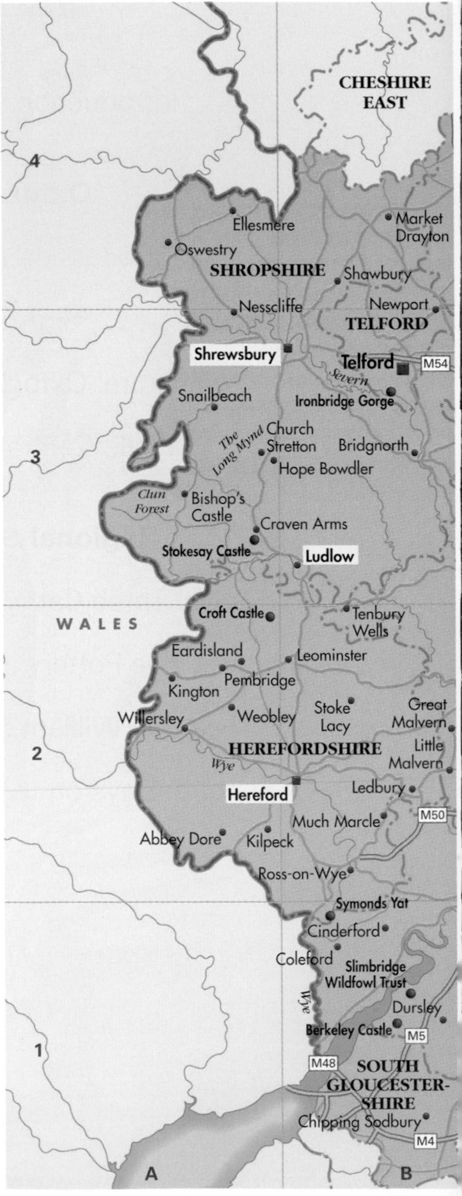

Oxfordshire share the Cotswolds, a low rolling range of hills considered by many to be the most appealing stretch of country in southern England.

Regional Architecture

These southern regions of the Heart of England show very distinctive styles of building that reflect the underlying stone in some parts, the growth of brick-making in others. Shropshire, Herefordshire and Worcestershire are famous for their black-and-white, half-timbered houses that look as if they have existed since medieval times – as many have, in fact. Around Weobley

(pronounced "Webley") and Leominster ("Lemster") in west Herefordshire, you can follow a specially marked 40-mile route through the best of these "black-and-white" villages.

Many of the churches in this region are built of dark red sandstone, with squat fortress-like towers that are reminders of bitter Anglo-Welsh conflict in days gone by. Other fortified buildings include castles and sturdy manor houses; Stokesay Castle, just north of Ludlow in Shropshire, is the oldest and finest in England. Grand and graceful ecclesiastical buildings are here, too, notably the "three cathedrals" of Hereford, Gloucester and Worcester, which encircle the Malvern Hills.

The buildings of east Gloucestershire and west Oxfordshire are of a different order, for here they are made mostly of the limestone that underlies the Cotswolds, varying from palest silver to the deepest gold. The buildings in the university city of Oxford, far and away the most stunning city in the Heart of England region, exemplify the beauty of this Cotswold stone.

Cotswold Delights

The Cotswold towns and villages are havens for antiques shops and local crafts – Stow-on-the-Wold and Broadway are particular hotspots. The idyllic village of Chipping Campden boasts its own group of "Morris Men" who, dressed in white, and decorated with bells and ribbons, perform the traditional English Morris Dance in the market square on May Day (May 1) and some summer weekends. They dance to the fiddle and accordion.

There are lovely pubs all through this region; the Falkland Arms in Great Tew is one of the most charming. The city of Cheltenham has elegant shopping streets decorated with hanging baskets; it also plays host to the Cheltenham Music Festival in July and the National Hunt Festival in March, one of Britain's best steeplechase events.

Rivers and Waterways

North of the Cotswold belt lies green and pleasant Warwickshire, bisected by the slow-flowing River Avon, on whose banks William Shakespeare grew up in Stratford-upon-Avon. The shadow of Shakespeare lies long in his home town, which draws millions of visitors each year, and it is an undisputed center for theater. Warwick Castle, north of Stratford, is another immensely popular tourist attraction – a magnificent, grim medieval stronghold.

The River Thames threads and loops its way through the region, passing through Oxford before heading east to London. It is dotted with the market

There are two blocks of five locks at Foxton Locks along the Leicester Line of the Grand Union Canal

towns, villages, and their accompanying pubs, that grew up along its banks, and it is alive with boats, particularly on weekends. The crowning event of the river's year is the Royal Regatta in June at Henley-on-Thames, an international rowing and social event.

Canals crisscross this region, a legacy of the days before the railroads. You can go boating on the placid Grand Union Canal as it winds from London all the way to Birmingham. Farther north stretches the open countryside of Leicestershire, prime hunting territory, and the semi-agricultural, semi-industrial county of Nottinghamshire, where the leafy remnants of Robin Hood's Sherwood Forest rub shoulders with gritty coal-mining country.

Such scenes provide a hint of what you find when you arrive in the West Midlands – the sprawling industry of Birmingham and the neighboring towns of the appropriately named Black Country. This region is home to a lively and enjoyable multicultural society that has enriched the area through the music, arts, cuisine and indigenous culture of a dozen nations. There is a "can-do" atmosphere in Birmingham, where you will meet friendly people speaking with an accent as distinctive as a birthmark.

The honey-colored stone of the Chapel at New College is typical of Oxford's buildings

Oxford

Any visitor to Britain who aims farther than London should have Oxford at the top of the agenda. This is a truly extraordinary city, the seat of the most famous university in the world and one of Europe's richest ensembles of medieval architecture. The 19th-century poet Matthew Arnold wrote seductively of a "sweet city with her dreaming spires," a magnetic image in the minds of so many visitors making their way to Oxford. Yet one's first impressions are generally disappointing. So powerful are those images of timeless towers and dignified colleges that it will come as something of a shock to find yourself navigating the housing subdivisions, beltways and shopping malls with which Oxford has gradually become surrounded. But press on, and cheer up! The dreaming spires and the glorious architecture are still there, once you make your way to the heart of the city.

The Early University

Oxford developed around a ford on the Thames, and had probably already become a seat of learning by 1167, when English scholars cast out by the University of Paris settled here. The colleges were built more or less to a conventional monastic pattern of chapel, dormitories and refectory around a quadrangle. Until Elizabethan times college residence was reserved for dons (tutors) and graduates, and the students continued to lodge all over town. Pre-Reformation traditions persisted for centuries; for example, until 1877 dons were not permitted to marry, and women were not awarded degrees until as late as 1920.

Town and Gown

Church influence over the thinking of the undergraduates and dons did not last as long, however. During the Middle Ages Oxford became a hothouse for intellectual liberty, which at times translated into anarchic behavior on the part of students – hence the number of "town-versus-gown" confrontations that not infrequently led to serious injury or death. Before the colleges admitted undergraduates into residence, these disputes were exacerbated by the famously loose morals of the student lodgers around Oxford.

These days things are a lot quieter and less confrontational. Don't expect to see all the undergraduates in "Oxford bags" (loose flannel trousers), long scarves and billowing black gowns – this is the 21st century, after all! Don't be fooled by their casual appearance and bicycle transport, either. An Oxford degree is no longer the absolute "open sesame" to success in politics, business or the Church that it once was, but acceptance at Oxford and Cambridge between them continue even now to be the goal of the brightest students.

Getting Your Bearings

All the chief Oxford sights are within a 20-minute walk of the city center. You can stroll around them independently (see page 137), or join an Official Guided Walking Tour departing from the Oxford Tourist Information Centre on Broad Street. (Advance booking through the information center is highly recommended.) The train station is a 10-minute walk west of the center (shuttle buses take five minutes).

Orienting yourself is not difficult. The old city is bounded by water – the River

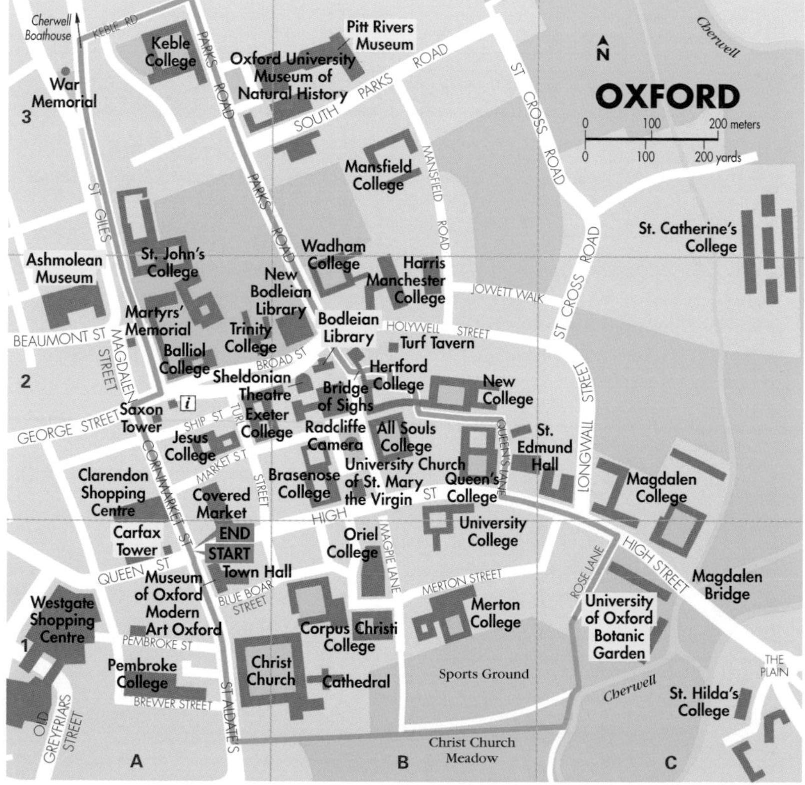

Cherwell on the east and the Oxford Canal on the west. Carfax Tower is the city's hub, with High Street (known as "The High") running east from the tower to Magdalen Bridge over the Cherwell. The High neatly divides the center into south and north; there are colleges on both sides, but most of the other attractions are located to the north of The High.

Eat, Drink and Enjoy

Given the number of undergraduates in Oxford, it's not surprising that there are dozens of inexpensive eateries in town – and some are quite good. The Covered Market off The High just north of Carfax Tower is a good bet for pleasant café-style nibbling, and on The High itself you'll find numerous places for tea and cakes. You can eat well by the river at the Cherwell Boathouse on Bardwell Road, then rent a punt (flat-bottomed boat) to work it all off.

Oxford's pubs range from the tacky to the atmospheric – of the latter, try the Eagle and Child on St. Giles Street or the diminutive Turf Tavern, on Bath Place off Holywell Street, not far from the city's much-used Bodleian Library.

The Covered Market is good fun for impromptu bric-a-brac purchases, as well as clothing, footwear and food. When in Oxford, buy books; new ones at Blackwell's on Broad Street, the university bookstore, or secondhand in various emporia (ask for details at the information center). Secure an unearned but authentic-looking university sweater, scarf or mug from the University of Oxford Shop on The High.

At night, try the college chapels or the Sheldonian Theatre for a concert, or the lively Oxford Playhouse on Beaumont Street for plays, opera or a concert. In summer, undergraduates sometimes put on open-air performances on the grounds of their colleges.

Essential Information

Tourist Information

✉ 15–16 Broad Street ☎ 01865 252200; www.visitoxfordandoxfordshire.com

Urban Transportation

The main railroad station is off Botley Road on Park End Street, half a mile west of the center. There is also a frequent bus link. For information and reservations contact the national rail information service ☎ 08457 484950. The bus station at Gloucester Green is where the longer-distance buses terminate. Most city buses leave from St. Aldates, Magdalen Street or Queen Street. For details on local travel contact The Oxford Bus Company ☎ 01865 785400; www.oxfordbus.co.uk. For long-distance bus services, contact Stagecoach Oxford ☎ 01865 772250; www.stagecoachbus.com, or National Express ☎ 08717 818178; www.nationalexpress.com. Taxis leave from the train station, Gloucester Green bus station and St. Giles, city center.

Airport Information

Oxford is linked by bus to Heathrow, Gatwick, Stansted and Luton airports. For Heathrow and Gatwick contact The Oxford Bus Company. See contact details above.

Climate – average highs and lows for the month

Jan.	Feb.	Mar.	Apr.	May	Jun.	Jul.	Aug.	Sep.	Oct.	Nov.	Dec.
6°C	6°C	9°C	12°C	16°C	18°C	21°C	21°C	17°C	13°C	9°C	7°C
43°F	43°F	48°F	54°F	61°F	64°F	70°F	70°F	63°F	55°F	48°F	45°F
1°C	1°C	2°C	3°C	6°C	9°C	12°C	11°C	9°C	6°C	3°C	2°C
34°F	34°F	36°F	37°F	43°F	48°F	54°F	52°F	48°F	43°F	37°F	36°F

Oxford Sights

Key to symbols
map coordinates refer to the Oxford map on page 131 admission charge: $$$ more than £6, $$ £2–£6, $ less than £2
See page 5 for complete key to symbols

Ashmolean Museum

The museum was founded in 1683 around the utterly eclectic collection of explorer John Tradescant, and has been expanding ever since. Exhibits include Michelangelo and Raphael, Egyptian mummies and Islamic ceramics, Impressionists and pre-Raphaelites and Oliver Cromwell's death mask. Since 2011, the new galleries of Ancient Egypt and Nubia, representing 5000 years of history, have proved to be two of the museum's main attractions.

A2 Beaumont Street 01865 278002; www.ashmolean.org Tue.–Sun. and public holidays 10–6 Restaurant and café Free

The Radcliffe Camera reading room

The Bodleian Library

Bodleian Library

Founded in Tudor times, this working library contains more than 7 million books. The fan-vaulted, 15th-century Divinity School played host to the English Parliament during the Civil War (1642–46) and is still used for university ceremonies. Frequent exhibitions display many of the library's treasures and there are a range of tours available.

The cylindrical room and dome of the Radcliffe Camera, now the reading room, were built in the mid-18th century with a bequest of the royal physician Sir John Radcliffe to house his scientific books. Admire the exterior; it is not open to the public except on one of the extended tours.

Bodleian Library B2 Broad Street 01865 277224; www.bodleian.ox.ac.uk Mon.–Fri. 9–5, Sat. 9–4:30, Sun. 11–5. Divinity School closes at 4 p.m. Free (Divinity School $) Guided tours and audio tours ($$$)

Oxford Colleges

The colleges of Oxford University are crammed together in the center of the old city. Brief descriptions of the best follow in the order in which they are encountered during the course of the Oxford walk (see page 137). Remember that these colleges are educational establishments, not museums. Opening times are displayed on boards at each college entrance, outside the Porter's Lodge. Carry cash so that you can pay whatever entrance fee is suggested, and try to phone the colleges you wish to visit in advance to avoid disappointment if they are closed.

Christ Church was founded in 1525 by Cardinal Thomas Wolsey. The college chapel doubles as Oxford's cathedral; it retains some Saxon work and a 12th-century nave and choir, along with 15th-century vaulting. The arcaded Tom Quad is the chief quadrangle; the gallery in Canterbury Quad contains paintings by Renaissance masters. "Great Tom" bell is rung 101 times beginning at 9:05 each evening from the Sir Christopher Wren-designed Tom Tower over the gateway, a ritual curfew disregarded by today's less tradition-bound undergraduates.

Magdalen, pronounced "Maudlin," has a foundation dating from 1458, with grotesque gargoyles around the cloisters, a fine paneled 15th-century hall and a beautiful tower rising over The High. On May Day (May 1) morning the choir sings hymns at sunrise (6 a.m.) from the tower top, a fine 500-year-old Oxford tradition.

University College is largely composed of handsome buildings from the mid-17th century. Tradition says this was the site of the first learned community in Oxford, established in AD 872 by King Alfred.

Queen's College consists of a 14th-century foundation rebuilt in the 17th and 18th centuries in fine baroque style, with input from Sir Christopher Wren and his pupil Nicholas Hawksmoor.

New College was founded in 1379 by William of Wykeham, Bishop of Winchester, who had founded Winchester College four years previously.

He wished to ensure a supply of well-educated priests to fill in the gaps in the ranks of the clergy caused by the disastrous Black Death plague some 30 years before. The college chapel contains the bishop's jeweled crozier, a study of St. James of Compestella by El Greco, a stained-glass Nativity in the west window designed by Sir Joshua Reynolds, and more recent treasures including a 1951 statue by Sir Jacob Epstein of Lazarus awakening from the slumber of death.

All Souls is unique in that it has no undergraduates, but only fellows (graduates elected for periods of research). A very fine restored 15th-century facade fronts The High. The chapel contains beautiful 15th-century stained glass and a handsome hammerbeam roof. Sir Christopher Wren was a fellow, and designed the sundial in the quad.

Trinity, set in beautiful grounds, was founded in 1555. Wren designed its lovely Garden Quad. In the chapel are exquisite late 17th-century carvings by master carver Grinling Gibbons.

Merton traces its origins back to 1264. It was the first college to bring students and tutors together under one roof. Mob Quad, dating from the 14th century, has the oldest library in England. Beautified with Tudor woodwork, it contains an astrolabe (an instrument used for navigating by the stars) once owned by Geoffrey Chaucer. The chapel features 13th- and 14th-century stained glass.

Christ Church ✉ St. Aldates ☎ 01865 276150; www.chch.ox.ac.uk
Magdalen ✉ High Street ☎ 01865 276000; www.magd.ox.co.uk
University College ✉ High Street ☎ 01865 276602; www.univ.ox.ac.uk ⓘ Entry at discretion of Lodge Porter
Queen's College ⓘ Closed to visitors except on official tours (ask at the tourist office); ☎ 01865 252200; www.queens.ox.ac.uk
New College ✉ Holywell Street/New College Lane ☎ 01865 279555; www.new.ox.ac.uk
All Souls ✉ High Street ☎ 01865 279379; www.all-souls.ox.ac.uk
Merton ✉ Merton Street ☎ 01865 276310; www.merton.ox.ac.uk

Above left to right: The view of All Souls College from the spire of the Church of St. Mary the Virgin; New College is usually open from March to early October

The Pitt Rivers Museum is housed in the Oxford University Museum of Natural History

Carfax Tower

The tower, all that remains of the 14th-century St. Martin's Church, is located in the center of town where Cornmarket Street and St. Aldates meet The High. Animated figures known as quarterjacks strike out the quarter-hours. You can climb the 99 steps to the top for a superb view.

A1 The High 01865 792653 Daily 10–5:30, Apr.–Sep.; 10–4:30, Oct. $$

Pitt Rivers Museum

This is a wonderfully anachronistic place, the absolute antithesis of the modern, high-tech, interactive museum. Here you will find case upon case of ethnic artifacts and scientific and archeological curiosities – including some South American shrunken heads – brought to Oxford from the corners of the earth during the great days of the British Empire. Or just admire the wonderful Victorian Gothic architecture.

B3 South Parks Road (enter from interior of the Oxford University Museum of Natural History, see page 137) 01865 270927; www.prm.ox.ac.uk Mon. noon–4:30, Tue.–Sun. 10–4:30 Free Audio tours available

University of Oxford Botanic Garden

The great greenhouse backing onto the River Cherwell near Magdalen Bridge was established nearly 400 years ago, the first garden in Britain devoted to the scientific study of plants. The formal flower beds and yew tree date from the garden's inception.

You can rent a punt from the parapet on Magdalen Bridge; this is where some undergraduates launch themselves into the Cherwell after learning the results of their final examinations.

C1 Rose Lane 01865 286690; www.botanic-garden.ox.ac.uk Daily 9–6, May–Aug.; 9–5, Mar.–Apr. and Sep.–Oct.; 9–4, rest of year. Last admission 45 minutes before closing $$ (donation Mon.–Fri., Nov.–Feb.)

Punting

Rent a punt (flat-bottomed boat) at Magdalen Bridge or at the Cherwell Boathouse on Bardwell Road north of the center, and pole gently downstream. The pole acts as a source of forward movement (push gently on the river bottom) and as a steering device (like the rudder on a boat). It is blissfully simple – unless you forget to withdraw the punting pole from the riverbed.

Cherwell Boathouse

A3 (off map) Bardwell Road Punting: 01865 515978; restaurant: 01865 552746; www.cherwellboathouse.co.uk Punting daily 10 a.m.–dusk, mid-Mar. to mid-Oct. Restaurant Punting $$$

Walk:
Central Oxford

Refer to route marked on city map on page 131

Allow a whole day for this walk, since there are many museums, libraries and college buildings to explore. Some of the best-known and most enjoyable are described on pages 133–136, but you are bound to discover others along the way.

Start at Carfax in the center of town.
Be sure to climb Carfax Tower (see opposite) before setting off to enjoy Oxford's treasures.
Walk south down St. Aldates to the Town Hall, housing the Museum of Oxford.
The museum gives an entertaining and informative look at the history of Oxford since Roman times, and is a good precursor to a walk around the city.
After visiting the museum, continue along St. Aldates past Christ Church College and turn left onto The Broad Walk through meadows to the River Cherwell, then proceed across Merton Field and up Rose Lane to The High.
Ahead is Magdalen College; to the right is the University of Oxford Botanic Garden and Magdalen Bridge.
Turn left onto The High and proceed until you turn right onto Queen's Lane. New College soon appears on the right, as the road becomes New College Lane.
Bath Place is on the right, with the Turf Tavern beckoning – one of Oxford's best pubs.
Proceed on New College Lane under the Bridge of Sighs until you reach Catte Street. Turn right on Catte Street to cross Broad Street, with the Sheldonian Theatre on your left.
The theater was an early design by the architect Sir Christopher Wren. Inside, a ceiling painting shows Ignorance and Jealousy cast out by Art and Science. Degree ceremonies and concerts are held here. Ahead on the right along Parks Road, past Wadham College, is the Oxford University Museum of Natural History with the Pitt Rivers Museum (see opposite) inside. Displays are in a glass-roofed hall and range from dinosaur skeletons to fossils.

Merton College was founded in 1264

Continue on Parks Road and turn left past Keble College onto Keble Road, then left onto broad St. Giles. Pass between the Ashmolean Museum on your right and Trinity College on your left. Continue on Magdalen Street.
On the corner of Broad Street is the Oxford Tourist Information Centre (information on guided walking tours of the city).
Turn right, then left onto Cornmarket Street and return to Carfax Tower.

Museum of Oxford A1 Town Hall, St. Aldates
01865 252761; www.museumofoxford.org.uk
Tue.–Thu., Sat. 10–5. Last admission 4:30
Café Free ($ donation suggested)
Audio tours ($$)

Oxford University Museum of Natural History B3
Parks Road 01865 272950; www.oum.ox.ac.uk
Daily 10–5 Free

Cheltenham

Cheltenham's medicinal spring was discovered in 1718, and by the time of King George III's visit in 1788 it had become an important spa town. But it was the patronage of the king's son, the fun-loving dandy George, Prince of Wales, that really set the town in the firmament of inland resorts. You can admire the Regency elegance of the green-roofed Rotunda and stroll down the wide pedestrian-only Promenade with its exclusive shops.

Cheltenham Art Gallery and Museum has an exhibition on William Morris, one of the leading lights of the English Arts and Crafts Movement in the late 19th century.

Round off your afternoon in Regency Cheltenham with tea at one of the numerous tearooms, then saunter to Pittville Park to take the rather nasty-flavored waters under the blue domed roof of the Pittville Pump Room.

C2

Tourist information 77 Promenade 01242 522878; www.visitcheltenham.com

Cheltenham Art Gallery and Museum Clarence Street 01242 237431; www.cheltenhammuseum.org

Pittville Pump Room East Approach Drive 01242 521621 Wed.–Sun. 10–4 Free

Cirencester

Cirencester is the capital of the Cotswolds, and its market, on Mondays and Fridays, draws people from the surrounding rural region. There are fashionable boutiques and antiques shops, and a converted Victorian brewery, New Brewery Arts, off Cricklade Street, is a good place to purchase art and crafts and you can watch artists at work in their studios.

The 15th-century parish church of St. John Baptist has a heavily buttressed tower and a mighty three-story south porch rich in fan vaulting. Wool wealth built and beautified the church, as it did the rest of Cirencester. Along Cecily Hill are the very grand town houses of Jacobean and Georgian wool merchants.

The Romans named the town they built here Corinium, and bits and pieces are continually being excavated. Many of the best – including some touching and evocative mosaics – are on display in the Corinium Museum.

C1

Tourist information Corinium Museum, Park Street 01285 654180; www.cotswold.gov.uk/go/tourism

Corinium Museum Park Street 01285 655611 Mon.–Sat. 10–5, Sun. 2–5, Apr.–Oct.; Mon.–Sat. 10–4, Sun. 2–4, Nov.–Mar. Café $$

Regency splendor in Cheltenham: You can take the waters at the Pittville Pump Room

Cotswold Villages

The Cotswolds owe their reputation among lovers of the subtler forms of English landscape to the beautiful limestone that underlies them, so productive when it comes to making attractive dips and hollows, so eye-catching when used for building. Oak and beech woods clothe the Cotswolds, interspersed with cornfields and open grazing land. These hills nurtured sheep to enrich medieval wool masters, and the wool men, in gratitude and self-advertisement, built beautiful churches. Chipping Campden, Cirencester, Fairford, Northleach, Painswick and Winchcombe are among the best. The wool masters also built fine gabled and mullioned houses for themselves, and handsome wool barns that still stand under stone-tiled roofs. The landscape is cross-hatched by mile upon mile of drystone walls (built without mortar), some of them tumbledown nowadays, others kept in wonderful repair.

Of the dozens of gorgeous Cotswold towns and villages you should at least try to see Bourton-on-the-Water, the "Venice of the Cotswolds," with its tiny bridges and plentiful gift shops and tearooms. Chipping Campden is perhaps the most appealing small town in the Cotswolds. The villages of Broadway, Stanton and Stanway are heavenly. Try to wander away from the main street to get glimpses of beautiful gardens.

Broadway ✚ C2

Tourist information ✉ Unit 14, Russell Square ☎ 01386 852937; www.beautifulbroadway.com

Bourton-on-the-Water ✚ C2

Tourist information ✉ Victoria Street ☎ 01451 820211; www.bourtoninfo.com

Chipping Campden ✚ C2

Tourist information ✉ The Old Police Station, High Street ☎ 01386 841206; www.chippingcampdenonline.org

Cheese Rolling

Six miles southwest of Cheltenham, Coopers' Hill is the venue for one of central England's oddest events. Despite recent attempts to ban it, the annual Cheese Rolling festival takes place on the public holiday at the end of May; it involves an enormous Double Gloucester cheese being rolled down a steep hill, followed excitedly by dozens of villagers in hot pursuit. It's a serious matter, however; the prize goes to the first brave person to grab the cheese!

Stone-built cottages line the streets of the small village of Stanton, near Broadway

The fan-vaulted ceilings of Gloucester Cathedral's cloisters date back to the 14th century

Drive:

Three Cathedrals Country

Distance: 65 miles

This drive leads you in a ragged circle around the south Midlands countryside, and takes in three medieval cathedrals, an abbey church and a beautiful Saxon chapel along the way – not to mention England's own "mini-Alps" and the one-time home of American poet Robert Frost.

Start in the city of Worcester.

Worcester has a sandstone cathedral occupying a superb location on the bank of the River Severn. The early Norman chapter house is worth seeing, as is the Norman crypt and the marble effigy of King John, who died in 1216 and lies buried here. Worcester is one of three neighboring cathedrals – Gloucester and Hereford are the others – which host the Three Choirs Festival each August (alternating locations each year). On Worcester's Severn Street stand the former factory and showroom of the Royal Worcester porcelain company, makers of fine china since 1751.

From Worcester A449 runs southwest and skirts the Malvern Hills.

The Malverns are a 9-mile-long chain of little mountains. Malvern spring water is famed for its purity, and there are still spa wells here.

A449 continues to Ledbury.

Ledbury is a charming small town, with its ancient Market Hall standing proud on tall wooden legs in the center. Cobbled Church Lane, a feast of

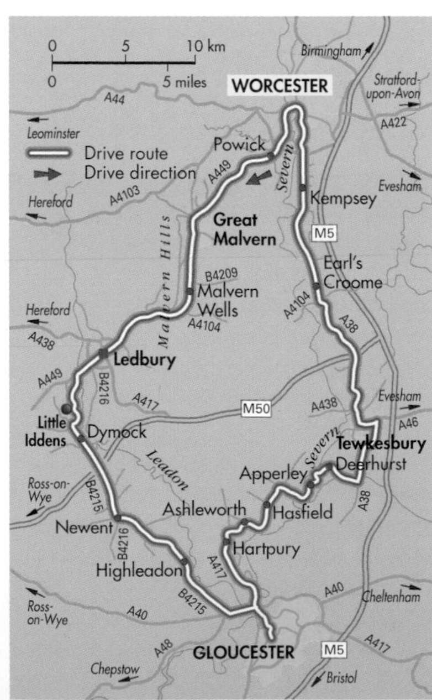

medieval buildings, leads to the Church of St. Michael and All Angels. This is a splendid building with a detached tower and spire, and a Norman west front. Hereford (see page 144) is 15 miles west along A438.

From Ledbury, take A449 (in the Ross-on-Wye direction) southwest. After 1 mile you'll reach B4216 branching off to the left; Continue on the A449 and take the second left, a winding lane. After 1 mile you'll pass a black-and-white farmhouse on your right at the brow of a short hill.

This farmhouse was Little Iddens, where Robert Frost came to stay as a young unpublished poet before World War I. For a few golden months in the summer of 1914 Little Iddens was a powerhouse of poetry, with eminent poets gathering under the charming spell of Frost. They included Rupert Brooke, Lascelles Abercrombie, Wilfred Gibson, Eleanor Farjeon and Edward Thomas, who died in the Battle of Arras in 1917, leaving behind some exquisite poetry. They were known as the "Dymock Poets."

Continue along the lane to Dymock, then follow B4215 to Gloucester.

Here Gloucester's glorious Norman cathedral stands under a graceful 225-foot spire. Inside are wonderful 14th-century fan-vaulting in the cloisters, and the tomb of King Edward II, gruesomely murdered with a red-hot poker in nearby Berkeley Castle in 1327.

Take A417 (the Ledbury road) north from Gloucester. After 5 miles, at Hartpury, bear right on a series of local roads through Ashleworth.

Here a medieval farm and a fine riverside pub, the Boat, are down a side lane.

After Hasfield, turn right on B4213 to cross the River Severn at Haw Bridge. After 1 mile turn left, pass through Apperley and continue to the Saxon church at Deerhurst, a mile farther on. A minor road joins Deerhurst with B4213 and then A38; turn left at A38 to reach Tewkesbury.

This handsome town has a superb abbey. The Norman structure is rich in fan-vaulted chantry chapels and tomb effigies. Climb the tower for views over the countryside.

Return to Worcester via A38 or M5.

Worcester ✚ B2
Tourist information ✉ The Guildhall, High Street ☎ 01905 726311; www.visitworcester.com
Worcester Cathedral ✉ College Green ☎ 01905 732900 ⌚ Daily 7:30–6; Tower: Sat., public holidays and school holidays 11–5 (last admission 4:30), Easter–Oct. 🍴 Café 🎫 Free; Tower $$ ℹ Tours Mon.–Sat. 11 and 2:30, Easter–Oct. ($$)
Gloucester ✚ B1
Tourist information ✉ 28 Southgate Street ☎ 01452 396572; www.gloucester.gov.uk/tourism
Gloucester Cathedral ✉ College Green ☎ 01452 528095 ⌚ Daily 7:30–6 🍴 Café 🎫 Free ($$ donation suggested); Tower $$; Exhibition and Whispering Gallery $$ ℹ Guided tours Mon.–Sat. 10:45–3:15, Sun. noon–2:30 🎫 ($$); Tower tours ($$)

Worcester Cathedral across the River Severn

Hereford

Hereford suffered numerous sackings and burnings throughout the Middle Ages. During the 17th century it entered quieter times, and this more prosperous era is reflected in the solid furnishings and fine decoration of The Old House, a museum of Herefordshire life in Jacobean times. Nearby stands the city's cathedral, with its Norman interior, and Tudor chantry with elaborate fan-vaulting. The most outstanding feature is the Mappa Mundi ("map of the world"), drawn by Richard de Bello in 1289. The big circular map writhes with beasts both real and legendary – centaur and salamander, Minotaur and Golden Fleece. Mappa Mundi shows an imagination stimulated by the tension between the certainties of Holy Scripture and the tales of medieval adventurers.

B2

Tourist information 1 King Street 01432 268430; www.visitherefordshire.co.uk

Hereford Cathedral and Mappa Mundi Cathedral Close 01432 374200; www.herefordcathedral.org Cathedral: daily 9:15–evensong. Mappa Mundi and Chained Library: Mon.–Sat. 10–5, Easter–late Oct. (also Sun. 11–4, late May–Aug.); Mon.–Sat. 10–4, rest of year. Last admission 30 minutes before closing Café Cathedral free ($$ donation suggested); Mappa Mundi $$ Guided tours Mon.–Sat. at 11:15 and 2:15, Easter–Oct.

The Old House High Town 01432 260694 Tue.–Sat. 10–5, Sun. 10–4, Apr.–Sep.; Tue.–Sat. 10–5, rest of year Free

Ludlow

Ludlow is south Shropshire's showpiece town, straddling a sharp-spined ridge and dominated by the Church of St. Laurence. Ludlow Castle overlooks ancient gardens known as the Linney and a permanent market is held in the streets between the castle and the church. On Corve Street you can admire ornate black timberwork on the front of the 17th-century Feathers Hotel, so named because of an old local industry making feathered arrows.

B3

Tourist information Castle Street 01584 875053; www.ludlow.org.uk

Ludlow Castle Castle Square 01584 873355; www.ludlowcastle.com Daily 10–7, in Aug.; daily 10–5, Apr.–Jul. and in Sep.; daily 10–4, Feb.–Mar. and Oct.–Nov.; Sat.–Sun. 10–4, rest of year. Last admission 30 minutes before closing Café $$

A winter-time view of the exterior of 11th-century Hereford Cathedral

Fine Pottery and Elegant China

The great potteries of Staffordshire are known the world over. Wedgwood, Spode, Minton and Royal Doulton have become household names; their best and most venerable pieces – superbly delicate, painstakingly hand-crafted and painted – change hands for a fortune these days.

Pottery Towns

The potteries of the six neighboring Staffordshire towns of Tunstall, Burslem, Hanley, Stoke, Fenton and Longton – known collectively as Stoke-on-Trent – operated throughout the 18th and 19th centuries. Stoke-on-Trent owed its prosperity to a location atop rich deposits of marl clay suitable for pottery-making, as well as coal, sandstone, gravel and sand. Excellent transportation links by canal and later by railroad meant that fragile pottery could be taken to the ports and then onto ships taking it to the export markets of the world without risk of being broken by jolting on the rough roads of those times.

Classic Designs

Josiah Wedgwood (1730–95) was the king of the pottery-owners, producing celebrated stoneware designs of white classical scenes in relief on a blue, green or black background. The region's other famous potters included Josiah Spode, who produced coveted bone china dining services painted with an old Chinese "willow-pattern" legend, and later Henry Doulton and his beautiful Royal Doulton ware.

You may be able to join a fascinating tour around Wedgwood and Spode to see just how hard-earned skills are put to work creating masterpieces of fine china. Marked by brown signposts, the Heritage Trail will guide you around the potteries of the towns. Fabulously expensive and more affordable pieces rub shoulders in the showrooms maintained by each pottery along the museum trail.

B1

The Wedgwood Visitor Centre and Museum Barlaston, Stoke-on-Trent 01782 282986; www.thewedgwoodvisitorcentre.com Mon.–Fri. 9–5, Sat.–Sun. 10–4 Restaurant $$$ Reservations prior to visit are essential

Classic Spode pottery can be seen in the Spode Visitor Centre

Shrewsbury Cathedral was designed by Edward Pugin and was completed in 1856

Oundle

Oundle is a harmonious old town of silver-gray buildings. The mostly 13th-century Church of St. Peter has a fine spire 203 feet high. The spire's crockets (decorative projections) are set just far enough apart to tempt rash boys from Oundle School to climb to the summit and touch "Peter," the weathercock at the tip. One lad achieved the feat in 1880, but when he reached ground level again it was to find his headmaster waiting grimly for him. He was first soundly thrashed for disobeying the school rules, then presented with a golden sovereign to reward his daring.

In the 17th-century Talbot Inn there is a wide staircase, said to have been brought here from nearby Fotheringhay Castle and to be the one that Mary, Queen of Scots descended on her way to execution at Fotheringhay in 1587. On the bank of the River Nene just downstream from Oundle stands a grassy mound, all that remains of the castle, its flat top aptly covered with thistles (the Scottish national emblem) – a poignant reminder of the most tenacious of Scottish queens.

E3

Tourist information 4 New Street 01832 274333; www.east-northamptonshire.gov.uk

Shrewsbury

Shrewsbury lies in a bend of the River Severn, a hunched defensive position appropriate to such an important Welsh Border town. Shrewsbury was attacked, sacked and burned numerous times during the Middle Ages. There are some handsome old buildings, notably the twin timber-framed Elizabethan houses of Owen's Mansion and Ireland's Mansion on High Street, reminders of the prosperity that the wool trade once brought to the town.

Shrewsbury Castle dates mostly from the 14th century, as does much of the stained glass in St. Mary's Church. A statue opposite the castle commemorates naturalist Charles Darwin, born here in 1809. Shrewsbury Abbey dates from the 11th century.

B3

Tourist information Shrewsbury Museum and Art Gallery, Rowley's House, Barker Street 01743 281200; www.visitshrewsbury.com

Shrewsbury Castle and The Shropshire Regimental Museum Castle Street 01743 358516; www.shrewsburymuseums.com Castle grounds: Mon.–Sat. 9–5 (also Sun. 10:30–5, late May–late Sep.). Museum: Fri.–Wed. 10:30–5, Jun.–Sep.; 10:30–4, rest of year Castle grounds free; museum $$

Shrewsbury Abbey Abbey Foregate 01743 232723; www.shrewsburyabbey.com Daily 10:30–3 Free (donation suggested)

William Shakespeare

What is astonishing about the English language's greatest playwright is not so much the sheer volume of brilliant work he produced – 37 plays over a 20-year period, not to mention dozens of sonnets – but that such sustained genius could have flourished in a sketchily educated boy from an obscure Warwickshire market town.

William Shakespeare was born in a timber-framed house in Stratford-upon-Avon on April 23, 1564. He probably attended the local grammar school, and may have had scrapes with the law and with local landowners over poaching expeditions. In 1582, while still a teenager, he married his pregnant girlfriend Anne Hathaway, a yeoman farmer's daughter from nearby Shottery. They quickly produced a son and two daughters. Then, at some time between 1585 and 1592, William left his young family and moved away to London to carve out a career for himself as an actor-manager and playwright in the lively theater scene then thriving in the raffish red-light district of Southwark.

Within a few years Shakespeare had become joint owner of the wooden-walled Globe Theatre (see page 41), which saw many of his plays launched. In 1603, shortly after the death of Queen Elizabeth I and the accession of King James I, he became patron of the royal theater troupe, the King's Men, a welcome opening of the door of royal approval. But in 1610 Shakespeare sold the theater, moved back to Stratford and hung up his quill. On his own birthday six years later he died, comfortably well off and respected but not lionized, and was buried in the town's Holy Trinity Church, where he had been baptized 52 years before.

These bald facts are what we know for certain about the Bard. After his death Shakespeare's reputation languished in the shadows for well over a century until the actor David Garrick inspired a rekindling of interest in the playwright's works in the 1760s and '70s.

Anne Hathaway's cottage in Shottery, childhood home of Shakespeare's wife

Stratford-upon-Avon

Stratford-upon-Avon lies approximately 20 miles south of Birmingham. That its Shakespearean associations make it one of England's most popular tourist destinations after London is a testament to the internationally effective magic of the Bard's genius.

Everyone who comes here wants to seek out the Shakespeare sites. These are well kept and of great intrinsic interest, and a day's stroll will allow you to cover all that are within the town boundaries. If you prefer a guided tour, a number of tour buses take in most of the sites – ask at the tourist information center for details. One word of warning, though: You will greatly increase your enjoyment if you can avoid visiting on holiday weekends, and especially during the months of July and August.

If you want to take in a play while you're in Stratford, the Royal Shakespeare Theatre (tel 0844 800 1110; www.rsc.org.uk) is home to the prestigious Royal Shakespeare Company which stages performances here. The repertoire ranges from classical playwrights to modern drama, so take your pick. There are several restaurants on the riverside, and many offer good-value pre-theater dinners.

On Henley Street stands Shakespeare's Birthplace, a handsome half-timbered building that must have been nearly new when John Shakespeare, William's wool-merchant father, moved in. In subsequent centuries it did duty as a pub, the Swan and Maidenhead Inn. It was bought for the nation in 1847 and refurbished to give a good impression of Shakespeare's life. Apparently David Garrick, while in Stratford in 1769 to fan some flames of interest in the long-neglected playwright, arbitrarily chose the "birth" room in time for the Shakespeare Festival he was organizing. Famous signatures scratched with diamond rings on a windowpane include Sir Walter Scott, Henry Irving and Ellen Terry.

One of the Bancroft Gardens Shakespearian statues

On the corner of High Street stands Judith Shakespeare's House (now a shop – Crabtree & Evelyn), where the playwright's daughter lived. A bit farther along High Street is Harvard House, built in Tudor times, where the mother of Harvard University founder John Harvard was born.

Nash's House stands on Chapel Street next to the site of Shakespeare's retirement home, New Place, where he died in 1616. New Place was torn down in the 18th century on the orders of its owner, who was tired of Shakespeare fans knocking on his door. There is a beautiful Elizabethan Knot Garden on the site of the house, down Chapel Street on the left.

Chapel Street soon becomes Church Street; on the left is King Edward VI Grammar School (not open to the public), where Shakespeare probably studied as a boy. It is possible, though, to visit the beautiful medieval house of Hall's Croft, where Shakespeare's daughter Susanna lived after her

This Tudor building was once a school, founded by the Guild of the Holy Cross

marriage to Dr. John Hall. Here you can admire the fine furnishings and paintings of the period and wince over an exhibition about medical practices back in those primitive days.

Holy Trinity Church on Trinity Street is where Shakespeare lies buried beside his wife within the altar rails. The walk from here back along the River Avon is pretty, passing the Royal Shakespeare Theatre before reaching Clopton Bridge, where you bear left along Bridge Street to return to Henley Street.

Two other notable sites lie outside Stratford-upon-Avon. Mary Arden's Farm, a Tudor farmhouse where Shakespeare's mother was born, is in Wilmcote, three miles north of town, and houses the Shakespeare Countryside Museum. At Shottery, one mile west of town, is Anne Hathaway's Cottage, charmingly thatched and half-timbered.
C2

Tourist information Bridgefoot 01789 264293; www.discover-stratford.com

Shakespeare's Birthplace Henley Street 01789 204016; www.shakespeare.org.uk Daily 9–6 Jul.–Aug.; 9–5, Apr.–Jun. and Sep.–Oct.; 10–4, Nov.–Mar. $$$ (includes Hall's Croft and Nash's House and New Place)

Harvard House High Street 01789 204507 Restricted opening. Phone for details

Nash's House and New Place Chapel Street 01789 292325 Daily 10–5, Apr.–Oct.; 11–4 Nov.–Mar. $$$ (includes Shakespeare's Birthplace and Hall's Croft)

Hall's Croft Old Town 01789 292107 Daily 10–5, Apr.–Oct; 11–4, Nov.–Mar. $$$ (includes Shakespeare's Birthplace and Nash's House and New Place)

Holy Trinity Church Trinity Street, Old Town 01789 266316; www.stratford-upon-avon.org Mon.–Sat. 8:30–6, Sun. 12:30–5, Apr.–Sep.; Mon.–Sat. 9–5, Sun. 12:30–5, Mar. and Oct.; Mon.–Sat. 9–4, Sun. 12:30–5, rest of year Free (Shakespeare's grave $ donation suggested)

Mary Arden's Farm Wilmcote 01789 293455; www.shakespeare.org.uk Daily 10–5, Apr.–Oct. Café (seasonal) $$$

Anne Hathaway's Cottage Cottage Lane, Shottery 01789 292100 Daily 9–5, Apr.–Oct.; 10–4 Nov.–Mar. Café opposite (seasonal) $$

Imposing Warwick Castle rises from the grounds landscaped by "Capability" Brown

Warwick Castle

One of the most impressive of Britain's great medieval fortresses, Warwick Castle looms over the River Avon like a statement of strength, impregnability and permanence. No castle in England so perfectly epitomizes the power and influence of medieval nobility – and also their dinosaur-like vulnerability to social change, which simply bypassed them and left them behind.

The original Norman castle was captured and burned in 1264 by Simon de Montfort, leader of the rebellious barons. The remains still stand on their mound within the castle grounds. But it is the solid, gray stone towers and outer walls, added in a 14th-century rebuilding, that are seen today, visible signs of the glory of the Beauchamp and Neville families, earls of Warwick. The most powerful of all the earls of Warwick was Richard Neville, who as "Warwick the Kingmaker" tried to serve both sides during the 15th-century Wars of the Roses.

There is a mighty turreted gatehouse pierced with arrow slits; it also holds concealed "murder holes" for the anointing of attackers' heads with boiling oil. The original portcullis still hangs high over the gateway. Five-story battlemented towers rise at the corners of the outer wall: Caesar's Tower, Guy's Tower and Watergate Tower, the last likely walked by the restless ghost of Sir Fulke Greville. Sir Fulke was murdered in 1628 by a servant who believed that his master had left him nothing in his will. In the dungeon of Caesar's Tower is an *oubliette*, a cell where prisoners, brought back from the battlefields of France, were forgotten and left to perish.

There are several exhibitions and displays in the castle, including an armory that has pieces of Oliver Cromwell's armor, ghastly looking torture instruments and a display telling the story of Warwick the Kingmaker. Parts of the castle were refurbished during the 17th and 18th centuries and turned into state rooms with fine carved fireplaces, plasterwork, furniture and paintings. The castle is part of the company that operates Madame Tussauds, and features several attractions with waxwork models and a program of events throughout the year.

In the 1750s "Capability" Brown landscaped the extensive grounds. The 60 acres of rolling countryside include a defensive mound built by William the Conqueror in 1068, a magnificent conservatory and the Victorian Rose Garden, seen at its best in June and July.

C2

Castle Hill, Warwick 0871 265 2000; www.warwick-castle.com Daily 10–6, Apr.–Sep.; 10–5, Oct.–Mar. Last admission 30 minutes before closing Restaurants and cafés $$$ Audio tours ($$)

Days on the River Thames

Between Oxford and London the River Thames passes through its most delectable stretch, winding through meadows and soft green lowlands.

Abingdon is the first place of any size you come to, a pretty old town with a lovely riverfront and some notable buildings, especially the 17th-century County Hall, which houses a museum about the area. A few miles downriver is Dorchester (not to be confused with the county town of Dorset), where the Norman abbey church has glorious east windows full of medieval stained glass.

Moving on south and east, you pass through Goring and Pangbourne on a thickly wooded stretch of the river. Kenneth Grahame, author of the children's classic *The Wind In The Willows* (1908), lived the last few years of his life here. Grahame had this section of the Thames in mind as a setting for his tales of Ratty, Mole, Mr. Toad and friends. Artist Ernest Shephard used scenes here for his charming illustrations for the book.

Mapledurham's lock, weir and mill have a picturesque setting, and the manor house of Mapledurham is worth a visit for its Elizabethan staircase, Jacobean plaster ceilings, Georgian private chapel and grounds. Farther along are Henley, site of the annual Royal Regatta rowing events, and Cookham, with a gallery celebrating local artist Sir Stanley Spencer and displaying his *Christ Preaching At Cookham Regatta*, an eccentric masterpiece with the river as its setting.

Mapledurham House D1 Mapledurham, 4 miles northwest of Reading 0118 972 3350; www.mapledurham.co.uk Sat.–Sun. and public holidays 2–5:30, mid-Apr. to late Sep. Last admission 30 minutes before closing Café House and mill $$$

Stanley Spencer Gallery E1 The Kings Hall, High Street, Cookham 01628 471885; www.stanleyspencer.org.uk Daily 10:30–5:30, Apr.–Nov.; Thu.–Sun. 11–4:30, rest of year $$

The 184-mile Thames Walk National Trail passes Goring Lock

Wales

There is a new mood afoot in Wales today, a fresh self-confidence and sense of "Welshness" that will be very apparent to anyone visiting this beautiful and character-filled country. Wales is a country in its own right, as well as a part of Britain along with England and Scotland. It has its own language, entirely distinct from English, as well as its own culture, literature, mythology and history.

Dramatic Landscapes

The Welsh landscape is hilly, rising to the north and west toward the elevated Snowdonia National Park. The Welsh coastline is mostly steep and craggy, cut with great sandy estuaries and sheltered fishing havens. In Snowdonia, at the upper end of the great westward-opening pincer of Cardigan Bay, are some of the oldest rocks in Britain, volcanic solidifications mixed with hard slates and schists pushed up in titanic upheavals some 400 million years ago. Wind and weather have shaped them into mountain ranges, superb for walking and climbing, whose slate hearts were intensively quarried during the Industrial Revolution for building materials.

Slate quarrying in the north, sheep and cattle raising in the interior, coal mining and iron smelting in the south, fishing along the magnificent coast: Wales' traditional industries defined its regions for hundreds of years. But no longer. Most of the slate quarries, and all of the coal mines except for a tiny handful have closed. Farmers are having hard times, and inshore fishing is on the decline.

Even the "soft" fifth mainstay industry, seaside tourism, has lost out to cheaper, sunnier vacations abroad. It would be enough to crush the spirit of a less resilient people, but the Welsh have fought back energetically.

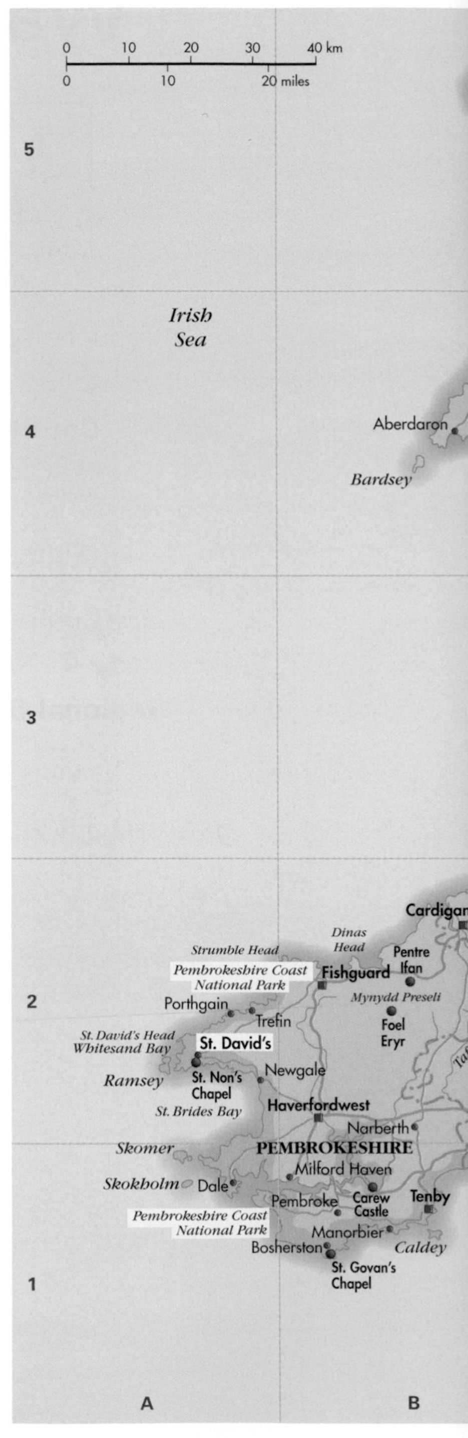

Holyhead Bay
Holyhead
Anglesey
Oriel Ynys Môn
Beaumaris
Holy Island
Llangefni
Llanfairpwll
Bryn Celli-Ddu
Penrhyn
Bangor
Newborough
Menai Strait
Caernarfon
Caernarfon Bay
Great Ormes Head
Llandudno
Colwyn Bay
Conwy
Bodnant
CONWY
Bethesda
Llanrwst
Llanberis
Snowdon Mountain Railway
3560ft
Snowdon
Capel Curig
Betws-y-Coed
Sygun Copper Mine
Nant Gwynant
Beddgelert
Blaenau Ffestiniog
Ffestiniog Railway
Nefyn
Lleyn Peninsula
Porthmadog
Portmeirion
Pwllheli
Abersoch
Trawsfynydd
Snowdonia National Park
Harlech
GWYNEDD
Rhyl
Prestatyn
Rhuddlan
Dee
St. Asaph
Clwyd
Flint
FLINTSHIRE
Denbigh
1821ft
Moel Famau
Mold
DENBIGHSHIRE
Llyn Brenig
Ruthin
Gresford
Wrexham
Erddig
Cerrigydrudion
Horseshoe Pass
Valle Crucis Abbey
Pontcysyllte Aqueduct
WREXHAM
Llyn Celyn
Corwen
Llangollen
Plas Newydd
Bala
Berwyn
Llyn Tegid
Pistyll Rhaeadr
Llyn Vyrnwy
Llanfyllin
Llanymynech
Dolgellau
Barmouth
2927ft
Cader Idris
Mallwyd
Centre for Alternative Technology
Castell y Bere
Vyrnwy
Powis Castle
Welshpool
Llanfair Caereinion
Tywyn
Machynlleth
Carno
Montgomery
Cardigan Bay
Aberdyfi
Dovey
Dylife
Caersws
Severn
Newtown
Offa's Dyke
ENGLAND
2467ft
Plynlimon
Rheidol
Llanidloes
Aberystwyth
Llangurig
Cambrian Mountains
Devil's Bridge
Wye
POWYS
Knighton
Rhayader
Claerwen Reservoir
Elan Village
Radnor Forest
Aberaeron
CEREDIGION
Llandrindod Wells
Presteigne
New Quay
Tregaron
Newbridge on Wye
Temple Bar
Beulah
Aberporth
Lampeter
Builth Wells
Llangammarch Wells
Teifi
Llanwrtyd Wells
Erwood
Hay-on-Wye
Newcastle Emlyn
Llandovery
Talgarth
Sennybridge
Brecon
CARMARTHENSHIRE
Usk
Mountain Centre
Black Mountains
Llanthony Priory
Llandeilo
Brecon Beacons National Park
2907ft
Pen-y-Fan
Carmarthen
Towy
Carreg Cennen Castle
Tretower
Crickhowell
St. Clears
Dan-yr-Ogof Caves
Ystradfellte
Abergavenny
Pontyberem
Brynmawr
Big Pit: National Coal Museum
Monmouth
Laugharne
Ammanford
Tredegar
Ebbw Vale
Blaenavon
Raglan
Kidwelly
Merthyr Tydfil
MONMOUTHSHIRE
Burry Port
Llanelli
Pontarddulais
NEATH & PORT TALBOT
Aberdare
Abertillery
Tintern Abbey
Carmarthen Bay
M4
Mountain Ash
Bargoed
Usk
Gorseinon
Neath
RHONDDA CYNON TAFF
Pontypool
Cwmbran
Llanrhidian
Killay
Swansea
CAERPHILLY
Chepstow
Rhossili
Gower
SWANSEA
Pontypridd
Worms Head
Port Talbot
Caerphilly
Newport
Caldicot
Port Einon
Oxwich
Mumbles Head
Swansea Bay
Taff
Castell Coch
NEWPORT
BRIDGEND
Bridgend
CARDIFF
St. Fagans
Llandaff
Porthcawl
VALE OF GLAMORGAN
Severn
Llantwit Major
Barry
C
D
E

Transformation and Tourism

The once semi-derelict Cardiff docklands have been transformed into an extensive waterside development for work, leisure and residence. The coal-mining valleys have taken on new, lighter industry, some of it high-tech. Black spoil heaps and scummy reservoirs are being converted into green hillocks and lakes for recreational activities, and many of the former coal pits and blast furnaces are being turned into tourist attractions. The same is true of the abandoned slate mines in Snowdonia. And former industrial railroad lines are now used for leisure purposes, the diminutive steam locomotives hauling carriages filled with visitors.

In 1997, the Welsh voted to have their own National Assembly, located in the capital city of Cardiff. Initially it wielded only limited powers, but in 2011 the Welsh voted to extend these to create their own laws. This move toward autonomy reflects a new optimism in Wales. It is partly a brave and necessary response to adversity, but indicative as well of a strong feeling of nationalism that is also resurgent in Scotland.

Males of Wales

The macho ethic of heavy labor in the valleys of South Wales during the Victorian era contributed to two very Welsh cultural icons – the male voice choir and the no-holds-barred village rugby team.

The Welsh still love their rugby; a flood tide of men, women and children pours into the national stadium in Cardiff whenever Wales is playing at home, and each town in the valleys has its own fanatically supported team.

Male voice choirs, strongly influenced by the tradition of singing in chapel, could be heard from one valley to the next in their heyday in the 19th century. The echo of their unique sound still reverberates. Performances are advertized locally, and heavily attended; if you can get tickets, you will experience the power and emotion generated by dozens of male voices in multi-part harmony, from quiet as a whisper to exultantly loud.

Strong Traditions

Adversity historically came from centuries of skirmishing between the Welsh and English. Evidence of the tensions is still scattered thickly across Wales in the form of castles and fortifications. But despite the depredations of English oppressors from across the border, you can't keep a good man down, and the roots of indigenous Welsh culture have proved extremely deep and enduring. The Welsh language continued to live in the rural west; so did the tale-telling and the strong traditions of poetry, song and independent religious thought. Meanwhile, radical politics flourished in the hothouse atmosphere of the crowded, vigorous coal and steel towns of southern Wales. They spawned a

Low tide on the beach at Three Cliff's Bay on the Gower Peninsula, near Swansea

hard-working, hard-playing society of choral-singing, rugby-playing, beer-drinking masculinity, left wing in politics and nonconformist in religion.

As for the English castles, fortified towns and Offa's Dyke (a massive earth bank and trench dug along the border in the eighth century) – they remain part of the Welsh landscape, historic monuments to be explored for fun by visitors, but powerful reminders of a turbulent past.

Welsh Culture and Language

Today the Welsh language is in good health and widespread. It appears on every road sign and map, and you'll see it the moment you enter Wales, on the welcoming sign *Croeso i Cymru* (Welcome to Wales). Your enjoyment and appreciation of Wales will be greatly enhanced if you learn the meaning of the country's highly descriptive and poetic place names (see page 283).

In northern and central Wales you will frequently hear the language spoken, but English is understood everywhere.

The Welsh are famously musical, and the country has produced some well-known musicians, poets and actors. Singers, dancers, musicians, actors and writers all participate in eisteddfods – celebrations of culture – culminating in the National Eisteddfod, held each year in early August.

Seafood and Oatcakes

On the culinary front, Wales has some dishes all of its own. Roast lamb with mint sauce, served with leeks, is traditionally Welsh, but so are salmon, trout and shellfish. Try laverbread for breakfast (an oatmeal and seaweed cake, often served with a cooked breakfast); Welsh cakes for tea (flat dough pancakes with raisins); and Welsh rarebit for lunch (bread topped with grilled, crumbly Caerphilly cheese and beer).

Cardiff

Cardiff is a lively, friendly city with a variety of interesting architecture. There is a warren of intriguing Victorian shopping arcades in the center. The Edwardian-style Civic Centre in Cathays Park encompasses the National Museum Cardiff, City Hall, Law Courts and the University of Wales, a fine assemblage of neoclassical structures. Cardiff Castle, on the other hand, boasts one of Britain's truly eccentric interiors. Nearby rises the futuristic bulk of the Millennium Stadium, home to Wales' much-worshiped national rugby team as well as the football (soccer) team. Medieval Llandaff Cathedral contains some wonderful craftsmanship and artistry spanning eight centuries, while along Cardiff Bay innovative modern architects have let their imaginations run riot – to varied effect.

Mapping the City

Orientation in Cardiff is mostly a matter of north and south. The spine of the city center is the street that starts as St. Mary Street and changes to High Street as it runs north, throwing off famous

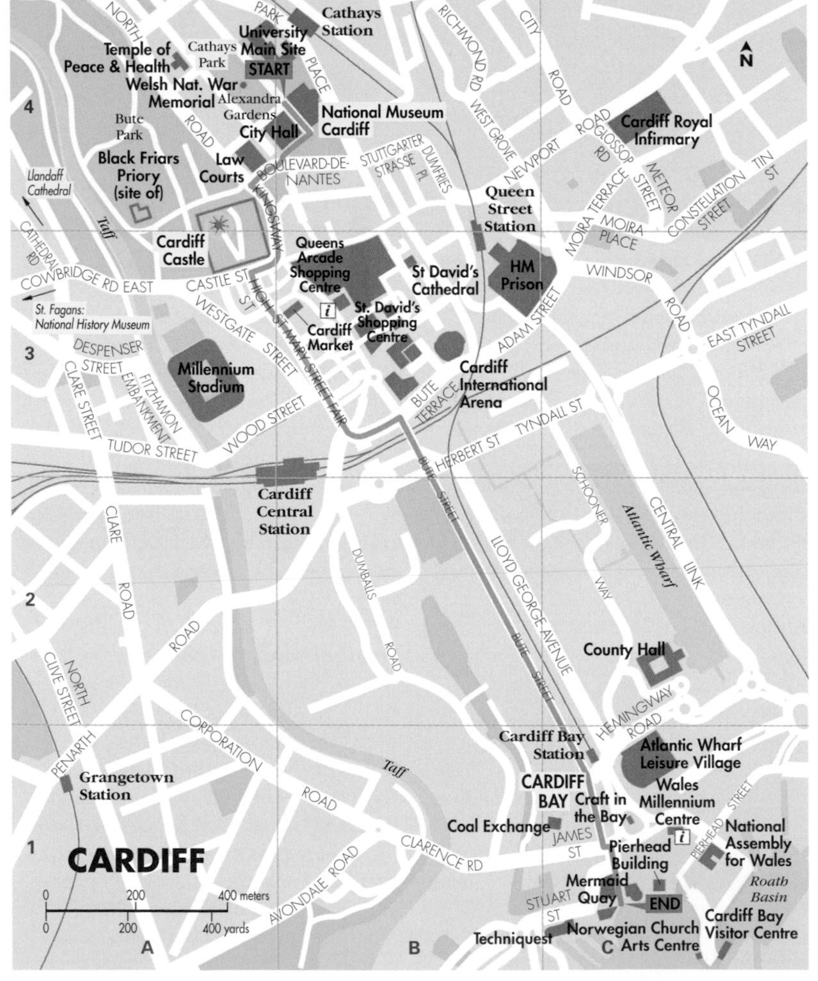

Cardiff's futuristic Millennium Centre hosts a range of music and arts events

Victorian shopping arcades left and right, until it reaches the gates of Cardiff Castle. Farther north is the Civic Centre, while Llandaff Cathedral is 2 miles northwest – a nice hour's stroll along the banks of the River Taff. The Millennium Stadium is a couple of blocks west of St. Mary Street.

Cardiff Cuisine

Cardiff has long been a cosmopolitan city with a wide range of ethnic cuisines. You can find anything from Thai to Japanese to classic French in or near the city center, with cheap curry houses toward Roath, just east of the center. Along the Cardiff Bay waterfront are plenty of trendy cafés and brasseries. Genuine Welsh cooking with regional ingredients is not hard to find. Try Welsh lamb or Welsh black beef, sewin (a delicious fish similar to salmon), Penclawdd cockles (small shellfish) from the Gower Peninsula in south Wales, or laverbread, made from seaweed. Cardiff-brewed Brains SA is a popular beer.

Arcades and Cafés

The main shopping district is right in the city center, a maze of pedestrian-only streets, Victorian and Edwardian arcades and brand-name shops. St. Mary Street/High Street forms its left flank; Duke Street/Queen Street is the northern boundary. The arcades are fun, narrow alleyways with high glass and cast-iron roofs; shops tend to be either frothy gift emporia or boutiques. The Royal Arcade is best for antiques, and the best cafés

Cardiff's Welsh Assembly Building

Welsh Pronunciation

If you're asking for directions in Wales, your one stumbling block could be in the pronunciation of place names.
Here are a few hints:
c is always hard, as in *c*ow
dd is th, as in *th*at
ch is similar to the Scottish lo*ch*
ll is similar to the Scottish lo*ch*, followed by an *l* sound
f is *v* as in *v*ole
s is *s*, never *z*
y at the end of a word is *ee* as in Mar*y*;
y elsewhere, or by itself, is *er* as in m*y*rtle
w, as a consonant, is *w* as in *w*ater
w, as a vowel, is *oo* as in b*oo*t or c*oo*k

and bars are in Castle Arcade. You can watch crafts being made, and then purchase them, at the bustling Victorian Cardiff Market, an indoor market (Monday to Saturday 8 a.m. to 5:30 p.m.) off High Street and at Craft in the Bay, a shop at the lower end of Bute Street. Welsh gold is always a good bet, as well as the traditional, intricately carved wooden lovespoons (see sidebar). At Jacob's Market you can buy period clothes, furniture and curios, and for food exotica, try the splendid Wally's, a Polish delicatessen in the Royal Arcade.

Lovespoons

Welsh arts and crafts traditionally rely on available natural materials (clay, wood, slate, wool and gold) and often reflect the country's traditions and folklore. The intricately designed wooden lovespoons are one of the best examples of this. Traditionally made from a single piece of wood, the entwined spoons are patterned with images from old myths and poems: keys, ships, dragons, hearts and flowers. The spoons originated in the 17th century and were made by young men as a gift for a sweetheart. If the spoon was accepted, it was a sign that an offer of marriage would be, too. In some places the tradition still lives on.

Sports and Singing

Cardiff's Millennium Stadium, with the first retractable roof in the U.K., hosts both international rugby and football (soccer) matches, where being surrounded by up to 74,500 ardent fans singing can be quite an experience. It was a venue for the 2012 Olympics, featuring football (soccer). You can enjoy Welsh singing in greater comfort at the Welsh National Opera in its home in the Wales Millennium Centre on Cardiff Bay, or by attending one of the stirring male voice choir performances frequently advertised around the city.

Essential Information

Tourist Information

Cardiff Visitor Centre ✉ The Old Library, The Hays ☎ 029 2087 3573; www.visitcardiff.com
Cardiff Bay Visitor Centre ✉ Wales Millennium Centre, Bute Place, Cardiff Bay ☎ 029 2087 7927; www.cardiffharbour.com

Urban Transportation

From Cardiff Central railroad station in Central Square, there are services to London Paddington (about 2 hours), and elsewhere. For reservations ☎ 0845 6061 660. Cardiff Bus Station is in Wood Street. Cardiff Bus (Bws Caerdyy) serves the city. There are frequent buses to the city and suburbs. Water taxis operate between the center and Cardiff Bay. Taxi stands are at rail and bus stations.

Airport Information

Cardiff International Airport is 12 miles west of the city at Rhoose. For information ☎ 01446 711111; www.tbicardiffairport.com. There is a direct train service (hourly) as well as Cardiff Bus Service X91 (every 2 hours daily) to central Cardiff. Taxis are expensive and line up outside the arrivals hall.

Climate – average highs and lows for the month

Jan.	Feb.	Mar.	Apr.	May	Jun.	Jul.	Aug.	Sep.	Oct.	Nov.	Dec.
7°C	7°C	9°C	12°C	15°C	18°C	20°C	20°C	17°C	13°C	10°C	8°C
45°F	45°F	48°F	54°F	59°F	64°F	68°F	68°F	63°F	55°F	50°F	46°F
3°C	2°C	3°C	4°C	7°C	10°C	12°C	12°C	11°C	8°C	5°C	4°C
37°F	36°F	37°F	39°F	45°F	50°F	54°F	54°F	52°F	46°F	41°F	39°F

Cardiff Sights

Key to symbols
map coordinates refer to the Cardiff map on page 158 admission charge: $$$ more than £6, $$ £2–£6, $ less than £2
See page 5 for complete key to symbols

Cardiff Bay

Modern housing developments, marinas and small businesses have sprouted all around the rejuvenated shoreline of Cardiff Bay. There are trendy wine bars and brasseries, waterfront walkways and high-tech museums such as Techniquest, a science discovery center incorporating a planetarium and excellent interactive displays. Atlantic Wharf and Mermaid Quay are "leisure villages," complete with movie theaters, bowling alleys and nightclubs. The Wales Millennium Centre hosts music and dance performances and is the home of the Welsh National Opera, while the Welsh government, the National Assembly for Wales (open to the public), is also here. This whole area lies about a mile south of the city center, at the foot of Bute Street, and is reached by that street or Lloyd George Avenue, a pleasant tree-lined boulevard, a 20-minute stroll from the city center.

Among the shiny new buildings around the bay are some interesting older ones; the Norwegian Church is an arts center converted from a weatherboarded church once used by Scandinavian seamen docked at Cardiff. The big redbrick and terra-cotta Pierhead Building on the Inner Harbour and the giant Coal Exchange (now used as an arts and entertainment center) tucked away in the heart of Butetown are monuments to Victorian pride and prosperity.

C1 Cardiff Bay Visitor Centre Wales Millenium Centre, Harbour Drive 029 2087 7927; www.visitcardiffbay.com Daily 10–6 Free

Cardiff Castle

An object lesson in what happens when a clever and dreamy 18-year-old inherits a lot of money and a whole castle to spend it on, Cardiff Castle's overblown Victorian Gothic grotesqueries will not be to everyone's taste. But this unique exercise in mock-medieval, over-the-top style is one of the highlights of any visit to Cardiff.

The 3rd Marquess of Bute was bright, brooding and fabulously rich through inherited coal and docks money. In 1867, while still a teenager, he commissioned the singular architect William Burges – not much over 4 feet

The rejuvenated Cardiff Bay area is a center for daytime and evening entertainment

A splendid staircase at Cardiff Castle

tall, and given to carrying a parrot on his shoulder – to "do up" the castle, already a mishmash of building styles spanning 800 years. Together the two men spent eight years letting their imaginations and the Marquess' money go.

The guided tour will take you through lavishly decorated suites, many of them cramped in size and exuding more than a whiff of claustrophobic paranoia. The Winter Smoking Room in the clock tower is painted with signs of the zodiac, the Labors of the Seasons, songbirds and satyrs, with a splendid black-faced devil leering down from the ceiling of the entrance lobby.

The Summer Smoking Room has a gold-painted gallery and a sumptuously inlaid floor. In the nursery, handpainted wall tiles depict fairy tales. There is a heavily Moorish "stalactite" ceiling in the Arab Room (decorated by imported Arab craftsmen with gold leaf, marble and lapis lazuli), and a beautiful wooden angel roof over the banqueting hall.

This genuine medieval hall was given the full Burges treatment, with a castle-like fireplace telling the story of King Stephen's struggle with his cousin Matilda in three-dimensional relief sculpture.

The Marquess' bedroom has a mirrored ceiling – "to reflect the beauty of the furnishings," grins the guide – and a unifying religious theme based around St. John (the 3rd Marquess also was named John). The blood-red dining room contains one nice human touch: unsophisticated but beautiful wood-carvings on the backs of the window shutters, executed by the 14-year-old son of Bute's master carver.

A stretch of the original Roman wall can be seen by the Black Tower on Castle Street, with modern three-dimensional murals providing a glimpse of everyday life in a Roman fort.

A4 Castle Street 029 2087 8100; www.cardiffcastle.com Daily 9–6, Mar.–Oct.; 9–5, rest of year (last tour 1 hour before closing); call ahead as times may change due to events Café $$$ Guided tours ($)

Cathays Park and the Civic Centre

The grand cluster of Edwardian civic buildings laid out in spacious style in Cathays Park, just north of the city center, is a monument to the aspirations of Cardiff around the turn of the 20th century, when the city's prosperity was at its height.

On the southern side of this great square of Portland stone buildings stand the Law Courts and the National Museum Cardiff (see page 163). They flank City Hall, which has an enormous clock tower, a sculptured exterior celebrating worldwide trade, and a Marble Hall full of statues of Welsh heroes.

The buildings of the University of Wales dominate the other sides of the park, with the Crown Buildings and the Temple of Peace and Health set between them. Within the square of buildings are

the Alexandra Gardens, with the National War Memorial at the center.
✚ A4 ✉ Cathays Park

Llandaff Cathedral

Half-hidden in a hollow in the quiet suburb of Llandaff, just two miles northwest of the city center, Llandaff Cathedral is a strikingly diverse building. It has undergone hard times in its 900 years of existence, including a long period of dereliction in the 17th and 18th centuries.

Oliver Cromwell's soldiers drank and gambled in the nave during the 1642–46 English Civil War, and John Wood (Georgian architect of the city of Bath) built a complete Italianate temple within its ruined walls in 1734. The cathedral was later lovingly restored by the Victorians. A German bomb shattered whole sections of the cathedral in 1941; the restoration was finally completed in 1960.

Drama grabs you as soon as you enter the west door, with Sir Jacob Epstein's elongated aluminum statue of *Christ in Majesty* floating on a bold, modern concrete arch at mid-nave level. Other notable highlights are medieval and Victorian stone carvings; Pre-Raphaelite stained-glass windows by William Morris, Edward Burne-Jones and Ford Madox Brown; and a painted triptych by Dante Gabriel Rossetti. Above the chancel arch a beautiful 1959 John Piper window and amazing round ornamental panel captivate with their rich, burning colors.
✚ A4 (off map) ✉ Cathedral Green, Llandaff ☎ 029 2056 4554; www.llandaffcathedral.org.uk 🕐 Daily 9–7 (check times online) 🚌 25, 33, 33A and 62 from Cardiff Central Bus Station ✋ Free (donation suggested)

National Museum Cardiff

Housed in a splendid Portland stone building on the south side of Cathays Park, these collections are divided between two floors. Downstairs is an absorbing "The Evolution of Wales" exhibition, with a good selection of animated prehistoric creatures and dinosaur skeletons. Here, too, is the Clore Discovery Centre where you can get your hands on some of the museum's exhibits.

Upstairs is the comprehensive archeology section, featuring examples of gold, bronze and stonework from Wales' deep and distant past, and an impressive collection of paintings and sculpture. The sculpture ranges from Rodin (a version of *The Kiss* cast in bronze) and Degas (a dancer gracefully balanced) to work by Barbara Hepworth and Henry Moore.

The National Museum Cardiff displays works by Gainsborough, J.M.W. Turner and Van Gogh

Paintings include classic 18th- and 19th-century landscapes and seascapes by painters such as Thomas Gainsborough, J.M.W. Turner and Wales' own Richard Wilson; Pre-Raphaelite scenes; and modern abstract art. A highlight is the collection of Impressionists – Monet's views of the Thames, Renoir's *La Parisienne*, Alfred Sisley's river views along the Seine, Cézanne in Provence – and a despairing *Rain – Auvers* by Vincent Van Gogh, painted shortly before his suicide.

B4 Cardiff Civic Centre, Cathays Park 029 2039 7951; www.museumwales.ac.uk Tue.–Sun. 10–5 Restaurant and café Free

St. Fagans: National History Museum

St. Fagans: National History Museum is set on the 100-acre grounds of St. Fagan's Castle, an Elizabethan manor house built on the site of a ruined Norman castle on the outskirts of Cardiff. The castle is worth exploring in its own right, as are its well-kept gardens. The museum's collection was started in 1946, when ordinary buildings redolent of Welsh life were being demolished all over Wales with little appreciation of their historic value. The museum opened two years later on July 1, 1948.

More than 40 buildings provide snapshots of life in Wales over the centuries. There are grand farmhouses furnished in Jacobean and Edwardian style, which contrast with the basic amenities of humble farm laborers' cottages. A severe Victorian school is the scene of many a mock-terrifying lesson re-enacted for young visitors by stern "schoolmistresses."

The tiny 18th-century chapel from northern Pembrokeshire evokes the stark simplicity of nonconformist religion in rural Wales. A tollhouse from 1772 once stood on the road to Aberystwyth. A particularly imaginative touch is shown in a row of ironworkers' houses from Merthyr Tydfil, in the valleys; each of the six cottages has been furnished in the style of a different decade between the early 19th century (open fires, no running water) and the late 20th century (electricity and plastic). A row of 19th-century shops displays the simple goods of those days: There's a bakery, which sells freshly made goods daily.

Costumed guides are on hand to get you into the mood of the "good old days." There are also a number of craft experts demonstrating coopering, clogmaking and other skills, and the workings of such small-scale industries as a corn-mill and a blacksmith's forge.

A3 (off map) St. Fagans, 4 miles west of city center 029 2057 3500; www.museumwales.ac.uk Daily 10–5 Restaurant and cafés 32 and 320 (at least hourly) from Cardiff Central Bus Station Free

A reconstructed house at St. Fagan's National History Museum

The restaurants of Mermaid Quay are just a short walk from Cardiff's city center

Walk:
Central Cardiff

Refer to route marked on city map on page 158

Cardiff's city center is compact, and you could see all the sights on this tour within an hour's stroll. It would be a two- to three-hour trip to walk through parks out to the cathedral at Llandaff. Cardiff Bay is a 20-minute stroll along Bute Street.

Starting among the grand civic buildings of Cathays Park (see page 162), cross the Boulevard de Nantes just south of City Hall to reach the Hilton Cardiff hotel. Continue along the sidewalk, with the walls of Cardiff Castle on your right.

A pedestrian crossing takes you over to the castle gates, and farther along Castle Street you'll reach a lodge from which footpaths lead through Bute Park and then through gardens and fields beside the River Taff to Llandaff Cathedral.

If you don't want to visit the castle and cathedral, turn left opposite the castle gates down High Street/St. Mary Street, detouring down any of the Victorian and Edwardian shopping arcades (mostly on your left). At the bottom of St. Mary Street turn left onto Custom House Street.

The so-called Café Quarter is on the left here, if you feel in need of a coffee stop.

Then it's a right turn onto Bute Street, which leads straight as an arrow to Cardiff Bay. At the foot of Bute Street you will emerge on the Inner Harbour beside the grand Pierhead Building, with Cardiff Bay spread right and left.

If you have done enough walking by now, a "bendy" number 8 or 9 bus will return you to the city center.

Conwy Castle is approached by Thomas Telford's suspension bridge

Conwy

Conwy stands on an estuary at the northern tip of Snowdonia National Park, a tiny town composed of medieval and later buildings drawn tight inside the protective circle of an astonishingly complete set of late 13th-century town walls. Even without the picturesque castle rising from the southeastern angle of the walls, Conwy would be breathtakingly attractive in its setting between mountains and sea.

In the cobbled Old Town, Plas Mawr is a superb Elizabethan mansion, and St. Mary's Church a pleasing jumble of architecture, part monastic.

You can walk a circuit of the walls and their regularly spaced guard towers before turning your attention to the castle, one of eight built after 1283 by King Edward I to form an "Iron Ring" around the mountainous retreats of the rebellious Welsh. The castle is massively built, with eight round towers forming vantage points around its walls. A walkway lets you look down into the interior of the roofless Great Hall, as well as the king's bedroom and drawing room. Some of the towers conceal dungeons, a chapel and a baking oven of suitable proportions to feed a hungry garrison. Children will love the high walkway, and the warren of hide-and-seek passages within the walls.

D5

Tourist information Rosehill Street 01492 577566; www.visitconwy.org.uk

Conwy Castle Castle Square 01492 592358; www.conwy.com Daily 9:30–6, Jul.–Aug.; 9:30–5, Mar.–Jun, Sep.–Oct; Mon.–Sat. 10–4, Sun. 11–4, rest of year. Last admission 1 hour before closing $$

Gower Peninsula

The Gower Peninsula, ragged-edged and irregular, protruding west from the underside of the South Wales coast, is one of Britain's special places – popular but seldom crowded, peaceful and blessed with a mild climate, green and pastoral. The coast has spectacular sandy beaches, particularly at Oxwich, where there is also a fine nature reserve, with trails through dunes and woods. Mumbles, in the southeast, is a nice old seaside resort.

At Rhossili Bay the Gower is at its most glorious, with 4 miles of beautiful sand, a spectacular cliff and ridge coastline, and the strange double-humped promontory of Worm's Head ("worm" is Norse for dragon). You can scramble along the promontory's causeway at low tide (it is covered at high tide) to a thrilling perch at the seaward tip among seabirds and wave spray.

C1

Swansea tourist information Plymouth Street, Swansea 01792 468321; www.visitswanseabay.com

Llangollen

Llangollen lies deep in the valley of the River Dee in northeastern Wales, a slate-roofed town beside a rushing river. It is renowned for the Llangollen International Musical Eisteddfod of music, dance and poetry, which takes place during the second week in July, attracting competitors from around the world. During the festival, performances are held at venues all over town, both indoors and out. The green slopes of the Berwyn Hills look down on Llangollen from the south. The dramatic limestone crags of Creigiau Eglwyseg (now there's a challenging Welsh pronunciation – "craig-ee-igh egg-loo-iss-egg") rise to the north, overlooking the ruins of Castell Dinas Brân, a 12th-century castle perched on a knoll.

Take a ride through the Dee valley on the steam-hauled Llangollen Railway, or on one of the horse-drawn barges that glide along the Llangollen Canal. And don't forget a visit to Plas Newydd, the house where the celebrated Ladies of Llangollen, the eccentric Lady Eleanor Butler and Sarah Ponsonby, lived their chosen life of "friendship, celibacy and the knitting of blue stockings." They lived here from 1780, transforming the cottage into a handsome house, and were visited by William Wordsworth, Sir Walter Scott, the Duke of Wellington and everyone who was anyone around the turn of the 19th century.

E4

Tourist information Y Capel, Castle Street 01978 860828; www.gonorthwales.co.uk

Plas Newydd Hill Street, Llangollen 01978 862834; www.denbighshire.gov.uk Wed.–Sun. and public holidays 10–5, Apr.–Oct. Café $$ Audio tours

A barge on Pontcysllte Aqueduct, Britain's highest and longest aqueduct, near Llangollen

Great Little Trains of Wales

Wales is a mecca for steam railroad enthusiasts, with more than a dozen lines operating. Many of these are narrow-gauge, using the trackbeds of long-abandoned industrial railroads. Among the best-known Welsh steam railways are:

- The Llangollen Railway (01978 860979)
- The Snowdon Mountain Railway, a rack-and-pinion railroad stretching from Llanberis to the summit of Wales' highest mountain (0844 493 8120)
- The 13-mile Ffestiniog Railway, a scenic former slate-quarrying line between Porthmadog and Blaenau Ffestiniog (01766 516000)
- The Vale of Rheidol Railway, 12 miles from Aberystwyth to Devil's Bridge (01970 625819)
- The Talyllyn Railway, a 27-inch gauge line traversing wonderful mountain scenery near Cader Idris (01654 710472)
- The tiny one-foot gauge Fairbourne Railway, connecting Fairbourne and Barmouth on opposite sides of the Mawddach Estuary with the help of a ferry (01341 250362)

Great Castles of Wales and the Borders

It was the Lords Marcher, powerful independent barons sent to control the Welsh shortly after the 1066 Norman Conquest of England, who initiated castle-building in Wales and along the Welsh border with England. Their first efforts were of wood, but as their power and confidence grew they began to build in stone. Some of these "private" castles were more like fortified houses than mighty strongholds. Many saw their final moments of action during the Civil War of 1642–46.

Typical is Hopton Castle near Knighton, some four miles from the English border, a crumbling stone keep on a diminutive mound in a field, peaceful yet poignant in its all-but-forgotten circumstances. Hopton had a most dramatic swan song, when a three-week siege by Royalist forces in 1644 ended in the capture of the castle and the slaughter of all but one of the 33-member Parliamentarian garrison. The captives were allegedly tied back to back in pairs and thrown in the moat to drown.

It is the great classic castles of Wales that draw visitors, however – and deservedly so, for these complex, cleverly designed mini-townships are truly fascinating places. They, like the smaller castles, are in varying states of repair; their condition mostly depends on what befell them during the English Civil War. Those that were held by supporters of the king, and had to be captured, were mostly "slighted" after the war – blown up or torn down to the point where they were considered sufficiently ruinous to be militarily useless.

A good example is Raglan Castle in Monmouthshire, built during the 15th and 16th centuries; another is sturdy Denbigh Castle, on the crest of a hill in northeast Wales, built at the end of the 13th century to exert further control over natives already crushed by the onslaught of King Edward I. In fact, the Welsh turned out to be not so crushed after all; the castle had not even been completed when they captured it (albeit briefly) in 1294. It was abandoned at the end of the English Civil War after holding out against a Parliamentary siege that lasted almost a year.

Many of the strongest stone castles were built by the barons during the uprisings earlier in the 13th century, before Edward I launched his decisive campaign. In this category falls Caerphilly Castle near Cardiff, a sprawling complex inside an enormous moat that was begun in 1268 in response to raids by Prince Llewellyn the Last. White Castle is another, a fortress built in the 1260s when Llewellyn allied himself with Earl Simon de Montfort in the Barons' Rebellion. White Castle's great curtain walls and drum towers are all the more impressive for its isolation in lonely country west of Monmouth. Chepstow Castle predates these two by a couple of centuries; it is the oldest stone-built castle in Britain, begun just after the Normans arrived. Its location on a clifftop perch near the mouth of the River Wye provided very visible proof of the powerful new order.

The most impressive of all the Welsh castles are those built under orders of King Edward I from 1283 onward to form the Iron Ring around western and northern strongholds in Wales. Eight were built, of which four are in excellent repair. Harlech, on Cardigan Bay, has 40-foot walls and a dominant position atop a crag; Conwy (see page 168) has a superb walkway circuit of its walls and a breathtaking backdrop of mountains. Caernarfon, on the Menai Strait, is the biggest and most impressive of them all, a grim and strong fort. Across the Menai Strait on the island of Anglesey is Beaumaris, the last of the Iron Ring to be built – strategically located, eye-catchingly symmetrical and brilliantly engineered to snuff out an attack from any quarter.

Beaumaris C5 ☎ 01248 810361; www.beaumaris.com

Caernarfon C5 ✉ Castle Ditch ☎ 01286 677617; www.caernarfon.com

Caerphilly D1 ☎ 029 2088 3143; www.visitcaerphilly.com

Chepstow E1 ✉ Bridge Street ☎ 01291 624065; www.chepstow.co.uk

Conwy D5 ✉ Rose Hill Street ☎ 01492 592358; www.conwy.co.uk

Harlech C4 ✉ Castle Square ☎ 01766 780552; www.harlech.com

Raglan E1 ☎ 01291 690228; www.raglanvillage.co.uk

Above left to right: Harlech Castle overlooks the hills of Snowdonia National Park; In 1969 Caernarfon Castle hosted the investiture of Prince Charles as Prince of Wales

Offa's Dyke

Offa, King of Mercia (a southern region of what is now England) between AD 757 and 796, had an uneasy relationship with the Welsh on the western border of his kingdom. He ordered the building of an 80-mile-long dyke (embankment) and ditch to delineate the boundary between the two peoples, and to keep the Welsh out. Situated on western-facing slopes and ridges, it was easily patroled. Offa's Dyke has survived for more than 1,200 years. Some sections are all but intact; others have been reduced to ground level. The actual border between England and Wales, although now a little farther east at the northern end of the dyke, largely follows its course, the two boundaries crossing and recrossing all along the Welsh Borders.

A 177-mile footpath, Offa's Dyke Path National Trail, was established along the course of the dyke in the early 1970s, linking the southern coast of Wales at Chepstow with the northern coast on the Dee Estuary at Prestatyn. In the course of its northward run the route encompasses the Wye Valley and Tintern Abbey; the Black Mountains and Llanthony Abbey; the beautiful tumbled country of the Herefordshire, Shropshire and Powys border counties; the towns of Knighton and Montgomery; the cliffs and bluffs of the Dee Valley at Llangollen; and the airy uplands of the Clwydian Hills.

The market town of Knighton, located at the halfway point along the route, is a good base from which to explore the area. The Offa's Dyke Centre there has informative interactive displays and friendly and helpful staff can supply visitors with maps, guidebooks, and details of the history and geography of the area.

E2–E3

Offa's Dyke Centre and Knighton Tourist Information Centre West Street, Knighton 01547 528753; www.offasdyke.demon.co.uk Daily 10–5, Apr.–Oct., (closes for 30 minutes at lunchtime); check website for opening hours for rest of year Free

Pistyll Rhaeadr Waterfall

Four miles northwest of the village of Llanrhaeadr-ym-Mochnant ("the church by the falls of the stream where the pigs are"), the River Disgynfa pours over a

Walking to the summit of Hay Bluff on Offa's Dyke Path in the Brecon Beacons National Park

Italianate-style buildings perch on a rockly ledge in the intriguing "village" of Portmeirion

rock lip in the eastern flank of the Berwyn Hills and crashes down in the most spectacular waterfall in Wales. Its upper stage is a straight tumble of more than 100 feet into a rock pool, from which it gushes out under an arch of rock to leap on down in spray and thunderous noise into a frothing pool at the foot of the fall. A footbridge near the bottom is a prime spot from which to view the full 240 feet of fall.

D4 4 miles from Waterfall Street, Llanrhaeadr-ym-Mochnant 01691 780392; www.pistyllrhaeadr.co.uk Daily, open access Restaurant Free

Portmeirion

Portmeirion is a bizarre place, reflecting its creator's sense of fun and love of the theatrical. It was after World War I that architect Clough Williams-Ellis began rescuing buildings in danger of demolition or decay and installing them on a peninsula between the rivers of Glaslyn and Dwyryd, in the northern part of Cardigan Bay. His idea was to prove that the beauty of man-made architecture could enhance rather than diminish the beauty of nature. Over the next half-century a strange, surrealistic little Italianate town took shape, with an architectural surprise around every street corner.

You enter Portmeirion through the Triumphal Arch to find more than 50 displaced buildings tightly huddled around a central square, or scattered along the hillside and shore. There's a telescopic-looking Italian bell tower, a splendid colonnade from a Georgian bath house in Bristol, temple furnishings from India and the Far East, a Jacobean town hall with Hercules featured in its ceiling, classical Greek columns, rococo plasterwork, and a hotel with a bar fitted out in Rajastani opulence.

You can rent a vacation cottage in Portmeirion itself, stay at the waterfront Hotel Portmeirione, or just come for the day to wander the streets and hillside gardens which are beautifully laid out with eucalyptus and cypress trees. You can enjoy a cup of tea and a Welsh cake at one of the cafés and browse the shops selling Portmeirion pottery.

C4 Minffordd, 2 miles east of Porthmadog 01766 770000; www.portmeirion-village.com Daily 9:30–7:30 Restaurants and cafés $$$

Tintern Abbey fell victim to Henry VIII's Dissolution of the Monasteries in September 1536

Drive: The Southern Borders

Distance: 150 miles

You will dip in and out of Wales and England during this drive through the southernmost Welsh Borders: up the Wye Valley and across to Raglan Castle; on through the Brecon Beacons; and skirting the Black Mountains to descend to the gentle landscape of the "Golden Valley."

Begin the drive in Chepstow.

This is an old river port where the River Wye flows down to meet the River Severn under the high walls of Chepstow Castle. The castle contains some of the earliest Norman stonework in Britain.

Follow A466 up the thickly wooded Wye Valley, with England on the east bank and Wales on the west, to Tintern.

Here you will find one of the glories of monastic architecture, the roofless but still magnificent ruins of Tintern Abbey. The tall east, west and south windows frame beautiful woodland views.

From Tintern take the side road to the left, marked "Raglan," and follow the lanes past Star Hill and Llansoy to cross over the A449 highway to reach Raglan.

Visit Raglan's ruined castle (see page 170).

Head west along A40, turning left just before Abergavenny to continue west on A465.

To the left are a series of once-industrial valleys. The Big Pit: National Coal Museum at Blaenavon allows visitors to experience mining conditions 300 feet below ground.

A465 skirts the northern edge of the former mining town of Merthyr Tydfil, then A470 heads north through the heart of Brecon Beacons National Park.

These hills are not quite mountains, but they are certainly impressive – particularly the summits of Cribyn, Corn Du and Pen y Fan (at 2,907 feet the highest summit in southern Wales). To climb all three, start by way of the minor road to Pontsticill and the Neuadd Reservoir, which climbs north from the intersection of A465 and A470 just northwest of Merthyr Tydfil. Up at the reservoir parking lot you'll have conifers, hills and water for company; it's a beautiful, silent place.

Stay on A470 north to Brecon.

This pleasant market town with its Georgian architecture is home to the South Wales Borderers Museum.

Proceed northeast on A470/A438 to Talgarth. Leave Talgarth on A4078 for 1 mile, then bear right to Hay-on-Wye.

Literary Hay-on-Wye is famous for its secondhand books and many book stores. Spring 2012 saw the 25th anniversary of the world renowned Hay Festival of Literature and the Arts.

B4348 curves east and then southeast from Hay-on-Wye, to descend the "Golden Valley" of the River Dore.

Here there is a string of medieval churches: St. Peter's at Peterchurch, St. Bartholomew's at Vowchurch and Dore Abbey at Abbey Dore.

At the village of Pontrilas you reach A465. For a diversion, turn left toward Hereford and proceed for 3 miles, then turn right at Wormbridge to reach Kilpeck village.

The 12th-century Church of St. Mary and St. David at Kilpeck contains the most expressive church sculpture in Britain. The south doorway is embellished with dragons, huntsmen and other patterns, and a corbel table is carved with the personification of sins.

Backtrack to Pontrilas and take the B4347 past Grosmont Castle and Rockfield to Monmouth, before returning to Chepstow.

Chepstow E1

Tourist information Castle Car Park, Bridge Street 01291 623772; www.visitwyevalley.com

Chepstow Castle Bridge Street, Chepstow 01291 624065; www.chepstow.co.uk Daily 9:30–6, Jun.–Sep.; 9:30–5, Oct. and Apr.–May; Mon.–Sat. 9:30–4, Sun. 11–4, rest of year. Last admission 30 minutes before closing $$

Tintern Abbey E1 Tintern 01291 689251; www.cadw.wales.gov.uk Daily 9:30–-6, Jul.–Aug.; 9:30–5, Mar.–Jun., Sep.; Mon.–Sat. 10–4, Sun. 11–4, rest of year $$

Big Pit: National Coal Museum E1 Blaenavon, Torfaen 01495 790311; www.museumwales.ac.uk Daily 9:30–5 (underground tours 10–3) Restaurant Free

South Wales Borderers Museum D2 The Barracks, Brecon 01874 613310 Mon.–Fri. 10–5, Sat. 10–4, mid-Apr. to Sep. Free

Hay-on-Wye E2

Tourist information Oxford Road 01497 820144; www.hay-on-wye.co.uk

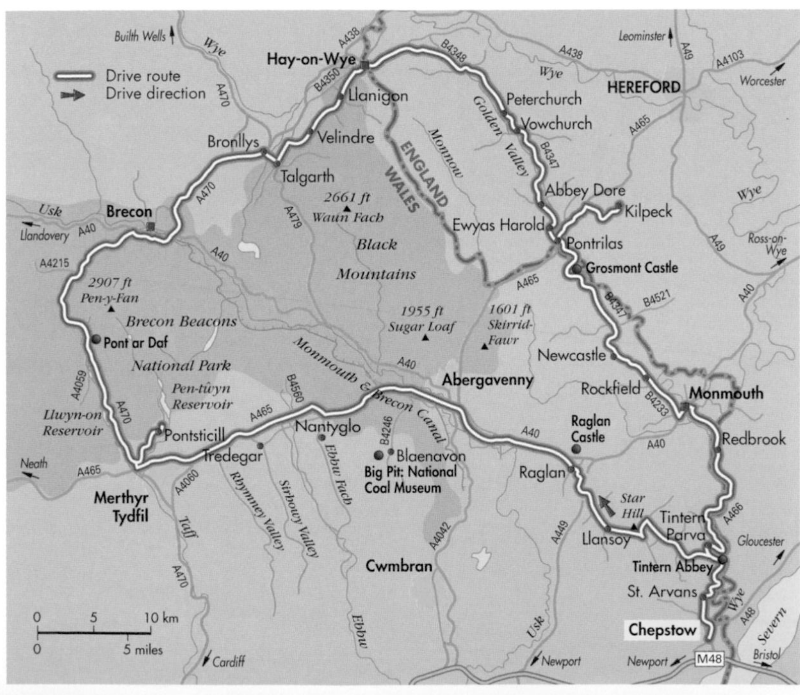

Snowdon Horseshoe from Llyn-y-Mymbyr in Snowdonia National Park

St. David's and Pembrokeshire Coast National Park

St. David's is Britain's smallest city. No larger than a village, it is the ecclesiastical center of Wales, and as such it was officially granted city status in 1995. The squat but beautiful cathedral lies half-buried in a hollow alongside the ruins of a 14th-century bishop's palace. Inside the cathedral, the shrine to Wales' patron saint is always decorated with fresh flowers, and music recitals and concerts are sometimes played here.

The city itself is a charming place to stroll around; there are plenty of tearooms, cafés, shops and art galleries. The enchanting setting attracts many artists, and you will find local pottery, weaving and wood-carvings for sale.

St. David's is within Pembrokeshire Coast National Park, 225 square miles of beautiful and unspoiled coastline encompassing the southwest tip of Wales. The Pembrokeshire Coastal Path traces the ins and outs of this coast for nearly 200 miles, through seaside towns as charming as Tenby and Fishguard and pretty villages such as Manorbier and Little Haven, or you can explore it via the Puffin coastal bus services.

St. David's A2

Pembrokeshire Coast National Park Visitor Centre The Grove, St. David's 01437 720392; www.pcnpa.org.uk

Tenby B1

Tourist information Unit 2, Upper Park Road 01834 842404; www.visitpembrokeshire.com

Snowdonia National Park

The most impressive mountain scenery south of the Scottish Highlands is found in Snowdonia National Park – 840 square miles of high country, lakes, mountains, dramatic valleys and coastline that fill the northwest corner of Wales.

The pride of the region is Snowdon, at 3,560 feet the tallest mountain in England and Wales. You can ascend Snowdon from the town of Llanberis the lazy way, aboard the steam-hauled rack-and-pinion Snowdon Mountain Railway; or you can climb it in three to four hours by one of six routes.

Snowdonia's main industry these days is tourism, but a century ago it was slate quarrying. Many of these gloomy caverns are open to the public. At Llechwedd Slate Caverns in Blaenau Ffestiniog, you can try your hand at the art of splitting slate. From Blaenau Ffestiniog the steam trains of the Ffestiniog Railway descend for 13 twisty and dramatic miles to the coast at Porthmadog, only a couple of miles from Portmeirion (see page 173).

Llanberis C5

Tourist information 41B High Street 01286 870765; www.llanberis.org

Betws-y-Coed D5

Tourist information Royal Oak Stables 01690 710426; www.eryri-npa.gov.uk

Llechwedd Slate Caverns C4 Crimea Pass, **Blaenau Ffestiniog** 01766 830306 Tours daily 10:15–5:15, Mar.–Sep.; 10:15–4:15, rest of year Café; pub (Mar.–Sep. only) $$$

Market Towns

A drive northward through the central Welsh Borders from Hay-on-Wye up to Welshpool reveals a string of charming market towns in the heartland of this pastoral but wild region, so attractive to the visitor who loves landscape, legend and history intertwined.

Hay-on-Wye (see page 175) is famous for its secondhand bookstores, which have proliferated since the so-called "King of Hay," Richard Booth, established a business in Hay Castle more than 30 years ago. The town also hosts the hugely successful Hay Festival of Literature and the Arts from the end of May to early June.

North of Hay the border leaves the broad River Wye and snakes through the tighter little valleys of the River Arrow. Around Gladestry it enters a landscape filled with history, from the ancient standing stones and hill forts around Old Radnor to the broad back of Hergest Ridge. Under shelter of the ridge are two notable houses: Hergest Croft, with beautiful gardens painstakingly tended by three generations of the Banks family; and medieval Hergest Court, whose erstwhile owner, wicked Black Vaughan, is said to haunt the area in the guise of a hellish black dog.

Black Vaughan was beheaded in 1469 after suffering defeat at the Battle of Banbury during the Wars of the Roses. But legend maintains that he continued to roam the Borders in ghostly form. It was in St. Andrew's Church at nearby Presteigne – so the stories say – that 13 clergymen gathered to exorcise the troublesome spirit. The clerics managed to shut him in a snuffbox for 100 years, but he eventually escaped.

Presteigne itself is an agreeable little town with Edwardian wood-and-glass fronts to its stores and a fine old beamed coaching inn, the Radnorshire Arms.

Knighton, to the north, has steep streets with antiques shops and tearooms, a clock tower, and a former school converted into the Offa's Dyke Centre and Knighton Tourist Information Centre (see page 172).

North of Knighton the border bulges westward, bequeathing a wide swath of lonely uplands to England. Offa's Dyke twists and turns toward Welshpool, the site of stunning Powis Castle. This charming market town has held a Monday livestock market for more than 500 years. It also has an ornate Victorian railroad station and a canal-side wharf. The steam-hauled Welshpool and Llanfair Light Railway makes an 8-mile jaunt from here to the friendly village of Llanfair Caereinion.

Hay-on-Wye is best known for its annual literary festival

Northern England

Opposite: The attractive village of Muker in the Yorkshire Dales

Northern England

There are many preconceptions about the north of England. To many an English southerner, the idea of the north is still bound up with images that were true of large parts of this region a couple of generations ago, but have since become obsolete. Slate-roofed rows of redbrick workers' houses, vast textile mills, great factories with tall factory chimneys pumping out smoke, and coal mines and spoil heaps, shipyards and steelworks – all can be attributed to the manmade ugliness and environmental degradation of heavy industry bequeathed to the north by the Industrial Revolution of the 18th and 19th centuries. And the no-nonsense character attributed to "The Northerner" – bluff, honest, blunt but neighborly, impatient with frills and courtesies – is fixed in the southerner's mind as well. Indeed, some northerners are happy to foster this "plain but proud" image.

If Britain is in part a divided society, it is less along class lines these days than along this north–south fault line, illusory though it may be.

The Modern North

It is certainly true that the heavy industries of the north gave rise to the prosperity on which Britain's Georgian and Victorian feats of empire-building were founded. It is true, too, that industry blighted sizable chunks of England between Liverpool and Leeds, and around the coalfields of South Yorkshire and County Durham. Any traveler with an eye for industrial architecture will have a field day in the north. But times have moved on in a very big way. The palls of smoke and grime that used to overhang the region's

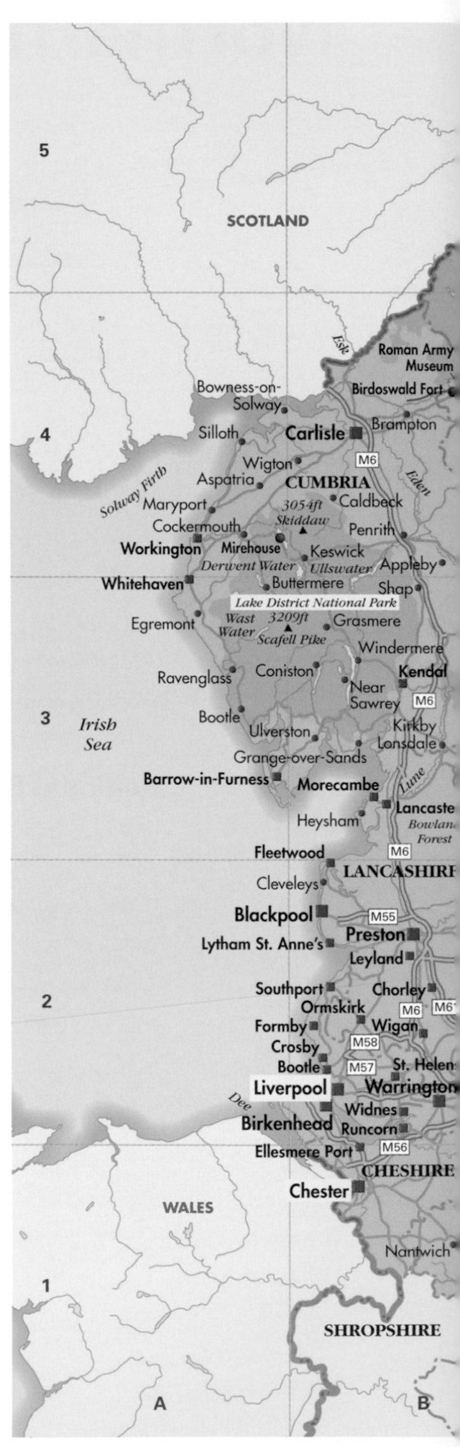

Berwick-upon-Tweed
Holy Island
Lindisfarne Castle
Farne Islands
Etal
Bamburgh
Bamburgh Castle
Ford
Seahouses
Wooler
Dunstanburgh Castle
Craster
2677ft
The Cheviot
Aln
Alnwick
Coquet
Warkworth
Rothbury
NORTHUMBERLAND
Northumberland National Park
Morpeth
Newbiggin-by-the-Sea
Hadrian's Wall
Blyth
Housesteads Fort
Chesters Fort
Ponteland
Whitley Bay
Vindolanda
Corbridge
Newcastle upon Tyne
Hexham
Tyne
Gateshead
Beamish Museum
Sunderland
Washington
Alston
Derwent Reservoir
Consett
Chester-le-Street
Durham
Peterlee
Stanhope
A1(M)
Hartlepool
Wear
DURHAM
Bishop Auckland
Middleton-in-Teesdale
Sedgefield
Middlesbrough
Newton Aycliffe
Barnard Castle
Staithes
Stockton-on-Tees
Tees
Darlington
Bowes
Whitby
Scotch Corner
Stokesley
North York Moors National Park
Robin Hood's Bay
Kirkby Stephen
Swale
Richmond
Goathland
Northallerton
Sedbergh
Leyburn
Rievaulx Abbey
Hutton-le-Hole
Scarborough
Bedale
Thirsk
Helmsley
Rye
Pickering
Filey
Yorkshire Dales National Park
Masham
2310ft
Great Whernside
2274ft
Pen-y-Ghent
NORTH YORKSHIRE
Staxton
Malton
Ripon
Ure
Flamborough Head
Castle Howard
Bridlington
Fountains Abbey
Boroughbridge
Settle
Malham
Grassington
Knaresborough
Stamford Bridge
Driffield
Skipsea
Harrogate
A1(M)
YORK
Pocklington
Skipton
Wharfe
Wetherby
Ouse
Derwent
EAST RIDING OF YORKSHIRE
Hornsea
Ribble
Otley
Keighley
Harewood House
Beverley
Haworth
Shipley
Burnley
Bradford
Leeds
Selby
Howden
Kingston upon Hull
M65
Accrington
South Cave
Withernsea
Blackburn
Halifax
Dewsbury
Castleford
Goole
Hessle
M62
Humber
Pontefract
Easington
Rochdale
M62
Huddersfield
Wakefield
Thorne
N LINCS
Spurn Head
M66
M1
Barnsley
Bolton
Holmfirth
A1(M)
M18
Oldham
Doncaster
Salford
Manchester
Chapeltown
Rotherham
Sale
Peak District National Park
Stockport
Sheffield
Cheadle
Castleton
Retford
Trent
LINCOLNSHIRE
Worksop
Macclesfield
Chatsworth House
Buxton
Chesterfield
M1
Sherwood Forest Visitor Centre
Middlewich
Arbor Low
Haddon Hall
Ollerton
Congleton
DERBYS
Mansfield
Crewe
Hardwick Hall
Southwell
Kidsgrove
Matlock
Sherwood Forest
Newark-on-Trent
Hucknall
Ashbourne
Nottingham
Derby
NOTTS
Long Eaton
STAFFORDSHIRE
NORFOLK
LEICESTERSHIRE
The Pennines
North Sea
0 10 20 30 40 km
0 10 20 miles
C
D
E

Bamburgh Castle, once the seat of the kings of Northumbria, rises out of a gray day

cities are long gone. Steelmaking, coal mining, textile manufacturing and shipbuilding are either gone or on their way out, swept aside by foreign competition or use of modern technology. The sprawling urban areas – Liverpool, Leeds, Bradford, Manchester, Newcastle upon Tyne – take pride in their industrial heritage and are turning it to their advantage, creating hands-on museums that tell the stories of their once-great industries. Visitors may arrive somewhat skeptical, but they leave fascinated.

Mountains and Castles

Parts of the north have never been industrial – hills, moors, valleys and coasts – which make up some of Britain's finest landscapes. There are the mini-mountains of the Lake District, the rugged glories of the Peak District, the Yorkshire Dales and the North York Moors, the lonely Pennine hills and the wild uplands of Northumberland. There are fewer crowds in the north and more space for those who like to explore.

The cultural and architectural delights of the north are wide-ranging, from the huge temples of commerce – factories, warehouses, mills – of Liverpool and Manchester to the great ruined abbey churches of Yorkshire (Fountains Abbey, Rievaulx, Whitby, Bolton Abbey) and the splendid cathedrals of York Minster, Durham and Beverley Minster.

There are famous residences to visit – country mansions such as Burton Agnes Hall and Castle Howard in Yorkshire, and Northumbrian castles like those at Bamburgh, Dunstanburgh and Warkworth. The museums in this part of the country are also excellent. Beamish Museum in County Durham

is the best of its kind in Britain, a fascinating open-air reconstruction of community life as it was in the northeast of England from the 1800s until the early 20th century. Two very different annual events take place in this region, too: Early April sees the Grand National steeplechase at Aintree racetrack, near Liverpool, while York hosts the JORVIK Viking Festival every February, complete with a "long ships" race, folk dancing and Viking feasts.

Regional Flavors

As you travel through the northern counties, you'll encounter subtle differences in accents and dialects and a (usually) friendly rivalry between the regions. Different cities and counties boast their own brands of beer and ales, and there are distinct local dishes. Cumberland sausages are delicious, accompanied by mashed potatoes and gravy. For tea, try a piece of rich fruit cake with some crumbly white Wensleydale or Cheshire cheese, or a Derbyshire Bakewell pudding (jam pastry with an almond-flavor filling). Yorkshire's most famous lunch is roast beef and Yorkshire pudding, served with hot horseradish sauce – a meal that you will see on pub menu boards across Britain, especially on a Sunday. This is also the county where Harry Ramsden set up his first fish-and-chip "restaurant," an innovation for an everyday dish that had traditionally been served as a takeout in a paper wrapper. Today there is a chain of Harry Ramsden restaurants across the country.

Many northern cities – particularly Leeds, Bradford and Manchester, with their strong Asian communities – have excellent Indian restaurants and takeouts. Mild chicken curry was supposedly invented in Bradford to cater to those unfamiliar with spicy foods, and curry has now overtaken fish and chips as Britain's premier takeout. However, a curry takeout is really for taking to your own kitchen, where you can assemble the components of the meal (rice, meat and sauce, naan bread, etc.) on a plate. For impromptu refueling on park benches, stick to fish and chips. Enjoy your curry in an Indian restaurant – usually inexpensive and tasty.

Take Your Time

Probably the best way to get into the heart and spirit of the north is to spend a few relaxing days wandering – on foot in the Peak District or along the Pennine Way; by train along the wonderfully scenic Settle–Carlisle Railway through the heart of the Pennines; or by car along the back roads and country lanes of the Yorkshire Dales or the Northumbrian hills.

Don't forget to stop at a pub or two to savor some locally brewed beer and engage in conversation. Northerners are famously friendly: That part of the cliché, at any rate, is true.

York

York is the best-known small city in northern England, and one of Britain's premier sights. It draws flocks of visitors, and it's easy to see why – the magnificent York Minster, the largest Gothic building in northern Europe, is second to none, and the 2.5 miles of almost complete medieval walls that encircle York are some of the finest of their kind anywhere in Britain.

A two-hour-long stroll around the walls and their four great fortified gates, or "bars," – Boothham Bar, Micklegate Bar, Monk Bar and Walmgate Bar – is one of Europe's classic town walks (see pages 190–191). The city is laid out along a photogenic tangle of medieval streets with enchanting names – Goodramgate, The Stonebow, Whip-ma-whop-ma-gate – which are attractively lined with houses ancient and not quite so ancient. Everything within the walled city, including a large number of excellent museums and some beautiful medieval churches, is within a 10-minute stroll of the center.

Leadership Confirmed

York stands on one of the main through routes between England and Scotland, and as such has been an important stronghold and center for trade since the Romans first established their garrison town of Eboracum here in AD 71. Through its Saxon incarnation as Eoforwic, and later a Danish phase as Jorvik, the town prospered. The Normans built two castles here, and the fortified circle of city walls was added and improved upon in later centuries. With the building of the great Minster cathedral (see page 187–188), York confirmed its spiritual as well as its military and commercial leadership. Later, in Georgian times, York became a fashionable inland resort for northerners just as Bath did for southerners. In the Victorian era the city

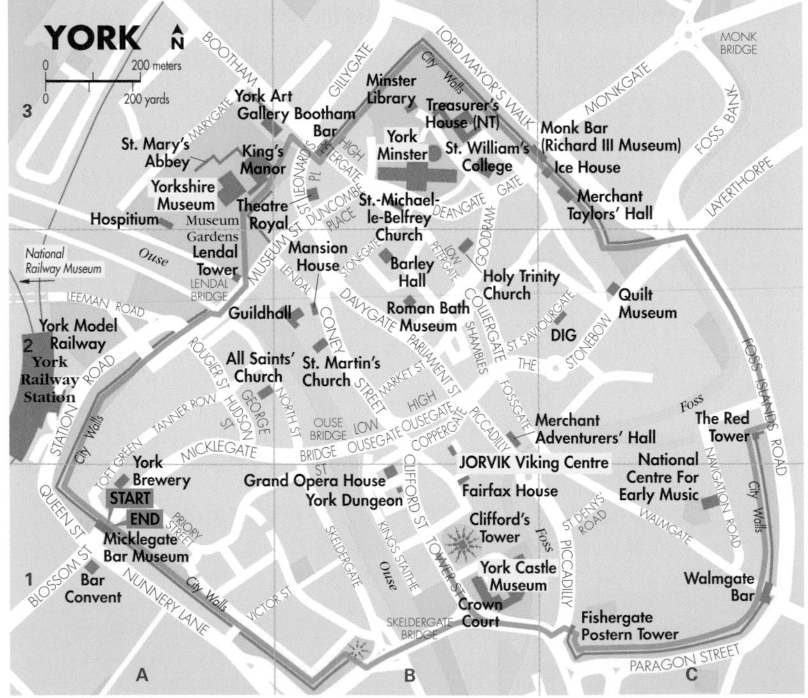

Some parts of the Merchant Adventurers' House in central York date back to the 14th century

was the base for the powerful North-Eastern Railway company. Nowadays tourism keeps the money flowing through the coffers of this ancient city.

Traffic-Free Center

The city center is a vehicle-free zone. If you arrive by car, you will find parking lots only sporadically interspersed along the medieval walls. It is advisable, however, to use one of the "park and ride" parking lots on the approach roads (well marked by signs). From there, an inexpensive bus will take you right into the center. The train station is just outside the western angle of the city walls, while most buses start from just inside on Rougier Street – both a 10-minute walk from the center.

The old city can be crossed on foot in 20 minutes. With its narrow, crooked streets, it is ideal for exploring on foot. Getting your bearings can be a problem at first because of the confusing tangle of those streets. The city walls form a diamond shape, with the Minster within the northern angle, the York Castle Museum within the southern angle and JORVIK Viking Centre on a straight line between these two points. Davygate, Parliament Street and Piccadilly progress north to south through the center; Micklegate, Bridge Street, Low Ousegate, High Ousegate, Pavement, The Stonebow and Peaseholme Green progress roughly west to east.

The River Ouse flows through the city from Lendal Bridge, at the northwestern section of the walls, to Skeldergate Bridge in the southern part. If in doubt, you can always find north by looking for

The Yorkshire Pass

Once purchased, the Yorkshire Pass allows free entry for one, two, three or six days into more than 70 tourist attractions, plus a range of discounts around York. It is available from the York Visitor Centre (see page 186) or online at www.yorkshirepass.com.

Rise and Fall

Two famous men in York's history, both avid gamblers who rode their luck to wild success and then to downfall, were Dick Turpin and George Hudson.

Turpin, a butcher's apprentice from London, had a notoriously productive career as a highway robber in the 1730s. Eventually he fled to York, where he was arrested for the minor crime of shooting a pheasant. Then his previous crimes came to light. Turpin was hanged in York on April 7, 1739, and took five long minutes to die.

George Hudson, the "Railway King," became a towering figure in York as Lord Mayor and also as the immensely rich boss of a giant railroad empire in early Victorian days. The crash, prompted by Hudson's dodgy business dealings, came in 1849, and he found himself a broken pauper in the city's prison.

the towering Minster. A good way to explore the city is on a free two-hour guided walking tour (daily at 10:15; also 2:15, Apr.–Oct., and 6:45, Jun.–Aug.) or on an open-top guided bus tour – both depart from Exhibition Square.

Eating and Drinking

Walking around York will make you hungry and thirsty, two states of mind and body well catered to in the city center. There are plenty of restaurants along Micklegate and Goodramgate, as well as dozens of pubs for a snack and a drink. Try the Kings Arms on Kings Staithe, near the Ouse Bridge in the center, where you can sit outside and watch the river.

York's own York Brewery (12 Toft Green; Mon.–Sat. tours at 12:30, 2, 3:30 and 5; also Sun., May–Sep.) produces a tasty bitter beer. For traditional afternoon tea, try Bettys Café Tea Rooms, on St. Helen's Square at the top of Davygate, or Little Bettys, just around the corner in Stonegate.

Essential Information

Tourist Information

De Grey Rooms, Exhibition Square
01904 550099; www.visityork.org

Urban Transportation

York's main railroad station is on Station Road. For rail information and reservations, contact the 24-hour national inquiry line (08457 484950). Most buses converge on Rougier Street; information line 01904 551400. The main taxi stand is outside the railroad station.

Visitors can obtain transportation information from the York Visitor Information Centres.

Airport Information

Leeds/Bradford International Airport (0871 288 2288; www.leedsbradfordairport. co.uk) is 11 miles northwest of Leeds. A regular bus service connects to Leeds City rail station. Manchester International Airport (0871 271 0711; www.manchesterairport.co.uk), 56 miles southwest, has a train service to York.

Climate – average highs and lows for the month

Jan.	Feb.	Mar.	Apr.	May	Jun.	Jul.	Aug.	Sep.	Oct.	Nov.	Dec.
6°C	7°C	9°C	13°C	16°C	19°C	21°C	20°C	18°C	14°C	9°C	7°C
43°F	45°F	48°F	55°F	61°F	66°F	70°F	68°F	64°F	57°F	48°F	45°F
0°C	1°C	2°C	4°C	7°C	10°C	12°C	11°C	10°C	7°C	4°C	2°C
32°F	34°F	36°F	39°F	45°F	50°F	54°F	52°F	50°F	45°F	39°F	36°F

York Sights

Key to symbols
map coordinates refer to the York map on page 184 admission charge: $$$ more than £6, $$ £2–£6, $ less than £2
See page 5 for complete key to symbols

The Shambles Area

The Saxons called them "shamel," and medieval Englishmen "shambles" – the word meant slaughterhouses, places that in most towns were confined to one bloody and stinking quarter. The Shambles of York, at the heart of the city, is no longer a scene of dung and death. Far from it: This is York's most picturesque and photogenic street, where crazily bent and leaning timbered houses jut their upper stories so far over the flagstoned sidewalk that occupants could almost shake hands across the roadway. Today antiques emporia and bookstores fill the first floors of the old butchers' shops, but fixed in the beams above you can still see the hooks from which carcasses of meat were hung.

From The Shambles, the narrow streets of York spread out along their haphazard medieval layout. Here the suffix "gate," legacy of ninth-century Danish settlers, means a street; a snickelway, or snicket, is an even narrower alley. Such is Whip-ma-whop-ma-gate, a snickelway off Fossgate, southeast of The Shambles. Farther along Fossgate stands the 14th-century Merchant Adventurers' Hall, a cavernous structure 40 feet wide under a really magnificent timber roof. The wool dealers, known as Merchant Adventurers, formed York's most influential guild during the Middle Ages, and this superb building, reflects their prosperity.

Colliergate runs northwest from Fossgate toward the Minster, soon meeting Goodramgate. Here stands Holy Trinity Church, its 14th-century pillars and 18th-century box pews leaning this way and that. Next to the church is a

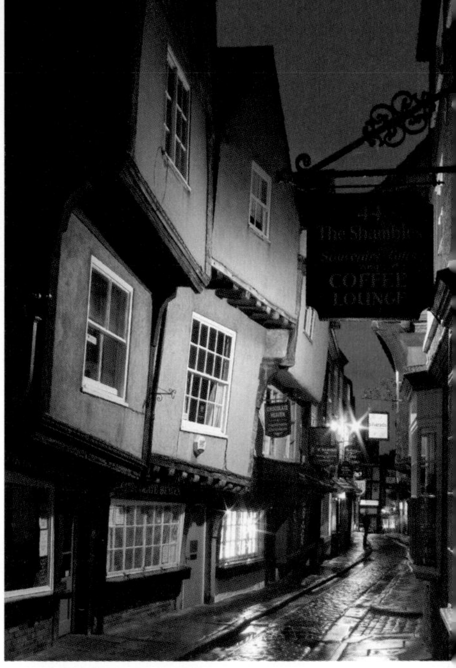

The Shambles after an evening rain shower

little row of early medieval houses, Our Lady's Row – built in 1316, they are York's oldest dwellings. A little west of Goodramgate runs Stonegate, built along the course of one of the roads laid out by the Romans in their garrison town. Look up outside No. 33 to spot the red-skinned, horned devil chained by his waist to a wooden post, some medieval carver's little joke.

B2
Merchant Adventurers' Hall Fossgate
01904 654818; www.theyorkcompany.co.uk
Mon.–Thu. 9–5, Fri.–Sat. 9–3:30, Sun. 11–4, Easter–Sep.; Mon.–Fri. 9–4, Sat 9–3:30, rest of year
$$ Audio tour (free)

York Minster

This magnificent cathedral, the largest medieval Gothic church in northern Europe, dominates York from its position in the northern angle of the city walls. It seems that from every vantage point in town you catch a glimpse of its great square central tower and rocket-like west towers, soaring high above roofs and walls. By sheer bulk and length – 534 feet – it draws the eye, yet the whole effect is light and graceful.

Take binoculars inside to appreciate the beauty and fine workmanship on display. York Minster was begun in 1220 and took 252 years to complete, so the mixture of architectural and aesthetic styles is fascinating. The 100-foot-high nave and the octagonal Chapter House are full of carvings on roof bosses and the capitals of the slender pillars. Those in the Chapter House include funny beasts (one is of a monkey making a ridiculous face) and even funnier grotesques of Church figures.

The choir screen, carved in 1461 at the end of the long construction process, shows English kings from William I to Henry VI with wild hair and luxuriant beards. Downstairs in the undercroft, treasury and crypt you can see the sturdy columns and vaulting that upheld the Norman cathedral that predated the Minster.

The glory of this church, though, is in its stained-glass windows, a collection unmatched in Britain for size, color and antiquity. In the great west window, 54 feet tall, the 14th-century glass is held in delicate stonework tracing the form of a heart. The north transept's window, made in 1260 shortly after work started on the building, contains more than 100,000 pieces of grisaille (gray- and green-tinted) glass of great although muted beauty. The south transept holds a beautiful Tudor rose window in glowing reds and blues.

The magnificent great east window is the size of a tennis court (78 feet by 31 feet). Between 1405 and 1408 it was installed with the largest display of medieval stained glass in the world – the stories of creation and doomsday depicted in glorious color and intricate detail. It is a superb spectacle of art.

B3 Minster Yard 0844 939 0011 (0844 939 0016 information Sat.–Sun.); www.yorkminster.org Minster: Mon.–Sat. 9–5:30, Sun. noon–3:45. Undercroft, Treasury and Crypt: Mon.–Sat. 9:45–5, Sun. 12:45–5. Tower: Mon.–Sat. 9:45–5, Sun. 12:30–5, Apr.–Oct.; Mon.–Sat. 10–30 minutes before dusk, Sun. 12:45–30 minutes before dusk, rest of year Restaurant in adjacent St. William's College Minster $$$ (including undercroft, treasury and crypt); Tower $$ Guided tours (Mon.–Sat., free); audio tours

Don't miss the carved limestone cloisters on a tour of York Minster

Museums of York

York is particularly well endowed with excellent museums, and you could happily spend hours in them. Four of the best are:

JORVIK Viking Centre

York's most popular museum offers an enjoyable glimpse into everyday life in Viking York some 1,000 years ago. You travel on a "time-car" through tableaux complete with appropriate sounds and smells – wattle huts, dirty streets, cooking smoke, animals and children everywhere.

JORVIK Viking Centre B2 Coppergate 01904 615505; www.jorvik-viking-centre.co.uk
Daily 10–5, Apr.–Oct.; 10–4, rest of year $$$ (ticket valid for 1 year)

Yorkshire Museum

The Crucifixion scene beautifully etched in the gold of the 15th-century Middleham Jewel is only one of the archeological treasures here. Also on display are Roman mosaics, carvings and artifacts, Viking silver bowls and fossils from the Yorkshire coast.

Yorkshire Museum A3 Museum Gardens 01904 687687; www.yorkshiremuseum.org.uk
Daily 10–5 $$$ (ticket valid for 1 year)

York Castle Museum

Here are reconstructed Victorian streets, shops and houses, agricultural work and crafts, and archeological finds, including the best-preserved Anglo-Saxon helmet in the country. A wide-ranging collection of everyday domestic objects is housed in the former debtors' and women's Prisons.

York Castle Museum B1 Eye of York 01904 687687; www.yorkcastlemuseum.org.uk
Daily 9:30–5 Café $$$ (ticket valid for 1 year)

National Railway Museum

The largest railroad museum in the world, this is a guaranteed delight for all. More than 60 juggernauts of steam loom large amid all the posters, models and memorabilia. Here you may be able to see the *Mallard* (although sometimes it is on loan), the holder of the world speed record for steam locomotives – 126 mph, set in 1938 and as yet unbroken.

You can also see a working replica of George Stephenson's 1829 Rocket; the world's most famous steam locomotive, the *Flying Scotsman* (currently under restoration); and the only Bullet Train (Shinkansen) outside Japan.

National Railway Museum A2 (off map) Leeman Road 08448 153139; www.nrm.org.uk
Daily 10–6 Restaurants Free (charge for special events) Audio guides (charge)

Displays of domestic Victoriana in the York Castle Museum

Walk:
The Walls of York

Refer to route marked on city map on page 184

The 2.5-mile circuit of the medieval city walls of York is fascinating, not just for the historical interest of the walls themselves, but also for the stunning views they offer across the tight huddle of medieval streets within their orbit.

The walkway is even underfoot, but there are some steep flights of steps to negotiate and unguarded drops of up to 20 feet at many points inside the walls. The walls form a rough diamond shape, with York Minster at the top or northern angle, and York Castle toward the bottom or southern angle. They are pierced with four great medieval "bars," or gates, from which roads radiate out to other points of the compass.

Start at Micklegate Bar, on the southwestern side of the diamond.

Micklegate Bar is flanked by two tall 14th-century drum towers on Norman foundations. In the days of robust punishments the severed heads of traitors would be displayed on spikes on the top of the bar as a grisly example to others; it is now a museum (☎ 01904 634436 🕒 Daily 10–4, Apr.–Sep.; 11–3, Oct.–Nov., Feb.–Mar. $$).

From here turn north along the raised walkway inside the ramparts of the wall.

These city walls follow much the same shape as the walls built by the Romans around their city of Eboracum, but they are considerably stronger, a forbidding girdle of stone built on the orders of King Edward III to protect the medieval city from attacks by the then-insurgent Scots. From Lendal Bridge there is a great view ahead to York Minster. Beyond the river the original walls disappear. A pleasant stroll through the Museum Gardens leads to the Multangular Tower, which stands on a Roman base next to the arches of the ruined St. Mary's Abbey. The abbey was founded around 1080, and Benedictine monks left from here to found Fountains Abbey (see page 208).

Rejoin the wall at Bootham Bar and continue above the lovely green parkland of the gardens behind York Minster, with the giant towers and walls of the Minster standing majestically on your right.

Your perspective of the church will change almost 180 degrees between Bootham Bar on the west and Monk Bar on the east. Monk Bar displays dummy soldiers at the parapets of its twin flanking towers; it houses the Richard III

Museum (☎ 01904 634191 ⌚ Daily 9–8, mid-Jul. to mid-Oct., 9–5 Mar. to mid-Jul.; 9:30–4, rest of year ✋ $$). From here you walk in a southeasterly direction, looking inward across the jumbled roofs of medieval York and outward to the domed roof of the city's Ice House. Built around 1800, it held tons of ice collected each winter and insulated in straw until needed. Beyond the Ice House the walls disappear again. Here you find the River Foss, and the King's Fishpool, a small lake created for William the Conqueror.

A short stretch of road reaches a brick-built Tudor watchtower, the Red Tower, where the wall reappears to take you on to Walmgate Bar.

Walmgate is the only bar to retain its barbican, or defensive courtyard – the others were pulled down in the 1820s and '30s. The bar contains a Calvary Chapel with a café that is open to visitors. Next comes the tall outlook tower of Fishergate Postern, and then York Castle, next to the moody-looking Clifford's Tower, a 13th-century stronghold atop a knoll (☎ 01904 646940 ⌚ Daily 10–6, Apr.–Sep.; 10–5 in Oct.; 10–4, rest of year ✋ $$).

From the tower it is a short stroll back to Micklegate Bar.

There are excellent views from Walmgate Bar, one of the higher points on the medieval city walls

Regional Sights

Key to symbols
map coordinates refer to the Northern England map on pages 180–181 admission charge: $$$ more than £6, $$ £2–£6, $ less than £2
See page 5 for complete key to symbols

Beamish Museum

This is a vast, living and working experience of life as it was in northeast England in the 1800s and early 1900s. Set in 300 acres of beautiful countryside, a typical early 20th-century town has been re-created, made up of houses, a general supplies store, candy shop, pub, bank, a printer's shop, dentist's office, lawyer's office, tavern, garage, carriage house and a Masonic temple. A colliery (coal) village of the same period is also here, including a terrace row of miners' houses complete with outside toilets ("netties"). You can tour the mine with guides who have themselves worked in coal mines. There's also a working farm and a manor house dating from 1825. Beamish boasts its own railroad with steam engines and carriages, and a tramway with restored, running trams.

C4
Beamish, County Durham 0191 370 4000; www.beamish.org.uk Daily 10–5, Easter–Oct.; Tue.–Thu. and Sat.–Sun. 10–4, rest of year (parts of museum closed). Last admission at 3 Cafés
$$$ (admission reduced early Nov.–Easter)

Castle Howard

This Palladian mansion near York was built between 1699 and 1712 by then untried architect Sir John Vanbrugh (with the help of Nicholas Hawksmoor, a pupil of Sir Christopher Wren). It was commissioned by Charles Howard, the 3rd Earl of Carlisle; his descendants still live in the east wing. There is a giant north facade topped by a cupola, which forms the roof for the enormous great hall. The grounds contain a lake as well as an array of follies and fancies: obelisks and towers; the Temple of the Four Winds, with four porticoes; and the circular Howard family mausoleum.

D3
Malton, 15 miles northeast of York 01653 648444; www.castlehoward.co.uk House: daily 11–4, end Mar.–Nov. 1 and Nov. 26–Dec. 18. Garden: daily 10–5:30, Apr.–Oct.; 10–4, rest of year; shops and café daily 10–4 Restaurant and cafés $$$ (gardens only $$); shops and café only free

Above: Castle Howard is still occupied by the family of the 3rd Earl of Carlisle who commissioned it
Opposite: The Brontë Way is a bleak walk through heathland on Haworth Moor

Chatsworth House is set on a beautiful landscaped park of 1,000 acres

Chatsworth House

By far the finest house in the Peak District National Park, Chatsworth, a classic baroque mansion near the town of Bakewell, was built between 1687 and 1707 for the 1st Duke of Devonshire. Impressive Palladian facades look to all quarters of the compass, but it is the west front and its imposing giant pediment that dominates the long driveway approach.

In the state rooms hang paintings by Anthony van Dyck, Rembrandt and Frans Hals. There are richly frescoed ceilings by Louis Laguerre and Antonio Verrio, and a clever *trompe l'oeil* fiddle painted by Jan Van der Vaart as if hanging on the back of a door. You can see grand table settings as once laid for King George V and Queen Mary in the great dining room. The library contains around 17,000 books.

The 1,000-acre park was landscaped by "Capability" Brown in the 1760s. Nearer at hand are superb formal gardens with beautiful water features. Joseph Paxton, who designed the Crystal Palace in London for the Great Exhibition of 1851, was head gardener here; his 1848 "Conservative Wall," a line of iron-framed greenhouses, flourishes.

C1

Near Bakewell, Derbyshire 01246 565300; www.chatsworth.org Daily 11–5:30 (house closes at 5:30), mid-Mar. to late Dec. Last admission 1 hour before closing Restaurants and cafés $$$ (garden only $$); Park free

Chester

Chester, capital of Cheshire, is a small city perfect for strolling around, with carved medieval woodwork adorning its buildings. Walk along the medieval walls to get an overview of the city or take one of the themed guided walking tours arranged by the tourist office. Be sure to see the partly excavated Roman Amphitheatre and the Dewa Roman Experience to discover what life was like in Roman Chester. Also visit Chester Cathedral, with its Norman decorations.

The medieval Rows is a galleried arcade of enticing shops, while Watergate Street has plenty of antiques shops. Stop for afternoon tea at Katie's (a real Old World tea shop), or enjoy a lunch served in the 13th-century monks' dining room in the cathedral refectory.

B1

Tourist information Town Hall Square, Northgate Street 0845 647 7868; www.visitchester.com

Roman Amphitheatre Vicar's Lane 0870 3331181; www.english-heritage.org.uk Daily 24 hours Free

Dewa Roman Experience 1–2 Pierpoint Lane, off Bridge Street 01244 343407; www.dewaromanexperience.org.uk Mon.–Sat. 9–5, Sun. 10–5, Feb.–Nov.; daily 10–4, Dec.–Jan. $$

Haworth and the Brontës

Visiting the Brontë Parsonage Museum at the top of Haworth's steep, Church Street, it is hard to imagine the currents of creation that swirled through this plain gritstone West Yorkshire house in the 1830s and '40s. But it was here that Charlotte, Emily and Anne Brontë wrote their childhood chronicles of the imaginary lands of Angria and Gondal. Then, in 1847, each published a first novel that would immortalize their names: Charlotte's *Jane Eyre*, Emily's *Wuthering Heights* and Anne's *Agnes Grey*.

The Parsonage Museum contains a priceless archive of Brontë papers, as well as items of memorabilia such as Charlotte's dress, a bracelet of Anne's hair and a watercolor by Emily of her dog, along with amateurish portraits by their brother Branwell, a sad victim of alcohol abuse and consumption (tuberculosis). Emily and Anne also died of consumption within two years of publishing their books. Charlotte outlived them by a few years, but died in 1855 at the age of 38.

To see where so much of the sisters' inspiration came from, you should step out across the wild moors that roll west of the village. From the cobbled lane outside the parsonage, a paved path marked "Haworth Moor" crosses a field to join West Lane through a narrow stone stile. After about 130 feet, fork left and follow the road beneath a slab of rock engraved "Penistone Hill Country Park." Cross the Stanbury-to-Oxenhope road. Step over a metal grid designed to prevent cattle from straying and follow a lane marked "Brontë Waterfalls." This was a favorite place of the sisters – the water tumbles down under a stone clapper bridge known as Brontë Bridge, overlooked by the Brontë chair, a rock with a natural seat shape. West of here is a ruined farmhouse that gave Emily Brontë the inspiration for Heathcliff's dour dwelling, Wuthering Heights. Ask at the tourist office for directions or for a map of the area.

You can travel to Haworth by steam train aboard the Keighley and Worth Valley Railway. The 5-mile route runs between Keighley and Oxenhope.

C2

Tourist information 2–4 West Lane, Haworth 01535 642329; www.visitbradford.com/bronte-country

Brontë Parsonage Museum Church Street, Haworth 01535 642323; www.bronte.org.uk Daily 10–5:30, Apr.–Sep.; 11–5, rest of year $$$

Keighley and Worth Valley Railway 01535 645214; www.kwvr.co.uk Railway Station, Haworth Schedules vary; call for details Buffet car (Sat.–Sun.) $$$

Haworth Moor, close to Top Withins on the Pennine Way

Durham

On a high bluff over the River Wear stand Durham's cathedral and castle, commanding the slate roofs below in lofty grandeur. There are splendid views of both from many places around Durham. All reinforce the impregnability of the site, a steep-sided peninsula caught in a tight loop of the Wear. Durham Cathedral is the finest and most handsomely situated Norman building in Britain. Combined with the castle, it radiates magnificence and a sense of defiance, fitting for an ensemble that Sir Walter Scott memorably described as "half church of God, half castle 'gainst the Scot."

The city's modest size and the region's recent history of workaday heavy industry might lead one to wonder why such a grand cathedral was built here. One reason was the turbulence of northern England after the Norman Conquest. In an effort to bring order into the region, the king granted the "Prince Bishops" of Durham almost unlimited powers, which were wielded freely and ruthlessly all through the Middle Ages.

The Prince Bishops controlled the garrison at Durham Castle to such effect that the city was never captured, and peace of a kind lay over this volatile corner of northeast England. They also minted their own money, made their own laws and built a cathedral to trumpet forth their power and prestige.

Most of Durham's sights are on or near the short peninsula on which the cathedral and castle stand. The cathedral looms over Palace Green, on the spine of the peninsula. Begun in 1093, it was built in classic Norman style. The nave is flanked by immensely sturdy, squat round pillars, their surfaces incised with wide chevrons and dogtooth patterns. Some arches are rounded in true Norman fashion; others are pointed, reflecting the changes in building style that took place before the completion of the cathedral in 1274. The choir reaches high, its aisle roofs ribbed in stone. Everything here is bulky, massive and built to last forever. In contrast are the two elegantly beautiful chapels located at either end of the building.

At the east end in the Chapel of the Nine Altars lies St. Cuthbert, hermit and reluctant bishop, who died in AD 687. His well-preserved body was brought here three centuries later by disciples from the island of Lindisfarne, off the Northumbrian coast (see page 205). In the delicately carved and constructed 12th-century Galilee Chapel at the west end is buried the Venerable Bede, a learned monk who wrote Cuthbert's life story.

In the Cathedral Treasury you can see, among many treasures from the cathedral's long life, the bejeweled pectoral cross that St. Cuthbert wore

The square Norman towers of Durham Cathedral rise steeply above the River Wear

when he was buried, and the wooden coffin in which he was first interred. There are some superbly decorated manuscripts, and curators hope that the Lindisfarne Gospels – exquisitely illuminated gospels dating from St. Cuthbert's time and presently housed in the British Library in London – will some day find a permanent home here.

The castle is worth a tour for the beautiful woodwork in its Tudor chapel, a fine 17th-century staircase, and the ancient kitchen with fireplaces big enough to roast an entire ox. The old streets around the castle and cathedral, packed with shops, pubs and cafés, are also as fascinating to explore.

On the east bank of the river below the cathedral, Durham University's excellent Museum of Archaeology is housed in an attractive medieval mill. From here you can either walk around the peninsula on a gentle riverside footpath or take a river cruise or rowboat ride from Elvet Bridge and enjoy the memorable views of the cathedral and castle from the water.

C4

Tourist information 2 Millennium Place 0191 384 3720; www.durhamcathedral.co.uk

Durham Cathedral Palace Green 0191 386 4266 Mon.–Sat., 7:30 a.m.–8 p.m., Sun. 7:45 a.m.–8 p.m., mid-Jul. to late Aug.; Mon.–Sat. 7:30–6, Sun. 7:45–5:30, rest of year. Treasury: Mon.–Sat. 10–4:30, Sun. 2–4:30 (4:15 Dec.–Jan.) Restaurant Free (donation suggested); Treasury $$ Guided tours, Mon.–Sat., Easter–early Nov. ($$)

Museum of Archaeology Old Fulling Mill, The Banks 0191 334 1823 Daily 11–4, Apr.–Oct.; Fri.–Mon. 11:30–3:30, rest of year $

Hadrian's Wall

Hadrian's Wall was built across the neck of northernmost England from AD 120 on the orders of the Roman Emperor Hadrian to mark the northern limit of the Roman Empire. Originally it stood some 20 feet high, with observation and signal turrets spread evenly along its 73-mile length. A garrisoned fort, or "milecastle," was located at the point of every Roman mile. The wall ran from the North Sea at Wallsend in the east to the Solway Firth in the west.

For 1,500 years after the Romans left Britain, Hadrian's Wall was seen only as a source of ready-shaped building stone. Now it has been restored and is treated with the respect it deserves.

You can walk its full length along the 84-mile-long National Trail, or explore the individual excavated forts and associated museums at various points: Chesters, Housesteads, Vindolanda and Birdoswald. The Hadrian's Wall Country Bus (No. AD122; daily Apr.–Oct.; call 01434 322002 for times) links each of the sites.

B4–C4

Tourist information B4 Railway Station, Station Road, Haltwhistle, Northumberland 01434 322002; www.hadrians-wall.org

Housesteads Roman Fort C4 Haydon Bridge, Hexham 01434 344363 Daily 10–6, Apr.–Sep.; 10–4, Oct.; Sat.–Sun. 10–4, rest of year $$

Hardwick Hall

Second only to Chatsworth House (see page 194) among Peak District houses, 16th-century Hardwick Hall in eastern Derbyshire is a fine Elizabethan mansion set in well-wooded and rolling parkland. "Hardwick Hall, more glass than wall," so the saying goes, is a reference to the house's large windows.

The real fascination about Hardwick Hall is the story of the remarkable woman who had it built between 1591 and 1597. Elizabeth Hardwick,

The 84-mile Hadrian's Wall Path stretches from coast to coast and follows the route of Hadrian's Wall

The Settle–Carlisle Railway

The Settle–Carlisle Railway, which opened in 1875, is England's most spectacular and exciting line. The building of the 72-mile track through the inhospitable moorlands and uplands of the Pennines was dangerous work, costing the lives of dozens of workers. The 24-arch Ribblehead Viaduct, north of Horton-in-Ribblesdale, is a triumph of Victorian engineering. The trip takes an hour and 40 minutes; there are regular daily scheduled trips as well as occasional steam-hauled trains, or you can drive the byroads that follow the line. The pleasant towns of Settle, Kirkby Stephen and Appleby each have stations and make good bases from which to explore the Pennine hills.

B3–B4

Train stations Settle and Carlisle

08457 484950; www.settle-carlisle.co.uk

Daily (call or consult website for time)

Cafés at stations and buffet car on some trains $$$

Countess of Shrewsbury – better known as "Bess of Hardwick" – possessed a will fully as strong as her sovereign, Queen Elizabeth I.

Having hauled herself up from humble origins through a series of advantageous marriages, including to her last husband, the Earl of Shrewsbury, Bess commissioned the building of Hardwick Hall. Her initials, E.S. (Elizabeth Shrewsbury), appear in stonework, woodwork and tapestries all over the house. Tapestries embroidered by Bess and her staff hang in nearly every room, making them claustrophobically dark. Portraits of her reveal an imperious stature.

C1

Doe Lea, near Chesterfield, Derbyshire

01246 850430; www.nationaltrust.org.uk

Hall: Wed.–Sun. noon–4:30, mid-Feb. to Oct.; Sat.–Sun. 11–3 in Dec. Old Hall: Wed.–Sun. 10–5, Apr.–Oct. Garden: Wed.–Sun. 11–5, mid-Feb. to Oct.; Sat.–Sun. 11–3 in Dec. Restaurant $$$ (garden only $$)

Harrogate

As a spa town, Harrogate appeared very late on the scene. It was not until the late Victorian era that this pleasant gray-stone town in central Yorkshire had its heyday.

Sufferers and pleasure-seekers alike flocked to taste the waters in the Pump Room, to lie and sweat in a Turkish bath at the Royal Baths, and to dance and flirt at social parties in the Assembly Rooms. The healing springs were discovered in 1571 on The Stray, a big, grassy common located south of the town center.

Almost 100 additional springs were unearthed over the following centuries. Strolling on The Stray or in Valley Gardens west of the town center, you can see the temple-like structures erected over these well heads over the years.

These days the Royal Pump Room houses a museum with exhibits depicting Harrogate's healing past, as well as a water fountain that will deliver a glass full of eggy, sulfurous water guaranteed to sort out any troubles in your digestive system – if you can drink it.

Harrogate is a great strolling town with a wealth of Victorian architecture. You can also take a Turkish bath in the Royal Baths building or just continue a pleasurable piling on of the pounds with afternoon tea at elegant Bettys Café Tea Rooms on Parliament Street, which serves irresistible local bakery goodies.

C3

Tourist information Royal Baths, Crescent Road 0845 389 3223; www.harrogate.gov.uk

Royal Pump Room Museum Crown Place 01423 556188 Mon.–Sat. 10–5, Sun. 2–5 (noon–5 in Aug.), Apr.–Oct.; Mon.–Sat. 10–4, Sun. 2–4, rest of year $$

Turkish Baths and Health Spa Royal Baths, Parliament Street 01423 556746 Mon.–Tue. and Fri. 9:30–9, Wed. 10–9, Thu. 1–9, Sat.–Sun. 9–8:30 Café $$$ Guided tours Wed. ($$)

Bettys Café Tea Rooms 1 Parliament Street 01423 814070; www.bettys.co.uk Daily 9–9

Fall colors in Little Langdale in the Lake District National Park in Cumbria

Lake District

The tight little circle of the Lake District, England's best-known mountainous landscape, measures only about 30 miles from side to side as the crow flies. It contains nearly 200 fells (the local word for high hills or small mountains) that top 2,000 feet, but only four over 3,000 feet. These are statistics that instantly give you an idea of the lay of the land – a tumbled, undulating mass of fells pressed close together, with deep dales (valleys) between them. Lakes, long and thin, are scattered in the dales; tarns (small lakes) lie in hollows of the upper fells. None of the fells has the majesty of a full-blown Alpine mountain, but they have something better – intense individual character, so that visitors return again and again.

This is prime walking country, from the cultivated grazing fields of the dale bottoms to the wild moorland that clothes the upper slopes of the fells. Farming hamlets and individual farms of gray stone are sprinkled throughout the district, and there are several villages – Ambleside, Grasmere, Hawkshead – as well as a couple of well-appointed small towns, Windermere and Keswick. These places are thoroughly prepared to welcome visitors who want to explore the fells and dales that surround them. In Ambleside in the south and Keswick in the north you can buy all the gear, footwear, clothing and maps that you will need to get out and about on foot. And you'll certainly see Kendal Mint Cake for sale – a very sweet, strongly flavored mint candy, the perfect energy-booster for walkers.

Windermere in the southeast is the largest and longest lake, with the very popular town of the same name on its east bank. On the opposite side of the

Walking in the Lake District

Common-sense walking rules apply; the fells are not dangerous places, but you should treat them – and the rapidly changeable weather – with respect. Find out the local weather forecast (☎ 0844 846 2444), and equip yourself properly with weatherproof clothes and boots. Take food and a hot drink, a compass and a map. Tell someone your planned route and stick to it.

The best guides are still the seven pocket-size books in the *Pictorial Guide to the Lakeland Fells* series by master fellwalker Alfred Wainwright – hand-drawn and written, bossy but knowledgeable, and reliable.

lake is Near Sawrey, where Beatrix Potter lived from 1905 to 1913. Here she wrote and illustrated *Tom Kitten*, *Jemima Puddle Duck* and other much-loved children's tales. Just north is Hawkshead, where William Wordsworth attended grammar school, and where you will find the Beatrix Potter Gallery.

The shadow of Wordsworth lies long over Grasmere (northwest of Ambleside), where England's great Romantic poet came to live in 1800. You can look around Dove Cottage, where he began his Lake District sojourn with sister Dorothy, and Rydal Mount, where he lived toward the end of his life, before paying your respects at his grave in St. Oswald's churchyard.

Helvellyn, 3,116 feet high and one of the Lake District's best-known fells, is north of Grasmere. Farther northwest is Cockermouth, where Wordsworth was born in 1770 – his birthplace, Wordsworth House and Garden, is a museum. It is south of Keswick that the main excitements of the Lake District await you. The steep and narrow B5289 road that loops southward through Borrowdale brings you to the feet of the highest fells – Bow Fell, Great Gable, Scafell Pike – and the high passes that connect them. Farther on are Buttermere and Crummock Water, heavenly twin lakes framed by fells of great beauty.

In the southwestern section of the Lake District are the wild and lonely valleys of Wasdale, with its dark lake, and rugged Eskdale, where the steam-hauled Ravenglass and Eskdale Railway runs down to the coast.

A3–B3

Lake District Visitor Centre at Brockhole B3 Brockhole, Windermere 015394 46601; www.brockhole.co.uk Daily 10–5, Apr.–Oct.; 10–4, rest of year. Gardens and grounds: daily dawn–dusk all year Café Free

Beatrix Potter Gallery B3 Main Street, Hawkshead 015394 36355; www.nationaltrust. org.uk Sat.–Thu. 10:30–5, mid-May to early Sep.; 11–5, Apr. to mid-May, Sep.–Oct.; 11–3:30, mid-Feb. to Mar. $$

Dove Cottage, the Wordsworth Museum and Art Gallery B3 On A591, Grasmere 015394 35544; www.wordsworth.org.uk Daily 9:30–5:30, Mar.–Oct.; 9:30–4:30, rest of year. Last admission 30 minutes before closing Restaurant and café $$$ Guided and audio tours

Wordsworth House and Garden A4 Main Street, Cockermouth 01900 820884; www.wordsworthhouse.org.uk Sat.–Thu. 11–5, mid-Mar. to Oct. Last admission 1 hour before closing Cafés nearby $$$

Dove Cottage, near Grasmere, was once the home of poet William Wordsworth

Leeds

The city of Leeds reached the peak of its prosperity during the height of the 19th-century wool trade, and the wealth of that era is evident in the Victorian civic buildings that grace the city center. The grand, colonnaded facade of the Town Hall dominates the Headrow; inside, ornate Victoria Hall plays host to classical music concerts. The neighboring Leeds Art Gallery has a good selection of 19th- and 20th-century British art, including some curvaceous Henry Moore sculptures, while the Royal Armouries, once displayed in the Tower of London, have been rehoused in an excellent museum.

Leeds is home to the eminent Opera North company, and offers a choice of restaurants and some excellent shopping. The prestigious London department store Harvey Nichols has a branch in the city, and the Victorian arcades are a pleasure to peruse. The renovated Corn Exchange is graced with a two-tiered gallery of stores; craft and clothes stands fill its central hall.

C2

Tourist information The Arcade, Leeds City Station 0113 242 5242; www.visitleeds.co.uk

Leeds Art Gallery The Headrow 0113 247 8256; www.leeds.gov.uk Mon.–Tue. 10–5, Wed. noon–5, Thu.–Sat. 10–5, Sun. 1–5 Café Free

Royal Armouries Museum Armouries Drive 0113 220 1999 (24 hours); www.royalarmouries.org Daily 10–5 Restaurant and cafés Free (charge for some events)

Liverpool

Liverpool is one of Britain's great seaports. It was natural for docks and wharves to develop along the deepwater estuary of the River Mersey, which faces the Atlantic. Rum, tobacco, cotton and sugar poured in from Britain's Caribbean and American colonies in the 17th and 18th centuries, and from here the manufactured goods of the cities went to the rest of the world. The slave trade flourished, too, as did emigration to the United States and Canada, mainly by the poor and disillusioned seeking a fresh start.

These aspects of the city's colorful history are explored in the Merseyside Maritime Museum. The giant Port of Liverpool Building, Cunard Building and Royal Liver Building – grand expressions of Liverpool's importance – stand at the Pier Head, where you can board one of the famous Mersey ferries for a delightful river cruise.

The Walker Art Gallery houses a superb collection of paintings, including several European masters, pre-Raphaelites and modern British art. Tate Liverpool also is an impressive showcase of contemporary and modern art.

Liverpool's skyline, with the twin towers of the Liver Building, seen across the Mersey from Birkenhead

Tour the sites made famous by world-renowned group The Beatles and other Liverpool beat groups in the 1960s with Cavern City Tours (☎ 0151 236 9091; www.cavernclub.org).

The impressive Museum of Liverpool opened in 2011 in a landmark building on the city's waterfront. Varied displays in a series of state-of-the-art galleries relate to Liverpool's unique history, geography and culture.

B2

Tourist information ✉ Albert Dock ☎ 0151 233 2008; www.visitliverpool.com

Merseyside Maritime Museum ✉ Albert Dock ☎ 0151 478 4499; www.liverpoolmuseums.org.uk Daily 10–5 Café Free

Walker Art Gallery ✉ William Brown Street ☎ 0151 478 4199; www.liverpoolmuseums.org.uk Daily 10–5 Café Free

Tate Liverpool ✉ Albert Dock ☎ 0151 702 7400; www.tate.org.uk Daily 10–5:50 Café Free (charge for special exhibitions)

Museum of Liverpool ✉ Pier Head, Liverpool Waterfront ☎ 0151 478 4545; www.liverpool-museums.org.uk Daily 10–5 Café Free

Manchester

Manchester slid a long way downhill when its textile trade collapsed in the mid-20th century. But this great northern city has pulled itself back up to celebrate a heritage of magnificent Victorian industrial architecture. The Museum of Science and Industry is on the site of the world's oldest surviving railroad station. The highlight of Manchester Art Gallery is its collection of paintings by Pre-Raphaelite artists. The Lowry at Salford Quays is an arts center housing paintings by L.S. Lowry; his "matchstick men" were inspired by the city's factory workers.

The Castlefield area boasts trendy canal-side bars and chic eateries. For a taste of the Far East, seek out Chinatown (between Princess and York streets) for its excellent restaurants. The Royal Exchange is bursting with shops. The new National Football Museum opened in 2012, with more than 140,000 objects displayed over three floors. Highlights include a shirt from the world's first international match, played in 1872, and a footballers' hall of fame.

B2

Tourist information ✉ Piccadilly Plaza, Portland Street ☎ 0871 222 8223; www.visitmanchester.com

Museum of Science and Industry ✉ Liverpool Road, Castlefield ☎ 0161 832 2244; www.mosi.org.uk Daily 10–5 Restaurant and café Free (charge for special exhibitions)

The Lowry ✉ Pier 8, Salford Quays ☎ 0843 208 6001; www.thelowry.com Sun.–Fri. 11–5, Sat. 10–5 Restaurant and café Free

National Football Museum ✉ Urbis Building, Cathedral gardens ☎ 0161 605 8200; www.nationalfootballmuseum.com Free

The Lowry at Salford Quays in Greater Manchester has theaters, galleries, bars and restaurants

The view down steeply curving New Road into the village of Robin Hood's Bay

North York Moors

The Yorkshire Heritage Coast runs north from the coastal resort of Scarborough for some 30 miles, with Whitby as its jewel. This little seaport is protected by the moors on all sides, except where its harbor looks out over the North Sea. Spectacular abbey ruins stand high on a cliff, and you can visit the house where South Seas explorer Captain James Cook lodged as an apprentice.

You are also following in Dracula's footsteps around here: Bram Stoker based some of the scenes in his novel in Whitby – ask at the tourist office about the Dracula Trail. South of town is Robin Hood's Bay, a fishing village that tumbles down a cleft in the cliffs. Visitors must park in the parking lot at the top of the village. The main street leads down to the bay.

Inland, the atmosphere of the North York Moors can be very bleak in rain or the not infrequent sea mists, but beautiful in fair weather. The town of Pickering, on the southern edge of North York Moors National Park, is a good base for exploring; from here the steam-hauled North Yorkshire Moors Railway will take you north through the moors for 18 miles to Grosmont. West of Pickering is the big moorland village of Helmsley; the fine ruined abbey of Rievaulx (pronounced "Ree-voe") is in Ryedale, a few miles beyond. Hutton-le-Hole has an idyllic village green and boasts the Ryedale Folk Museum, which includes a reconstruction of a glassworks and a blacksmith's shop.
C3–D3

The Moors National Park Centre D3
Lodge Lane, Danby, Whitby 01439 772737; www.northyorkmoors.org.uk

North Yorkshire Moors Railway D3 Pickering Station, Park Street, Pickering 01751 472508; www.nymr.co.uk Daily, Apr.–Oct.; call for details for rest of year Restaurant on train $$$

Ryedale Folk Museum D3
Hutton-le-Hole 01751 417367; www.ryedalefolkmuseum.co.uk Daily 10–5:30, mid-Mar. to late Oct.; 10–dusk, mid-Jan. to mid-Mar. and late Oct.–early Dec.; closed rest of year $$$

Whitby D3

Tourist information Langborne Road 01723 383636; www.discoveryorkshirecoast.com

Pickering D3

Tourist information The Ropery, Pickering 01751 473791; www.yorkshire.com

Northumberland

Much of Northumberland is a national park, a region of moors and coniferous forests. The beaches are largely deserted. Two castles sit atop the low cliffs: Dunstanburgh, a spectacular 14th-century ruin, and Bamburgh, located on a crag a few miles farther north, with a Norman keep and the extensive remains of a curtain wall. The castle looks out on the Farne Islands, shelves of volcanic rock inhabited by seals and seabirds. Bamburgh village, where the Northumbrian kings were crowned, is a nice place to stop, and there is a good pub with a fire in winter. Also here is the Grace Darling Museum, which tells the tale of a Longstone lighthouse keeper's daughter who in 1838 spotted a ship aground. Grace, age 23, and her father rowed out to the rescue, saving nine passengers – 43 were drowned. The lighthouse still stands on Longstone.

Lindisfarne, or Holy Island, is 5 miles up the coast and accessible by a causeway over the sands. This is submerged at high tide; contact the tourist office at Alnwick for tide times. On Holy Island you will find Lindisfarne Castle perched on a rocky crag and the impressive ruins of Lindisfarne Priory, built in Norman times on the site of the monastic community led by St. Cuthbert in the seventh century. The tradition of brewing mead (an alcoholic drink made from honey and herbs) is still carried out on the island.

Lindisfarne Castle overlooks Holy Island

B4, C4, B5, C5

Alnwick tourist information C5
2 The Shambles 01665 511333;
www.visitalnwick.org.uk

Northumberland National Park Visitor Centre C5
Church Street, Rothbury 01669 620887;
www.northumberlandnationalpark.org.uk

Dunstanburgh Castle C5 Craster, Alnwick
01665 576231; www.nationaltrust.org.uk Daily 10–5, Apr.–Sep.; daily 10–4 in Oct.; Thu.–Mon. 10–4, rest of year $$

Bamburgh Castle C5
Bamburgh 01668 214515;
www.bamburghcastle.com Daily 10–5, mid-Feb. to Nov. 1 (last admission 4); Sat.–Sun. 11–4, rest of year Café $$$

Grace Darling Museum C5
Radcliffe Road, Bamburgh 01668 214910
Daily 10–5, Easter–Oct.; Tue.–Sun. 10–4, rest of year $$

Lindisfarne Castle C5 Lindisfarne (Holy Island)
01289 389244; www.nationaltrust.org.uk
Tue.–Sun. either 10–3 or noon–5 depending on tides, mid-Mar. to Nov. 1; daily 10–3 in mid-Feb.; Sun.–Tue. 10–3 in late Dec. $$$

Nottingham and Sherwood Forest

Nottingham is a historic town with a great sense of its past. Nottingham Castle is not a traditional English castle, but instead a 17th-century ducal palace standing where the medieval castle once stood, on a wonderfully dramatic site, a great crag overlooking the town. The building is forever associated with the epic archery contests, imprisonments and escapes of folk hero Robin Hood in his struggles with the satisfyingly wicked Sheriff of Nottingham. Another tale, dating from 1330, has King Edward III leading a band of friends through a 300-foot-long passage in the rock below the castle in order to capture his mother, Isabella, and her lover

Robin Hood

The legends of Robin Hood and his Merry Men, who stole from the (usually wicked) rich to give to the (invariably hard-working and good) poor, have survived and been elaborated on through seven centuries of storytelling, but even today it is not known for certain whether these stories have a basis in fact or are merely pure fiction. Perhaps because of the durability of the folk tale, it is quite possible that there was such a character as Robin Hood who lived the life of an outlaw in Sherwood Forest, poaching the king's deer. More likely his character and story are a mix of many such real-life outlaws, heroes of medieval ballads.

Statue of Robin Hood, Nottingham

Sir Roger Mortimer. Today the castle is both museum and art gallery, with temporary exhibitions as well as the permanent collections. The ancient tunnels in the rock can be explored during a tour of the castle. Hacked from the thick walls deep beneath the castle is England's oldest pub, Ye Olde Trip to Jerusalem. Dating from 1189, it was in use during the 13th-century Crusades.

Sherwood Forest is only a shadow of its extensive medieval self after many centuries of tree felling, but you can still find some of it standing near Ollerton, 20 miles north of Nottingham.

C1

Tourist information 1–4 Smithy Row 0844 477 5678; www.visitnottingham.com

Nottingham Castle Friar Lane, off Maid Marian Way 0115 915 3700 Tue.–Sun. 10–5, Mar.–Sep.; 10–4, rest of year (last admission 30 minutes before closing). Cave tours: Tue.–Sat. 11, 2, 3, Sun. noon, 1, 2, 3, Mar.–Sep. Café $$ (includes Brewhouse Yard Museum of Nottingham Life, valid for 1 week); Cave tour $$

Sherwood Forest Country Park and Visitor Centre C1–D1 Edwinstowe, near Mansfield 01623 823202 Country park: daily dawn–dusk. Visitor Centre: daily 10–4, Easter–Oct. Times may be longer in summer Restaurant Free (charge for parking)

Peak District

The Peak District is yet another of northern England's splendid national parks. The Dark Peak, or more northerly section of the park, takes its atmosphere from the brooding heather uplands of the Derbyshire/South Yorkshire border between Sheffield and Manchester. Here you can stride the lonely moors along the most southerly section of the Pennine Way. For caving fanatics, there are spectacular caves at nearby Castleton, where feldspar was once mined in deep caverns.

Buxton, to the south, is a charming spa town with notable Georgian buildings, while neighboring Bakewell is famous for Bakewell pudding, a delicious jam-and-almond cake. East of these towns is the great mansion of Chatsworth (see page 194); to the south are the water-cut limestone dales of the White Peak, marvelous for walking. Dovedale, the best known and most photogenic, has mighty rock pinnacles; also make time to seek out Lathkilldale, south of Bakewell, where medieval Haddon Hall waits to be discovered.

C1–C2

Peak District National Park Authority C1 Aldern House, Baslow Road, Bakewell

The countryside view from the Roaches, a stunning gritstone outcrop in the Peak District

☎ 01629 816200; www.peakdistrict.gov.uk

Buxton ✚ C1

Tourist information ✉ Pavilion Gardens, St. John's Road ☎ 01298 25106; www.visitpeakdistrict.com

Haddon Hall ✚ C1

✉ Bakewell ☎ 01629 812855; www.haddonhall.co.uk ⊕ Daily noon–5, May–Sep.; Sat.–Mon. noon–5 in Apr. and Oct. (last admission 1 hour before closing); daily 10:30–4 in early Dec. (last admission 30 minutes before closing) 🍴 Restaurant $$$

The Pennines

The Pennine chain of hills forms the north–south backbone of northern England. Aside from one or two serious hills, this is mostly a rolling, undulating landscape. The Pennine Way National Trail runs the entire length of the chain, starting in Derbyshire on the Dark Peak moors between Sheffield and Manchester, and ending up just across the Scottish Border, 268 miles north.

You can travel miles through the hills and see some of its loneliest landscapes aboard the Settle–Carlisle Railway (see page 199). Towns strung along the railroad line include Settle, Kirkby Stephen, Appleby and Penrith, all stone-built, modest and friendly settlements. There are several towns and villages further afield worth seeking out, too – Brough, Alston, Allendale Town and Kirkoswald.

There are uplands around Malham, where there is a spectacular curved cliff formation, and in Upper Teesdale near Middleton-in-Teesdale, where the River Tees plummets over a lip of rock and becomes High Force waterfall. Farther north in western County Durham are moors and dales around lovely Weardale and the brooding Derwent Valley, where you'll find a choice of real country pubs. ✚ B2–C2–B3–C3–B4–C4

This stone bridge at Muker in Swaledale is typical of the Yorkshire Dales National Park

Drive:
The Yorkshire Dales

Distance: 200 miles

The classic view of a Yorkshire dale is of a fertile valley bottom set with stone barns and farm buildings and divided up by distinctive "drystone" walls (built without mortar). These walls snake up the sides of the dale and over the clearly defined boundary where pasture meets moorland. It is this mixture – rough grazing on the upper slopes and intervening hills and pastureland down in the valleys – that gives the Yorkshire Dales their character. This drive will show you some of the loveliest places in the dales, but there are others waiting to be discovered up side roads and in odd corners. Take your time and perhaps stop overnight along the way.

Skipton, a bustling market town a few miles north of Haworth and the Brontë moors (see page 195), is the starting point. Proceed east along A59 to Blubberhouses; 2 miles farther, turn left on B6451/B6165 to Pateley Bridge.

If you have a couple of hours to spare, bear left along Nidderdale and past the long Gouthwaite Reservoir to the village of Lofthouse. The narrow cleft of How Stean gorge is just beyond. Beautiful Nidderdale attracts few visitors along this wild road, but the 16-mile detour is definitely worth the extra effort.

Continue from Pateley Bridge on B6265 toward Ripon, turning right before you reach the town.

Here are the impressive remains of Fountains Abbey, a 12th-century monastery, and the beautiful water gardens and landscaped grounds at nearby Studley Royal.

Ripon itself has a glorious late Norman cathedral. If you arrive in the evening, attend the blowing of curfew on the Wakeman's horn in the market square at 9 p.m.

From Ripon, A6108 takes you to Masham. Stop and tour the traditional Theakston Brewery in Masham.

Richmond, the next town, is one of Yorkshire's most appealing, with its huge Norman castle and steep streets.

From Richmond, proceed along A6108, bear west toward Swaledale via B6270 and continue to Reeth.

Here you can make a counterclockwise loop on the minor road through the valley of Arkengarthdale, with its intriguingly named settlements of Booze and Whaw, then on through rugged moorland scenery through the valley of Swaledale, passing the villages of Keld and Muker on the way back to Reeth.

From Reeth, turn south on the moorland road over the fells to the villages of Redmire and Wensley in broad, green Wensleydale, famous for its cheese. From Wensley a side road runs up ever-narrowing Coverdale, a little-visited dale under the bulk of Great Whernside hill. Drop steeply into the village of Kettlewell and turn right on B6160 to Buckden, then bear left to Hubberholme.

At Hubberholme there is an excellent inn, The George. The little Church of St. Michael and All Angels stands next to a humpbacked bridge, and contains a Tudor rood screen and wooden pews made by craftsman Robert Thompson; look for his trademark – long-tailed mice – carved into the furniture.

Continue from Hubberholme up the glorious valley of Langstrothdale beside the River Wharfe, admiring the distinctively elongated farmhouses. Eventually the moorland road takes you back to Wensleydale at the cheerful market town of Hawes. Turn right down Wensleydale on A684 to Aysgarth.

Stop here to admire the waterfalls.

Turn right on B6160 up Bishopdale; then descend the full length of Wharfedale, passing again through the village of Kettlewell and onward through Threshfield and Burnsall.

Near the foot of the dale, park and take a stroll upriver from the scenic ruins of Bolton Abbey to the Strid, a dramatic, rocky narrows where the river comes tumbling through.

Return to your car and turn right on A59 for the 5-mile drive back to Skipton.

C3

Yorkshire Dales National Park Authority Yoredale, Bainbridge, Leyburn, North Yorkshire 01969 652300; www.yorkshiredales.org.uk

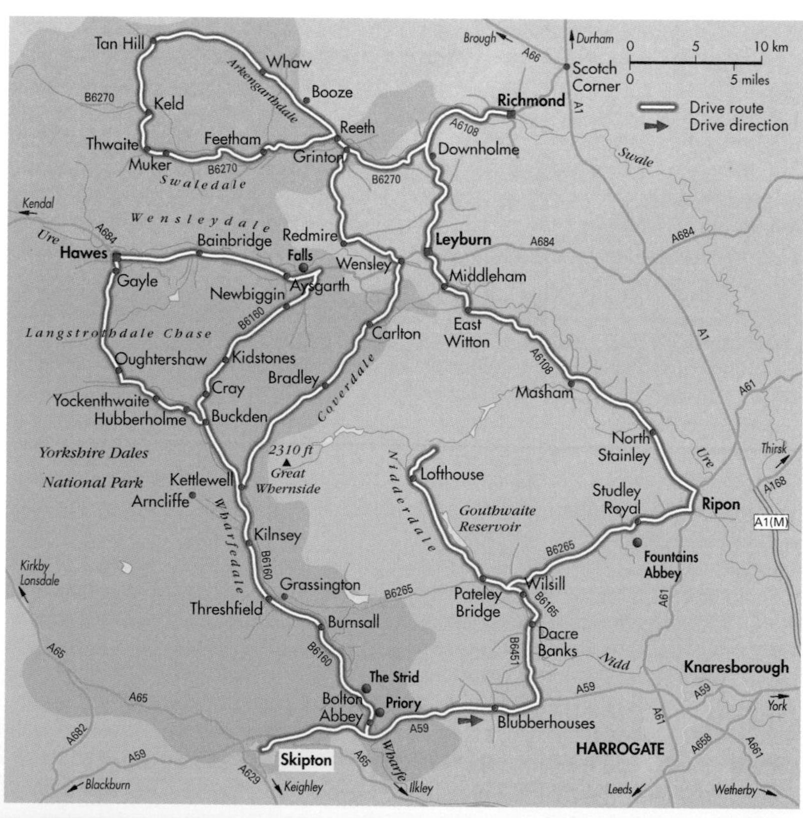

Scotland

Opposite: Eilean Donan Castle

Scotland

Scotland, more than any other region of Britain, projects itself in the minds of visitors in a series of strong and clearly defined images – red-bearded men in kilts and bonny women in tartan, bagpipes and wild Highland dancing, whiskey and haggis, empty glens sweeping up to mountains purple with heather. Scots are dour, reliable, close with the pennies but open-handedly hospitable, quick to anger, practical, hardy and endlessly antagonistic to the English, the "Auld Enemy."

The Proud Scots

So run the stereotypes – and there is a grain of truth in them. You will indeed find elements of all these characteristics if you peer and probe hard enough. But there is a whole lot more to Scotland and the Scots than a string of picture-postcard views and an inclination to take a gloomy relish in the darker episodes of the nation's history. For Scotland is indeed a nation again; it has had its own parliament, vested with significant powers, since 1997 (although central British government is still based in London). Scottish national pride is currently running high, and the mood among Scots is to look forward rather than back. Scotland remains within the United Kingdom for the time being, but the old ties seem to be loosening.

Highlands and Lowlands

Just as there is a "north–south divide" in England, one exists in Scotland, but more geographical than social. Everyone seems to have heard of the Scottish Highlands (although exactly where they begin and end is a moot point, even among Scots), and most visitors, once they have "done" Edinburgh, tend to gravitate north and west as quickly as possible to get to the mountains, castles, islands, red deer and golden eagles. That the lowlands and border regions also

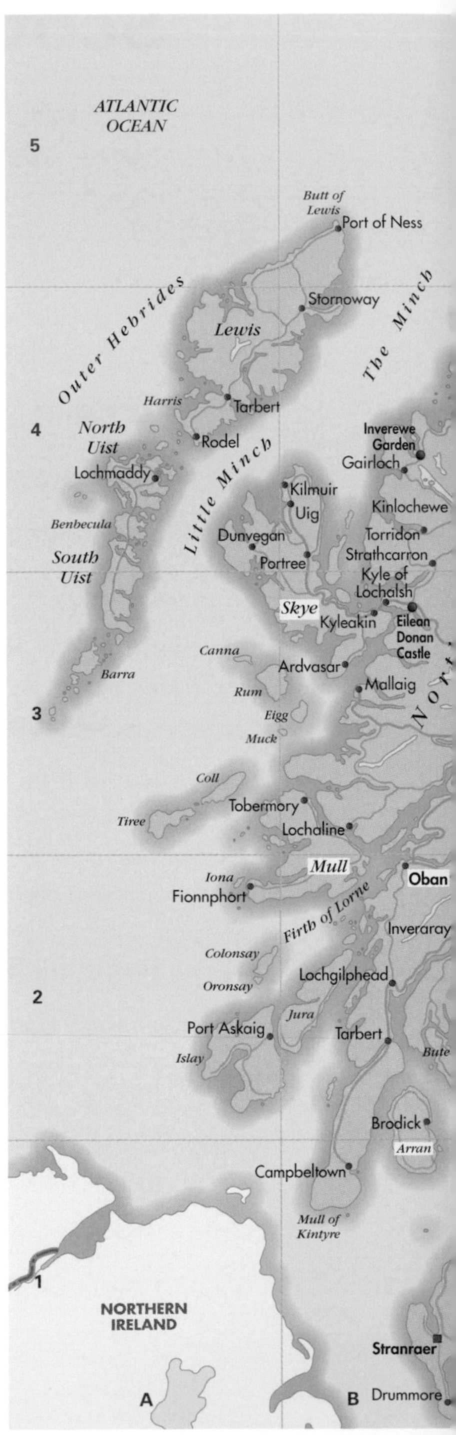

Orkney Islands
Westray
Rousay
Sanday
Stronsay
Redland
Shapinsay
Kirkwall
Stromness
St Mary's
Hoy
South Ronaldsay
Burwick
Durness
Scrabster
Thurso
John o'Groats
Tongue
Laxford Bridge
Wick
3146 ft
Ben Klibreck
Lochinver
3274 ft
Latheron
North Sea
Lairg
Helmsdale
Ullapool
Dornoch
Moray Firth
3429 ft
Ben Wyvis
Lossiemouth
Cromarty
Banff
Fraserburgh
Achnasheen
Dingwall
Elgin
Nairn
Keith
3773 ft
Sgurr na Lapaich
Inverness
Culloden
New Byth
Dufftown
Peterhead
Grantown-on-Spey
Loch Ness
Huntly
Oldmeldrum
Spey
Invermoriston
Aviemore
Inverurie
Kingussie
Cairngorms National Park
Strathdon
Drum Castle
Aberdeen
Invergarry
Ballater
Crathes Castle
Fort William
Laggan
Braemar
Balmoral Castle
Banchory
4406ft
Ben Nevis
Grampian Mountains
Blair Atholl
Stonehaven
Pitlochry
Glencoe
Brechin
Aberfeldy
Montrose
Glamis
Forfar
Blairgowrie
Tyndrum
3842 ft
Ben More
Arbroath
Carnoustie
Crieff
Perth
Dundee
Loch Lomond and the Trossachs National Park
Callander
Auchterarder
St. Andrews
Aberfoyle
M90
Glenrothes
Loch Lomond
Kinross
Stirling
Kirkcaldy
Firth of Forth
Dunfermline
Dumbarton
Falkirk
Linlithgow
Dunbar
Greenock
GLASGOW
Haddington
Grantshouse
Paisley
M8
EDINBURGH
Dalkeith
Eyemouth
East Kilbride
Motherwell
Ardrossan
M74
Lauder
Berwick-upon-Tweed
Troon
Kilmarnock
Lanark
Peebles
Melrose
Mauchline
Coldstream
Abington
Ayr
Ettrick Forest
Jedburgh
Kelso
Burns National Heritage Park
Culzean Castle
Hawick
Cheviot Hills
Turnberry
Moffat
Girvan
A74(M)
Scottish Borders
Southern Uplands
New Galloway
Langholm
Newton Stewart
Lockerbie
ENGLAND
Dumfries
Castle Douglas
Gretna Green
Solway Firth
Kirkcudbright
Whithorn
West Highlands
C
D
E
Shetland Islands
Baltasound
Unst
Gutcher
Isbister
Fetlar
Yell
Toft
Voe
Walls
Lerwick
Foula
Scalloway
Bressay
Fladdabister
Toab
Fair Isle
North Sea
0 20 40 60 80 km
0 10 20 30 40 50 miles

Loch Lomond stretches out within Loch Lomond and the Trossachs National Park

contain more than their share of beautiful, dramatic landscapes, quiet and tucked-away places, wild animals and birds, and romantic lakes and castles is a fact unknown to many of those who come to Scotland. And just as well, think lowland enthusiasts who treasure the peace and absence of tourists in these southerly regions of Scotland.

History's Bloody Conflicts

The national boundary between England and Scotland stretches northeast from Carlisle to Berwick-on-Tweed through the lonely country of the Borders. Ownership of these parts was disputed with fire and sword for many centuries – between English and Scots, who took and retook the Border towns and valleys, and also between Scottish landowners themselves. These conflicts led their retainers into many a bloody skirmish and siege with neighbors in dispute over cattle and land, and their "pele towers" (defensive strongholds, half house and half castle) dot the landscape.

The little Border towns – Peebles, Kelso, Melrose, Hawick (pronounced "Hoik"), Moffat, Jedburgh – are neat, orderly places where shopkeepers delight in offering personal service and local gossip. West Ayrshire is Robert Burns country, where Scotland's humorous national poet enjoyed his short life at the end of the 18th century with bottle and bedchamber – there are Burns sites galore here.

Cities and Mountains

Across the neck of southern Scotland sit Edinburgh and Glasgow, the country's two biggest and liveliest cities. North of them is a rising landscape of high hills and broken ridges, vigorous country full of lakes and fast rivers. There are the wild moors of Rannoch and the fearsome canyon of Glencoe in the west, the long lakes and hills of the Trossachs, and lumped together in the center the Grampians, rising to the most formidable mountains of all, the Cairngorms, famous among skiers and climbing enthusiasts.

Compared with the great ranges of the world, the remote and wild Cairngorms may be only toy mountains – the highest peaks barely top 4,000 feet – but conditions on top can be as tough as anywhere, especially in winter when subarctic temperatures and fierce blizzards make them worthy of any mountaineer's respect.

Lochs and Islands

Even here, some would say, the real Highlands have yet to be reached. For diehard romantics the Highlands really start north and west of the Great Glen, that decisively straight slash of the geological sword from northeast to southwest, from the North Sea up on the Moray Firth to the Atlantic Ocean down on Loch Linnhe, below Fort William.

Beyond dark Loch Ness (with its mythical monster) spread the wide glens and sweeping mountain landscapes beloved by every Scottish calendar photographer, but far more beautiful, impressive and mournful when seen in person. You have to leave your car and walk here, along the glen rivers and into valleys where the ruins of abandoned settlements still lie, to experience fully the emptiness of this landscape, cleared of its people and its Gaelic way of life in the 18th and 19th centuries.

Then there are the islands, where people still make a precarious living in unbelievably bare but beautiful surroundings. Four great archipelagos lie off of mainland Scotland – the Inner Hebrides off the west coast, the Outer Hebrides 30 miles farther out, and Orkney and Shetland stretching north from the northernmost tip of the mainland. Here you will find the wildest scenery and music, the coldest winds and seas, and the warmest hearths and hospitality in Britain.

Scottish Culture

The Scottish accent and dialect change perceptibly between regions. Visitors will find that English is spoken everywhere, although Gaelic is still spoken in the far north and Outer Hebrides (see page 283).

The language survives in place names, poetry and also song, which you'll encounter frequently in Scotland. Many pubs offer live folk music, while "ceilidhs" (pronounced "kay-lees," dances accompanied by fiddle and pipe music, usually at a cracking pace) take place year-round.

Visitors usually come to Scotland during the warmer months of summer (May through August); because of the country's northern latitude, this time of year is blessed with long days and short nights. It is also the season for Highland Games, held countrywide, where you watch Scottish dancing and "tossing the caber" (a sport that involves throwing a large log end over end as far as possible).

The Real Taste of Scotland

Watch for the "EatScotland" sign in restaurant windows if you're looking for authentic food cooked with the best local ingredients. Aberdeen Angus beef and wild salmon are both of high quality here, and you'll see game on the menu in many pubs and restaurants.

For the hungry, huge fried breakfasts can include hot porridge (oatmeal cooked in milk and seasoned with a pinch of salt), eggs, bacon, square slice (a type of flat beef sausage), black pudding (blood sausage), potato cakes and tomatoes.

Haggis is Scotland's most famous dish; it consists of sheep's organ meat (liver, lungs and heart) cooked in spices and oatmeal and boiled in a sheep's stomach. Vegetarian varieties are also available.

Edinburgh

Whatever the pretensions and aspirations of Glasgow, its near neighbor and rival, Edinburgh is unquestionably Scotland's premier city, the capital of the Scottish nation. You feel an air of grandeur the moment you reach the city center. Edinburgh Castle is every inch the dark and dominant fortress, perched high over the city atop a basalt crag as it frowns down the Royal Mile to the Palace of Holyroodhouse, while Princes Street is a splendidly wide Georgian thoroughfare with handsome civic buildings and a solidly impressive layout of Georgian town houses, row houses and squares under its influence.

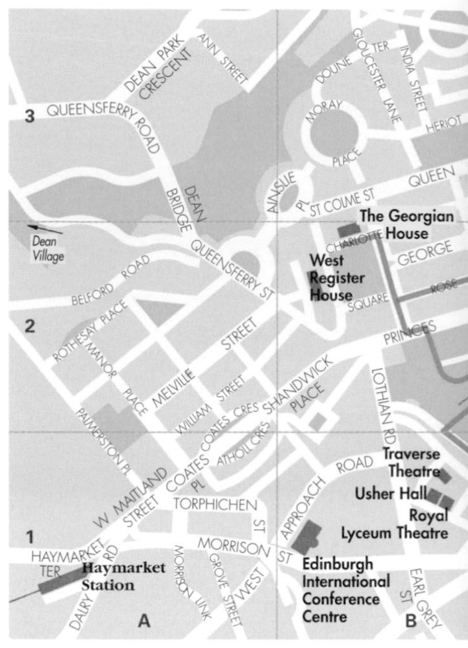

Two Faces of the City

Castle and palace reflect the older, historic side of this split-personality city. Along the Royal Mile you will see ancient tall houses, cramped little courts, churches and bent old inns that made up "Auld Reekie," the atmospheric but unsanitary medieval city where Mary, Queen of Scots plotted, traitors and honest men alike rotted in the castle's dungeons, John Knox preached Reformation, and Scottish Presbyterian Covenanters signed a declaration of religious dissent in their own blood. The student pubs and clubs here today have a strange ambience, both deeply historical and completely modern.

The Café Royal restaurant in West Register Street

But along Princes Street and streets farther north Edinburgh shows another face. This part of town was built in the late 18th century, when Auld Reekie became too old and reeking to be tolerated any longer. This New Town had a grand and visually pleasing building plan, with its galleries, monuments and academy buildings, its spacious layout, its gardens and solid, prosperous-looking architecture. It exudes a solemnity and gravitas that used to make Edinburgh, along with its mannerly and upright citizens and their rather precise accents, seem stiff and pompous. No longer, however – there are enough students, visitors, media and artsy types around to give the city an agreeably light and positive atmosphere,

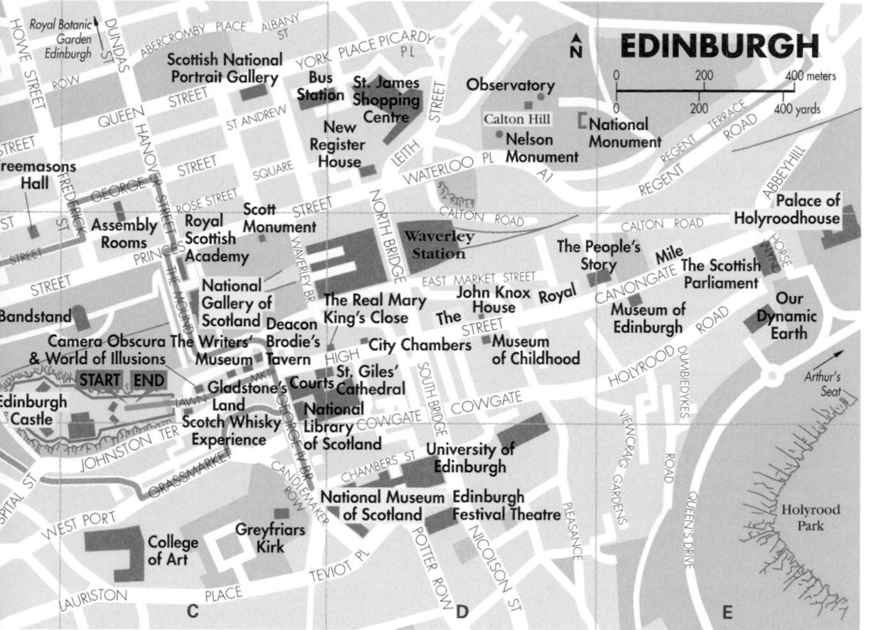

boosted by the ever-growing popularity of the annual summertime Edinburgh International Festival and its irreverent "Fringe" offshoot.

Center of Attractions

The layout of central Edinburgh is simple to grasp. The west side of the city center is bounded by the Water of Leith, the east by Holyrood Park and the fine basalt rampart of Salisbury Crags. The Old Town clusters along the Royal Mile, which runs from Edinburgh Castle east to the Palace of Holyroodhouse.

Below and to the north of the Old Town (and separated from it by Waverley railroad station and some sunken gardens) lies the New Town; the main artery and shopping place, Princes Street (parallel to the Royal Mile), runs east to Calton Hill. All the city's main attractions are within a 20-minute walk of Waverley Station. However, there are so many that you may want to save your feet and take one of the frequent red-and-white Lothian buses that serve the city center.

Hunger for a High Tea

As you would expect from a major capital city, Edinburgh has a great number of cafés, restaurants and pubs. Cafés tend to be for tea and light snacks; hotels and restaurants may also serve the famous Scottish high tea. Consider your state of hunger honestly before ordering this, as it consists of cookies, jam, cakes and pastries, plus a cooked dish of eggs, ham and kippers or haddock.

The once-rowdy dock area of Leith, a mile north of the center, has cleaned up its act and become a trendy place to enjoy a brasserie-style meal with a view over the Firth of Forth. As for pubs, noisy student hangouts abound along the Royal Mile and around the Grassmarket. To experience beautiful Victorian "high-pub" decor, try one of the pubs along Rose Street, north of Princes Street.

Music and Dancing

Princes Street has the standard chain stores, and some that are more elegant. Tourist-oriented but amusing Scottish

Edinburgh International Festival

The Edinburgh International Festival is one of the world's biggest and most famous arts festivals. It is held during the last two weeks in August and the first week in September. Opera, dance, theater and music are performed at a variety of venues across the city. The Edinburgh Festival Fringe (last three weeks of August) is a more irreverent event featuring student theater companies and some excellent, and unusual, comedy.

If you're visiting Edinburgh during the festivals, make sure you reserve accommodations well in advance.

For information on the Edinburgh International Festival call ☎ 0131 473 2099; www.eif.co.uk

For information on The Edinburgh Festival Fringe call ☎ 0131 226 0026; www.edfringe.com

goods – haggis, tartan kilts, sporrans (a leather pouch worn over a kilt), tam-o'-shanters (tartan hats), malt whiskey (spelled "whisky" in Scotland) are plentiful along the Royal Mile. Edinburgh Rock is a crumbly, soft fruit-flavored candy-stick that comes in various pastel colors.

Music is very important in Edinburgh – everything from classical concerts to guitars and dancing in dozens of small clubs. You will also find traditional Scottish music being played in many bars – try the inviting Royal Oak on Infirmary Street or seek out Sandy Bell's on Forrest Road.

Essential Information

Tourist Information

Edinburgh and Scotland Information Centre, ✉ 3 Princes Street ☎ 0131 473 3868; www.edinburgh.org

Urban Transportation

The main railroad station is Waverley Station on Princes Street, in the heart of the city. For schedule information and reservations ☎ 08457 484950. There are numerous city buses; for information contact one of the Lothian Buses Travelshops at Waverley Bridge, Hanover Street or Shandwick Place ☎ 0131 555 6363 (24 hours). First buses also operate within the city and surrounding area ☎ 0870 872 7271, Mon.–Fri. 8–6. The main taxi stands are at Waverley Station, or hail a cab on the street or call ☎ 0131 229 2468 or 0131 228 1211.

Airport Information

Edinburgh International Airport is 8 miles west of the city center (☎ 0844 481 8989; www.edinburghairport.com).

There is a Tourist and Airport Information Centre in the main hall. Frequent buses (every 10 minutes; or every 20 minutes off peak) go to and from Waverley Station (journey time 25 minutes), and taxis can be hired right outside the terminal.

Climate – average highs and lows for the month

Jan.	Feb.	Mar.	Apr.	May	Jun.	Jul.	Aug.	Sep.	Oct.	Nov.	Dec.
5°C	6°C	7°C	10°C	13°C	16°C	18°C	17°C	15°C	12°C	9°C	6°C
42°F	43°F	45°F	50°F	55°F	61°F	64°F	63°F	59°F	54°F	48°F	43°F
1°C	1°C	2°C	4°C	6°C	9°C	11°C	11°C	9°C	6°C	4°C	2°C
34°F	34°F	36°F	39°F	43°F	48°F	52°F	52°F	48°F	43°F	39°F	36°F

Edinburgh Sights

Key to symbols

map coordinates refer to the Edinburgh map on pages 216–217 admission charge: $$$ more than £6, $$ £2–£6, $ less than £2

See page 5 for complete key to symbols

Calton Hill

The eastern end of Princes Street is cut off by the volcanic upthrust of Calton Hill, a green and tree-covered mound that you can climb for some excellent views across Edinburgh. Below the south slope of Calton Hill stand the grand old Royal High School and a round, classical temple dedicated to Robert Burns.

The upper slopes of the hill are adorned with a splendid collection of mainly 19th-century monuments. The Dugald Stewart Monument of 1837 resembles the upper tiers of a sandstone wedding cake and commemorates a professor of philosophy at Edinburgh University who left no other trace behind him. The National Monument, "Edinburgh's Disgrace," was an attempt (begun in 1822) to build a replica of the Parthenon to honor Scotland's dead from the Napoleonic Wars. Money and enthusiasm ran out after the erection of the 12 columns that stand here today. The Nelson Monument, constructed between 1807 and 1815 and based on the appropriate design of an upturned telescope, purports to honor Admiral Horatio Nelson, who fell at the Battle of Trafalgar in 1805. You can climb the 143 steps of the monument for more city views. Note: This site should be avoided at dusk and after dark.

D3

Nelson Monument Calton Hill 0131 556 2716; www.edinburghmuseums.org.uk Mon.–Sat. 10–7, Sun. noon–5, Apr.–Sep.; Mon.–Sat. 10–3, rest of year $$

Dean Village

Down below Thomas Telford's 1832 bridge and huddled in the narrow valley of the Water of Leith, Dean was once an industrial settlement with 11 mills. Today this secret little village, reached from the city center end of the bridge by way of steep Bell's Brae, has become a desirable place to live. The handsome old mill buildings here have been converted into upscale apartments. Above the village is the famous Dean Bridge, designed by Thomas Telford in 1833, with Holy Trinity Church standing at the end of it.

A2 (off map)

The view across Edinburgh from the Dugald Stewart Monument on Calton Hill

Edinburgh Castle

Standing in lordly disdain on its volcanic crag high above both Old and New Town, this is one of Britain's really great castles. The site can't be beat for dramatic effect – nor for military effectiveness, as one quickly discovers when looking over the ramparts from the King's Bastion and down impregnable cliffs.

The surrounding view commands nearly 100 miles, from the hills of the Borders to the distant Grampian peaks. Encapsulated here, from the grim cells and dungeons in the bowels of the castle to the ramparts and their all-embracing view of any approaching friend or foe, are eight centuries of Scotland's history.

The obvious defensive site of the castle's crag has been fortified since Bronze Age times, and the present castle's datable structure (going back to the 12th-century Chapel of St. Margaret) probably conceals far older and earlier buildings. Sieges have been many, and it changed hands several times in the Anglo-Scots wars of the Middle Ages.

The castle houses various regimental museums, as well as the 15th-century bombard, or siege cannon, called Mons Meg – "the great iron murderer, Muckel Meg."

The beautifully simple chapel, high up in the castle, is a must-see, as are the Honours of the Kingdom, a collection of royal regalia that includes the priceless crown, sword and scepter of the monarchs of Scotland. After 100 years in obscurity following the 1707 Act of Union between England and Scotland, the detective work of Sir Walter Scott discovered their whereabouts in 1818, locked away and forgotten in the castle. Scott might have written that particular romantic denouement himself in one of his Waverley novels.

Displayed nearby is the Stone of Destiny, also called the Stone of Scone, a sandstone block on which Scottish monarchs traditionally rested their feet during the coronation ceremony. This

Dramatic Edinburgh Castle guards the city from its high lookout of Castle Rock

Explore a 19th-century kitchen at the Georgian House in Charlotte Square

important Scottish symbol was returned to Scotland in 1996 after 700 years in Westminster Abbey in London following its abduction by the English King Edward I.

B1–C1–B2–C2 Castlehill 0131 225 9846; www.edinburghcastle.gov.uk Daily 9:30–6, Apr.–Sep.; 9:30–5, rest of year. Last admission 45 minutes before closing; opening times of museums may vary Restaurant and cafés $$$ Guided tours (free); audio tours $$

The Georgian House

In 1796 Robert Adam designed Charlotte Square to be the New Town's architectural masterpiece. No. 7, The Georgian House, has been refurbished to show the lifestyle of its first owner, John Lamont, Chief of the Clan Lamont, a typical citified gentleman. His dining room and parlor are furnished with Wedgwood and Spode china and you can see the wine cellar and kitchens. Fine portraits by contemporary Scottish artists Henry Raeburn and Allan Ramsay hang among others on the walls.

B2 Charlotte Square 0844 493 2118; www.nts.org.uk Daily 10–6, Jul.–Aug.; 10–5, Apr.–Jun. and Sep.–Oct.; 11–4 in Mar.; 11–3 in Nov. Last admission 30 minutes before closing $$

Greyfriars Bobby

Descending the Royal Mile from Edinburgh Castle, turn right at the first crossroads onto George IV Bridge. You will soon reach Greyfriars Kirk on the right (0131 225 1900; www.greyfriarskirk.com Mon.–Fri. 10:30–4:30, Sat. 11–2, Apr.–Oct. and other times by arrangement). In the churchyard dissenting Presbyterians signed the National Covenant in 1638, pledging to keep their religion free from monarchical taints and the doctrines of the Roman Catholic Church. Thousands of Covenanters died in the ensuing persecutions.

The churchyard's most famous recumbent incumbents are "Auld Jock" Gray and his little Skye terrier, Bobby. Jock died in 1858, and for the next 14 years Greyfriars Bobby stayed on guard beside his grave. The people of Edinburgh tended the little dog. He was granted the Freedom of the City and became an international celebrity before his own death and burial in the churchyard in 1872. "Auld Jock" lies beside the path northeast of the church; Bobby lies near the gate. On top of a memorial drinking fountain outside the gate is an effigy of Bobby, his head cocked as if listening for his master's voice.

The Palace of Holyroodhouse is the Queen's official Edinburgh residence

National Gallery of Scotland

The National Gallery of Scotland stands in an impressive location on The Mound, off Princes Street. The works of Renaissance Italians here include Raphael, Tintoretto and Veronese; Flemish and Dutch masters are represented by Frans Hals, Rembrandt, Van Dyck and Vermeer. There are notable collections of J.M.W. Turner watercolors, landscapes by John Constable, and some fine American landscapes and portraits. Scottish painters have their own wing, with seascapes by Alexander Nasmyth and portraits by Allan Ramsay.

C2 The Mound 0131 624 6200; www.nationalgalleries.org Daily 10–5 (also Thu. 5–7); extended hours during Edinburgh International Festival Restaurant and café Free; charge for special exhibitions $$

National Museum of Scotland

Mixing traditional and boldly new architecture, Scotland's National Museum rises above the Old Town. The exhibits cover the earliest times through to the development of the medieval Kingdom of Scotland, with galleries continuing through Scotland's role in the British Empire and on into modern times. The Grand Gallery is a soaring Victorian atrium with impressive natural history, science and cultural exhibits and the Artist Rooms, an interesting new collection of international art.

D1 Chambers Street 0300 123 6789; www.nms.ac.uk Daily 10–5 Restaurant and café Free Guided tours (free)

Palace of Holyroodhouse

The grand Palace of Holyroodhouse stands against a backdrop of the rock curtain of Salisbury Crags. This is the official Edinburgh residence of the British monarch, part country house, part palace, built from 1500 around the nucleus of the guesthouse of Holyrood Abbey. Grand ironwork gates and a fountain are your introduction to the palace. Inside are ornamental ceilings and beautiful antique furniture. Up a winding staircase you can see the antechamber of Mary, Queen of Scots. It was here that the Queen's jealous husband Lord Darnley had her Italian secretary, David Rizzio, stabbed to death on March 9, 1566. Behind the palace lies Holyrood Park, Edinburgh's largest natural park. Climb from Dunsapie Loch to the summit of Arthur's Seat, the remains of a 325-million-year-old volcano, for fine city views.

E2 Canongate, Royal Mile 0131 556 5100; www.royalcollection.org.uk Daily 9:30–6, Apr.–Oct.; 9:30–4:30, rest of year (last admission 1 hour before closing). Closed for some state functions Café $$$ Audio tours (free)

Walk:
Central Edinburgh

Refer to route marked on city map on pages 216–217

Allow at least three hours for this walk, more if you spend time at the attractions along the way.

Starting at Edinburgh Castle (see page 220), walk down Castlehill at the top of the Royal Mile.
You'll see the Edinburgh Old Town Weaving Company, with kilts and tartan material for sale. The Outlook Tower is on the left, housing a camera obscura that provides a panoramic preview of your walk (see page 224).
Turn right at Lawnmarket along the George IV Bridge, with the National Library of Scotland on your left. Soon Chambers Street runs off to the left, with the striking National Museum of Scotland on the right.
The museum tells the story of Scotland's history, people, culture and achievements from the oldest treasures to modern, everyday items.
Return to George IV Bridge and turn left down Victoria Street. Continue through West Bow into the Grassmarket. From here, it is a short walk below the castle and through West Princes Street Gardens to Princes Street, Edinburgh's showcase boulevard. Turn left and walk to the end of Princes Street, then cross and turn right up Hope Street to reach Charlotte Square, named for Queen Charlotte, the wife of King George III.
The square is architect Robert Adam's Georgian masterpiece, with The Georgian House (see page 221) at No. 7 on the north side.
From the east side of Charlotte Square turn left onto Rose Street.
Pop into one of the magnificent Victorian pubs here – perhaps try the Abbotsford or Milnes, an historic and welcoming spot – for a pint or other refreshment.
Turn left at Frederick Street and then make a right turn along elegant George Street in the heart of the New Town. At Hanover Street, turn right. Cross Princes Street, traverse The Mound, and then climb back to reach the Royal Mile and return to Edinburgh Castle.

National Museum of Scotland D1 Chambers Street 0131 225 7534; www.nms.ac.uk Daily 10–5 Restaurant and café Free Guided tours and audio tours (free)

There are plenty of restaurants and independent stores on Grassmarket, in the heart of the old town

The Royal Mile

The so-called "Royal Mile" is composed of four streets – Castlehill, Lawnmarket, High Street and Canongate, which run in that order downhill from Edinburgh Castle to the Palace of Holyroodhouse. This was the spine of the Old Town. Some features of the Royal Mile are:

Scotch Whisky Experience

The new Scotch Whisky Experience takes visitors on an insightful journey. You can sample a few of the different malts before you buy.

C2 354 Castlehill 0131 220 0441; www.scotchwhiskyexperience.co.uk Daily 10–6:30, Jun.–Aug.; 10–6, rest of year. Last tour 1 hour before closing Restaurant $$$

Camera Obscura & World of Illusions

Enjoy panoramic views of the city here. Upper stories were added to the 17th-century building in 1853 when it first housed a camera obscura.

C2 Outlook Tower, Castlehill 0131 226 3709; www.camera-obscura.co.uk Daily 9:30–8:30, Jul.–Aug.; 9:30–7, Apr.–Jun. and Sep.–Oct.; 10–5, rest of year. Last presentation 1 hour before closing $$$

Gladstone's Land

This is a cramped, crowded and fascinating restoration of a six-story "land," or apartment building, of 1617.

C2 477B Lawnmarket 0844 493 2120; www.nts.org.uk Daily 10–6:30, Jul.–Aug.; 10–5, Apr.–Jun. and Sep.–Oct. Last admission 30 minutes before closing $$

The Writers' Museum

Displays and memorabilia pertaining to poet Robert Burns and writers Sir Walter Scott and Robert Louis Stevenson are exhibited in a house dating from 1622. Among the objects on display is a cast of Burns' skull.

C2 Lady Stair's House, Lawnmarket 0131 529 4901; www.edinburghmuseums.org.uk Mon.–Sat. 10–5 (also Sun. noon–5 in Aug.) Free

Deacon Brodie's Tavern

Murals tell the story of Councillor William Brodie, respectable by day but a burglar by night. Brodie was hanged in 1788, and inspired Robert Louis

Stevenson with the idea for *The Strange Case of Dr. Jekyll and Mr. Hyde*.
C2 435 Lawnmarket 0131 225 6531 Sun.–Thu. 10 a.m.–11 p.m., Fri.–Sat. 10 a.m.–1 a.m.

St. Giles' Cathedral

The cathedral, dedicated to the patron saint of Edinburgh, is a treasure house of stained glass and monuments.

C2–D2 Off High Street 0131 225 9442; www.stgilescathedral.org Mon.–Fri. 9–7, Sat. 9–5, Sun. 1–5, May–Sep.; Mon.–Sat. 9–5, Sun. 1–5, rest of year Café Free ($$ donation suggested) Guided tours

The Real Mary King's Close

Guided tours of Edinburgh's underground streets show life in Edinburgh from the 16th to 19th centuries.

D2 2 Warriston's Close, Writers Court 0845 070 6244 Daily 9–9 in Aug.; daily 10–9, Apr.–Jul. and Sep.–Oct.; Sun.–Thu. 10–5, Fri.–Sat. 10–9, rest of year $$$

The People's Story

Ordinary citizens' lives from the late 18th century to the present day are shown with audiovisual displays.

D2–E2 Canongate Tolbooth, 163 Canongate 0131 529 4057; www.edinburghmuseums.org.uk Mon.–Sat. 10–5 (also Sun. noon–5 in Aug.) Free

Museum of Edinburgh

The city's life over the centuries is traced through a display of artifacts.

E2 Huntly House, 142 Canongate 0131 529 4143 Mon.–Sat. 10–5 (also Sun. noon–5 during Edinburgh Festival) Free

The Scottish Parliament

The controversial Holyrood building of Scotland's parliament is an architectural celebration of devolution.

E2 Canongate 0131 348 5200; www.scottish.parliament.uk Mon., Fri. (also Tue. and Thu. when parliament is in recess) 10–5:30, Apr.–Sep.; 10–4, Oct.–Mar.; Tue.–Thu. 9–6:30 (when parliament is sitting); Sat. and public hols 11–5:30 Free

Above left to right: Deacon Brodie's Tavern was named after the man who inspired *Dr. Jekyll and Mr. Hyde*; The spire of St. Giles' Cathedral rises above Royal Mile buildings

Glasgow

In the 1970s anyone comparing the merits of Edinburgh and Glasgow would have had no hesitation placing Glasgow far below the Scottish capital. In contrast to Edinburgh's solidity and atmosphere of cultural self-confidence, there was a real air of depression and decay about the shipbuilding city on the River Clyde, just 30 miles west. The shipyards and heavy engineering industries were in terminal decline, and fine old warehouses and commercial buildings were in disrepair.

But there has since been a remarkable upswing in Glasgow's image. Today the city projects renewed self-confidence, loudly trumpeting its unquestionably superb galleries and museums, lively nightlife, new trendy eateries and watering holes, and legacy of Georgian and Victorian architecture. There are walkways along the banks of the Clyde and newly refurbished urban green spaces. Tall sailing ships docked at the city wharves wait to be visited, and architectural and heritage trails take visitors to the best pockets of the city. While Glaswegians have always loudly acclaimed their own worth, there now seems to be a genuinely exciting buzz about this once run-down city.

Glasgow is now a gourmet destination

Boom and Decline

An initial flourishing of culture and self-confidence took place in the 18th century, when the merchants of Glasgow became rich through transatlantic trade. Streets, squares and fine Georgian churches sprang up. During the 19th century shipbuilding boomed, bringing with it a market in financial services. Ornate offices and warehouses were the

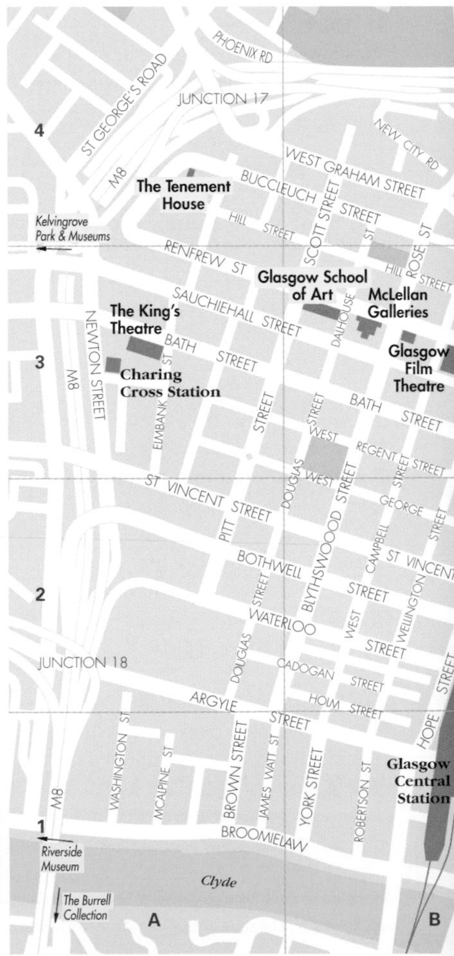

temples of commerce in the city center. As long as iron foundries, shipyards and engineering works along the river continued to roar – which they did until after World War I – it was boom time for Glasgow.

The long decline in the 20th century, exacerbated by industrial slumps in the 1930s and '70s and by wartime bombing, was hard to bear and had a dramatic effect on the morale of city residents. All this makes the renaissance of an attractively buoyant Glaswegian spirit all the more astonishing. Glasgow, in fact, was designated the Cultural Capital of Europe in 1990 and the U.K. City of Architecture and Design in 1999.

Seeing the Sights

This is a sprawling place, and orientation is a matter of remembering that the grid of streets around the center run east–west (the wide ones) and north–south (the narrower ones). Almost every sight worth seeing is located north of the River Clyde. The center's hub is George Square (Buchanan Street subway station), with the elegant streets and squares of the 18th- and 19th-century city to the west. To the north is the Glasgow School of Art, high above Sauchiehall (pronounced "Sockie-hall") Street (Charing Cross railroad station); farther north is The Tenement House on Buccleuch

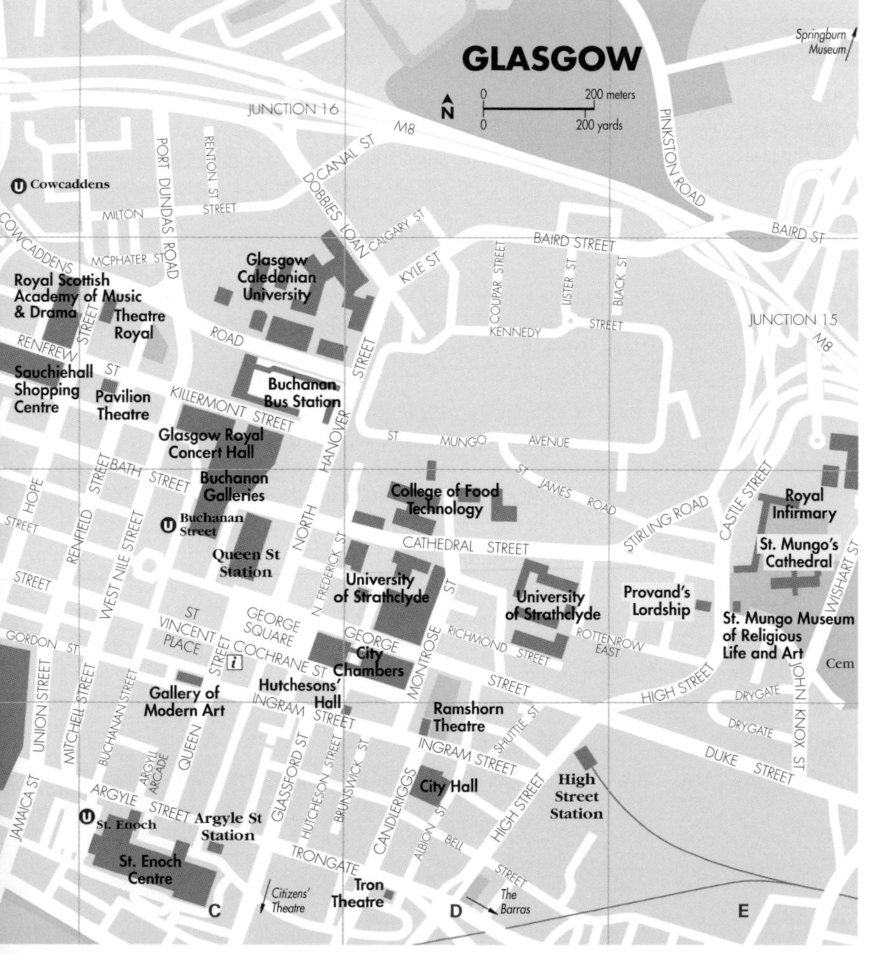

("B'cloo") Street. Farther west, Kelvingrove Park (Kelvinhall or Hillhead subway stations) has great museums and art galleries. A short walk east of George Square (High Street railroad station) are more attractions – Glasgow Cathedral and its museum, and the ancient house of Provand's Lordship.

Finally, 3 miles southwest of the city and a half-mile walk from Pollokshaws West railroad station, The Burrell Collection in Pollok Country Park is a must-see, with rare and stunning art and artifacts from around the world, including paintings from major international artists, antique Chinese ceramics and ancient artifacts.

Shopping and Entertainment

By far the best shopping fun you'll have is at the stands of The Barras, the busy weekend market situated near Glasgow Green (High Street railroad station).

Entertainment varies from mainstream music at Glasgow Royal Concert Hall on Sauchiehall Street to adventurous plays at the Citizens' Theatre on Gorbals Street (just south of the river) to the perpetual theater of loud and friendly Glasgow pubs.

For enthusiastic shoppers and fashionistas, three of the city's most important shopping streets: Argyle, Buchanan and Sauchiehall Street are now known as the Style Mile.

Essential Information

Tourist Information

✉ 11 George Square ☎ 0141 204 4400; www.seeglasgow.com

Urban Transportation

There are two main railroad stations: Glasgow Central (off Gordon Street) for services from the south and England, and Queen Street for services from Edinburgh and the north. For train schedules and reservations ☎ 08457 484950; www.nationalrail.co.uk. A small subway (metro) system ensures smooth but limited travel around the city. Strathclyde Partnership for Transport provides a comprehensive travel center within Buchanan Bus Station on Killermont Street. For information about local bus, rail, subway and ferry services, call ☎ 0141 333 3708; www.spt.co.uk. It also sells tickets for long-distance bus tours. Four types of travel tickets provide unlimited use of local transportation. The Discovery Ticket, for the subway only, is valid for one day. The Mackintosh Trail gives one-day unlimited travel and free access to all Charles Rennie Mackintosh attractions in Glasgow. The Daytripper Ticket, valid for one day, all day, is for families. It encompasses rail services (including the subway), most buses and some ferries for unlimited travel throughout the region of Strathclyde. For a taxi ☎ 0141 429 7070.

Airport Information

Glasgow International Airport, in Paisley, is 8 miles west of the city center (☎ 0844 481 5555; www.glasgowairport.com). The Glasgow Airport Shuttle (No. 500) runs up to every 10 minutes to Glasgow Central train station; journey time 15 minutes. Services 747 and 757 run up to every 20 minutes with several stopping places; travel time 25 minutes. Taxis are available at the front of the terminal.

Climate – average highs and lows for the month

Jan.	Feb.	Mar.	Apr.	May	Jun.	Jul.	Aug.	Sep.	Oct.	Nov.	Dec.
6°C	7°C	8°C	11°C	15°C	17°C	19°C	18°C	16°C	12°C	9°C	7°C
43°F	45°F	46°F	52°F	59°F	63°F	66°F	64°F	61°F	54°F	48°F	45°F
1°C	1°C	2°C	3°C	6°C	9°C	11°C	11°C	8°C	6°C	3°C	2°C
34°F	34°F	36°F	37°F	43°F	48°F	52°F	52°F	46°F	43°F	37°F	36°F

Glasgow Sights

Key to symbols
map coordinates refer to the Glasgow map on pages 226–227 admission charge: $$$ more than £6, $$ £2–£6, $ less than £2
See page 5 for complete key to symbols

The Burrell Collection

Any city in the world would be proud to claim this astonishing priceless collection of art and artifacts, gathered singlehandedly by Sir William Burrell. Enormously well-off thanks to ship-owning interests, in 1944 Burrell presented his native city with 6,000 items, continuing to add to them until his death in 1958. Burrell's only stipulation was that the collection be displayed in a rural setting, far enough from Glasgow to escape pollution. Those conditions were met in 1967, when Mrs. Maxwell Macdonald gave the Pollok Estate (now Pollok Country Park) to the city.

The collection is housed in a low, modern building 4 miles south from the city center. There are striking pieces of European art dating from the early Middle Ages onward; entire church doorways; medieval German religious carvings in beautiful limewood; very well-lit stained glass; and tapestries, glass and silver.

Paintings include a self-portrait by Rembrandt, as well as other portraits by William Hogarth, George Romney and Frans Hals; some beautiful Impressionist paintings by Monet, Cézanne, Degas and Alfred Sisley; and earlier masterpieces such as *Judith with the Head of Holofernes* (1530) by Lucas Cranach the Elder.

Items in the Ancient Civilizations section include Etruscan mirrors and Greek perfume bottles, a giant Roman bowl, mosaics and Egyptian busts. Outstanding exhibits in the Oriental Art collection are Persian carpets and Islamic tiles, delicate Chinese porcelain and jade, Japanese prints and a set of Tang dynasty tomb guardians. There are recreations of three of the rooms at Hutton Castle near Berwick-upon-Tweed, which Burrell bought in 1916 to house his then smaller collection – all heavy furniture and dark draperies. Bronzes by Auguste Rodin (including *The Thinker*) and Jacob Epstein are in the collection.

A1 (off map)
Pollok Country Park, 2060 Pollokshaws Road
0141 287 2550; www.glasgowlife.org.uk/museums
Mon.–Thu. and Sat. 10–5, Fri. and Sun. 11–5
Café Pollokshaws West Station, then 10-minute walk 45, 47, 48, 57 Café Free Guided tours twice daily (free)

Modern architecture blends with historical items

Looking west between the tall columns of Glasgow Cathedral's nave

Glasgow Cathedral

St. Mungo's ought to have been destroyed, along with the other Roman Catholic cathedrals of mainland Scotland, during the religious upheavals of the 16th-century Reformation. But this 13th-century Gothic masterpiece survived, thanks to the agreement of Glasgow's guilds to ensure Protestant worship in the church.

The cathedral is built on two levels, due to the slope of its site, and is divided into an upper and a lower church. The Lower Church, at the east end, is the crypt where the tomb of the original founder, St. Mungo, stands. Descending into the Lower Church, you find yourself among a thicket of columns rising to rib-vaulting around the saint's tomb. Mungo was a sixth-century ascetic, and his tomb became one of Britain's great medieval pilgrimage destinations. Even the iron-hard King Edward I, famed "Hammer of the Scots," came here three times to pray.

In the cathedral grounds is the unique St. Mungo Museum of Religious Life and Art, designed to bypass sectarian and religious bigotries and celebrate all of the world's religions. Particularly striking are a huge, many-armed statue of a dancing Shiva, exquisite Taoist porcelain, glorious Islamic prayer rugs and richly glowing stained-glass pieces collected from medieval churches.

E2 · Cathedral Square · 0141 552 8198; www.glasgowcathedral.org.uk · Mon.–Sat. 9:30–5:30, Sun. 1–5, Apr.–Sep.; Mon.–Sat. 9:30–4:30, Sun. 1–4:30, rest of year · Free

St. Mungo Museum of Religious Life and Art

2 Castle Street · 0141 276 1629; www.glasgowlife.org.uk/museums · Tue.–Thu. and Sat. 10–5, Fri. and Sun. 11–5 · Café · Free · Guided tours (free)

Glasgow School of Art

This fine sandstone building – still in use as Glasgow's prestigious art school – is a prime example of the style of its art nouveau architect, Charles Rennie Mackintosh (see page 233). In 1896 he won a competition to design the building and embarked on the project with confidence and vigor.

Entry is by guided tour only, led by well-informed student guides. The tour explains how Mackintosh strove to utilize every space to the utmost, to emphasize with dark-colored wood the brilliance of light pouring down from above or through tall windows, and to bring the vivid colors of Scottish nature

Kelvingrove Art Gallery and Museum is one of Glasgow's best-loved public galleries

and the smooth elegance of uncluttered lines to every corner of his building.

Mackintosh completed the art school in two stages, the eastern facade in a stern Scottish baronial style from 1897 to 1899, and the western end in a far less severe fashion between 1907 and 1909. The second phase saw the installation of a fabulous two-story library where angular dark wood columns support the reading galleries and light floods down on readers at the central tables from brightly colored lamps.

The Furniture Gallery contains a collection of stored Mackintosh artifacts, from his trademark tall-backed chairs to a model for a "House for an Art Lover" – which was finally built in 1996 in Bellahouston Park, south of the river.

B3 167 Renfrew Street 0141 353 4500; www.gsa.ac.uk Guided tours: daily at 10, 10:45, 11:30, 12:15, 1, 1:45, 2:30, 3:15, 4 and 5, mid-Jun. to mid-Sep.; 11, 3 and 5, mid-Sep. to Feb. Café $$$

Kelvingrove Park: Museums and Galleries

Kelvingrove Park, 1.5 miles west of the city center, houses the Gothic mini-palace of Glasgow University in addition to a number of first-class museums. The university itself, on the north side of the park, is home to the Hunterian Art Gallery and Hunterian Museum. The Hunterian Art Gallery underwent major refurbishment in 2012 and contains fine examples of Scottish oil and watercolor painting, as well as paintings and drawings by James McNeill Whistler. Upstairs is a reconstruction of several rooms in the house of Charles Rennie Mackintosh. The Hunterian Museum, across University Avenue, contains archeological finds and zoological material, as well as a display on the Roman occupation of Scotland.

The Kelvingrove Art Gallery and Museum, one of Glasgow's premier public galleries, on the southern edge of the park, is housed in a huge red Edwardian mock castle. There are sections on natural history and Scotland's wildlife, and arms and armor. But it is the paintings that most visitors come to see. Here are Scottish works galore, with the Massacre of Glencoe a popular subject, along with pre-Raphaelite and 19th-century genre paintings. A new gallery dedicated to the "Glasgow Boys" – late 19th-century outdoor realists – opened in 2011. Also here are fine Constable and Turner

Glasgow's new Riverside Museum of Transport

landscapes, some French Impressionist works, and plenty of Dutch and Flemish landscapes and portraits by such artists as Rembrandt, Lely and Van Dyck.

Kelvingrove Park A4 (off map) Otago Street 0141 287 5918 Daily dawn–dusk Cafés Free

Hunterian Art Gallery A4 (off map) University of Glasgow, 82 Hillhead Street 0141 330 4221; www.gla.ac.uk/hunterian Tue.–Sat. 10–5, Sun. 11–4 Café Free ($$ Mackintosh House; free Wed. after 2)

Hunterian Museum A4 (off map) University of Glasgow, University Avenue 0141 330 4221; www.hunterian.gla.ac.uk Tue.–Sat. 10–5, Sun. 11–4 Café in University Visitor Centre Free

Kelvingrove Art Gallery and Museum A4 (off map) Argyle Street 0141 276 9599; www.glasgowlife.org.uk/museums Mon.–Thu. and Sat. 10–5, Fri. and Sun. 11–5 Café Free (charge for special exhibitions) Guided tours (free)

Provand's Lordship

The tall, sandstone Provand's Lordship is Glasgow's oldest dwelling, built in 1471. It has served many functions in its life, from a drinking den to a shop, and the displays within tell the story of some of them. The low ceilings and simple furnishings of the 16th century show the plain nature of a medieval cleric's life. Mary, Queen of Scots came to the house in 1566, allegedly to meet her husband, Lord Darnley, who was sick with poison and shortly to be murdered mysteriously in Edinburgh.

E2 3 Castle Street 0141 276 1625; www.glasgowlife.org.uk/museums Tue.– Thu. and Sat. 10–5, Fri. and Sun. 11–5 Café Free Guided tours (free)

Riverside Museum

Glasgow's new iconic Riverside Museum on the River Clyde includes the Museum of Transport at the Kelvin Hall. The broader theme of travel and transport is explored through more than 3,000 objects, such as the South African locomotive and a restored local ship.

A1 (off map) 100 Pointhouse Place 0141 287 2720; www.glasgowlife.org.uk Mon.– Thu. and Sat. 10–5, Fri. and Sun. 11–5 Free Guided tours (free)

The Tenement House

The National Trust for Scotland has restored the extraordinary interior of this Victorian tenement (apartment) building. Here, between 1911 and 1965, lived Miss Agnes Toward, a typist in a shipping firm who changed almost nothing in her house and threw away even less. It is a perfect time capsule, with every old-fashioned item in the parlor, kitchen and bedroom bespeaking an orderly, waste-not-want-not lifestyle that has long vanished in Britain.

A4 145 Buccleuch Street, Garnethill 0844 493 2197; www.nts.org.uk Daily 1–5, Mar.–Oct. $$

Charles Rennie Mackintosh

Charles Rennie Mackintosh was born in 1868 in the Townhead area of Glasgow, not far from St. Mungo's Cathedral. This inner-city boy, one of 11 children, entered Glasgow Art School at the age of 16 and quickly became absorbed by the principles of art nouveau, with its stylized images from nature, flowing lines and subtle contrasting coloring. Mackintosh loved the outdoor colors of Scotland – green, purple and pink – and added to them a sense of form influenced by Japanese art, a big source of interest in Britain at that time. What he also realized was the artistic potential of a building designed as one harmonious whole – structure, furniture, glasswork, fixtures and fittings.

By 1896 Mackintosh was on his way as an independent designer, after winning a competition to design the new Glasgow School of Art on Renfrew Street. Many commissions around Glasgow followed – notably the Willow Tea Rooms on Sauchiehall Street, where everything from the elegant spoons to the tall-backed chairs and highly colored glass windows was designed to give Glaswegians something to admire and talk about over the teacups, in a building itself long, elegant and light.

Another grand Mackintosh building that links various facets of his style is Queen's Cross Church on Garscube Road. This distinctive sandstone church – the only religious building that Mackintosh designed from beginning to end – is the headquarters of the Charles Rennie Mackintosh Society (☎ 0141 946 6600; www.crmsociety.com). Viewed from outside, the building seems to be tapering up to heaven. Inside, the appearance is dark and solemn, except where the light enters through cheerful pink and purple windows inlaid with Mackintosh's characteristic tall lilies and stylized hearts.

Toward the end of his life Mackintosh fell out with some of his colleagues and abandoned Scotland. He left behind a legacy of fascinating city buildings, including (in addition to the three mentioned above) the Daily Record Building on Renfield Lane; Martyrs' school on Parson Street (where he was born); and The Hill House on Upper Colquhoun Street, which retains its original furnishings and decorations.

Brightly colored glass windows at the Willow Tea Rooms are typical of Mackintosh's style

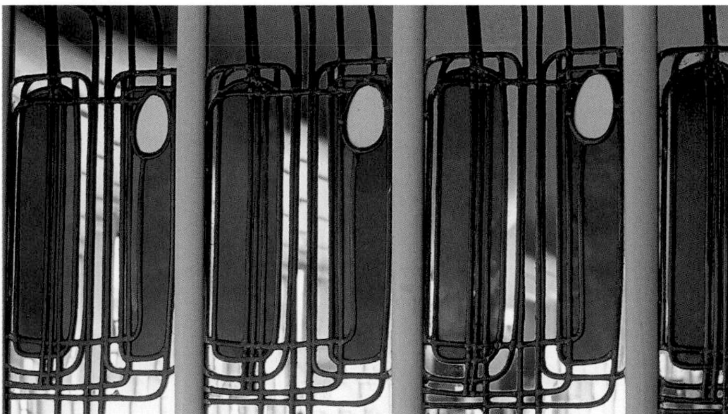

Regional Sights

Key to symbols
map coordinates refer to the Scotland map on pages 212–213 admission charge: $$$ more than £6, $$ £2–£6, $ less than £2
More symbol information on page 5

Aberdeen and Royal Deeside

Aberdeen, known as the "Granite City," is on Scotland's eastern coast. It is a city of two faces – grimly impressive under clouds and rain, fresh-faced and sparkling in sunshine. It is a lively university city with plenty of restaurants, bars and nightlife.

Stroll along the large fishing harbor, especially when the early morning fish auction is in full swing, to the Aberdeen Maritime Museum on Shiprow. The chief tourist attraction is the 16th-century Provost Skene's House on Guestrow, with rooms furnished and decorated in the styles of different centuries. The Satrosphere Science Centre is an excellent interactive science and technology exhibition. For a real Scottish experience you can learn to "curl" at Curl Aberdeen on Eddy Walk (tel: 01224 810369); curling involves bowling a granite stone across an ice rink to reach a target.

Aberdeen stands at the mouth of the River Dee, whose scenic valley descends gradually from the Cairngorm mountains. The valley is known as Royal Deeside because of its strong connections with the British royal family. They have been honorary Deesiders since 1852, when Queen Victoria and Prince Albert bought the huge Balmoral estate.

Balmoral Castle, near Ballater, is the British monarch's summer holiday home, a baronial-style castle built for Queen Victoria. West of Balmoral is Braemar, where the Highland Gathering is held in September.

The beautiful Dee valley is home to a number of superb castles. Drum Castle is a 17th-century house added to a 13th-century stronghold and Crathes Castle is a 16th-century tower house.

Opposite: The slopes around Crathes Castle are a riot of spring color
Right: The River Dee rushes through the Cairngorms National Park

Aberdeen D3
Tourist information 23 Union Street 01224 288828; www.aberdeen-grampian.com
Aberdeen Maritime Museum Shiprow 01224 337700; www.aagm.co.uk Tue.–Sat. 10–5, Sun. noon–3 Café Free
Provost Skene's House Guestrow, Broad Street 01224 641086; www.aagm.co.uk Mon.–Sat. 10–5 Café Free
Satrosphere Science Centre The Tramsheds, 179 Constitution Street 01224 640340; www.satrosphere.net Daily 10–5 Café $$
Ballater D3
Tourist information Old Royal Station, Station Square 01339 755306; www.aberdeen-grampian.com
Braemar C3
Tourist information The Mews, Mar Road 01339 741600; www.aberdeen-grampian.com
Balmoral Castle C3
Balmoral 013397 42534; www.balmoralcastle.com Grounds, gardens and exhibitions: daily 10–5, Apr.–Jul. Castle not open to public Café $$$ Audio tours (free)
Drum Castle D3
Drumoak, by Banchory 0844 493 2161; www.nts.org.uk Daily 11–4:45, Jul–Aug; Thu.–Mon. 11–4:45, Apr.–Jun. and Sep. Grounds: daily dawn–dusk. Garden: daily 11–5, Apr.–Oct. Café $$$
Crathes Castle D3 On A93, 3 miles east of Banchory 0844 493 2166; www.nts.org.uk Daily 10:30–4:45, Apr.–Oct.; Sat–Sun 10:30–3:45, Jan.–Mar., Nov.–Dec. Garden: daily 9–dusk. Grounds: daily dawn–dusk Restaurant and café $$$

The grave of Burns' father at Alloway Old Kirk

Ayrshire and Robert Burns Country

The county of Ayrshire, southwest of Glasgow, is the home of national poet Robert Burns (1759–96). Scots feel passionately about the "heaven taught ploughman" whose temperament during his short life summed up so many characteristics perceived to be typically Scottish – anti-authority, dryly humorous, by turns reckless and cautious, deeply romantic, and fond of a dram or three.

Burns sites are numerous in Ayrshire. On B7024 in Alloway village, just south of the county town of Ayr, is the cottage where he was born, now the Robert Burns Birthplace Museum. The Grecian temple shape of the Burns Monument stands beside the village's Brig O'Doon, a medieval humpbacked bridge over which, in Burns' comic masterpiece *Tam O'Shanter*, the drunken Tam escapes from witches on his gray mare, Maggie. Tam had interrupted the witches at an orgy in Alloway Old Kirk, and this roofless old church can also be seen just by the bridge.

B744 and B730 intersect at Tarbolton, 5 miles northeast of Ayr, where the National Trust for Scotland administers a museum in the Bachelors' Club, a house where Burns and his friends enjoyed themselves. At Mauchline, about 4 miles east of Tarbolton, there are several Burns sites: Poosie Nansie's Tavern, where he drank; Burns House, where his mistress, Jean Armour (later his wife), entertained him; and Mauchline Church, where he did public penance for the sin of fornication.

Ayrshire is not all Burns, however. There are waterfront golf courses at the towns of Troon and Prestwick and the village of Turnberry, and a grand clifftop castle at Culzean (pronounced "Cull-ain"), designed in 1777 by architect Robert Adam. There is also a sandstone coast of beautiful beaches.

Inland there is some invigorating high country such as the hills of Kyle Forest, where many rivers spring – among them the Coyle Water, or "Coila," as Burns styled it:

O, sweet are Coila's haughs an' woods,
When lintwhites chant amang the buds,
And jinkin hares, in amorous whids,
Their loves enjoy,
While through the braes the cushat croods
Wi' wailfu' cry!

Ayr B1

Tourist information 22 Sandgate 0845 2255121; www.ayrshire-arran.com

Robert Burns Birthplace Museum B1
Robert Burns Birthplace Museum, Murdoch's Lone, Alloway 0844 493 2601; www.burnsmuseum.org.uk Daily 10–5:30, Apr.–Sep.; 10–5, rest of year Café (Jun.–Sep.) $$$

The Borders

To rush through the Scottish Borders is to miss half of what Scotland is all about. The landscape between the border and the cities of Edinburgh and Glasgow, generally known as the Borders, is hilly country – not wild like the great mountains and glens of the northwest, but both intimate and grand. There are small towns such as Kelso, a trim little place where the rivers Tweed and Teviot meet; Melrose, with its tangle of narrow lanes and roadways and its magnificent abbey; snug Victorian Peebles; and farther west the town of Moffat, surrounded by great swaths of lovely countryside.

These towns have a well-earned reputation for quality woolen knitwear and textiles ("tweed" means cloth), and the region is dotted with mills and shops selling woolen, cashmere and tweed goods. Many of the Border towns have "Common Riding" events every year, when riders on horseback follow the town's boundaries – a reminder of the days when the area's borders were continually under threat by raids from south of the border.

There are tourist offices in Melrose and Selkirk (although the office in Selkirk is open April through October only), which can provide information about various drives and walks through the hill and valley country of Teviotdale and Eskdale.

There are four 12th-century abbey ruins to visit hereabouts. The abbey in the town of Jedburgh has wonderfully carved, many-tiered Norman arches and a monastic garth (garden) behind the cloisters. To the north, the Tweed valley encloses the other three: Kelso's lofty north transept; the chapter house and extensive abbey church remains at Dryburgh (Sir Walter Scott is buried here); and farther upriver at Melrose, many rose-pink arches. Here lies buried the heart of that scourge of England and self-proclaimed King of Scotland, Robert the Bruce, who died in 1329.

Jedburgh D1

Tourist information Murray's Green 01835 863170; www.visitscottishborders.com

The abbeys listed below are administered by Historic Scotland, www.historic-scotland.gov.uk

Jedburgh Abbey D1

Abbey Bridge End, Jedburgh 01835 863925; Daily 9:30–5:30, Apr.–Sep.; 9:30–4:30, rest of year $$ Audio tours (free)

Kelso Abbey D1

Kelso 0131 668 8600 Daily 9–5 Free

Dryburgh Abbey D2

Near St. Boswells 01835 822381 Daily 9:30–5:30, Apr.–Sep.; 9:30–4:30, rest of year. Last admission 30 minutes before closing $$

Melrose Abbey D1

Abbey Street, Melrose 01896 822562 Daily 9:30–5:30, Apr.–Sep.; 9:30–4:30, rest of year $$

The evocative ruins of Dryburgh Abbey lie near woods, not far from the River Tweed

The rocky outcrop of Bass Rock can be seen from the beach at North Berwick

Drive:

East Lothian Coast

Distance: 85 miles

The East Lothian coast is a little-visited corner of the Scottish Borders. All the better, then, for anyone who enjoys exploring rugged sea cliffs, fishing villages and magnificent castle ruins.

Start at Berwick-upon-Tweed.

Make sure you walk a circuit of the famous walls around this tenacious little town, just across the border in England. Between 1147 and 1482, Berwick changed hands 13 times between England and Scotland.

From Berwick, proceed north on A1; after 5 miles turn right and wind down to the tiny fishing hamlet of Burnmouth, typical of this craggy coast. Back on A1, turn right after another mile on A1107 to reach Eyemouth, another fishing village.

The excellent museum at Eyemouth tells the story, partly through a locally woven commemorative tapestry, of the Great East Coast Fishing Disaster of October 14, 1881, when 189 fishermen drowned, 129 of whom were from Eyemouth.

From A1107, side roads lead eastward to the cliffs.

Here are St. Abbs Head and its lighthouse, the jagged ruins of Fast Castle on a headland, and a million wheeling and shrieking seabirds. Footpaths along the clifftops offer memorable views of coast and sea.

Return to A1107 and drive for 11 miles before rejoining A1. After 5 miles, turn right on a side road to Barns Ness.

Follow the walking trail along the beach and you'll see strange and beautiful fossils in the cliffs and shore rocks.

Beyond Dunbar, turn right on A198 and head for North Berwick.

North Berwick is a pleasant coastal and golfing resort. Nearby is North Berwick

magnificent abbey; snug Victorian Peebles; and farther west the town of Moffat, surrounded by great swaths of lovely countryside.

These towns have a well-earned reputation for quality woolen knitwear and textiles ("tweed" means cloth), and the region is dotted with mills and shops selling woolen, cashmere and tweed goods. Many of the Border towns have "Common Riding" events every year, when riders on horseback follow the town's boundaries – a reminder of the days when the area's borders were continually under threat by raids from south of the border.

There are tourist offices in Melrose and Selkirk (although the office in Selkirk is open April through October only), which can provide information about various drives and walks through the hill and valley country of Teviotdale and Eskdale.

There are four 12th-century abbey ruins to visit hereabouts. The abbey in the town of Jedburgh has wonderfully carved, many-tiered Norman arches and a monastic garth (garden) behind the cloisters. To the north, the Tweed valley encloses the other three: Kelso's lofty north transept; the chapter house and extensive abbey church remains at Dryburgh (Sir Walter Scott is buried here); and farther upriver at Melrose, many rose-pink arches. Here lies buried the heart of that scourge of England and self-proclaimed King of Scotland, Robert the Bruce, who died in 1329.

Jedburgh D1

Tourist information Murray's Green 01835 863170; www.visitscottishborders.com

The abbeys listed below are administered by Historic Scotland, www.historic-scotland.gov.uk

Jedburgh Abbey D1

Abbey Bridge End, Jedburgh 01835 863925; Daily 9:30–5:30, Apr.–Sep.; 9:30–4:30, rest of year $$ Audio tours (free)

Kelso Abbey D1

Kelso 0131 668 8600 Daily 9–5 Free

Dryburgh Abbey D2

Near St. Boswells 01835 822381 Daily 9:30–5:30, Apr.–Sep.; 9:30–4:30, rest of year. Last admission 30 minutes before closing $$

Melrose Abbey D1

Abbey Street, Melrose 01896 822562 Daily 9:30–5:30, Apr.–Sep.; 9:30–4:30, rest of year $$

The evocative ruins of Dryburgh Abbey lie near woods, not far from the River Tweed

The rocky outcrop of Bass Rock can be seen from the beach at North Berwick

Drive:
East Lothian Coast

Distance: 85 miles

The East Lothian coast is a little-visited corner of the Scottish Borders. All the better, then, for anyone who enjoys exploring rugged sea cliffs, fishing villages and magnificent castle ruins.

Start at Berwick-upon-Tweed.
Make sure you walk a circuit of the famous walls around this tenacious little town, just across the border in England. Between 1147 and 1482, Berwick changed hands 13 times between England and Scotland.

From Berwick, proceed north on A1; after 5 miles turn right and wind down to the tiny fishing hamlet of Burnmouth, typical of this craggy coast. Back on A1, turn right after another mile on A1107 to reach Eyemouth, another fishing village.
The excellent museum at Eyemouth tells the story, partly through a locally woven commemorative tapestry, of the Great East Coast Fishing Disaster of October 14, 1881, when 189 fishermen drowned, 129 of whom were from Eyemouth.

From A1107, side roads lead eastward to the cliffs.
Here are St. Abbs Head and its lighthouse, the jagged ruins of Fast Castle on a headland, and a million wheeling and shrieking seabirds. Footpaths along the clifftops offer memorable views of coast and sea.

Return to A1107 and drive for 11 miles before rejoining A1. After 5 miles, turn right on a side road to Barns Ness.
Follow the walking trail along the beach and you'll see strange and beautiful fossils in the cliffs and shore rocks.

Beyond Dunbar, turn right on A198 and head for North Berwick.
North Berwick is a pleasant coastal and golfing resort. Nearby is North Berwick

Law, a 613-foot volcanic plug worth climbing for the view from the summit. Just offshore, in the Firth of Forth, Bass Rock (350 feet high) is a vital nesting place for gannets.

Nearby on the edge of the cliffs stands grim Tantallon Castle, a stronghold of a Scottish clan, Douglas. The castle was built in 1375 and never captured until General Monk, commander of the Royalist army in Scotland, besieged and battered it in 1651, the year that Charles II was crowned at Scone. Just west of North Berwick is Dirleton Castle, eye-catching 13th-century ruins on a knoll. There are beautiful grounds and a garden within the castle walls themselves.

Continue on A198 to Aberlady.

In Aberlady Bay there are vast numbers of geese and other seabirds in winter, and much to delight bird-watchers year-round.

From Aberlady, follow A6137 southeast to Haddington.

Haddington is a pretty little market town set in prime agricultural country that has carefully preserved its ancient houses and church. You can stretch your legs here on a stroll about town.

Take B6369 south to Gifford.

Gifford is laid out in the shadow of the Lammermuir Hills. One of the rebels who put his signature to the American Declaration of Independence in 1776, the Reverend John Witherspoon, was born in Gifford in the manse (minister's house) near the church.

The Lammermuir Hills are crossed by a network of marked footpaths, several of which begin at Gifford.

Leave Gifford on B6355, which runs across the shallow passes and through the valleys of the Lammermuirs for 20 miles to Duns. Alternatively, take the narrow hill road that leaves B6355 5 miles southeast of Gifford and snakes through the remote heart of the hills by way of Longformacus to Duns. It is then a 15-mile trip east from Duns on A6105 back to Berwick-upon-Tweed.

Berwick-upon-Tweed D2
Tourist information 106 Marygate
01289 301780; www.visitnorthumberland.com

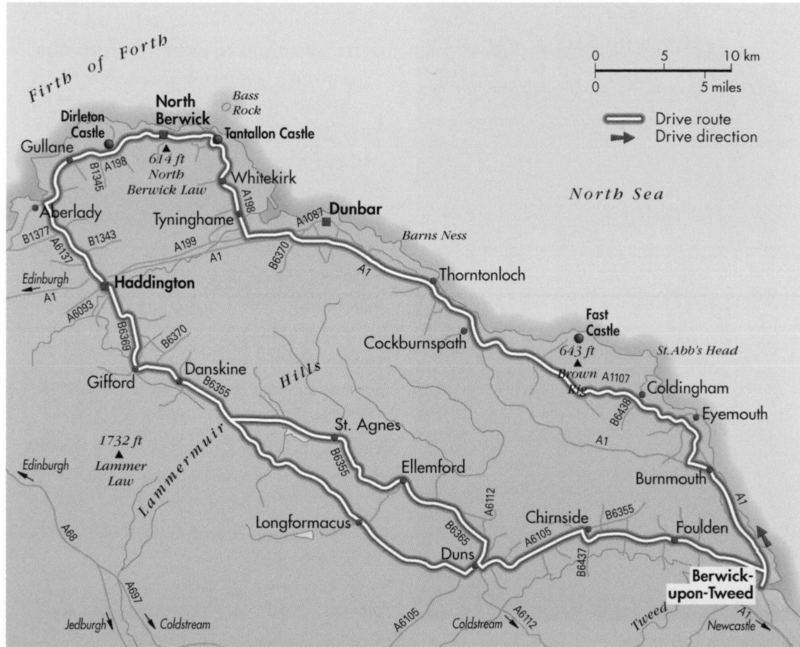

Dumfries and Galloway

In the southwestern corner of Scotland, the region of Dumfries and Galloway is an area that visitors tend to drive past rather than explore. Yet here is a marvelous coast, a clutch of small towns, plenty of historic interest, and an interior of hills and forests.

The main town is Dumfries, built from the local red sandstone. Here you can take up the Robert Burns trail again (see page 236), for Burns spent his last few years as an excise officer in Dumfries. The Robert Burns Centre relates the story of his stay in town. Burns House, on Burns Street, is where he lived and died, and the Burns Mausoleum at St. Michael's Church is where he lies buried. At The Globe Inn, tradition says if you sit in Burns' chair you must recite a line of his poetry, or treat everyone present to a drink.

The Globe Inn is one of several places to visit on the Burns Heritage Trail

Burns' house in Dumfries

J.M. Barrie, author of *Peter Pan*, went to school in Dumfries, and it was here that the ideas for his book originated while playing pirates with his friends. His math teacher is supposedly the character on whom he based the sinister Captain Hook. You can see some of Barrie's writings in Dumfries Museum.

The pretty town of Kirkcudbright (pronounced "Ker-coo-bree") consists of Georgian houses and fishermen's cottages in attractive disarray around the town center and harbor – perfect for the painters who established an "artistic colony" here in the early 20th century. Some of their works, mostly of local scenes, are on display in Broughton House, on High Street.

Dumfries C1
Tourist information 64 Whitesands 01387 253862; www.visitdumfriesandgalloway.co.uk
Robert Burns Centre C1 Mill Road, Dumfries 01387 253374; www.dumgal.gov.uk Mon.–Sat. 10–5, Sun. 2–5, Apr.–Sep.; Tue.–Sat. 10–1 and 2–5, rest of year Café Free ($ for audiovisual theater)
Kirkcudbright C1
Tourist information Harbour Square 01557 330494; www.visitdumfriesandgalloway.co.uk Apr.–Oct.

The sun shines down on the ruins of Old St. Peter's Kirk in Thurso

Inverness and the North

Once across the Great Glen, Inverness is the only sizable town in all of northern Scotland, a mini-capital that shoulders its historical weight with dignity. Beyond Inverness stretches the most northerly portion of mainland Britain, mountainous and wild in the west, rolling and bare in the east.

Inverness is a handsome town, and compact enough to stroll around in an hour or two. The castle is a huge 19th-century edifice, still used for court sessions. The Cathedral of St. Andrew on the opposite bank of the River Ness dates back to the 1860s. The town's museum and art gallery, back to back with the tourist office on Castle Wynd, houses Highland memorabilia, including a collection of bagpipes and relics relating to the 1745 Jacobite rebellion.

North of Inverness via the A9 road lies the Black Isle, a broad and fertile peninsula separating the Moray and Cromarty firths. From here, the A9 runs north to Dornoch Firth, then up the eastern seaboard through the fishing villages of Brora and Helmsdale.

Around Britain's northernmost town, the Norse-named Thurso, the fields lie low, crisscrossed with flagstone walls, and the wind blows constantly. Another 15 miles farther east is John O' Groats, named after Dutchman Jan de Groot, who lived here in 1509. You can have your photograph taken next to a sign quoting the number of miles to your home town. Another mile east is Duncansby Head, the end of mainland Britain, a vista of dramatic cliffs plunging into wild water.

Inverness C3

Tourist information Castle Wynd 0845 225 5121; www.visithighlands.com

Inverness Museum and Art Gallery Castle Wynd 01463 237114; http://inverness.highland.museum Tue.–Sat. 10–5, Apr.–Oct. Café Free

Thurso C5

Tourist information Riverside 0845 225 5121; www.visithighlands.com Apr.–Oct.

St. Andrews, Home of Golf

St. Andrews is a mecca for golfers the world over. It was here on the grassy dunes that the game developed in early medieval times. The Stuart kings of 15th-century Scotland banned it, lest young men should waste their leisure chasing the wee ball. But Mary, Queen of Scots gave golf a boost when she tried the game in 1567.

In 1754, the Society of St. Andrews Golfers was established to hold an annual competition. In 1834, King William IV became patron of the society, which then renamed itself the Royal and Ancient Golf Club. Today it is every golfer's dream to play a round on the Old Course in front of the R&A's grand clubhouse.

St. Andrews is not all golf, though. This is a civilized, historic university town with a fine castle and the notable 12th-century ruins of St. Andrews Cathedral. North Street is lined with the dignified buildings of St. Andrews University, while South Street boasts numerous fine Georgian houses and the delicate stone skeleton of the 16th-century Blackfriars Chapel.

D2

Tourist information 70 Market Street, St. Andrews 01334 472021; www.visitfife.com

British Golf Museum Bruce Embankment, St. Andrews 01334 460046; www.britishgolfmuseum.co.uk Mon.–Sat. 9:30–5, Sun. 10–5, Apr.–Oct.; daily 10–4, rest of year $$

Where to Play

Golf is considered the "people's game" in Scotland, and there is little of the exclusivity associated with the game in England. There are more than 600 courses in Scotland, most of them comparatively inexpensive. At many public courses you can show up and play – advance tee times are not required. If you want to try your luck on a private championship course you will need to reserve a tee time in advance and bring your handicap certificate with you.

Turnberry B1 Turnberry, Ayrshire, 50 miles south of Glasgow 01655 334032; www.turnberryresort.co.uk

St. Andrews D2 St. Andrews 01334 466718; www.standrews.org.uk

Carnoustie D3 Links Parade, Carnoustie, 10 miles east of Dundee 01241 802270; www.carnoustiegolflinks.co.uk

Gleneagles C2 Off A9 near Auchterarder, between Stirling and Perth 01764 662231; www.gleneagles.com

Royal Dornoch C4 Golf Road, Dornoch, 65 miles north of Inverness 01862 810219; www.royaldornoch.com

The website www.scotlands-golf-courses.com features a comprehensive listing of golf courses in Scotland, as well as details of accommodations.

Above left to right: A golfer tees off toward the clubhouse on the Old Course at St. Andrews; Auchterlonies of St. Andrews golf shop was established by three brothers in 1895

Whiskey on Speyside and Sports in the Cairngorms

The River Spey, one of Scotland's most beautiful rivers, rushes northeast in a series of majestic curves on its journey into the Moray Firth in Spey Bay, halfway between Fraserburgh and Inverness. The Spey is a world-class salmon-fishing river, fast-flowing and relatively shallow, and you may see fly fishermen up to their wader-tops in the water almost anywhere along the river.

The many burns (mountain streams) that hurry their pure, peat-filtered water from the hills into the Spey make this classic malt whiskey country. (The drink is spelled "whisky" in Scotland.) The soft water of the burns is as much an essential ingredient of the liquid gold as are the carefully selected and malted barleys used by the string of whiskey distilleries along the valley of the Spey. These distilleries, many of them dating back over 100 years, produce single malt whiskeys that are more expensive and exclusive – and, say the connoisseurs, a far subtler drink – than the more common blended whiskeys.

Well-known names along this beautiful river valley include Glenfiddich, Glen Grant, Glenlivet, Macallan and Glenfarclas, while smaller distilleries such as Knockando and Tamdhu are sought out by whiskey buffs.

There is a marked Malt Whisky Trail, and a brochure guide is available from most local tourist information centers.

In its northward run to the Moray coast the River Spey shadows the western edge of the Cairngorms. These impressive mountains are a winter and summer playground for outdoor enthusiasts and became Scotland's second National Park in 2003.

Walkers, climbers, snowboarders and skiers base themselves at Aviemore, in the valley of Strathspey to the northwest, or at Glenmore Lodge in the mountains. Ski lifts and a funicular railway go to the upper ski runs. There are marked walking trails; details at the Glenmore Visitor Centre.

Note: If you intend to walk in the Cairngorms, make sure you are properly equipped. Summer conditions can be unpredictable; winter conditions on the upper plateau and slopes can be subarctic, with 100 m.p.h. winds and whiteouts. These mountains are not tame.

Aviemore C3

Tourist information Unit 7, Grampian Road 0845 225 5121; www.visithighlands.com

Glenmore Forest Park Visitor Centre C3 Glenmore 01479 861220; www.forestry.gov.uk

Daily 9–5 Café Free

Traditional whiskey barrels pile up outside the Speyside Cooperage at Craigellachie

The Battlefield of Culloden

Prince Charles Edward Stuart, or "Bonnie Prince Charlie" as he came to be called, landed in Scotland in July 1745 from exile in France as the young and dashing claimant to the British throne. Charles' grandfather James Stewart, as King James II, had been deposed in 1688, and the Catholic Jacobites, supporters of the House of Stuart – both Scottish and English – longed to see their man crowned king.

The prince led his army as far south as Derby in central England in a march on London. But then he retreated, losing men and morale along the way back to Scotland. It was on Drummossie Moor, 4 miles east of Inverness (well marked from town) that the Bonnie Prince's dream came to a bloody and disastrous end on April 16, 1746. On the moorland battlefield the well-disciplined soldiers of the English Crown under the Duke of Cumberland overcame 5,000 wildly charging Highland clansmen with ease.

Terrible slaughter of fugitives and a scorched-earth policy followed quickly. The prince fled abroad to a long, sad decline in exile. The Gaelic-speaking clans were ruthlessly suppressed and their chiefs stripped of power. Within a century most of their lands had been sold, and the ordinary clan members scattered across the world by eviction and emigration. These infamous "highland clearances" brought a way of life to an end.

Today, the battlefield is a national monument, which you are free to wander at will and it is very well explained in the excellent Visitor Centre, and on a battlefield guided tour.

Culloden C4

Culloden Moor On B9006, 5 miles east of Inverness 0844 493 2159; www.nts.org.uk/culloden
Site: daily, dawn–dusk. Visitor Centre: daily 9–6, Apr.–Sep.; 9–5, Oct.; 10–4, rest of year (closed 3 weeks in Jan.) Restaurant Site free; Visitor Centre $$$ (including battlefield tour)

Stone markers on the battlefield help explain the events of Culloden

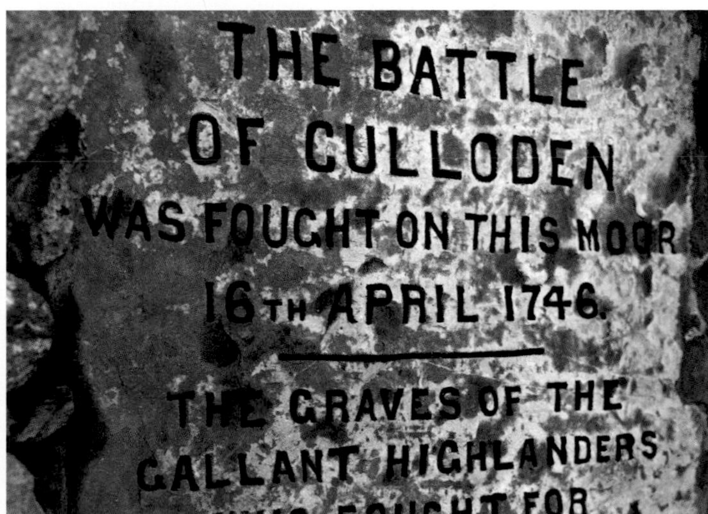

Drive:
The Western Highlands

Distance: 230 miles

This drive from Inverness through the wild and grand scenery of Wester Ross could be accomplished in a day. But it would be far better to allow yourself a night's break around Dornie or Plockton in order to enjoy fully the mountain scenery.

From Inverness, it is worth making the 4-mile trip to Culloden Battlefield (see page 245) to appreciate what underlies the silence and emptiness of the Highlands, before traveling west.

You can spend an hour or so discovering what life was like for the Highlanders before and after the 1745 Jacobite Rebellion. Their subsequent fate is reflected in the abandoned strips of cultivated land and empty glens of Wester Ross. This is an empty landscape missing its people, and all the more poignant in its sublime beauty because of that.

Returning to Inverness, head northwest on A835, crossing the mouth of Beauly Firth and then the neck of Cromarty Firth. Soon a right turn offers a little detour to Strathpeffer.

Strathpeffer is a neat Victorian spa town where you can still take the stinking sulfurous waters – should you wish.

Back on A835, continue west for 25 miles through countryside that soon becomes wild and hilly. Shortly before you reach Braemore, turn left on A832 to wriggle north and west until Little Loch Broom opens an arm of the sea. Now the road winds through beautiful, harsh coastal scenery past Gruinard Bay and Gruinard Island, then Loch Ewe and the Isle of Ewe, before reaching the remarkable Inverewe Garden.

Here rhododendrons and azaleas bloom in mid-May, along with other shrubs and flowers – testimony to the warmth of the Gulf Stream just offshore.

Next come the villages of Poolewe and Gairloch, and a last look west at the island-scattered ocean. Continue a long southeasterly descent along the south shore of beautiful Loch Maree as far as Achnasheen, then turn right on A890 and descend into majestic Glen Carron.

You'll traverse this wide, sweeping valley in company with the Skye and Dingwall Railway. At the top of Loch Carron there is an opportunity to extend the drive, to follow A896 to Kishorn and then bear left at Tornapress on a narrow mountain road to the remote village of Applecross and on around the Torridon peninsula – a side trip of about 60 miles through beautiful scenery.

A890 proceeds through the village of Auchtertyre; turn left on A87 here.

You will see the picturesque, fairy-tale castle of Eilean Donan standing on a rock in Loch Duich.

A87 sweeps east along Glen Shiel between mountains and Loch Cluanie; then A887 continues through Glen Moriston and drops down into the Great Glen on the west bank of Loch Ness. Turn right here on A82 to Fort Augustus.

You will pass the gaunt gray Benedictine abbey and the head of the Caledonian

Eilean Donan Castle on Loch Duich is one of Scotland's iconic images

Canal, where sailboats, trawlers and narrowboats (barges) wait their turn to pass.

B862 brings you back to Inverness up the quieter and more beautiful east bank of Loch Ness, with views across the loch to romantic-looking Castle Urquhart.

Every ripple in the peat-dark water of Loch Ness shapes itself into a monster to tease the overactive imagination.

Inverewe Garden B4
Off A832, near Poolewe 0844 493 2225; www.nts.org.uk Daily 10–4, Apr.–Oct.; 10–3, rest of year Restaurant (Apr.–Oct. only) $$$

Eilean Donan Castle B3
Off A87, near Dornie 01599 555202; www.eileandonancastle.com Daily 9–6, Jul.–Aug.; 10–6, mid-Mar. to Jun. and Sep.–Oct. Last admission 1 hour before closing Café $$

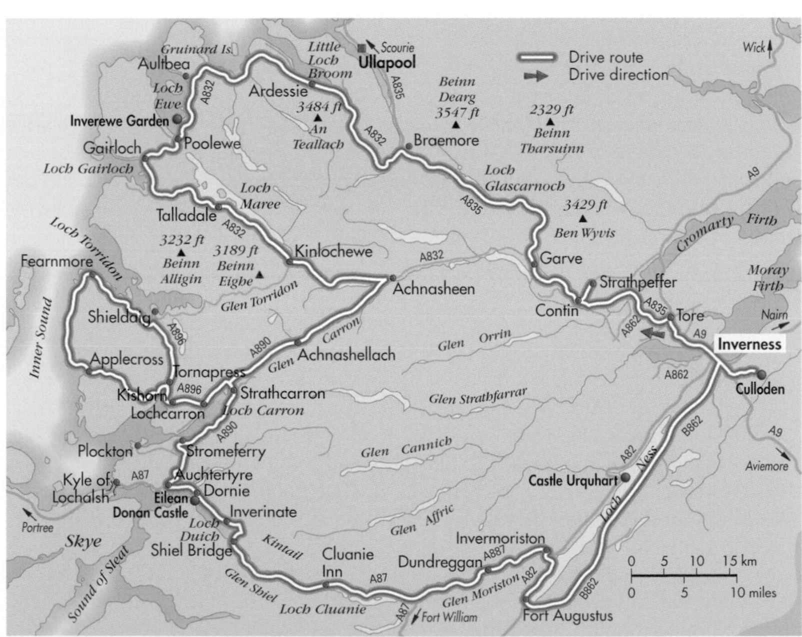

Colorful houses line the harbor at the fishing port of Tobermory on the Isle of Mull

Islands of Scotland

There is nowhere in Britain where the harsh realities of life are quite so much at odds with a romanticized image as in the Scottish islands. Life is genuinely hard for the islanders, as many fugitives from the city discover when they buy up an old ruin and come to live the "good life" – only to back out after the first winter. Facing fierce Atlantic or North Sea storms, trying to make a living from fishing, farming, running a bed-and-breakfast or whatever else they can manage, islanders stare isolation and hardship in the face. All the more remarkable, then, is their unstinting generosity and hospitality, and courtesy that never seems ruffled. Scottish islanders, whether they are Inner or Outer Hebrideans, Orcadians or Shetlanders, are among the most polite and genuine people you're likely to meet anywhere.

As for the wonderfully beautiful, impossibly romantic little "worlds in the water" that they inhabit – islanders know all about the magical effect on the visitor of that first sight of the Cuillin Hills of Skye, or the glory of a Western Isles sunset, or the thrill of hearing a Shetland fiddler at full gallop. When you cross that gap of water and step onto an island, you step into a different frame of mind and rhythm to life, where time is not measured by the clock but by the job or the drink or the dance – how long they last, and whether it is time to start a new one or not.

It is no good rushing through the Scottish islands – even if the weather, transportation and timekeeping would allow you to. The only way to appreciate the islands properly is to arrive, take a deep breath, relax, and let it all come to you in its own good time – the landscape, the wildlife, the people.

Scotland's islands fall into three main groups: the Inner Hebrides, just off the west coast; the Outer Hebrides or Western Isles, lying parallel but 30 miles farther out into the Atlantic, and the twin archipelagos of Orkney and Shetland off the northern coast, collectively known as the Northern Isles. Each group of islands has its own distinctive character, and only experience will tell you which pleases the most. The ferry company Caledonian MacBrayne operates westward to the Inner and Outer Hebrides; NorthLink Ferries sail north to Orkney and Shetland. There also are flights available.

Just before the Inner Hebrides, a few Clyde islands are sheltered between the mainland and the Kintyre peninsula – mountainous Arran; low-lying Bute and its resort town, Rothesay; and Great and Little Cumbrae.

Dramatic weather whips up waves on Loch Scavaig and threatens the view to the Cuillin Hills

The Inner Hebrides lie off the west coast, with Skye the chief island. Skye, although connected to the mainland at Kyle of Lochalsh by a road bridge, still has the romance lent to it by Bonnie Prince Charlie's flight "over the sea to Skye" with the help of Flora Macdonald after the Battle of Culloden (see page 245). Features include the magnificent volcanic Cuillin Hills; the great basalt rock curtain of the Trotternish peninsula; and dramatic Dunvegan Castle, on the island's western side.

Mull, the other big Inner Hebridean island, resembles a basalt layer cake. Off its southwestern tip lies the tiny island of Iona, from which Celtic Christianity spread all over Britain during the Dark Ages.

Across the rough channel called The Minch is the 130-mile-long chain made up of the Outer Hebrides, or Western Isles, a stronghold of the Gaelic language. Here you will find incredibly beautiful beaches called *machair* – thick, flower-spangled turf that lies on top of shell sand. The islands' east coasts are spectacularly mountainous. The northern island of Lewis is still a stronghold of the Free Church, a stern Presbyterian sect, while Barra, a southern island, is genially Catholic. Everyone on these islands, however, is extraordinarily hospitable.

The lush green Orkney islands shelter some of the world's most impressive prehistoric sites, from everyday dwellings to giant tombs thousands of years old. The Shetland archipelago, in contrast, has tremendous cliffs, seabirds, and hardy souls, living in a treeless landscape of windswept peaty moorland and heather.

Arran B1

Tourist information The Pier, Brodick
01770 303776; www.ayrshire-arran.com

Bute B2

Tourist information Isle of Bute Discovery Centre, Winter Garden, Victoria Street, Rothesay
0870 720 0619; www.visitscottishheartlands.com

Mull B2

Tourist information The Pier, Craignure
01680 812377; www.visitscottishheartlands.com

Skye B3

Tourist information Bayfield House, Bayfield Road, Portree 0845 225 5121; www.visithighlands.com

Orkney D5

Tourist information West Castle Street, Kirkwall
01856 872856; www.visitorkney.com

Shetland Map inset E4–E5

Tourist information Hay's Dock, Lerwick 01595 989898; www.visitshetland.org

Ferry operators:

Caledonian MacBrayne 0800 066 5000 (toll-free); www.calmac.co.uk

NorthLink Ferries 0845 600 0449; www.northlinkferries.co.uk

Loch Lomond and the Trossachs

An hour's drive north of Glasgow, Loch Lomond and the Trossach Hills are the city's country playground. This area became Scotland's first National Park in 2002. A narrow, poorly maintained road runs most of the way up the east side of the loch to the Rowardennan Hotel, below Ben Lomond. The A82 runs up the west bank, giving views of the slopes and mountain waterfalls across the lake. Northeast of Loch Lomond rise the Trossachs, offering the first real mountain scenery (although small in scale) that you encounter on your journey north. Much of the area is blanketed by the trees of Queen Elizabeth Forest Park; from the David Marshall Lodge Visitor Centre at Aberfoyle you can take the lovely Achray Forest Drive. North of here lies Loch Katrine, on which the steam cruiser SS *Sir Walter Scott* chugs about with visitors.

Callander is another visitor-oriented town with tearooms, outdoor equipment stores and souvenir outlets. Local hero Rob Roy – a dashing Robin Hood to myth-maker Sir Walter Scott but a vengeful cattle thief to historians – is romanticized in these parts and you will find connections with him everywhere.

East of Aberfoyle is the calm Lake of Menteith, where you can take a boat to Inchmahome Island, site of abbey ruins.

Aberfoyle C2

Tourist information Trossachs Discovery Centre, Main Street 01877 382352; www.visitscottishheartlands.com

David Marshall Lodge Visitor Centre Dukes Pass, on A821, Aberfoyle 01877 382283 Daily 10–6, Jul.–Aug.; 10–5, Apr.–Jun. and Sep.–Oct.; 10–4, Mar. and Nov.–Dec. Café Free; $ for parking

SS *Sir Walter Scott* Trossachs Pier, Loch Katrine 01877 332000; www.lochkatrine.com Operates most days early Apr.–early Oct. Café at pier $$$

Callander C2

Tourist information Ancaster Square 01877 330342; www.visitscottishheartlands.com

Safety in the Hills

Scotland's mountains, glens and rolling Border hills offer the best walking in Britain. There is something here for every outdoor enthusiast, from gentle pastoral strolls to the toughest possible mountain hikes.

Hiking tips:

- Find out the local mountain weather forecast (www.mwis.org.uk).
- Equip yourself properly, and know how to use your equipment.
- Go with a party of four at least, so that if someone gets hurt one person can stay with the injured party, keeping him or her warm and dry, and two can go for help.
- Be realistic about how experienced and fit you are, and be pragmatic about the weather. Discuss the route with a local expert – hiker, ranger or warden – if unsure. Be flexible enough not to set out if the weather is threatening or the route looks too tough.
- Tell someone where you are going, and when and where you expect to finish. Stick to that route, and phone to report your safe arrival.
- If bad weather or darkness threaten, find shelter quickly.
- If there is an emergency, keep calm and optimistic. If you have told someone where you are going, the rescue services will soon find you.
- Don't rely on a cell phone; it may not work when you want to use it.
- There is no substitute for these precautions.

Oban and the Southwest Highlands

The Southwestern Highlands, from Fort William south to the Mull of Kintyre, is an enormous region of dramatic sea-battered coasts and wild hills cut by deep glens.

Oban, a small, attractive seaside town toward the island-spattered mouth of Loch Linnhe, has a busy and thriving fishing harbor, and – more importantly for the region's prosperity – is the chief ferry port for the Hebrides. The town is dominated by a hillside folly resembling a Roman ruin.

This popular tourist center has a magnificent setting and plenty of facilities for visitors – stroll along the waterfront, shop for whiskey and tartan in the many gift shops, or enjoy freshly caught fish in one of the dockside cafés.

At the head of Loch Linnhe, nearly 50 miles north by road, Fort William is the gateway for those who want to explore the wonderfully wild and unfrequented peninsulas of the western coast. Just south of Fort William curves Glen Nevis, with the great bulk of Ben Nevis – at 4,406 feet, Britain's highest mountain – rising from its northern side. You can climb the mountain via a very well-marked path beginning at the Glen Nevis Youth Hostel. The trek is not especially difficult, but it will take a whole day and you must pay proper attention to the weather and take sensible precautions – see panel on opposite page.

Between Fort William and Oban the darkly dramatic valley of Glencoe cuts in eastward. Here can be seen the great hanging slopes up which survivors of the Massacre of Glencoe fled in the snow. This brutal act of ethnic cleansing took place on February 13, 1692, when 38 members of the local Macdonald clan – a thorn in the side of the authorities – were murdered in cold blood by soldiers billeted in their houses. It was a betrayal that has never been forgotten.

From Oban, A85 leads east. Just before reaching Dalmally, a right turn onto A819 will take you south to Inveraray, where a striking castle sits on Loch Fyne. A83 runs south from here via Lochgilphead for 100 miles, all the way to the southern tip of the Kintyre peninsula, the Mull of Kintyre. Ex-Beatle Paul McCartney bought a farm here to escape from the pressures of stardom, and you can appreciate his choice of location as you savor the peace.

Oban B2
Tourist information Argyll Square
01631 563122; www.visitscotland.com
Fort William B3
Tourist information 15 High Street
01397 701801; www.visitscotland.com
Glen Nevis Visitor Centre Glen Nevis, Fort William
01397 705922; www.highland.gov.uk Daily 9–5, Apr.–Sep.; 9–3, rest of year Free

Britain's highest mountain, Ben Nevis, rises above the calm waters of Loch Linnhe

St. Matthew's Church sits beside the River Tay near the 18th-century bridge that spans the dark waters

Perth

Perth, "The Fair City," is set on craggy hills above the River Tay, with the Grampian mountains as a northern backdrop. On the meadows of North Inch you can visualize the bloody championship contest fought in 1396 between the clans of Chattan and Quhale, as poetically described by Sir Walter Scott.

Northeast of Perth via A94 is the enormous pink fantasy castle of Glamis (pronounced "Glarms"). Shakespeare is said to have used Duncan's Hall as the setting for the murder of King Duncan by Macbeth, and there is evidence that King Malcolm II was murdered in or near the castle.

Another splendid castle is Blair, 35 miles north of Perth via A9. Turrets, gables and memorabilia bear witness to 700 years of history. Its owner, the Duke of Atholl, still maintains a private army and his own piper.

C2

Tourist information Lower City Mills, West Mill Street 01738 450621; www.perthshire.co.uk

Glamis Castle C3 Glamis 01307 840393; www.glamis-castle.co.uk Daily 10–6, Mar.–Oct. (last tour 4:30); 10–30–4:30, Nov.–Dec. (last tour 3). Restaurant $$$ ($$, Nov.–Dec.); gardens and grounds only $$; grounds only free, Nov.–Dec.

Blair Castle C3 Blair Atholl 01796 481207; www.blair-castle.co.uk Daily 9:30–5:30, Apr.–Oct.; Tue. and Sat. 9:30–2:30. Last admission 1 hour before closing Restaurant $$$ (grounds only $$)

The Wallace Monument marks the Scottish victory at the Battle of Stirling Bridge in 1297

Stirling

Attractive Stirling sits at Scotland's narrow waist, forming the apex of a triangle with Glasgow and Edinburgh. Stirling Castle, spectacularly perched on a crag, was used by the Scottish Stuart monarchs as their royal court from the 1480s until James VI became King of England in 1603.

The imposing castle houses the Argyll and Sutherland Highlanders Regimental Museum, a military regiment with plenty of dashing exploits to celebrate. The view from the battlements, some 250 feet up, is superb.

The town's historic buildings include Argyll's Lodging, a 17th-century residence of the Dukes of Argyll; the grand but never completed Mar's Wark; the 15th-century Church of the Holy Rude (Holy Cross); and the Stirling Old Town Jail.

The National Wallace Monument celebrates William Wallace, who led Scottish resistance against the English in 1297. There is an interesting audiovisual presentation, and for great views you can climb the 246 steps up the tower's spiral staircase.

C2

Tourist information 41 Dumbarton Road 08707 200620; www.visitstirling.org

Stirling Castle Castle Wynd 01786 450000; www.stirlingcastle.gov.uk Daily 9:30–6, Apr.–Sep.; 9:30–5, rest of year Café $$$ Guided tours (free) and audio tours (charge)

Hotels and Restaurants

Opposite: The timber-framed facade of The Feathers Hotel at Ludlow was built in 1603

Hotels and Restaurants

The hotels and restaurants in this book were selected by local specialists and include establishments in several price ranges. Since price is often the best indication of the level of facilities and quality of service, a three-tiered price guide appears at the beginning of the listings. Because variable rates will affect the amount of foreign currency that can be exchanged for dollars (and thus affect the cost of a room or a meal), price ranges are given in the local currency.

Although price ranges and operating times were accurate at press time, this information is always subject to change without notice. If you're interested in staying at a particular establishment, it is always advisable to call ahead to make a reservation.

Facilities suitable for travelers with disabilities vary, and you are strongly advised to contact an establishment directly to determine whether it will be able to meet your needs. Older buildings may not be adequately designed or equipped for visitors with limited or impaired mobility.

Accommodations

Accommodations have been selected with two considerations in mind: a particularly attractive character or sense of local flavor, or a central location that is convenient for sightseeing. Remember that centrally located hotels fill up quickly, especially during busy summer vacation periods; make reservations well in advance. In-room bathrooms (sometimes referred to as "en-suite facilities") may not be available in smaller budget hotels.

Room rates normally include breakfast. In British hotels, this is likely to be a full meal of bacon, sausage, eggs, fried potatoes, tomatoes and toast that should leave you feeling well fed most of the day. Some hotels offer a price for overnight accommodations that includes an evening meal (known as "half-board" in Britain).

The elegant entrance to The Bear Hotel at Woodstock

Eating Out

Listed restaurants range from upscale places suitable for an elegant evening out to small cafés where you can stop and take a leisurely break from a busy day of sightseeing. Other possibilities for getting a bite to eat are the cafeterias and restaurants on the premises of some museums, galleries and other tourist attractions.

The British used to be mocked about their culinary prowess and considered unimaginative when it came to food – but no longer. Today, there is a real interest and excitement about eating out. Chefs are feted both in their kitchens and as media personalities. New restaurants are opening, catering to all tastes and serving a variety of cuisine. Visitors will enjoy sharing this revival of British enthusiasm for good food.

KEY TO SYMBOLS

- hotel
- restaurant
- address
- telephone number
- days/times closed
- nearest metro/tube/subway station(s)

AX American Express
DC Diners Club
MC MasterCard
VI VISA

Hotels

Price guide: double room with breakfast for two people

$ less than £80
$$ £80–£175
$$$ more than £175

Restaurants

Price guide: dinner per person, excluding drinks

$ less than £25
$$ £25–£40
$$$ more than £40

Inviting and friendly

Don't always believe that paying more will guarantee you a better standard of accommodations. Unless you demand the lap of luxury and the widest possible range of amenities, you will often find well-run bed-and-breakfast houses and country pubs just as clean and inviting as an upscale hotel, and probably a lot more friendly.

SOUTHEAST ENGLAND

AMBERLEY

Amberley Castle $$$

Set in the South Downs, this delightful 11th-century castle has a gatehouse, an oak portcullis (one of the few remaining working ones in Europe), high walls, gardens and peacocks. It is also a hotel combining great charm and modern luxuries. The Queen's Room restaurant offers accomplished cooking in elegant surroundings – reservations are essential.
Amberley, West Sussex
01798 831992 AX, MC, VI

BOUGHTON LEES

Eastwell Manor $$–$$$

This Jacobean-style manor in Kent sits on 62 acres of gardens and woodland. The menu features luxurious dishes typical of British and French cuisine.
Eastwell Park, Boughton Lees, Kent 01233 213000 AX, DC, MC, VI

BRAY

Monkey Island $$

Idyllically located on an island in the River Thames near Windsor and within easy reach of major routes to other parts of the country, these accommodations are comfortable and stylish. The grounds are beautifully maintained and provide a peaceful haven for wildlife. The island can be reached only by footbridge or boat.
Old Mill Lane, Bray-on-Thames, Berkshire 01628 623400 AX, MC, VI

BRIGHTON

Amherst Hotel $$

This stylish boutique hotel offers lots of luxury but is very reasonably priced. Guests can expect personal and friendly service, which make this a real home away from home.
2 Lower Rock Gardens 01273 670131 AX, MC, VI

Drakes $$$

The seafront location is just one of the draws of this charming town house hotel with contemporary décor and lots of original features. The cocktail lounge and pleasant restaurant are a welcome bonus.
43–44 Marine Parade 01273 696934 AX, MC, VI

CANTERBURY

Canterbury Cathedral Lodge $$

This thoroughly modern hotel lies in the shadow of Canterbury's historic cathedral. Many rooms boast exceptional views of the cathedral's mellow medieval architecture and yet are light and comfortable.
The Precincts, Canterbury, Kent
01227 865350 AX, MC, VI

Ebury $$

The Ebury is a delightful family-run hotel surrounded by two acres of pretty gardens. Choose from a room with four-poster bed to a family suite. There is an indoor swimming pool.
65–67 New Dover Road, Canterbury, Kent 01227 768433
Closed for 10 days at Christmas and New Year AX, MC, VI

CHATHAM

Bridgewood Manor $$–$$$

This hotel has extensive leisure facilities, including an indoor pool. There is a choice of dining in the informal bar or the more formal Squires restaurant.
Bridgewood Roundabout, Walderslade Woods, Chatham, Kent
01634 201333 AX, DC, MC, VI

CHICHESTER

Comme Ça $–$$

This centrally located restaurant offers a superb selection of French-influenced recipes complemented by some excellent wine choices.
67 Broyle Road, Chichester, West Sussex 01243 788724
Closed Mon., Tue. lunch MC, VI

Millstream $$–$$$

Well-tended lawns surround this charming hotel, which has beautifully decorated bedrooms and public rooms. The highly regarded restaurant has a menu that changes frequently.
Bosham Lane, Bosham, near Chichester, West Sussex 01243 573234 AX, DC, MC, VI

The Ship $$

The only independently owned hotel within the walls of the Roman city, this Georgian hotel is furnished in a contemporary style. The restaurant serves bistro-style seasonal food.
57 North Street, Chichester, West Sussex 01243 788000 AX, DC, MC, VI

KEY TO SYMBOLS
hotel
restaurant
address
telephone number
days/times closed
nearest metro/tube/subway station(s)
AX American Express
DC Diners Club
MC MasterCard
VI VISA

Hotels
Price guide: double room with breakfast for two people
$ less than £80
$$ £80–£175
$$$ more than £175

Restaurants
Price guide: dinner per person, excluding drinks
$ less than £25
$$ £25–£40
$$$ more than £40

A Cholesterol Treat

Almost everywhere you stay in Britain you will be offered a "full English breakfast" of bacon, eggs, sausages and other trimmings to start your day. Few British households now eat like this at breakfast time; it is a treat reserved mainly for hotel guests. If you don't want such a cholesterol blast first thing in the morning, just tell your hosts; most places will be able to provide a healthier Continental breakfast (rolls, toast, fruit, yogurt).

CHILGROVE

The Fish House $$–$$$
The Fish House is a sumptuous fish restaurant in the village of Chilgrove, on the South Downs, convenient to Chichester and the Fishbourne Roman Palace. Choose from the tempting à la carte or the fixed-price lunch menu.
High Street, Chilgrove, near Chichester, West Sussex 01243 519444 AX, MC, VI

DEAL

Dunkerleys Restaurant and Hotel $$
Fresh fish is the specialty at this seafront restaurant located opposite the pier, but there are some good meat dishes to try, too.
19 Beach Street, Deal, Kent
01304 375016 Closed Mon.
AX, DC, MC, VI

Royal $$
Set on the seafront overlooking the beach, the spacious Royal Hotel has a vibrant brasserie.
Beach Street, Deal, Kent
01304 375555 AX, MC, VI

DOVER

Wallett's Court Country House Hotel, Restaurant and Spa $$
Formerly a Jacobean farmhouse with some original architectural features. Wallett's Court also has modern recreational facilities and English country cooking is a specialty.
Westcliffe, Dover, Kent 01304 852424 AX, DC, MC, VI

EAST GRINSTEAD

Gravetye Manor $$$
A shining example of a country hotel, this Elizabethan stone manor house is set amid extensive grounds with a beautiful garden. Gravetye Manor is famous for excellent food, using ingredients from its own walled kitchen garden. It is also a convenient base for exploring the castles and great houses of Kent and Sussex.
East Grinstead, West Sussex
01342 810567 AX, MC, VI

FOLKESTONE

Best Western Clifton $$
Overlooking the English Channel, this classic seaside hotel is down to earth, but assuredly comfortable and now has WiFi. Most rooms overlook the sea.
The Leas, Folkstone, Kent
01303 851231 AX, MC, VI

FORDINGBRIDGE

The Three Lions $$
The Three Lions offers attractively furnished accommodations, an excellent restaurant and is ideally located for exploring the New Forest.
Stuckton, Fordingbridge, Hampshire 01425 652489 MC, VI

HASLEMERE

Lythe Hill Hotel and Spa $$–$$$
This privately owned hotel is housed in a cluster of historic buildings, set amid 30 acres of grounds that include a bluebell wood and lakes. The Henry VIII Suite features a four-poster bed dating to 1614. The restaurant offers reliable local ingredients, while breakfast is served in the hotel dining room.
Petworth Road, Haslemere, Surrey
01428 651251 AX, DC, MC, VI

LONDON

Boyd's $$
Visit this newly refurbished restaurant for cocktails, cream tea or dinner. Classic British dishes are served in this historic building just off Trafalgar Square.
8 Northumberland Avenue, WC2N 5BY 020 7808 3344 Trafalgar Square AX, DC, MC, VI

Browns $$$
A perennially popular hotel that is both chic and classic, Browns has welcomed plenty of famous guests, who come to stay but also to eat at the superb HIX at The Albemarle.
Albemarle Street, Mayfair, W1S 4BP 020 7493 6020 Green Park AX, DC, MC, VI

Corinthia $$$
Old-school elegance and London's largest spa and wellness center are just two of the hallmarks of this impressive grand hotel, moments from Downing Street and the National Gallery.
Whitehall Place, SW1A 2BD
020 7930 8181 Embankment
AX, MC, VI

Double Tree Hilton Tower of London $$
This spectacular, great value hotel is highly recommended. The Tower View suites are particularly desirable,

and don't miss the rooftop bar offering fabulous city views.
7 Pepys Street, SE1 2BY 020 3002 4300 Tower Bridge AX, DC, MC, VI

Dukes Hotel $$$
This delightful spot in Mayfair is quiet yet right in the heart of things. Sip on a classic Martini, enjoy afternoon tea or dine in the acclaimed restaurant, THIRTY SIX.
St James Place, SW1A 1NY
020 7491 4840 Green Park
AX, DC, MC, VI

Lancaster London $$–$$$
Sweeping views over Hyde Park are just one of the draws of this fine central hotel. Its two restaurants, Nipa and Island Grill are excellent and it has strong eco credentials.
Lancaster Terrace, W2 2TY
020 7262 6737 Lancaster Gate
AX, DC, MC, VI

Langham $$$
Something of a London institution, this Victorian hotel boasts fine dining, one of the best spas in the city and a sophisticated cocktail bar.
1c Portland Place, Regent Street, W1B 1JA 020 7636 1000
Oxford Circus AX, DC, MC, VI

Mandarin Oriental $$$
Check in for luxury, spectacular views of Hyde Park, a world class spa and Heston Blumenthal's restaurant. The hotel offers a wide choice of different styles of room.
66 Knightsbridge, SW1X 7LA
020 7201 3833 Hyde Park Corner AX, DC, MC, VI

St. James Hotel and Club $$$
This Victorian town house and gentlemen's club offers a quintessential British experience. Expect slick service, use of a lovely day spa and London elegance.
7–8 Park Place, St. James, SW1A 1LS 020 7316 1600 Green Park AX, MC, VI

St. Pancras Renaissance $$–$$$
A sumptuous interior in a Gothic Revival building and an acclaimed spa give this Marriott hotel a unique and romantic identity. One of London's most exciting new hotels.
Euston Road, NW1 2AR
020 7841 3540 Kings Cross
AX, MC, VI

Texture $$
This excellent restaurant offers contemporary European cuisine with a Scandinavian flavor. The emphasis in the cooking here is firmly put on texture, hence the restaurant's name. The tasting menu and wine list are both a joy.
34 Portman Street, W1H 7BY
020 7224 0028 Closed Sun. and Mon. Portland Street AX, DC, MC, VI

The Wolseley $$
Brunch is an institution at this café-restaurant in the grand European style but with all-day dining there is not a bad time to come to eat. Reservations advised.
160 Piccadilly, WIJ 9EB 020 7499 6996 Green Park AX, DC, MC, VI

NEW MILTON

Chewton Glen Hotel and Spa $$$
A luxurious retreat within easy reach of the New Forest, Chewton Glen offers sumptuous accommodations in spacious rooms and elegant suites. Superior cooking in the restaurant uses excellent ingredients, and the wine list is impressive.
Christchurch Road, New Milton, Hampshire 01425 275341
AX, DC, MC, VI

PORTSMOUTH & SOUTHSEA

Queen's Hotel $$
This elegant hotel, with views across the sea to the Isle of Wight, is only a mile from Portsmouth city center. Many rooms have sea views and balconies, and there is a heated outdoor swimming pool. There is also a choice of bars and dining venues.
Clarence Parade, Osbourne Road, Southsea, Hampshire 023 9282 2466 AX, DC, MC, VI

The Wine Vaults $$
Wood-paneled walls, interesting paintings and artifacts all lend a relaxing atmosphere to this ale houses which boasts five bars. Ales come from Fullers of London, with up to eight different beers on offer at a time. The traditional English menu includes homemade soups and lamb stew, and traditional roasts are served on Sunday.
43–47 Albert Road, Southsea, Hampshire 023 9286 4712
MC, VI

RYE

Jeakes House $$
A 16th-century town house located on medieval, cobbled Mermaid Street, this bed-and-breakfast offers visitors a warm and friendly stay.
Mermaid Street, Rye, East Sussex
01797 222828 MC, VI

Mermaid Inn $$
This medieval smugglers' inn is full of character, with oak beams, historical paintings and huge open fireplaces. The modern menu includes good fish dishes.
Mermaid Street, Rye, East Sussex
01797 223065 AX, MC, VI

WINCHESTER

Mercure Wessex $$
This modern hotel is tucked away in the heart of the city and has magnificent views of the cathedral.
Paternoster Row, Winchester, Hampshire 01962 861611 AX, DC, MC, VI

Wykeham Arms $$
This famous old pub, right in the center of historic Winchester, has an innovative menu, an extensive wine list and a stylish atmosphere.
75 Kingsgate Street, Winchester, Hampshire 01962 853834
AX, MC, VI

WINDSOR

Mercure Castle $$
Rooms in the older part of this building, close to Windsor Castle, have been tastefully modernized and are traditionally furnished. The elegant restaurant offers a good seasonal menu. There is also a bar for light meals and snacks.
18 High Street, Windsor, Berkshire
01753 851577 AX, DC, MC, VI

Sir Christopher Wren Hotel and Spa $$$
Within easy walking distance of the Castle, this hotel boasts views of the Thames; some rooms have private courtyards overlooking the river.
Thames Street, Windsor, Berkshire
01753 861354 AX, DC, MC, VI

THE WEST COUNTRY

BATH

Bath Priory Hotel, Restaurant and Spa $$$
This intimate hotel in a Georgian building, includes a recreation center

KEY TO SYMBOLS

[hotel symbol]	hotel
[restaurant symbol]	restaurant
[address symbol]	address
[telephone symbol]	telephone number
[closed symbol]	days/times closed
[metro symbol]	nearest metro/tube/subway station(s)
AX	American Express
DC	Diners Club
MC	MasterCard
VI	VISA

Hotels

Price guide: double room with breakfast for two people

$ less than £80
$$ £80–£175
$$$ more than £175

Restaurants

Price guide: dinner per person, excluding drinks

$ less than £25
$$ £25–£40
$$$ more than £40

with a Roman Baths theme. Bedrooms are furnished with antiques, while the restaurant serves stylish, modern cuisine.
Weston Road, Bath, Somerset 01225 331922 AX, DC, MC, VI

Best Western The Cliffe $$
Set at the crest of a wooded hill in a quiet village 2 miles outside Bath, The Cliffe is a retreat from the hustle and bustle of the city. The gardens include an outdoor swimming pool.
Cliffe Drive, Crowe Hill, Limpley Stoke, Bath, Somerset 08457 767676 AX, DC, MC, VI

Dukes $$–$$$
This stylish hotel on a charming Georgian boulevard is near the beautiful Pulteney Bridge.
Great Pulteney Street, Bath, Somerset 01225 787960 AX, DC, MC, VI

Lansdown Grove $$
This historic building has high ceilings and delicate plasterwork and is surrounded by lovely gardens. The bedrooms have been renovated and offer a high standard of comfort.
Lansdown Road, Bath, Somerset 01225 483888 MC, VI

Lucknam Park $$–$$$
Lucknam Park is a member of Relais & Chateaux with a superb restaurant and equestrian center on the edge of the beautiful city of Bath.
Colerne, Wiltshire 01225 742777 AX, DC, MC, VI

Mercure Francis $$
This traditional hotel, located on elegant Queen Square in the heart of Bath, offers a warm welcome.
Queen Square, Bath, Somerset. 01225 424105 AX, DC, MC, VI

Queensberry $$–$$$
Enjoy beautifully appointed bedrooms and the fresh cuisine of the Olive Tree restaurant, located in a carefully restored Bath stone house a few minutes' walk from the town center.
Russell Street, Bath, Somerset 01225 447928 AX, MC, VI

Redcar Hotel $–$$
This is a comfortable hotel within striking distance of the city center. It offers good-value accommodations.
27–29 Henrietta Street, Bath, Somerset 01225 469151 AX, DC, MC, VI

The Royal Crescent $$$
Hospitality, service and fine cuisine are combined in this grand Bath setting – the curve of Georgian houses that is the Royal Crescent.
16 Royal Crescent, Bath, Somerset 01225 823333 AX, DC, MC, VI

Strada $
An historic Regency house, this is the former home of Beau Nash's mistress, Juliana Popjoy. The contemporary Italian restaurant is best known for its pizzas.
Beau Nash House, Sawclose, Bath, Somerset 01225 337753 AX, MC, VI

Tasburgh House $$–$$$
There are sweeping views over the Avon valley from this charming Victorian hotel offering elegant accommodations and friendly service. The lovely grounds slope down to the picturesque Kennet and Avon Canal, along whose towpath guests can walk right into the town center.
Warminster Road, Bath, Somerset 01225 425096 AX, MC, VI

Woods $$
Located just across the road from the Assembly Rooms, Woods has a short, well-balanced menu and is known locally for delicious, good-value lunches.
9–13 Alfred Street, Bath, Somerset 01225 314812 Closed Sun., Jan. 1 and Dec. 26 MC, VI

BRADFORD-ON-AVON

Bradford Old Windmill $$
Rooms at the Old Windmill, in the heart of town, are individually decorated to match the character of this unique property. Breakfasts include vegetarian options as well as a conventional English one.
4 Masons Lane, Bradford-on-Avon, Wiltshire 01225 866842 Closed Jan.–Feb. and Dec. 25 AX, MC, VI

Georgian Lodge $–$$
This historic-looking building occupies an ideal spot in the center of town. All the accommodations are reached from the central courtyard.

Traditional Cream Tea

One tradition you must observe when traveling in the West Country is the leisurely consumption of a cream tea. This features a yellow scone (fruit-studded or plain), a thick layer of jam and an even thicker dollop of cream. Then another. Better eat breakfast early and dinner late if you know you will be embarking on a Cream Tea Day.

The split-level restaurant serves classic dishes with a few saucy touches of modernity.
✉ 25 Bridge Street, Bradford-on-Avon, Wiltshire ☎ 01225 862268 MC, VI

BRIDPORT

Bridport Arms $$
Located on the beach at West Bay, 1 mile south of Bridport, this popular thatched inn offers warm hospitality. Rooms are simply furnished, and meals are available in the restaurant and bar.
✉ West Bay, Bridport, Dorset ☎ 01308 422994 MC, VI

BRISTOL

The Avon Gorge $$
This hotel occupies a commanding position overlooking the Avon Gorge and famous suspension bridge in the heart of fashionable Clifton. There is a choice of bars (one with a terrace above the gorge) and an attractive restaurant.
✉ Sion Hill, Clifton, Bristol ☎ 0117 973 8955 AX, MC, VI

Riverstation $–$$
Contemporary decor and a modern European menu prevail at this restaurant along Bristol's revitalized dockside.
✉ The Grove, Bristol ☎ 0117 914 4434 Closed Jan. 1 and Dec. 25 DC, MC, VI

CASTLE COMBE

Manor House $$$
Convenient for exploring Lacock and Avebury, this hotel is surrounded by 365 acres of gardens and parkland in the lovely village of Castle Combe. There are bedrooms in the main house and in a row of cottages on the grounds. Elegant cuisine is served in the restaurant.
✉ Castle Combe, Wiltshire ☎ 01249 782206 AX, DC, MC, VI

CHAGFORD

Gidleigh Park $$$
This mock-Tudor hotel, set on 54 acres within Dartmoor National Park, provides rooms of an exceptional standard. The grounds have streams, woodlands and a variety of recreational pursuits. The hotel restaurant offers outstanding dishes, many using local ingredients.
✉ Chagford, Devon ☎ 01647 432367 AX, DC, MC, VI

CORFE CASTLE

Mortons House $$–$$$
This hotel occupies an Elizabethan manor house in the shadow of Corfe's ruined castle. Features include an oak-paneled drawing room. Well-prepared cuisine is also available in the hotel restaurant.
✉ 49 East Street, Corfe Castle, Dorset ☎ 01929 480988 MC, VI

DORCHESTER

Casterbridge $$
This hotel is convenient to the town center. A bar, library, drawing room and conservatory are all options for relaxing during the day.
✉ 49 High East Street, Dorchester, Dorset ☎ 01305 264043 AX, DC, MC, VI

Yalbury Cottage $$
Located 2 miles east of Dorchester in the heart of Thomas Hardy's Wessex, this 350-year-old cottage was once a shepherd's home. The oak-beamed restaurant has an inglenook fireplace, and the cuisine is award-winning.
✉ Lower Bockhampton, Dorchester, Dorset ☎ 01305 262382 MC, VI

EVERSHOT

Summer Lodge Country House Hotel, Restaurant and Spa $$$
This country house hotel, set in four picturesque acres, including charming walled gardens, is personally owned and run. Log fires, antiques and watercolor paintings all add to the elegance. The hotel restaurant serves imaginative food.
✉ Evershot, Dorset ☎ 01935 482000 AX, DC, MC, VI

FALMOUTH

Royal Duchy $$–$$$
The Royal Duchy is an elegant Victorian seafront hotel, with such modern luxuries as a swimming pool, sauna, solarium and spa bath. Seafood features strongly on the restaurant menu.
✉ Cliff Road, Falmouth, Cornwall ☎ 01326 313042 AX, MC, VI

The Terrace $$–$$$
Originally a cheese and wine cellar, the Royal Duchy hotel's restaurant has been tastefully decorated in art deco style. The menu features excellent seafood.
✉ Cliff Road, Falmouth, Cornwall ☎ 01326 313042 AX, DC, MC, VI

GLASTONBURY

George and Pilgrim $$–$$$
This 15th-century inn is steeped in history. It offers accommodations as well as a cozy bar and brasserie.
✉ 1 High Street, Glastonbury, Somerset ☎ 01458 831146 AX, MC, VI

Who'd A Thought It $–$$
Unfussy, good food is served in a Georgian pub furnished with local artifacts and memorabilia.
✉ 17 Northload Street, Glastonbury, Somerset ☎ 01458 834460 MC, VI

LACOCK

The Red Lion $–$$
Located in the timeless, preserved village of Lacock (where photography was invented), this refurbished inn offers good fare.
✉ 1 High Street, Lacock, near Corsham, Wiltshire ☎ 01249 730456 AX, MC, VI

LYNMOUTH

Rising Sun $
This delightful thatched, wood-beamed 14th-century inn on the waterfront at Lynmouth offers comfortable rooms. The kitchen specializes in local Exmoor game and excellent seafood, using quality local products, such as crab bisque.
✉ Harbourside, Lynmouth, Devon ☎ 01598 753223 MC, VI

MALMESBURY

Whatley Manor $$$
This fine hotel and spa, and a fitting member of Relais & Châteaux, really is a destination in its own right where you can expect tranquility and luxury in a stunning setting.
✉ Easton Grey, Malmesbury ☎ 01666 822888 MC, VI

MOUSEHOLE

Old Coastguard Hotel $$–$$$
In the heart of the picturesque fishing village of Mousehole (pronounced "Mouzall"), this informal inn has a backdrop of subtropical gardens, which lead directly to a rocky beach. Most of the bedrooms have wonderful sea views.
✉ The Parade, Mousehole, Cornwall ☎ 01736 731222 MC, VI

POTTERNE

Blounts Court Farm $
Enjoy a taste of country living at this superbly converted barn, surrounded

KEY TO SYMBOLS

- hotel
- restaurant
- address
- telephone number
- days/times closed
- nearest metro/tube/subway station(s)

AX American Express
DC Diners Club
MC MasterCard
VI VISA

Hotels
Price guide: double room with breakfast for two people
$ less than £80
$$ £80–£175
$$$ more than £175

Restaurants
Price guide: dinner per person, excluding drinks
$ less than £25
$$ £25–£40
$$$ more than £40

by farmland and overlooking the village cricket field. Breakfast, featuring local products, is served in the farmhouse dining room.
Coxhill Lane, Potterne, near Devizes, Wiltshire 01380 727180 MC, VI

SALISBURY

Best Western Red Lion $$
Located just off Market Square, the Red Lion is older than the town's magnificent cathedral and offers traditional standards of hospitality. Several rooms have four-poster beds. The restaurant serves modern and traditional-style cuisine.
Milford Street, Salisbury, Wiltshire 01722 323334 AX, MC, VI

Howard's House Country Hotel $$$
This welcoming hotel in a picturesque village 4 miles west of Salisbury has spacious, comfortably furnished rooms. In the restaurant, simple presentations allow the flavors to speak for themselves.
Teffont Evias, Salisbury, Wiltshire 01722 716392 AX, MC, VI

SHEPTON MALLET

Charlton House Spa Hotelo $$$
This hotel occupies a 16th-century house on pretty grounds. All the bedrooms are decorated in individual style. Facilities include a spa, sauna and tennis courts.
Charlton Road, Shepton Mallet, Somerset 01749 342008 AX, DC, MC, VI

ST. IVES

Alba Restaurant $–$$
The old lifeboat house in this bustling Cornish fishing village is transformed into an airy harborside eatery where freshly caught fish is the star of an eclectic menu.
Wharf Road, St. Ives, Cornwall 01736 797222 MC, VI

STON EASTON

Ston Easton Park $$$
This 18th-century Palladian mansion occupies extensive grounds. Rooms are luxuriously furnished with antique pieces. Aperitifs are served in the elegant salon, dinner in the dining room. After-dinner drinks, and petits fours are taken in the library.
Ston Easton, Somerset 01761 241631 AX, DC, MC, VI

THORNBURY

Thornbury Castle $$$
Royalty have been among the guests here in the only Tudor castle in England to be opened as a hotel. It is conveniently located just 15 minutes from the M5. Visit for tea or a meal if not for an overnight stay.
Thornbury, Gloucestershire 01454 281182 AX, DC, MC, VI

TOTNES

The Waterman's Arms $–$$
Log fires, exposed beams and a riverside location make this a happily atmospheric place to stay. Pub meals are served in the bar.
Bow Bridge, Ashprington, near Totnes, Devon 01803 732214 MC, VI

WARMINSTER

Bishopstrow House $$–$$$
This lovely Georgian-house hotel (a convenient base for visiting Longleat) is furnished with English antiques and 19th-century paintings. Several suites have whirlpool baths and four-poster beds. The Mulberry Restaurant overlooks the gardens and offers contemporary British and Mediterranean cuisine.
Warminster, Wiltshire 01985 212312 AX, DC, MC, VI

WILLITON

The White House $–$$
There is a wonderfully relaxed and easy-going atmosphere at this friendly hotel on the Somerset coast, where fresh fish and local game feature on the menu.
11 Long Street, Williton, Somerset 01984 632306 AX, MC, VI

EASTERN ENGLAND

ALDEBURGH

Regatta $
Regatta is a bright and child-friendly bistro in the center of town. The lively menu features local fish and delicious fries.
171 High Street, Aldeburgh, Suffolk 01728 452011 AX, MC, VI

Wentworth $$
This popular hotel, just a short walk from the seafront, is family-run and has a welcoming atmosphere. The hotel does not have a lift.
Wentworth Road, Aldeburgh, Suffolk 01728 452312 AX, DC, MC, VI

Guide to Beer Part 1

Ale, beer, bitter, best...they all mean the same thing: what the British like to drink in a pint glass at a temperature slightly lower than that of the room they are drinking it in. It tastes best when pulled through a hand-pump, or poured into the glass straight from the barrel. Color, flavor and strength vary enormously from one district to the next – and from one day to the next, since beer is a living and ever-changing thing. Remember that the pint you order will be a British pint – 19 U.S. fluid ounces (instead of the U.S. 16 fluid ounces). If your thirst isn't up to a British pint, order a half (9 U.S. fluid ounces).

AYLESBURY

Hartwell House Hotel, Restaurant and Spa $$$
A grand country mansion with service to match. Rooms, some in a converted stable block, are full of character. The dining room offers an elegant atmosphere in which to appreciate an imaginative menu. Afternoon tea is served in a number of elegant salons.
Oxford Road, Aylesbury, Buckinghamshire 01296 747444 AX, MC, VI

Titchwell Manor $$–$$$
A luxurious hotel housed in an atmospheric Victorian farmhouse, Titchwell Manor is family owned with an acclaimed restaurant. It boasts wonderful original features and a charming courtyard herb garden.
Titchwell, Nr Brancaster, Norfolk 01485 210221 AX, MC, VI

BURNHAM MARKET

Hoste Arms $$
This combination pub, restaurant and hotel close to the north Norfolk coast is upscale and stylish in appearance, yet down-to-earth and unpretentious in atmosphere.
The Green, Burnham Market, Norfolk 01328 738777 MC, VI

BURY ST. EDMUNDS

Angel $$–$$$
This is an elegant Georgian house close to the cathedral. Bedrooms are tastefully decorated with period furniture and include such thoughtful extras as books and mineral water. There is also a bar and restaurant.
3 Angel Hill, Bury St. Edmunds, Suffolk 01284 714000 AX, DC, MC, VI

Best Western Priory $–$$
Convenient to town and popular with business guests, this hotel has a restaurant with an ambitious menu, a conservatory dining room and a lounge bar.
Mildenhall Road, Bury St. Edmunds, Suffolk 01284 766181 AX, DC, MC, VI

CAMBRIDGE

Arundel House $$
Converted from a row of Victorian town houses, this popular hotel is next to the River Cam and overlooks parkland.
Chesterton Road, Cambridge, Cambridgeshire 01223 367701 AX, DC, MC, VI

Restaurant 22 $$
Restaurant 22 emphasizes unfussy English cooking with touches of classic French cuisine, served in a relaxed atmosphere.
22 Chesterton Road, Cambridge, Cambridgeshire 01223 351880 Closed Sun.–Mon., daily lunch AX, DC, MC, VI

COLCHESTER

Best Western Rose and Crown $–$$
Located in the center of town, this lovely 14th-century house, with exposed beams and timbered walls, has trendy accommodations and a restaurant with an extensive menu.
East Street, Colchester, Essex 01206 866677 AX, DC, MC, VI

DEDHAM

Maison Talbooth $$$
This stylish Victorian country house hotel, offering warm hospitality, has a lovely riverside setting.
Stratford Road, Dedham, Essex 01206 322367 AX, DC, MC, VI

Le Talbooth $$–$$$
Half a mile west of Dedham, in a black-and-white timbered building, this restaurant has stunning river views. You can dine on the terrace in summer. The food is tasty and complemented by a good wine list. There are evening riverside barbecues Jun.–Sep.
Gun Hill, near Dedham, Essex 01206 323150 Closed Sun. dinner AX, DC, MC, VI

ELY

Anchor Inn $–$$
Just a few miles out of the cathedral city of Ely, this waterside inn was built by Scottish prisoners captured by Oliver Cromwell in the 1650s. Spacious rooms are well appointed and the food and drink offered in the bar and restaurant are outstanding.
Sutton Gault, Sutton, Ely, Cambridgeshire 01353 778537 AX, MC, VI

The Old Fire Engine House $$
Excellent regional English cuisine is on the menu at this friendly 18th-century restaurant-cum-art gallery. Try the rabbit with prunes and bacon or the roast guinea fowl.
25 St. Mary's Street, Ely, Cambridgeshire 01353 662582 Closed Sun. dinner AX, MC, VI

HOLKHAM

The Victoria Hotel $$–$$$
Just a short stroll from the Norfolk coast, this boutique hotel on the Holkham estate is utterly charming. The historic building is very family – and even dog – friendly.
Park Road, Holkham, Wells-next-the-Sea, Norfolk 01328 711008 AX, DC, MC, VI

IPSWICH

Hintlesham Hall $$–$$$
This fine country house hotel with health club is much applauded for its atmosphere, elegance, stylish restaurant menu and excellent wine list.
George Street, Hintlesham, near Ipswich, Suffolk 01473 652334 AX, DC, MC, VI

LAVENHAM

Angel Hotel $–$$
This 15th-century coaching inn in the center of medieval Lavenham offers traditional pub fare.
Market Place, Lavenham, Suffolk 01787 247388 Closed Dec. 25–26 MC, VI

Lavenham Priory $$
This is a prize-winning bed-and-breakfast in a 15th-century priory, tastefully furnished and set amid large, beautiful gardens.
Water Street, Lavenham, Suffolk 01787 247404 Closed Dec. 21–Jan. 2 MC, VI

LINCOLN

The White Hart $$
Located within the old city walls between Lincoln's magnificent cathedral and castle, this hotel is attractively decorated. Many rooms have lovely views over the city.
Bailgate, Lincoln, Lincolnshire 01522 526222 AX, MC, VI

Wig and Mitre $–$$
This 14th-century hostelry, on a cobbled medieval street close to the cathedral, offers a comprehensive menu of good British and international home cooking.
30–32 Steep Hill, Lincoln, Lincolnshire 01522 535190 AX, MC, VI

KEY TO SYMBOLS

hotel
restaurant
address
telephone number
days/times closed
nearest metro/tube/subway station(s)

AX American Express
DC Diners Club
MC MasterCard
VI VISA

Hotels

Price guide: double room with breakfast for two people

$ less than £80
$$ £80–£175
$$$ more than £175

Restaurants

Price guide: dinner per person, excluding drinks

$ less than £25
$$ £25–£40
$$$ more than £40

Guide to Beer Part 2

If you really get the taste for beer, consider investing in a copy of the Good Beer Guide, published annually by the advocacy group Campaign for Real Ale (CAMRA). The campaigners have successfully resisted the big breweries' attempts to replace traditional beer – which is difficult to maintain in tip-top condition, but rewarding to drink – with fizzy pasteurized stuff that tastes blandly chemical but keeps for months. The Good Beer Guide lists thousands of pubs that serve beer the old-fashioned – and best – way.

NORWICH

Beeches Hotel $–$$

A peaceful retreat within walking distance of the city center, with a noteworthy sunken Victorian garden. Bedrooms are well maintained. Dining options are available at sister establishments close by.

2–6 Earlham Road, Norwich, Norfolk 01603 621167 AX, DC, MC, VI

Bishops $$

This small restaurant is tucked away down a side street in the city center. Specialties include confit pork belly, perhaps followed by a selection of Norfolk cheeses.

8–10 St. Andrews Hill, Norwich, Norfolk 01603 767321 Closed Sun.–Mon., Jan. 1, 2 weeks in summer, Dec. 25–26 and 2 weeks in winter AX, MC, VI

By Appointment $$

Sumptuous furnishings and bold colors give this restaurant a theatrical and romantic setting. Excellent seafood is a feature, such as pan-fried John Dory.

25–29 St. George's Street, Norwich, Norfolk 01603 630730 Closed Sun.–Mon., daily lunch and Dec. 25 MC, VI

The Georgian House $$

An informal, friendly family hotel, The Georgian House is a short walk from the city center and includes a cozy bar and an elegant restaurant.

32–34 Unthank Road, Norwich, Norfolk 01603 615655 or 01603 703369 (reservations) AX, DC, MC, VI

Marriott Sprowston Manor Hotel and Country Club $$

Housed in a 19th-century manor on 170 acres of parkland, this hotel has family rooms and full suites. The leisure facilities are excellent, and there is an adjacent golf course. British and French cooking is served in Restaurant 1559.

Sprowston Park, Wroxham Road, Sprowston, Norwich, Norfolk 01603 410871 AX, DC, MC, VI

Park Farm $$–$$$

Located on 200 acres of farmland 3 miles southwest of Norwich, this hotel combines Georgian features with modern comforts.

Hethersett, Norwich, Norfolk 01603 810264 AX, DC, MC, VI

Ribs of Beef $

This riverside pub incorporates part of an original 14th-century building damaged in Norwich's Great Fire of 1507. Simple but pleasing bar food is served at lunchtime.

24 Wensum Street, Norwich, Norfolk 01603 619517 AX, DC, MC, VI

Roger Hickman's Restaurant $–$$

A charming restaurant on an atmospheric old street, Hickman specializes in British cuisine with a particularly local flavor.

79 Upper Giles Street, Norwich, Norfolk 01603 633522 Closed Sun.– Mon. and first week in Jan. AX, DC, MC, VI

The Wildebeest Arms $–$$

The decor is African in style at this dining pub, but the food is Provençal-influenced. There are real ales on tap.

82–86 Norwich Road, Stoke Holy Cross, Norwich, Norfolk 01508 492497 Closed Dec. 25–26 AX, DC, MC, VI

SAFFRON WALDEN

The Cricketers' Arms $$$

This inn consists of Elizabethan timber-framed cottages facing the village green. There are also comfortable accommodations in a modern extension and beds are king or super-king size. The restaurant offers decent gastro-pub food.

Rickling Green, Saffron Walden, Essex 01799 543210 AX, MC, VI

Rowley Hill Lodge $

This small country guest house offers a friendly retreat. Updated since it was first built in 1830, the modern facilities include rooms with baths and proper showers.

Little Walden, Saffron Walden, Essex 01799 525975 No credit cards

STAMFORD

Garden House $$

The comfortable rooms at Garden House are only a short walk from the town center. Light meals are served in the bar and conservatory; there is also a good restaurant.

High Street, St. Martins, Stamford, Lincolnshire 01780 763359 AX, MC, VI

The George of Stamford $$
The George, a delightful old coaching inn, offers excellent accommodations and service. The restaurant is enticing in the summer, when you can eat outside in the walled courtyard. A good wine list complements an imaginative menu; light meals are served in the bar.
71 St. Martins, Stamford, Lincolnshire 01780 750750 AX, DC, MC, VI

STOKE-BY-NAYLAND

The Angel Inn $
This deservedly popular 16th-century inn is surrounded by lovely countryside in the River Stour valley. Exposed brickwork, beams and open fireplaces provide a relaxed setting for superb pub-style meals.
Polstead Street, Stoke-by-Nayland, Suffolk 01206 263245 AX, MC, VI

Stoke by Nayland Hotel, Golf & Spa $$–$$$
A standout in the region, this new hotel has two 18-hole championship golf courses as well as a fully equipped spa. It offers a great location from which to explore Constable Country.
Keepers Lane, Leavenheath, Colchester, Essex 01206 262836 DC, MC, VI

SWAFFHAM

Strattons Hotel $–$$
In the center of this market town, this hotel in an historic building has 14 rooms to choose from, all with original features and plenty of contemporary luxury.
Ash Close, Swaffham, Norfolk 01760 723845 AX, MC, VI

TAPLOW

Cliveden Country House Hotel $$$
This is one of England's great country houses, located on a vast 376-acre estate with views over the River Thames, set in the heart of Berkshire. Visitors are treated as "house guests," and the staff perpetuates the country-house tradition of service. There are lovely views across the formal gardens while eating in The Terrace restaurant; or try Waldo's for serious dining in discreet luxury. Leisure facilities include cruises along Cliveden Reach.
Taplow, Buckinghamshire 01628 668561 AX, DC, MC, VI

WARE

Marriott Hanbury Manor Hotel and Country Club $$–$$$
The Marriott chain's British flagship, this Jacobean-style mansion occupies 200 acres of grounds and gardens. Original features include wood paneling, crystal chandeliers, antiques and open fireplaces. There also are outstanding leisure facilities including an 18-hole golf course.
Ware, Hertfordshire 01920 487722 or 0870 400 7222 AX, DC, MC, VI

HEART OF ENGLAND

BISHOP'S TACHBROOK

Mallory Court $$–$$$
This lovely English country house on 10 acres of grounds is only a short drive from Warwick Castle. Many rooms have garden views, and some have art deco bathrooms. The paneled restaurant serves innovative cuisine.
Harbury Lane, Bishop's Tachbrook, Royal Leamington Spa, Warwickshire 01926 330214 AX, DC, MC, VI

BUCKLAND

Buckland Manor $$$
Occupying extensive grounds near the lovely Cotswold village of Broadway, this 13th-century manor house has high-quality rooms and an excellent restaurant.
Buckland, near Broadway, Gloucestershire 01386 8526267 AX, MC, VI

BURFORD

The Lamb Inn $$–$$$
This vine-clad Cotswold inn, located in the pretty village of Burford, serves traditional, seasonal fare with flair. Flagstone floors, antique furnishings and open fireplaces all add to the character. Accommodations also are available.
Sheep Street, Burford, Oxfordshire 01993 823155 MC, VI

CHELTENHAM

Cowley Manor $$$
It is hard to imagine the grandeur of this wonderful country house set among its own gardens. Guests can really feel like the lord of the manor, with fine dining and superb spa facilities available.
Cowley, near Cheltenham, Gloucestershire 01242 870900 AX, MC, VI

Ellenborough Park $$
This luxury hotel boasts an enviable location on the original Cheltenham Racecourse estate while being only 10 minutes from Cheltenham. Exquisite design, a startlingly good spa and individually designed rooms are just part of the appeal.
Southam Road, Cheltenham Spa, Gloucestershire 01242 807947 AX, MC, VI

Le Champignon Sauvage $$$
Long-standing excellence in cooking, decor and hospitality are maintained at this respected city restaurant.
24–26 Suffolk Road, Cheltenham, Gloucestershire 01242 573449
Closed Sun.–Mon., 3 weeks in Jun. and 10 days at Christmas AX, DC, MC, VI

Hotel on the Park $$$
Polished service awaits visitors at this elegant town house in the heart of Cheltenham. Day rooms include a bar, restaurant and drawing room, all luxuriously furnished. The restaurant serves excellent food.
38 Evesham Road, Cheltenham, Gloucestershire 01242 518898 AX, DC, MC, VI

CHIPPING CAMPDEN

Noel Arms $$–$$$
Excellent food is served both in the restaurant and bar of this 14th-century inn in the heart of town. Rooms are individually furnished and have stylish en-suite facilities.
High Street, Chipping Campden, Gloucestershire 01386 840317 AX, DC, MC, VI

GREAT MILTON

Le Manoir Aux Quat' Saisons $$$
This 15th-century, mellow-stone manor house, surrounded by immaculate gardens, is 4 miles east of Oxford. Beautifully appointed bedrooms and suites offer superb comfort, and some have their own private terrace gardens. The restaurant's cuisine, overseen by chef Raymond Blanc, is outstanding.
Church Road, Great Milton, Oxfordshire 01844 278881 AX, DC, MC, VI

HENLEY-ON-THAMES

Red Lion $$–$$$
This attractively furnished hotel is on the riverside. Meals are served in

KEY TO SYMBOLS

hotel
restaurant
address
telephone number
days/times closed
nearest metro/tube/subway station(s)

AX American Express
DC Diners Club
MC MasterCard
VI VISA

Hotels
Price guide: double room with breakfast for two people

$ less than £80
$$ £80–£175
$$$ more than £175

Restaurants
Price guide: dinner per person, excluding drinks

$ less than £25
$$ £25–£40
$$$ more than £40

Local Recommendations

Bed-and-breakfast (commonly known as B&B) generally means exactly what it says: A private house where you can find a bed for the night and a good and hearty breakfast the next morning. Very often these are the most pleasant places to stay – not only because the host and hostess have their own personal pride and reputation on the line, but because they are only too happy to give you all the local gossip, along with their own worthwhile recommendations about what to see and where to eat.

both the bar and the restaurant.
Hart Street, Henley-on-Thames, Oxfordshire 01491 572161 AX, MC, VI

HEREFORD

Castle House Hotel $$–$$$
An elegant and luxurious boutique hotel, Castle House is right in the city center – its pretty garden abuts the castle moat. The hotel's restaurant serves outstanding food with international influences.
Castle Street, Hereford 01432 356321 AX, MC, VI

KINNERSLEY

Upper Newton Farmhouse $$
Pearl and John Taylor run this exceptionally friendly, well-organized and first-class bed-and-breakfast.
Kinnersley, near Hay-on-Wye, Herefordshire 01544 327727
No credit cards

LUDLOW

The Clive Bar $–$$
Beautifully presented, high-quality English fare is served at this elegant restaurant just north of Ludlow. Accommodations are also available.
Bromfield, near Ludlow, Shropshire 01584 856565
Closed Dec. 25–26 AX, MC, VI

The Feathers $$–$$$
This picturesque hotel is one of Ludlow's best-known landmarks. Rooms are furnished in traditional style; English and French cuisine is served in the restaurant.
The Bull Ring, Ludlow, Shropshire
01584 875261 AX, MC, VI

MUNSLOW

Crown Country Inn $–$$
This is a delightful old inn, abounding in interesting nooks and crannies. The modern British food is worth traveling for, too. Ingredients are locally sourced.
Munslow, near Craven Arms, Shropshire 01584 841205
Closed Sun. and Mon. eve.
AX, MC, VI

OAKHAM

Hambleton Hall $$$
The epitome of an English country house hotel, Hambleton Hall stands in beautiful gardens against the lake backdrop of Rutland Water. The kitchen turns out top-quality dishes using the best ingredients.
Hambleton, Oakham, Rutland
01572 756991 AX, DC, MC, VI

OUNDLE

Oundle Mill $–$$
The River Nene flows right under the bar at this converted watermill with rooms. Enjoy good pub food as you watch the boats go by or try the sophisticated restaurant upstairs.
Barnwell Road, Oundle, Northamptonshire 01832 272621
AX, DC, MC, VI

Talbot $$
An atmosphere of Old World charm prevails at this coaching inn in the heart of Oundle.
New Street, Oundle, Northamptonshire 01832 273621
AX, MC, VI

OXFORD

Brasserie Blanc $$–$$$
This restaurant boasts a stylish interior, good service and a punchy, modern menu. The pea and mint soup and the Loch Fyne mussels are favorites.
71–72 Walton Street, Oxford, Oxfordshire 01865 510999
Closed Dec. 25 AX, MC, VI

The Cherwell Boathouse $–$$
Enjoy an afternoon by the river at this popular restaurant. The menu offers modern English food and there is an excellent set-price lunch.
Bardwell Street, Oxford, Oxfordshire 01865 552746 MC, VI

Gables $–$$
A very comfortable and welcoming bed-and-breakfast on the western edge of the city, Gables has a conservatory and pleasant gardens.
6 Cumnor Hill, Oxford, Oxfordshire
01865 862153 Closed Dec. 22–Jan. 5 MC, VI

Gees $–$$
Occupying a splendid Victorian conservatory, this stylish restaurant offers skilfully prepared traditional British dishes based on the finest seasonal produce.
61 Banbury Road, Oxford, Oxfordshire 01865 553540
AX, DC, MC, VI

Macdonald Randolph $$–$$$
This landmark Victorian hotel, with its neo-Gothic architecture and tasteful decor, stands opposite the

Ashmolean Museum. Take afternoon tea in the drawing room, or enjoy formal dining in the restaurant.
✉ Beaumont Street, Oxford, Oxfordshire ☎ 01865 256400 AX, MC, VI

Mercure Eastgate $$
Eastgate is a relaxing hotel with an informal atmosphere. It's close to Magdalen Bridge and the city center and has views of the famous Examination Schools.
✉ 73 High Street, Oxford, Oxfordshire ☎ 01865 248332 AX, DC, MC, VI

Parklands $–$$
A delightful hotel and late-Victorian house in a leafy residential area near to the town center.
✉ 100 Banbury Road, Oxford, Oxfordshire ☎ 01865 554374 MC, VI

Quod Brasserie and Bar $–$$
Set in a former Georgian banking hall, with an amazing collection of contemporary British art, Quod is a chic, lively restaurant serving Italian-inspired, quality food. There's also an outdoor terrace.
✉ 92–94 High Street, Oxford, Oxfordshire ☎ 01865 202505 AX, MC, VI

SHREWSBURY

Cromwells Hotel, Restaurant and Bar $
The oak-paneled restaurant offers internationally inspired dishes, alternatively, there's a sheltered courtyard for summer dining. Leave room for the delicious desserts. Rooms are also available.
✉ 11 Dogpole, Shrewsbury, Shropshire ☎ 01743 361440 AX, MC, VI

Prince Rupert Hotel $$
With parts dating back to the 12th century, this central hotel was once the home of Prince Rupert, Royalist general and grandson of King James I. There's a health spa and a choice of dining rooms.
✉ Butchers Row, Shrewsbury ☎ 01743 499955 MC, DC, VI, AX

STRATFORD-UPON-AVON

Monk's Barn Farm $
A friendly bed-and-breakfast at a working farm, Monk's Barn is near the village of Clifford Chambers, just a mile south of Stratford.
✉ Shipston Road, Stratford-upon-Avon, Warwickshire ☎ 01789 293714 🕓 Closed Dec. 24–26 MC, VI

Thai Boathouse $
Eat lunch or dinner while enjoying the river views, then stroll along the River Avon to the Courtyard Theatre to see one of the Bard's plays.
✉ Swan's Nest Lane, Stratford-upon-Avon, Warwickshire ☎ 01789 297733 🕓 Closed Sat. lunch AX, MC, VI

TETBURY

Close $$
This hotel has a warm country-house feel, with log fires in winter and a terrace in a walled garden for summer relaxation. Bedrooms are traditional and there is a lovely garden restaurant.
✉ 8 Long Street, Tetbury, Gloucestershire ☎ 01666 502272 MC, VI

WALLINGFORD

Beetle and Wedge Boathouse $$
Beautifully located on the edge of the River Thames, this hotel has wonderful river views from many of the rooms and also from the dining rooms (brasserie-style or more formal).
✉ Ferry Lane, Moulsford, Wallingford, Oxfordshire ☎ 01491 651381 AX, MC, VI

WARWICK

Tudor House Inn $
This ornately timbered medieval inn at the gates of Warwick Castle serves good hearty bar food.
✉ 90–92 West Street, Warwick, Warwickshire ☎ 01926 495447 MC, VI

WALES

ABERDYFI

Penhelig Arms Hotel $–$$
Fresh local fish is a specialty at this delightful Georgian inn, overlooking the broad Dyfi Estuary on Cardigan Bay.
✉ Terrace Road, Aberdyfi, Gwynedd ☎ 01654 767215 🕓 Closed Dec. 25–26 MC, VI

ABERGAVENNY

Walnut Tree Inn $$
The Walnut Tree is famous for its daily specials, made using local ingredients. It's a convenient stop for those visiting the Black Mountains and the Brecon Beacons.
✉ Llandewi Skirrid, Abergavenny, Monmouthshire ☎ 01873 852797 🕓 Closed Sun.–Mon. and public holidays dinner MC, VI

ABERYSTWYTH

The Conrah $$
Beautifully located 3.5 miles south of Aberystwyth, The Conrah has spectacular views of the Cambrian Mountains. The hotel restaurant features local ingredients, including Black Welsh beef.
✉ Chancery, Aberystwyth, Ceredigion ☎ 01970 617941 🕓 Closed Dec. 24–26 AX, MC, VI

BETWS-Y-COED

Tan-y-Foel Country House $$–$$$
Many of the rooms in this well-maintained manor house have lovely country views of Snowdonia National Park as well as thoughtful extras (one room has a four-poster bed). An expert kitchen delivers a range of Welsh and international dishes.
✉ Capel Garmon, Betws-y-Coed, Conwy ☎ 01690 710507 🕓 Closed part of Dec. MC, VI

BONTDDU

Borthwnog Hall $–$$
This 17th-century country house adjoins Garth Gell nature reserve on the Mawddach Estuary, in the south of Snowdonia National Park. Rooms are spacious. With delightful views, this bed-and-breakfast is ideal for house parties.
✉ Bontddu, Dolgellau, Gwynedd ☎ 01341 430271 AX, MC, VI

BRECON

Felin Fach Griffin $$
This stylishly traditional inn serves up food of the highest caliber in a refreshingly simple setting. There's an excellent wine list and real ales to tempt you to stay over in one of the seven comfortable bedrooms.
✉ Felin Fach, Brecon, Powys ☎ 01874 620111 AX MC, VI

CAPEL CURIG

Cobdens $–$$
The mountaineering crowd frequents the bar at Cobdens, deep in Snowdonia. Hearty straightforward food is served and packed lunches are available on request.

KEY TO SYMBOLS

- hotel
- restaurant
- address
- telephone number
- days/times closed
- nearest metro/tube/subway station(s)
- AX American Express
- DC Diners Club
- MC MasterCard
- VI VISA

Hotels

Price guide: double room with breakfast for two people

$ less than £80
$$ £80–£175
$$$ more than £175

Restaurants

Price guide: dinner per person, excluding drinks

$ less than £25
$$ £25–£40
$$$ more than £40

More Than a Sandwich

In recent years there has been a revolution in pub food. Not long ago, very few pubs offered more than a cheese sandwich; nowadays the vast majority serve decent food at reasonable prices. Many have extensive menus with dozens of items listed on a chalk board. It's a relaxing way to eat, enjoying wholesome food that you can accompany with a pint of the local brew.

Capel Curig, Conwy 01690 720243 Closed Jan. 6–26 MC, VI

CARDIFF

Bellini's $–$$

This stylish Italian eatery has a real buzz about it and attracts locals and tourists alike, offering elegance without extravagance. There is also a children's menu.
Unit 10, Mermaid Quay, Cardiff 029 2048 7070 MC, VI

Best Western New House Country Hotel $–$$

This hotel has fantastic views across the city and Bristol Channel to the Somerset hills. The Sequoias restaurant offers an imaginative and ambitious menu.
Thornhill, Cardiff 029 2052 0280 AX, DC, MC, VI

Cardiff Marriott $$–$$$

Ideally located in the city center, this large, modern hotel features a fitness and leisure club. Eating options include the Chats Café Bar and the French-style Brasserie Centrale. The bedrooms are furnished to a high standard.
Mill Lane, Cardiff 029 2039 9944 AX, DC, MC, VI

Copthorne Hotel Cardiff-Caerdydd $$–$$$

Conveniently located for the city and the airport, this modern hotel overlooks a lake. Leisure facilities include a swimming pool, sauna, gym and steam room.
Copthorne Way, Culverhouse Cross, Cardiff 029 2059 9100 AX, DC, MC, VI

Holiday Inn Express – Cardiff Bay $

This stylish hotel is on the new Cardiff Bay waterfront. The hotel has proved so popular that it recently doubled in size.
Longueil Close, off Schooner Way, Atlantic Wharf, Cardiff 029 2044 9000 AX, DC, MC, VI

ffresh $–$$

Adjoining the Millennium Centre, this lively restaurant offers an interesting range of dishes, drawing on fresh local ingredients.
Wales Millennium Centre, Bute Place, Cardiff 029 2063 6465 AX, MC, VI

St. David's Hotel and Spa $$–$$$

Right on the Cardiff Bay waterfront, this stunning, stylish hotel has a seven-story atrium. The light, airy bedrooms have balconies looking over the bay. Leisure facilities here include a spa and hair salon, as well as a bar and restaurant.
Havannah Street, Cardiff 029 2045 4045 AX, DC, MC, VI

Y Mochyn Du $

Celebrating all that is Welsh, "the Black Pig" takes its name from an irreverent folk song. It's renowned for its excellent service, good Welsh food and selection of traditionally brewed beers.
Sophia Close, Cardiff 029 2037 1599 MC, VI

CHEPSTOW

Marriott St. Pierre Hotel and Country Club $$–$$$

Hospitable leisure hotel set in 400 acres of parkland. Rooms are either locaated in the main house, at the lakeside or in the cottage suites.
St. Pierre Park, Chepstow, Monmouthshire 01291 625261 AX, DC, MC, VI

CRICKHOWELL

The Bear $

This 15th-century inn sits at the foot of the Black Mountains. The restaurant's good cooking takes advantage of local ingredients.
Brecon Road, Crickhowell, Powys 01873 810408 AX, MC, VI

GELLILYDAN

Tyddyn-Du Farm Holiday Suites $–$$

This Tudor farmhouse, set amid spectacular scenery, is convenient to the nearby Ffestiniog Railway. Delicious farmhouse food is created by the hostess.
Gellilydan, Blaenau Ffestiniog, near Porthmadog, Gwynedd 01766 590281 No credit cards

HAY-ON-WYE

Old Black Lion $–$$

This fine old coaching inn was occupied by Oliver Cromwell during the English Civil War. The charming, cozy bar serves good pub food, and there is also a restaurant.
26 Lion Street, Hay-on-Wye, Powys 01497 820841 Closed Dec. 24–26 AX, MC, VI

The Swan-at-Hay $
Some accommodations at this hotel are in former cottages. There is also a good restaurant.
Church Street, Hay-on-Wye, Powys 01497 821188 MC, VI

LLANBERIS

The Legacy Royal Victoria $–$$
A large Victorian hotel retaining many of its original features, the property is set dramatically at the foot of Wales' highest mountain, Snowdon. There are two restaurants and bars.
Llanberis, Gwynedd 0844 411 9003 AX, DI, MC, VI

LLANDUDNO

The Lighthouse $$
This former lighthouse is set on the northern edge of Great Orme, the spectacular headland northwest of Llandudno. One of the rooms is in the lighthouse's glazed dome. Each room is equipped with a pair of binoculars so guests can peruse the stunning views of the Irish Sea.
Marine Drive, Great Orme's Head, Llandudno, Conwy 01492 876819 MC, VI

St. Tudno $$–$$$
In a prime seafront location, opposite the Victorian pier, this fine hotel has a popular restaurant with a good wine selection, and an indoor swimming pool.
The Promenade, Llandudno, Conwy 01492 874411 AX, DC, MC, VI

LLANGOLLEN

Britannia Inn Hotel $
At the foot of the scenic Horseshoe Pass, 1 mile from Llangollen, this old inn has beautiful gardens and serves enjoyable inn fare. Accommodations are also available here.
Horseshoe Pass, Llangollen, Denbighshire 01978 860144 AX, MC, VI

LLYSWEN

Llangoed Hall $$$
This imposing Edwardian country house is located amid Wye Valley parkland. Guests enjoy grandeur in the day rooms and bedrooms are furnished with antiques. The menu has a good mix of traditional and modern British and Welsh dishes.
Llyswen, Powys 01874 754525 AX, MC, VI

OLD RADNOR

Harp Inn $
This 15th-century pub, located beside a medieval church, has bags of character. A log fire roars in the bar on cold days and on warmer days you can sit outside and enjoy views of the beautiful Radnor Valley.
Old Radnor, Presteigne, Powys 01544 350655 Closed Mon., Tue.–Fri. lunch MC, VI

PARKMILL

Parc-Le-Breos House $
This 19th-century country house, the hub of a working farm, sits on 70 acres of grounds. Horseback riding is available.
Parkmill, Gower 01792 371636 AX, MC, VI

PORTMEIRION

The Hotel Portmeirion $$–$$$
This hotel is in the heart of the make-believe village of Portmeirion. Many rooms have balconies and private sitting rooms have spectacular views of the village and Traeth Bach Estuary. An art deco dining room offers modern Welsh cooking with a smattering of Mediterranean flavors.
Portmeirion, Gwynedd 01766 770000 AX, DC, MC, VI

ST. DAVID'S

Warpool Court $$–$$$
The main part of this Victorian hotel was originally the St. David's Cathedral's School for its choristers. The lovely landscaped gardens have views of the sea, as do some of the rooms.
St. David's, Pembrokeshire 01437 720300 Closed Jan. AX, MC, VI

NORTHERN ENGLAND

AMBLESIDE

Drunken Duck Inn $$
This remote but accessible pub is located in the scenic heart of the Lake District, and has a reputation for great food – expect wide choices of meat and fish – and ales.
Barngates, Ambleside, Cumbria 015394 36347 Closed Dec. 25 AX, MC, VI

BAKEWELL

Rutland Arms Hotel $$
Popular for the Tavern Bar and The Square restaurant, this Georgian inn on Bakewell's central square is said to be the place where Jane Austen revised some of *Pride and Prejudice*.
The Square, Bakewell, Derbyshire 01629 812812 AX, DC, MC, VI

BASLOW

Cavendish $$$
This is a 16th-century country house hotel with 24 rooms among wooded hills on the edge of Chatsworth Estate. Several of the works of art adorning the walls have been loaned by the Duke and Duchess of Devonshire (the estate's owners) and the views through the windows are works of art in themselves.
Church Lane, Baslow, Derbyshire 01246 582311 AX, DC, MC, VI

BEAMISH

Beamish Park $$
This hotel is near Beamish Museum. International bistro food is served in the conservatory. There is also a classically styled dining room.
Beamish Burn Road, Marley Hill, Beamish, Co. Durham 01207 230666 AX, DC, MC, VI

BLANCHLAND

Lord Crewe Arms Hotel $
One of England's oldest inns, the Lord Crewe Arms is full of ghosts and character. It's a convenient place to stop for lunch while exploring Hadrian's Wall country.
Blanchland, County Durham 01434 675251 AX, DC, MC, VI

BOLTON ABBEY

The Devonshire Arms Country House Hotel and Spa $$$
This very stylish country-house hotel, owned by the Duke and Duchess of Devonshire, is located at the foot of glorious Wharfedale, in the heart of the Yorkshire Dales. An indoor pool and tennis court complement the spa facilities on offer.
Bolton Abbey, Skipton, North Yorkshire 01756 710441 AX, DC, MC, VI

CHESTER

The Chester Grosvenor Hotel and Spa $$$
Located within the old city walls, the hotel serves elegant food. There is a choice of dining experiences from the Simon Radley restaurant to the Arkle Bar and lounge.
Eastgate, Chester, Cheshire 01244 324024 AX, DC, MC, VI

KEY TO SYMBOLS
hotel
restaurant
address
telephone number
days/times closed
nearest metro/tube/subway station(s)
AX American Express
DC Diners Club
MC MasterCard
VI VISA

Hotels
Price guide: double room with breakfast for two people
$ less than £80
$$ £80–£175
$$$ more than £175

Restaurants
Price guide: dinner per person, excluding drinks
$ less than £25
$$ £25–£40
$$$ more than £40

DURHAM

Bistro 21 $
A former farmhouse with stone-flagged floors and stone walls offers excellent value from a simple menu. There is a daily specials board and a private dining option too.
Aykley Heads House, Aykley Heads, Durham, County Durham 0191 384 4354 Closed Sun. dinner, Jan. 1, Dec. 25 and public holidays AX, MC, VI

Durham Marriott Hotel, Royal County $$–$$$
This is a centrally located, riverside hotel with extensive leisure facilities that include a swimming pool, sauna, gymnasium, Jacuzzi and spa. Daily Champagne Tea.
Old Elvet, Durham, County Durham 0191 386 6821 AX, DC, MC, VI

GOATHLAND

Mallyan Spout $$
Close to the famous Mallyan Spout waterfall, this ivy-clad Victorian hotel is in a scenic village in North York Moors National Park. Fresh fish from nearby Whitby is a feature of the restaurant menu.
The Common, Goathland, North Yorkshire 01947 896486 MC, VI

HARROGATE

The Boar's Head $$
The Boar's Head is an old former coaching inn convenient to Harrogate, which has been renovated by Sir Thomas and Lady Ingilby of nearby Ripley Castle.
Ripley Castle Estate, Harrogate, North Yorkshire 01423 771888 AX, MC, VI

Harrogate Brasserie $–$$
Making good use of local seasonal produce and offering some excellent value early-bird discounts, this lively eatery spills out on to the sidewalk on warmer Yorkshire evenings. Live jazz five days a week.
26–30 Cheltenham Parade, Harrogate 01423 505041 Closed Mon–Sat lunch AX, MC, VI

HAWORTH

Weavers $–$$
Set in a trio of weavers' cottages close to the Brontë Parsonage Museum (see page 195), this restaurant offers both modern and traditional British dishes featuring seasonal local ingredients.
15 West Lane, Haworth, West Yorkshire 01535 643822 Closed Mon., Tue. and Sat. lunch, Sun. dinner, and 10 days at Christmas and New Year AX, DC, MC, VI

HOPE

Cheshire Cheese Inn $
A 400-year-old inn in the heart of the Peak District, the Cheshire Cheese offers accommodations, and serves good food and local beers.
Edale Road, Hope, Derbyshire 01433 620381 MC, VI

LEEDS

Brasserie Forty 4 $–$$
In an old grain store overlooking a canal, this modern brasserie epitomizes the new Leeds. The food is eclectic, the wine list creditable.
44 The Calls, Leeds Closed Sun. 0113 234 3232 AX, MC, VI

Haley's $$
This elegant hotel, conveniently just north of the city center, offers a country feel. Its modern restaurant serves modern British cuisine.
Shire Oak Road, Headingley, Leeds, West Yorkshire 0113 278 4446 AX, MC, VI

LIVERPOOL

Liverpool Marriott Hotel City Centre $$
This modern hotel is located in the Queen Square area, close to St. George's Hall. Accommodations are well-equipped, elegant and spacious; there is also a recreation center and a restaurant.
1 Queen Square, Liverpool, Merseyside 0151 476 8000 AX, DC, MC, VI

MANCHESTER

Harvey Nichols Second Floor Restaurant $$
This super-chic department store restaurant has an accomplished team producing dishes such as Goosnargh duck, clam chowder or Cheshire lamb with carrot and cumin purée. Vegetarian options are interesting and afternoon teas are served.
21 New Cathedral Street, Manchester 0161 828 8898 Closed Sun. and Mon. dinner AX, DC, MC, VI

Fresh Ideas in Cuisine
The British have been self-conscious about their cooking for centuries, having been told by everyone else that it is stodgy and unimaginative. Don't believe it! A glance at the menu in a decent restaurant will show you what a long way British cooks have come in the last few years, operating kitchens that promise good fresh ingredients, especially local products such as fish near the coasts, mountain lamb in Wales and organic home-grown vegetables.

Marriott Worsley Park Hotel and Country Club $$
This modern hotel is within easy reach of the city center. The leisure facilities include a golf course.
Worsley Park, Walkden Road, Worsley, Manchester 0161 975 2000 AX, DC, MC, VI

MOLLINGTON

Crabwall Manor $$–$$$
A turreted manor house, parts of which date back to the 11th century, Crabwall Manor offers traditional country-house cuisine, gardens and a spa.
Parkgate Road, Chester, Cheshire 01244 851666 AX, DC, MC, VI

PICKERING

Best Western Forest and Vale $–$$
Several rooms in this pleasant hotel have four-poster beds; a variety of food is served in the bar and restaurant.
Malton Road, Pickering, North Yorkshire 01751 472722 AX, MC, VI

White Swan Inn $–$$
A welcoming inn in the marketplace between the church and the steam railroad station.
Market Place, Pickering, North Yorkshire 01751 472288 AX, MC, VI

RICHMOND

Charles Bathurst Inn $–$$
The "CB" inn, in remote and beautiful Arkengarthdale, features traditional open fireplaces, wooden floors and a relaxed atmosphere in which to enjoy freshly cooked locally sourced food.
Arkengarthdale, Richmond, North Yorkshire 01748 884567
Closed Dec. 25 MC, VI

Natural Retreats $$–$$$
Luxurious, fully equipped self-catering accommodations in a magical location, this superb spot is a wonderful base for local activities from cycling to horseback riding.
Aislabeck plantation, Hurgill Road, Richmond, North Yorkshire 0844 384 3166 AX, MC, VI

SETTLE

The Lion at Settle $
The Lion is located in Settle's old marketplace. Diners can choose between laidback informality in the dining room or quiet privacy in the "Lion's Den."
Duke Street, Settle, North Yorkshire 01729 822203 MC, VI

Whitefriars Country Guesthouse $
Just a short stroll from the town center and station is this family-run guesthouse with a pretty garden and leafy surroundings. There are 10 traditionally furnished bedrooms, and some are quite spacious. Most of the rooms have private bathrooms.
Church Street, Settle 01729 823753 Closed Christmas
No credit cards

WASDALE HEAD

Wasdale Head Inn $–$$
Filled with character, this inn boasts an incomparably beautiful and hauntingly lonely location in the Lake District. Rooms are available.
Wasdale Head, Gosforth, Cumbria 019467 26229 AX, MC, VI

WINDERMERE

Holbeck Ghyll Country House $$$
The dramatic profiles of the Langdale Pikes can be seen from this charming 19th-century hotel, often with a beautiful sunset providing a fine backdrop at dinner. Some rooms have private balconies.
Holbeck Lane, Windermere, Cumbria 015394 32375 AX, MC, VI

YORK

Best Western Dean Court $$–$$$
This city-center hotel opposite York Minster provides quiet, comfortable rooms in an ideal location for seeing the city sights.
Duncombe Place, York, North Yorkshire 01904 625082 AX, DC, MC, VI

The Blue Bicycle $$
A buzzy city-center eatery but with an intimate atmosphere, this is one of York's best-loved restaurants. It has a wide-ranging, modern European menu, emphasizing local ingredients.
34 Fossgate, York, North Yorkshire 01904 673990 Closed Mon.–Wed. lunch (except Dec.), Dec. 24–27, Dec. 28 lunch, Jan. 1–10, Jan. 11 lunch MC, VI

Bootham Guest House $–$$
A family-run bed-and-breakfast, quietly but centrally located just 5 minutes from the city center, with free WiFi internet access.
56 Bootham Crescent, York, North Yorkshire 01904 672123
No credit cards

The Grange $$–$$$
This classical Regency town house offers country-house elegance in the heart of the city. The individually designed bedrooms and stylish public rooms with blazing fires in winter create a relaxing atmosphere, while the Ivy Brasserie offers fine dining, making use of locally sourced ingredients, in lavish surroundings.
1 Clifton, York, North Yorkshire 01904 644744 AX, DC, MC, VI

Middlethorpe Hall and Spa $$$
This magnificent King William III country house, protected by the National Trust since 2008, is less than 2 miles from York city center. Guests can walk in the restored gardens, and the house contains fine paintings, furniture, and antiques.
Bishopthorpe Road, Middlethorpe, York, North Yorkshire 01904 641241 AX, MC, VI

Nineteen $–$$
Housed in one of York's oldest buildings (15th century), just 2 minutes' walk from the Minster, this restaurant combines old-world charm with modern furnishings. The table with a view along Swinegate is one of the most sought-after in the city. The food is modern British with a European twist.
19 Grape Lane, York, North Yorkshire 01904 636366 MC, VI

SCOTLAND

ABERDEEN

Copthorne Hotel Aberdeen $$
Centrally located, the Copthorne has a restaurant specializing in steaks and grills utilizing fresh local ingredients.
122 Huntly Street, Aberdeen 01224 630404 AX, DC, MC, VI

Dunavon House $$
The bedrooms in this Victorian villa are attractive and well equipped, and the inviting lounge bar and restaurant offer an excellent range

KEY TO SYMBOLS

- hotel
- restaurant
- address
- telephone number
- days/times closed
- nearest metro/tube/subway station(s)

AX American Express
DC Diners Club
MC MasterCard
VI VISA

Hotels
Price guide: double room with breakfast for two people
$ less than £80
$$ £80–£175
$$$ more than £175

Restaurants
Price guide: dinner per person, excluding drinks
$ less than £25
$$ £25–£40
$$$ more than £40

Homey Hotels
A familiar sight in remote Scottish landscapes is a lonely hotel, huge and baronial. In the storms and snows of winter these great dark ships of hotels come into their own, as a cozy "home away from home" for locals, and as a welcoming refuge for stormbound travelers at any hour of the day or night.

of dishes at both lunch and dinner.
60 Victoria Street, Dyce, Aberdeen 01224 722483 AX, MC, VI

ABERFELDY

Ailean Chraggan $–$$
Local game and salmon from the River Tay feature in the restaurant at this small hotel. Views take in the river and the hills beyond.
Weem, Aberfeldy, Perth and Kinross 01887 820346 MC, VI

AUCHTERARDER

The Gleneagles $$$
This renowned Edwardian luxury hotel is surrounded by championship golf courses and extensive grounds. There are several restaurants to choose between, from formal to more relaxed.
Auchterarder, Perth and Kinross 01764 662231 AX, DC, MC, VI

AVIEMORE

Ravenscraig $
This comfortable, small guesthouse, in the center of Aviemore, is an ideal base for exploring the Cairngorms National Park.
141 Grampian Road, Aviemore, Highland 01479 810278 MC, VI

AYR

Enterkine Country House $$
Just 10 minutes' from Prestwick International airport, Brownes Restaurant at Enterkine offers relaxed but stylish dining in a sumptuous country house estate. Good use is made of exceptional local ingredients. Try the home-smoked langoustines or the cepe mushroom and truffle lasagne.
01292 520580 VI, MC

Savoy Park $–$$
The restaurant in this family-run hotel is reminiscent of a Highland shooting lodge, complete with wood-paneled walls and an open fire, offering a welcoming retreat on cold days.
16 Racecourse Road, Ayr, South Ayrshire 01292 266112 AX, DC, MC, VI

BALLATER

Darroch Learg Hotel $$$
Perched on the "Hill of Oaks" above the scenic town of Ballater, this hotel has river views and a restaurant that offers modern Scottish dishes.
Braemar Road, Ballater, Aberdeenshire 013397 55443 Closed Mon.–Sat. lunch, last 3 weeks in Jan. and Dec. 25 AX, DC, MC, VI

BALLOCH

Cameron House $$$
Enjoy luxurious accommodations on the shores of Loch Lomond with legendary Scottish hospitality, a sublime spa and superb restaurant all thrown in. Cameron House caters to everyone, from families to business travelers.
Loch Lomond, Dunbartonshire 01389 755565 AX, MC, VI

BLAIRGOWRIE

Kinloch House $$
Part of the highly regarded Relais Chateau stable of hotels, Kinloch House offers fine food and wine, warm hospitality and a spectacular setting. Plan on staying here for at least several days.
Blairgowrie, Pertshire 01250 884237 AX, DC, MC, VI

CALLANDER

Roman Camp Country House $$
This former hunting lodge was built in 1625 for the dukes of Perth, and has a rich history. The hotel's own walled garden supplies vegetables to the formal restaurant and lounge.
Callander, Stirling 01877 330003 AX, DC, MC, VI

CANISBAY

Bencorragh House $
With fantastic sea views across the Pentland Firth to the Orkney Isles, this working farm offers value-priced accommodations and is ideally positioned for the island ferries.
Upper Gills, Canisbay, By John O'Groats, Highland 01955 611449 MC, VI

CULLODEN

Culloden House $$$
This historic mansion on 40 acres of wooded grounds and parkland is where Bonnie Prince Charlie left for the Battle of Culloden in 1746. It has been sensitively renovated, although many of the traditional features remain.
Culloden, Inverness, Highland 01463 790461 Closed Dec. 24–28 AX, MC, VI

EDINBURGH

The Balmoral $$$
An elegant Edwardian luxury hotel that is conveniently located on Princes Street. Afternoon tea is served in the Palm Court, and there is a light and lively atmosphere in the Bollinger Bar. Diners can choose between Hadrian's brasserie menu or more formal dining in the Number One restaurant.
1 Princes Street, Edinburgh
0131 556 2414 or 0800 7666 6667
AX, DC, MC, VI

The Bonham $$–$$$
This award-winning hotel is an imaginatively designed conversion of a former university building, and it oozes style. All bedrooms are spacious, and all have equally splendid bathrooms.
35 Drumsheugh Gardens, Edinburgh 0131 226 6050 or 0131 274 7400 AX, DC, MC, VI

Channings $–$$
A light, bright conservatory is part of this hotel's restaurant. Modern Scottish food with a Continental twist produces some adventurous recipes. The hotel, comprising five Edwardian terraced houses, has 41 rooms and suites.
15 South Learmonth Gardens, Edinburgh 0131 315 2226 AX, DC, MC, VI

George Hotel Edinburgh $$–$$$
A classical facade and marble foyer distinguish this city-center hotel. It is home to the popular bar and restaurant Tempus (reservations).
19–21 George Street, Edinburgh
0131 225 1251 AX, DC, MC, VI

Malmaison Edinburgh $$–$$$
Malmaison Edinburgh is a stylish conversion of a former seaman's mission in the harbor area. French fare with a Scottish flavor is served in the brasserie. The café/bar offers lighter meals.
1 Tower Place, Leith, Edinburgh
0131 468 5000 AX, DC, MC, VI

Rutland Hotel Edinburgh $$$
Almost certainly Edinburgh's best located hotel, this building is full of history while being utterly contemporary in terms of luxury. Enjoy spectacular views, superb service and one of the most highly regarded restaurants in the city.
1–3 Rutland Street, Edinburgh
0131 229 3402 AX, DC, MC, VI

Sheraton Grand Hotel & Spa in Edinburgh $$$
This newly renovated hotel includes an onsite restaurant, One Square, and a state of the art spa. It is perfectly situated, close to both the main stores and the castle.
1 Festival Square, Edinburgh
0131 229 9131 AX, DC, MC, VI

Stac Polly $$
Taking its name from a peculiar mountain in the Highlands, Stac Polly's labyrinth of stone-lined cellar rooms make this a memorable dining choice. Scottish food of the highest class is the specialty.
38 Dublin Street, Edinburgh
0131 556 2231 AX, DC, MC, VI

Tower Restaurant $$–$$$
The good Scottish food produced here, with an admirable attention to detail, vies with the dramatic setting on the top floor of the National Museum of Scotland to redefine museum restaurants.
Museum of Scotland, Chambers Street, Edinburgh 0131 225 3003 AX, MC, DC, VI

FORT WILLIAM

Inverlochy Castle $$$
The castle provides a grand setting for three elegant dining rooms with garden and loch views, serving very inventive dishes.
Torlundy, Fort William, Highland
01397 702177 AX, MC, VI

GAIRLOCH

Myrtle Bank $$
This hotel by Loch Gairloch has comfortably furnished bedrooms with views of the Isle of Skye.
Low Road, Gairloch, Highland
01445 712004 AX, MC, VI

The Old Inn $$
This delightful harborside inn has comfortable bedrooms. Hearty food is served in the bar and bistro.
Gairloch, Highland 01445 712006 MC, VI

GLASGOW

Argyll Hotel $–$$
This friendly hotel looks out over Kelvingrove Park, a central area near many of the city's museums. Rooms are simple but comfortable.
973 Sauchiehall Street, Glasgow
0141 337 3313 AX, MC, VI

Blythswood $$–$$$
Probably Glasgow's best hotel, this superb, five-star spa hotel ticks all the boxes. It is in a magnificent square, with charming service and luxurious rooms.
11 Blythswood Square, Glasgow
0141 248 8888 AX, MC, VI

Gamba $$–$$$
This modern basement restaurant is decorated with a striking sea mural to match the menu, which specializes in Scottish seafood. Local beef is also available.
225a West George Street, Glasgow
0141 572 0899 Closed Sun. lunch, Jan. 1–2, Dec. 25–26 and public holidays AX, MC, VI

Glasgow Marriott $$
The Glasgow Marriott combines a convenient city location with high-quality facilities.
500 Argyle Street, Glasgow
0141 226 5577 AX, DC, MC, VI

Hotel du Vin at One Devonshire Gardens $$$
This luxurious boutique hotel is located in four adjoining row houses. Rooms have bold decor and luxurious bathrooms. In one house there is a stylish lounge and bar; in another an elegant cocktail lounge. Restaurant menus change frequently.
1 Devonshire Gardens, Glasgow
0141 339 2001 AX, DC, MC, VI

The Kelvin $
The Kelvin bed-and-breakfast guest hotel occupies two Victorian houses near the Botanic Gardens.
15 Buckingham Terrace, Great Western Road, Hillhead, Glasgow
0141 339 7143 MC, VI

Malmaison Glasgow $–$$
This is a contemporary hotel conversion (from a church) with stylish rooms and an exceptionally friendly and helpful staff. Meals are served in the original crypt.
278 West George Street, Glasgow
0845 365 4438 AX, MC, VI

La Parmigiana $$
Mediterranean flair and fresh Scottish ingredients are the winning combination of the excellent food

KEY TO SYMBOLS

hotel
restaurant
address
telephone number
days/times closed
nearest metro/tube/subway station(s)
AX American Express
DC Diners Club
MC MasterCard
VI VISA

Hotels
Price guide: double room with breakfast for two people
$ less than £80
$$ £80–£175
$$$ more than £175

Restaurants
Price guide: dinner per person, excluding drinks
$ less than £25
$$ £25–£40
$$$ more than £40

here. Italian specialties include a fabulous risotto with seafood, and the desserts are equally as good.
447 Great Western Road, Glasgow 0141 334 0686 Closed Jan. 1–2, Easter and Dec. 25–26 MC, VI

Rab Ha's $–$$
Varied cuisine, including modern Scottish favorites such as chicken breast stuffed with haggis and pan-fried venison. Boutique hotel rooms are also available here.
81 Hutcheson Street, Glasgow 0141 572 0400 MC, VI

GLEN CLOY, ISLE OF ARRAN

Kilmichael Country House $$–$$$
Located in what is thought to be the oldest house on the island, the Kilmichael Country House is a charming hotel with attractive grounds. Bedrooms in the converted barn are particularly stylish. The dinner menu is simple but tasty.
Glen Cloy, By Brodick, Isle of Arran, North Ayrshire 01770 302219 Closed Nov.–Feb. MC, VI

INVERNESS

Best Western Inverness Palace Hotel and Spa $$–$$$
Located beside the River Ness in the heart of Inverness, with views of the castle, this hotel has a range of health and leisure facilities.
8 Ness Walk, Inverness, Highland 01463 223243 AX, DC, MC, VI

Culloden House $$–$$$
This historic house boasts a great location from which to explore the local tourist attractions. Relax next to open fires, enjoy fine service and take part in activities from fishing to golf or even whisky drinking.
Inverness, Highland 01463 790461 AX, MC, VI

Glenmoriston Town House $$
This stylish hotel overlooks the cathedral. The highly rated on-site Abstract restaurant serves modern French cuisine, and there's a chic brasserie and bar.
20 Ness Bank, Inverness, Highland 01463 223777 AX, DC, MC, VI

KIRKCUDBRIGHT

Best Western Selkirk Arms $$
This 200-year-old inn, where Robert Burns is said to have written his Selkirk Grace, is set in secluded gardens near the town center. Its elegant restaurant offers innovative Scottish cuisine.
Old High Street, Kirkcudbright, Dumfries and Galloway 01557 330402 AX, MC, VI

KIRKWALL, ORKNEY

Ayre $$
This family-run hotel stands on the harbor in the town of Kirkwall, the capital of the Orkney Islands. It's an ideal base for visitors to the islands.
Ayre Road, Kirkwall, Orkney 01856 873001 AX, MC, VI

MELROSE

Burts $$
This welcoming 18th-century hotel faces the attractive town square in Melrose, one of the most appealing small towns in the Scottish Borders.
Market Square, Melrose, Scottish Borders 01896 822285 AX, MC, VI

ST. ANDREWS

The Old Course Hotel, Golf Resort and Spa $$–$$$
This internationally renowned hotel overlooks the world-famous golf course; the conservatory and rooftop restaurants have great views.
St. Andrews, Fife 01334 474371 AX, DC, MC, VI

SALEN, ISLE OF MULL

Gruline Home Farm $$
A friendly bed-and-breakfast, in a former farmhouse, in the midst of beautiful mountain scenery. A country house-party atmosphere accompanies meals.
Gruline, Salen, Isle of Mull, Argyll and Bute 01680 300581 MC

STIRLING

Barcelo Stirling Highland $$
This hotel was originally a high school. Drinks are served in the old headmaster's study and diners eat in the Scholars restaurant upstairs.
29 Spittal Street, Stirling 01786 272727 AX, DC, MC, VI

TURNBERRY

Turnberry Resort, Scotland $$$
This world-famous hotel sits on 800 acres of stunning countryside, and has a renowned golf course.
Turnberry, South Ayrshire 01655 331000 AX, DC, MC, VI

Essential Information

U.S. CITIZENS

The information in this guide has been compiled for U.S. citizens traveling as tourists.

Travelers who are not U.S. citizens, or who are traveling on business, should check with their embassies and tourist offices for information on the countries they wish to visit.

Entry requirements are subject to change at short notice, and travelers are advised to check the current situation before they travel.

National flag

Before You Go

Passports
The most important document you'll need to arrange before you travel is a passport. Passport application forms can be obtained by contacting any federal, state or probate court, post office, public library, or county or municipal office authorized to accept passport applications. U.S. passport agencies have offices in major cities; check online or the Yellow Pages (U.S. Government, State Department) for the nearest. You can also request an application form by contacting the National Passport Information Center at (877) 487-2778 (toll free), Mon.–Fri. 8 a.m.–8 p.m. (EST). Passport information and application forms are available on the U.S. State Department internet site at http://travel.state.gov, where travel warnings and consular information can be accessed and in some cases a passport card applied for online. Each person must have a passport; apply early, since processing can take several months. Rush service is available for an extra charge. Make sure your passport is valid for at least six months after you are due to travel: Some European countries require this.

Visas
In addition to a passport, some countries require a visa as an entry requirement. Travel visas are not necessary for American nationals traveling to Britain for less than six months, but if you'll be traveling on to other nations, check entry requirements before you leave home.

Travel Insurance

It is recommended that you are covered by travel insurance. You should also have coverage for property loss or theft, emergency medical and dental treatment, and emergency evacuation. Before taking out insurance, check if your homeowners or medical coverage already covers you for travel abroad. If you make a claim, your insurer will need proof of the incident or expenditure. Keep copies of any police report and related documents, or doctor and hospital bills.

Essential for Travelers

Required ● Recommended ● Not required ●

Passport	●
Visa	●
Travel, medical insurance	●
Round-trip or onward airline ticket	●
Local currency	●
Traveler's checks	●
Debit or Credit cards	●
First-aid kit and medicines	●
Health inoculations	●

Essential for Drivers

Required ● Recommended ● Not required ●

Driver's license	●
International Driving Permit	●
Car insurance (for non-rental cars)	●
Car registration (for non-rental cars)	●

*see also Driving section

When to Go

The British Isles – infamous for damp weather – can actually have weeks of dry conditions in summer, although this is unpredictable. British winters are often rainy, although temperatures are rarely extremely cold. Snow is uncommon except in the higher elevations of northern England and Scotland. School vacations are another factor in planning when to schedule your trip. Schools in Britain are in session from early September until early July. This makes May and June good months to visit, both from a weather standpoint and the fact that there are likely to be fewer crowds at major attractions.

Important Addresses

Britain and London Visitor Centre (walk-in only)
Operator assisted visa information.
Callers from within the United Kingdom should dial
☎ 09042 450 100 from within the UK.
☎ 1 866 382 3589 from within the US, fixed rate US$16.

American Embassy
24 Grosvenor Square
London W1A 2LQ, U.K.
☎ 020 7499 9000
www.london.usembassy.gov

Customs

Duty-free limits on goods brought in from non-European Union countries:

200 cigarettes or 100 cigarillos or 50 cigars or 250 g. tobacco; 4 L still table wine; 16 L beer; 1 L. alcohol over 22% volume or 2 L. of fortified wine (such as port or sherry), sparkling wine or other alcohol under 22% volume; plus any other duty free goods (including perfume, aftershave and gifts) to the value of £390 ($576). You must be aged 17 or over to qualify for tobacco and alcohol allowance.

On returning to the United States, you will be required to complete a customs declaration. You are allowed $800 worth of personal goods or gifts; keep sales slips and have them ready for inspection.

✘ No unlicensed drugs, weapons, ammunition, obscene material, pets or other animals, counterfeit money and meat or poultry.

Money

Britain's currency is the pound sterling (£), which is divided into 100 pence (p). The denominations of pound bills are 5, 10, 20 and 50 (Scotland also has £1 and £100 bills). There are coins of 1, 2, 5, 10, 20 and 50p and £1 and £2. The most convenient way of obtaining foreign currency or paying for items is using your debit card at ATMs and banks or in stores. You can also exchange dollars or traveler's checks at banks, main post offices, exchange offices and some travel agencies. Credit cards are widely accepted throughout Britain, and ATMs are common in shopping areas.

Tips and Gratuities

Restaurants (where service is not included)	10–15%
Cafés/bars	change
Taxis	10%
Porters	£2–£5
Hairdressers	10%
Chambermaids	£2–£5
Cloakroom attendants	30p–50p

Communications

Post Offices

Buy stamps at post offices, gas stations, tobacconists and grocery stores. Out-of-town post offices often close 1–2 p.m. and Wednesday afternoon. Mailboxes (referred to as"pillar-boxes" or post boxes) are red. Pillar-boxes show who was monarch at the time of their installation (ER II, for instance, stands for Elizabeth Regina II).

Telephones

Public telephones are increasingly hard to find. Use cash, a credit card or a phone card. Public telephones take 10p, 20p, 50p and £1 coins and some accept £2 coins, but they do not give refunds if you do not use up your credit. There is a minimum charge of 60p, which includes a 40p connection charge. If using a credit card there is a £1.20 minimum fee which includes a £1 connection charge.

Phoning in Britain
All British numbers in this book include an area code: dial the number listed. To call the operator dial 100.

Phoning Britain from abroad
The country code for Britain is 44. Note that British numbers in this book do not include the country code; you will need to prefix it if you are phoning from another country. To phone Britain from the United States or Canada, omit the first zero from the British number and add the prefix 011 44. Example: 011 2233 4455 becomes 011 44 11 2233 4455.

Phoning from Britain
To phone the United States or Canada from Britain, prefix the area code and number with 00 1. Example: (111) 222-3333 becomes 00 1 111 222-3333. To call international information dial 153.

Emergency Numbers

Police	999 or 112
Fire service	999 or 112
Ambulance	999 or 112

Emergency calls are free from phone booths.

Hours of Operation

- Stores Mon.–Sat.
- Offices Mon.–Fri.
- Banks Mon.–Fri.
- Post offices Mon.–Fri.
- Museums/Monuments
- Pharmacies

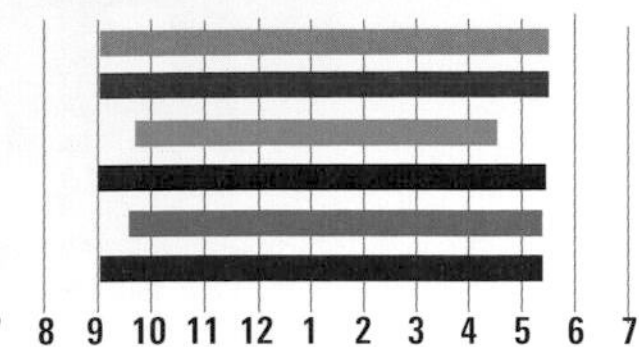

The times above show the traditional hours of operation. Many malls and city center stores stay open longer and also on Sunday. Some grocery stores stay open until late in the evening, and some supermarkets are open 24 hours (except Sunday, when they open 10–4 or 11–5).

Banks and post offices open on Saturday mornings, but some out-of-town services have shorter hours. Museum opening times vary. Some major sights close on Monday and stay open later one evening a week; more modest sights of interest may close off season, so it is advisable to check with the local tourist office.

Note that many restaurants do not open for dinner until around 6 or 7 p.m.

National Holidays

There are a number of national holidays in Britain (called bank holidays), when banks, businesses, smaller stores and many museums close for the day. Almost all attractions, many restaurants, and some hotels close on Christmas; check ahead.

Jan. 1	New Year's Day
Jan. 2	New Year's Day Bank Holiday (Scotland only)
Mar./Apr.	Good Friday
Mar./Apr.	Easter Monday (not Scotland)
1st Mon. of May	May Day Bank Holiday
Last Mon. of May	Spring Bank Holiday
First Mon. of Aug.	Summer Bank Holiday (Scotland only)
Last Mon. of Aug.	Summer Bank Holiday
Nov. 30	St. Andrew's Day (Scotland only)
Dec. 25	Christmas Day
Dec. 26	Boxing Day

Restrooms

Public restrooms (toilets, lavatories, WCs, or, colloquially, "loos") are generally easy to find and maintained to a high standard. Most are free, but there is a fee for those at major rail stations (30p). To use the restroom in a café or bar, buy a drink first.

Health Advice

Medical Services

Private insurance is recommended. Visitors can receive treatment in emergency rooms but are charged if admitted to a hospital.

You can seek advice from a doctor at a surgery or health center; you must make an appointment and you will be charged. Doctors are listed in the Yellow Pages, or ask at your hotel or tourist office.

Dental Services

Dentists charge for consultations or treatment. After-hours emergency treatment is available in towns and cities (see the Yellow Pages). Be sure to check if it is covered by your medical insurance.

Sun Advice

During the summer months extended spells of sunshine are possible. Visiting historic sights can involve being outside for prolonged periods, so cover up, apply sunscreen and drink plenty of water. Remember that even on overcast days, sunburn is possible.

Drugs

Prescription and nonprescription medicines are available from pharmacies (chemists). Pharmacists can advise on medication for common ailments. Notices in all pharmacy windows give details of emergency facilities open outside regular hours.

Safe Water

Tap water is safe to drink, even in remote areas. Mineral water is widely available but can be expensive in some restaurants.

Personal Safety

The cities, towns and villages of Britain are all generally safe places to be, and are regularly patrolled by police. British police are usually helpful, friendly and approachable. Sensible safety precautions should prevail, however:

- Keep valuables hidden when you're on the move; a money belt or neck purse worn inside clothing is the safest option. Many hotels provide safe deposit boxes.
- Never leave bags unattended.
- Avoid walking alone in dimly lit areas at night.
- If you have belongings stolen, report the incident to the police immediately and get a written police report to provide to your insurance company as evidence for your claim.

National Transportation

Air

There are airports in most major British cities and an extensive network of domestic flights, served by British Airways (☎ 0844 493 0787; www.britishairways.com) and other regional carriers. Flights can be expensive, but are a good option for covering long distances (for example, London to Edinburgh), or for those traveling to the Orkney or Shetland islands. Off-peak, stand-by and advance ticket discounts are available.

Train

Rail services are generally efficient in Britain and serve most major towns. Most lines radiate from London, so "cross-country" services to some provincial towns may require a number of changes. There is a rail inquiry line to help you plan your trip (☎ 08457 484950; www.nationalrail.co.uk), and it also is possible to reserve tickets in advance. There are a number of discount tickets available if you travel outside peak times. First class is comfortable but much more expensive than standard class. If you plan to use trains frequently, rail cards, such as BritRail passes, offer good discounts. You can only purchase BritRail passes prior to arriving in Britain: contact BritRail, 1 866 936 RAIL (US and Canada only); www.britrail.com.

Once you are in Britain, Rail Rover passes are another option: ☎ 08457 484950; www.railrover.org. The Eurostar train service runs regular daily services to Europe through the Channel Tunnel. Services depart from London St. Pancras International, Ebbsfleet and Ashford to Calais, Lille, Paris, Disneyland Resort Paris, Avignon, the French Alps and Brussels. Reserve in advance to avoid disappointment (☎ 08432 186186; www.eurostar.com).

Bus

Bus travel is less expensive than rail travel. The main operator for long-distance (coach) travel in England, and some parts of Wales and Scotland, is National Express. For details ☎ 08717 818181; www.nationalexpress.com. The Brit Xplorer pass offers unlimited travel on National Express services for 7, 14 or 28 days. It can be purchased in Britain through National Express agents or through VisitBritain Shop (VisitBritain's online shop for visitors to Britain) at www.visitbritainshop.com or ☎ (800) 462-2748 (toll-free).

In Scotland, Scottish Citylink (☎ 0871 266 3333; www.citylink.co.uk) covers most of the country; Wales has a number of regional operators. In remote areas of Britain there are small Postbuses, run by the Royal Mail, carrying mail and passengers to destinations off the beaten track (☎ 0845 774 0740; www.royalmail.com/postbus).

Ferry

Ferries serve the smaller British islands and France, Spain, Belgium, Netherlands, Ireland and Denmark. In Scotland, Caledonian MacBrayne (☎ 0800 066 5000 – toll free; www.calmac.co.uk) runs services to the main west coast islands, while NorthLink ferries (☎ 0845 600 0449; www.northlinkferries.co.uk) run services to the Orkney and Shetland islands from Aberdeen and Scrabster.

Electricity

Britain has a 240-volt power supply. Electrical sockets take plugs with three square pins, so an adapter is needed for American appliances. A transformer is also required for appliances operating on 110 or 120 volts.

Photography

All digital photography equipment and ancillaries are available throughout the U.K. and there are outlets in towns and cities for downloading photographs onto CDs. Traditional camera equipment stores can be found throughout the U.K. and specialty equipment stores are in major cities.

Media

National newspapers fall into three broad categories: the more sensationalist "tabloids" such as *The Sun, Daily Mirror* and *Daily Star,* the mid-range tabloids such as *Daily Mail* and Daily Express, and the serious "broadsheets" such as *The Times*, *The Daily Telegraph*, *The Independent*, *The Guardian* and *The Scotsman*. There are local daily papers in most cities, and weekly papers in towns.

For listings, *Time Out* is a useful weekly guide to what's on in London. In larger cities, American newspapers (usually previous-day editions) and magazines are available; the most common are *USA Today*, the international edition of the *New York Herald Tribune*, and *Newsweek* and *Time magazines*. They can be purchased at airports and central railroad stations as well as at newsstands and tobacconists.

British television is being transformed by switching to a digital terrestrial format. This has multiple channels including some international news stations. In Scotland and Wales some broadcasts are in Gaelic and Welsh respectively. Hotels often have satellite or cable TV with a range of news and other channels.

Driving Regulations

Drive on the Left

Drive on the left-hand side of the road and, at traffic circles (roundabouts), yield to traffic coming from your right.

Seat Belts

Must be worn in front seats at all times and in back seats where fitted.

Minimum Age

The minimum age for driving a car is 17. However, some car rental firms will often stipulate a minimum age of 25.

Blood Alcohol

The legal blood alcohol limit is 0.08%. Random breath tests on drivers are carried out frequently, especially late at night, and the penalties for offenders are severe.

Tolls

Limited-access highways are mostly free. Some bridges levy a toll, usually minimal. The Severn Bridge, joining England and south Wales, westbound is expensive (free eastbound) and there is a weekday congestion charge in central London (www.tfl.gov.uk).

Additional Information

An International Driving Permit (IDP) is a document confirming that you hold a valid driver's license in your own country. It is a useful document to carry if you plan to drive in Britain and is available from AAA travel agencies. Some rental firms require this document, and it can speed up formalities if you are involved in an accident.

A Green Card (international motor insurance certificate) is recommended if you are driving a non-rental car. Car rental agencies will provide this with the vehicle; most companies include it in the rental price.

Speed Limits

Regulations

Speed limits are stringently enforced by police patrols and also by strategically positioned cameras that detect speeding motorists.

Limited-access highways (motorways) 70 m.p.h.

Main roads 50 or 60 m.p.h.

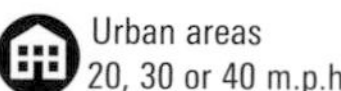

Urban areas 20, 30 or 40 m.p.h.

Car Rental

The leading rental firms have offices at airports, railroad stations and ferry terminals. Hertz offers discounted rates for AAA members. For reservations:

United States		Britain
Avis	(800) 331-1212	0844 5818181
Budget	(800) 527-0700	0844 5812231
Hertz	(800) 654-3001	0870 8448844
Rhino	888 882 2019	0845 5089845

To rent a car you will need a valid U.S. driver's license and preferably an IDP; you will probably be asked to show your passport, and possibly an additional credit card if you are renting a luxury car. Note that European cars are generally smaller than those in the United States, and usually have manual transmissions.

Find out exactly what insurance coverage is included, and check whether you need a collision damage waiver (CDW) – you may already be covered through your personal car insurance policy or credit card company. However, a CDW may not cover certain types of damage. Also note that reciprocal arrangements with European motoring clubs may not apply if you are driving a rental car.

Driving in busy British cities can be a daunting prospect if you are not used to the signs and driving habits. Rental companies should provide a chart of road signs and regulations and an area road map. They may also offer a GPS system for rent. AAA travel agencies can reserve a car for you before you leave the U.S. or provide prepayment arrangements. Rates are often lower if reservations are made in the U.S. prior to your departure, and guaranteed in U.S. dollars if you prepay.

Fuel

Gasoline (petrol) and diesel are priced in liters and are expensive. There are two grades of unleaded gas: super (98 octane) and ordinary (95 octane). Most gas stations are self-service, and 24-hour facilities are common in urban areas.

Parking

If you are visiting a city by car, it is often possible to use "Park and Ride" facilities. You leave your car in a well-marked parking area just outside the city center and use public transportation to proceed downtown. Wherever you park, always be sure that there are no parking restrictions, and that you pay for and display a parking sticker if necessary.

There is no parking at any time on double yellow lines, and limited hours of parking on single yellow lines. In London, roads marked with red lines

("Red Routes") mean that there is no stopping at any time.

If you are parked illegally, a fine may be left on the car windshield; the vehicle may also be towed away or wheel clamped.

AAA

AAA Affiliated Motoring Club
The Automobile Association (AA), Fanum House, Basing View, Basingstoke, Hampshire RG21 4EA ☎ 0870 550 0600 or 0870 544 8866, fax 01256 493389 (administration office); www.theaa.com. If you break down while driving ☎ 0800 887766 (24-hour AA breakdown service). Not all automobile clubs offer full services to AAA members.

Breakdowns/Accidents

There are emergency telephones at regular intervals on limited-access divided highways. If you are involved in an accident ☎ 999 or 112 for police, fire and ambulance assistance.

Most car rental firms provide their own free rescue service; if your car is rented, follow the instructions in the documentation. Use of a car repair service other than those authorized by your particular rental firm may violate your car rental agreement.

Road Signs

Signs that give orders and prohibitions are usually circular. Red circles prohibit; blue circles give positive instruction. Triangular signs carry messages warning of hazards ahead. They should never be ignored because they provide valuable information about what is just ahead or around the next corner.

National speed limit applies

No entry for vehicular traffic

Ahead only

Keep left

Vehicles may pass either side to reach same destination

No passing

One-way traffic

No through road

Crossroads

Yield to traffic on major road

Two-way traffic straight ahead

Other danger

Steep hill downwards

Double bend, first to the left

British and American English

Although on the surface the same language, there are some quirky differences between American and British English. Britons have become familiar with Americanisms through imported American television shows and movies, and on the whole will understand American visitors when they request a "check" in a restaurant, instead of the English "bill." However, it is still possible to misunderstand when a British sales clerk directs you to the "first floor" of a shop (which is the American equivalent of the second floor). English words and phrases are in the left column below, American words appear in the right column.

Hotels

bath	*bathtub*
book	*reserve*
porter	*bell-hop*
cot	*crib*
duvet	*quilt*
en suite	*with private bathroom*
foyer	*lobby*
ground/first floor	*first/second floor*
lavatory/loo/toilet	*restroom*
lift	*elevator*
reception	*front desk*

Eating Out

aubergine	*eggplant*
bacon rasher	*slice of bacon*
banger	*sausage*
bill	*check*
biscuit	*cookie*
broad bean	*lima bean*
chips	*french fries*
courgette	*zucchini*
crisps	*potato chips*
ice lolly	*popsicle*
jacket potato	*baked potato*
jelly	*Jell-O*
kipper	*smoked herring*
lager	*light beer*
porridge	*oatmeal*
pudding	*dessert*
rocket	*arugula*
runner beans	*string beans*
scone	*biscuit*
sweets	*candy*

Communications

phone box	*telephone booth*
post box	*mailbox*
post code	*zip code*
put through	*connect*
reverse charge	*call collect*
ring up	*call*

Money

bank note	*bill*
cashpoint	*ATM*
cheque	*check*
handbag	*purse*
quid (slang)	*pound sterling*
VAT	*value added tax*

Shopping

anorak	*parka*
bank holiday	*public holiday*
braces	*suspenders*
briefs	*jockey shorts*
carrier bag	*shopping bag*
chemist	*drugstore/pharmacy*
dinner jacket	*tuxedo*
ironmongers	*hardware store*
jumper/sweater	*pullover*
nappy	*diaper*
off licence	*liquor store*
pants	*briefs (underwear)*
plaster	*bandage*
plus fours	*knickerbockers*
queue	*line of people*
shop assistant	*sales clerk*
tights	*pantyhose*
trousers	*pants/slacks*

Transportation

coach	*long-distance bus*
left-luggage office	*baggage room*
lost property	*lost and found*
return ticket	*round-trip ticket*
single ticket	*one-way ticket*
timetable	*schedule*
underground/tube	*subway*

Driving

boot	*trunk (of a car)*
bonnet	*hood (of a car)*
car park	*parking lot*
caravan	*house trailer*
dual carriageway	*divided highway*
estate car	*station wagon*
filling station	*gas station*
flyover	*overpass*
garage	*gas station*
gear lever	*gear shift*
layby	*pull-off*
level crossing	*grade crossing*
lorry	*truck*
manual	*stick shift*
motorway	*freeway*
pavement	*sidewalk*
petrol	*gas*
roundabout	*traffic circle*
T-junction	*intersection*

Welsh Words and Phrases

English is spoken and understood almost everywhere in Wales, and in southern regions particularly there are many residents who don't speak or understand Welsh at all. However, the Welsh language is still very much alive in both its written and spoken form. In the north, visitors may hear it spoken among locals, and any visitor to Wales will certainly encounter it on bilingual road signs and maps. Understanding a few words can enrich a visitor's experience of the country and its culture. Here are just a few examples (see page 159 for a guide to pronunciation):

Meeting people

arfoll	*welcome*
boddhau	*please*
bore da	*good morning*
helô	*hello*
nos da	*good night*
prynhawn da	*good afternoon*

Place names

Caerdydd	*Cardiff*
Caernarfon	*Caernarvon*
Clawdd Offa	*Offa's Dyke*
Eryri	*Snowdonia*
Tyddewi	*St. David's*
Y Fenni	*Abergavenny*
Y Trallwng	*Welshpool*

Town and countryside

afon	*river*
ban, bannau	*peak*
betws/eglwys	*church*
caer	*fortress*
coed	*wood*
cwm/dyffryn	*valley*
dinas	*city, fortress*
garth	*hill*
llyn	*lake*
mynydd	*mountain*
porth	*harbor*
rhaeadr	*waterfall*
rhyd	*ford*
tre	*town*

Regional English

As you travel through England, you will encounter different accents and phrases. This is particularly noticeable in the way people (and maps) refer to the landscape, and it can be confusing. Following are a few of the most commonly encountered terms:

dales	*valleys*
downs	*undulating open land*
fells	*high hills*
moors	*open, uncultivated area of high ground*
screes	*loose rock slopes*
tarns	*small lakes*
uplands	*high, or hilly area*

Scottish Words and Phrases

Three languages are spoken in Scotland: Gaelic, Scots and English. Gaelic is still spoken in the Outer Hebrides, but is most commonly heard in partially anglicized place names or geographical features, such as "loch" or "glen." Modern Scots (originating from the borders, or lowlands) is very much diluted by its near kinship with English. Essentially, English is spoken everywhere, and visitors may not even hear Gaelic or Scots spoken at all. However, you will likely encounter linguistic nuances or expressions and regional accents (the Glaswegian accent being famously tricky to comprehend). Below are just a few words in everyday usage (but don't use them yourself, or the Scots will perhaps think you are showing off):

Meeting people

aye	*yes*
bonnie	*pretty*
ceilidh	*party or dance*
clan	*family group or tribe*
do ye ken?	*do you know?*
ken	*to know*
naw	*no*
sassenach	*non-Scot*
wee	*little*

Eating and drinking

bridie	*a spicy meat pie*
champit tatties	*mashed potatoes*
clootie dumpling	*rich fruit cake*
dram	*measure of whiskey*
gigot or shank	*a leg of lamb or pork*
haggis	*mixture of organ meat and oatmeal, boiled in a sheep's stomach*
jeelie piece	*jelly sandwich*
messages	*shopping for groceries*
neeps	*turnips*
piece	*sandwich*
stovies	*potato cooked with onion and meat*
tatties	*potatoes*

Weather

braw	*good*
dreich	*gray and dull*
droukit	*soaked*
glaur	*mud*
snell	*cold*

Geography

burn	*stream*
cairn	*pile of stones used as a marker on a hill*
clachan	*small Highland village*
croft	*small landholding*
firth	*large river estuary*
glen	*valley*
kirk	*church*
kyle	*inlet or strait*
loch	*lake*

Acknowledgments

The Automobile Association wishes to thank the following photographers and organizations for their assistance in the preparation of this book.

Abbreviations for the picture credits are as follows – (t) top; (b) bottom; (l) left; (r) right; (c) center; (AA) AA World Travel Library

3 AA/A Burton; 5 AA/C Jones; 8/9 AA/L Noble; 10/11 AA/J Hunt; 12/13 AA/R Duke; 14 AA/J Tims; 15 AA/J Tims; 16/17 AA/K Blackwell; 18/19 AA/K Blackwell; 20 AA/L Noble; 22 AA/H Palmer; 23 AA/M Kipling; 24 AA/M Kipling; 26 AA/L Noble; 30 AA/D Croucher; 31 AA/M Busselle; 35 AA/J Tims; 36 AA/J Tims; 37 AA/J Tims; 38/39 AA/J Tims; 40 AA/C Sawyer; 41 AA/N Setchfield; 42 AA/J Tims; 43 AA/M Jourdan; 44/45 AA/J Tims; 46 AA/N Setchfield; 47 AA/S Montgomery; 48 AA/J Tims; 49 AA/D Forss; 50 AA/J Miller; 51 AA/P Baker; 52 AA/L Noble; 53 AA/L Noble; 54 AA/D Forss; 55 AA/P Brown; 56 AA/N Setchfield; 57 AA/A Burton; 59 AA/L Noble; 60 AA/A Burton; 61 AA/N Setchfield; 62/63 AA/D Forss; 63 AA/M Moody; 64 AA/John Miller; 65 AA/J Tims; 66 AA/A Burton; 70 AA/A Newey; 70/71 AA/A Burton; 75 AA/R Duke; 76 AA/R Duke; 77 AA/E Meacher; 78 AA/M Birkitt; 79 AA/R Duke; 80 AA/R Duke; 81 AA/C Jones; 82 AA/A Lawson; 83 AA/R Duke; 84 AA/A Burton; 85 AA/A Burton; 86 AA/A Burton; 87 AA/A Newey; 88 AA/J Tims; 89 AA/M Moody; 90 AA/J Tims; 91 AA/J Tims; 92/93 AA/M Moody; 93 AA/J Tims; 94 AA/T Mackie; 98 AA/T Mackie; 99 AA/L Noble; 100 AA/R Ireland; 102 AA/T Mackie; 103 Chris Bull / Alamy; 104 AA/A Baker; 105 Anthony Smith / Alamy; 106 AA/L Whitwam; 107 AA/T Mackie; 108 AA/T Mackie; 109 AA/T Mackie; 110 AA/T Souter; 111 AA/T Mackie; 112 AA/L Noble; 114 AA/M Birkitt; 115 AA/T Mackie; 116 AA/J Miller; 117l AA/M Birkitt; 118/119 AA/M Birkitt; 119 AA/T Mackie; 120 AA/T Mackie; 121 AA/N Setchfield; 122/123 AA/T Mackie; 124 AA/R Duke; 128/129 AA/J Tims; 130 AA/J Tims; 133t AA/J Tims; 133b AA/J Tims; 134 AA/J Tims; 135 AA/J Tims; 136 AA/J Tims; 137 AA/J Tims; 138 AA/C Jones; 139 AA/M Birkitt; 140 AA/R Duke; 141 AA/S Day; 142 AA/S Day; 143 AA/C Jones; 144 AA/C Jones; 145 Antiques & Collectables / Alamy; 146 Robin Weaver / Alamy; 147 AA/C Jones; 148 AA/M Moody; 149 AA/M Moody; 150 AA/C Jones; 151 AA/J Tims; 152 AA/S Lewis; 156/157 AA/M Sterling; 159t AA/R Duke; 159b AA/R Duke; 161 AA/R Duke; 162 AA/R Duke; 163 AA/R Duke; 164 AA/I Burgum; 165 AA/R Duke; 166 AA/D Croucher; 167 AA/C Molyneux; 168 AA/N Jenkins; 169 AA/M Bauer; 170 AA/M Bauer; 171 AA/M Bauer; 172 AA/D Santillo; 173 AA/T Timms; 174 AA/R Duke; 176 AA/N Jenkins; 177 AA/H Williams; 178 AA/T Mackie; 182/183 AA/J Hunt; 185 AA/C Clapp; 187 AA/C Clapp; ; ; 188 AA/C Clapp; 189 AA/C Clapp; 190/191 AA/C Clapp; 192 AA/J Tims; 193 AA/J Morrison; 194 AA/P Baker; 195 AA/J Tims; 196/197 AA/J Hunt; 198 AA/J Hunt; 200 AA/T Mackie; 201 Brian Stark / Alamy; 202 AA/S Day; 203 Mark Sunderland / Alamy; 204 AA/M Kipling; 205 AA/J Hunt; 206 AA/P Baker; 207 AA/T Mackie; 208 AA/T Mackie; 210 AA/J Smith; 214/215 AA/S Day; 216 AA/K Blackwell; 219 AA/K Blackwell; 220 AA/K Blackwell; 221 AA/K Blackwell; 222 AA/K Blackwell; 223 AA/K Blackwell; 224 AA/S Whitehorne; 225 AA/J Smith; 226 Neil Setchfield / Alamy; 229 AA/S Whitehorne; 230 AA/S Gibson; 231 AA/S Whitehorne; 232 Scott Rae / Alamy; 233 AA/S Whitehorne; 234 AA/J Beazley; 235 AA/R Weir; 236 AA/K Paterson; 237 AA/K Blackwell; 238 AA/K Blackwell; 240l AA/S Anderson; 240r AA/M Alexander; 241 AA/J Henderson; 242/243 AA/J Smith; 243 AA/A Baker; 244 AA/E Ellington; 245 AA/R Weir; 246/247 AA/S Whitehorne; 248 AA/S Whitehorne; 249 AA/S Whitehorne; 251 AA/S Whitehorne; 252/253 Imagestate Media Partners Limited - Impact Photos / Alamy; 253 AA/S Day; 254 AA/I Burgum; 256 AA/D Hall; 277t AA/J Tims; 277c AA/S Montgomery

Every effort has been made to trace the copyright holders, and we apologise in advance for any unintentional omissions or errors. We would be pleased to apply any corrections in a following edition of this publication.